HANDS-ON

STUDY GUIDE FOR

EXAM 70-411

ADMINISTERING WINDOWS SERVER 2012 R2

VICTOR ASHIEDU

Copyright and Disclaimer

Published by: ITechGuides.com
Copyright © Victor Ashiedu
Edited by: Victor Ashiedu with help from the following websites:
 www.onlinecorrection.com and www.spellcheckplus.com

Cover design by: www.coverdesignstudio.com

Victor Ashiedu & ITechguides.com
2014

About The Author

Victor has deployed, managed and optimized Windows Servers since 2001. He has over 12 years' hands-on, real-life enterprise-level experience in Microsoft Infrastructure Server Administration and support. He is currently focusing on Active Directory and Windows PowerShell.
Victor lives and works in London, England. When he is not writing codes and Administering Windows Servers, he reads autobiographies, plays table tennis and visit museums.
To get in touch, email 70411Guide@iTechguides.com.

Why You Need This Book

Hands-On Study Guide For Exam 70-411 is written in a simple language to ensure you pass the exam and gain real-life skills to apply to your job.
This exam reference guide emphasizes a hands-on approach that you can take to your day-to-day job.

Dedication

To Bunmi Titiloye, for motivating and supporting me to pursue and achieve my dreams.

Acknowledgements

I would like to thank Olujide Olosunde for his contributions throughout the over 10 months it took me to write this book. I also want to thank Biola Bolaji and Ken Akinmade. Special thank you to Bunmi Titiloye for allowing me pick her brain. Bunmi is one of the smartest women I have ever met and her contributions were invaluable.

I appreciate my previous employers: Computer Warehouse, MTN Nigeria, and many others. Without you, I would not have become a great Windows Pro that I am today. I am thankful for all the training and development opportunities I received from you. I also appreciate my current employer for the opportunity to continue to build great skills.

Finally, I would like to thank my family for supporting me to be my best. I appreciate my late Dad, Mr. Lawrence Ashiedu and my mum Mrs. Philomena Ashiedu. I also appreciate my siblings: Onyeka and his wife Nkechi, Tonia, Christie and Joy. I thank you all for being there for me.

Introduction

I set out to write this book when I was preparing for my MCSA Windows Server 2012 exams, but could not find a suitable hands-on study guide. This book is very hands-on. Though you are preparing to pass the 70-411: Administering Windows Server 2012 exam, this Hands-On training guide goes beyond passing the exam. It is designed to train you to become a pro. Over and above passing the 70-411 exam, this book is designed to become a reference guide to support you in your day-to-day work as a professional Windows Systems Administrator.

When you complete the studies and meticulously perform the practices outlined in this material, you will definitely become a better Systems administrator. In fact, your knowledge of all the technologies covered in this book and the 70411 exam will literally skyrocket! You will require a lab to benefit fully from this hands-on material. I took time to prepare the lab environment to cover all aspects of the guide. It is very important to follow the steps as outlined. Ensure every server is created, every folder created and all applications installed as outlined.

I recommend that you read the guide and practice the labs in sequence. This is essential as you will require some Server 2012 R2 roles and features in the order outlined. Also, pay particular attention to notes and exam tips. To maximize knowledge gained, during any installation, I recommend that you form the habit of reading notes included by Microsoft in all installation Wizards. You will be amazed by the amount of information included in these Wizards. Do not just click Next, Next, Finish!

Finally, while I was writing this Hands-On guide, I created a comprehensive practice test that covers every objective in this book as well as the 70-411 exam. This is not a dump. It is intended to be used side-by-side this book to reinforce your knowledge and prepare you for the exam. Please visit www.ITechguides.com and subscribe so you can take the practice tests as you study. This book entitles you to one month free subscription. Please email your order number to 70411Guide@ITechguides.com for your free code. I recommend that you set aside three months of intensive study and practice. This is not a quick-fix solution. You will not only pass the exam, but you would have acquired knowledge that you can sell to employers and improve your earning power.

Before you commence the lab setup, please visit ITechguides.com for latest information.

Victor Ashiedu

How to read this book

This book is written with two things in mind:

1. Pass Microsoft Exam 70-411: Administering Windows Server 2012 R2.
2. Gain practical, hands-on experience in all the objectives of the exam.

The second aim will definitely achieve the first but not vice versa. With this in mind, I structured the book as outlined below:

Lab Setup

You will set up your own lab. Details are provided from the first page after table of contents. To get the best out of this book, it is strongly recommended that you create your own lab. You should still be able to read the book without the lab, but to maximize the benefit; it is strongly recommended that you set up the lab.

Chapter Structure

Every chapter follows the structure outlined below:

Sections & Sub-sections

The sections are key exam objectives for example **1.1 Deploy and manage server images.** Every section has an **Introduction** followed by the exam objectives covered in that section. The exam objectives in each section are used as the sub-sections in this book. For example, **1.1.0 Install the Windows Deployment Services (WDS) role**.

How sub-sections are written

Every sub-section will have a short overview of the content. This creates the knowledge required in the exam and provides you with the requisite knowledge to proceed with the lab.

Once I have given a quick overview of the sub-section, I proceed to provide the procedure to complete the lab for the sub-section, for example **To install the Windows Deployment Services role with Server Manager**. The steps will come in the numbering format, 1, 2, 3, etc. If I need to break-down a procedure into sub-procedure, I present the sub-procedure with letters a, b, c. Further breakdown will be followed by bullet points. See example below:

To install the Windows Deployment Services role with Server Manager

1. Launch server manager and click Next.
2. To select the Windows deployment feature:
    a) Perform tasks abc.
    b) To drill further:
        i) Perform tasks xyz.

Notes & Exam Tips

I use **Notes** & Exam Tips to emphasize key points. It is very important to pay attention to them.

Welcome to Hands-On Study Guide For Exam 70-411: Administering Windows Server 2012 R2.

Table of Contents

Lab Setup

If you experience any problem with the lab setup, please email: 70411Guide@ITechguides.com

Lab Requirement & Important Information

To set up the lab for this study guide, you require the following:

1. A Windows 7 PC or Laptop with a minimum of 6GB RAM and 250GB hard drive.
2. PC or laptop must support hardware virtualization (Enable this feature in BIOS).
3. A 2-port hub - Configure the leg that connects to your laptop with IP address 192.168.0.1 (This will be your default gateway on all servers).
4. A Microsoft login account (A Hotmail or a Live ID).
5. Install Google Chrome and use for downloads (Optional).
6. The lab is built with PowerShell commands.

Note

I set up my lab on a Windows 7 laptop so I cannot guarantee that it will work on a Windows 8 or 8.1 laptop or PC. I suppose it will. If you have a Windows 8.1, you can explore running the Hyper-V feature directly from the Windows 8.1 PC or laptop.

Important

PowerShell supports command completion. When you type the first few letters of a command and press the tab key, the shell provides suggestions.

Recommended Setup

Connect the hub between your laptop (or desktop) and your ADSL switch. This will give you control over your IP address management and separate it from your internet connection. With this setup, the IP address of your hub will be your default gateway. Enable hardware virtualization from the BIOS of your laptop or desktop.

Virtual Computer Configuration: All the virtual computers in this lab will be created with the following configuration:

1. Startup RAM: 768MB, Minimum RAM: 512MB, Maximum RAM: Default.
2. NIC: Connected to the Virtual switch, VLAN1 (To be created in step 5 below).
3. Dynamic RAM will be enabled for all VMs.

4. Any of the Virtual Machine with a different configuration will be specified.

Follow the steps below to prepare your lab:
Perform the tasks outlined below from your Windows 7 PC or laptop. When you complete the task, you will be able to dual boot your Windows 7 (or Windows 8) with Windows Server 2012 R2 VHD.

1. To create the required folders, run the PowerShell scripts below:

```
New-Item -type directory C:\Labfiles\VHD
New-Item -type directory C:\Labfiles\VHD-Used
New-Item -type directory 'C:\Labfiles\ISO\8.1 Enterprise'
New-Item -type directory 'C:\Labfiles\ISO\7 Pro'
New-Item -type directory 'C:\Labfiles\ISO-Used\8.1 Enterprise'
New-Item -type directory 'C:\Labfiles\ISO-Used\7 Pro'
```

2. Download Windows 8.1 ISO:
   a) Open the URL
      http://technet.microsoft.com/en-gb/evalcenter/hh699156.aspx.
   b) When the link opens, Select Windows 8.1 Enterprise ISO (64-bit (x64) and click GET STARTED NOW.
   c) Provide log in details and complete the required registration form, scroll down and click **Continue**.
   d) Install **Akamai NetSession Interface** and continue download.
   e) If Windows Firewall blocks the Akamai NetSession Interface, allow it and continue. (If the download returns an error message, restart the download).
   f) Save the ISO image to **C:\Labfiles\ISO\8.1 Enterprise**. Monitor download progress bar on the top left corner of the page.
   g) When the download completes, rename the ISO file **Windows 8.1 Ent x64** and copy it to **C:\Labfiles\ISO-Used\8.1 Enterprise**.

3. Download Windows 7 Professional ISO:
   a) Open the URL: http://msft.digitalrivercontent.net/win/X17-24281.iso.
   b) When download completes, move **X17-24281.iso** to **C:\Labfiles\ISO\7 Pro** and rename the file as **Windows 7 Pro x64.iso**.
   c) Copy Windows 7 Pro x64.iso to C:\Labfiles\ISO-Used\7 Pro.

4. Download Windows Server 2012 R2 VHD:
   a) Open the URL: http://www.microsoft.com/en-us/evalcenter/evaluate-windows-server-2012-r2.
   b) Click **Sign In** and enter your Microsoft ID to login.
   c) On the Please choose a file type screen, select VHD and click **Register** to continue.

d) Complete the required registration form, scroll down, and click **Continue**.

e) If the download returns an error message, restart the download.

f) Save the file to C:\Labfiles\VHD. Monitor download progress bar on the top left corner of the page.

g) When the download completes, rename the VHD file to **WindowsSRV2012R2.vhd.**

h) Copy WindowsSRV2012R2.vhd to **C:\Labfiles\VHD-Used** and rename the file to **70411HPV.vhd**.

5. Attach the **70411HPV.vhd** file with the following steps:

a) Open Disk Management (Administrative Tools – Computer Management, then Disk Management).

b) From Disk Management, click **More actions,** then click **Attach VHD.**

c) Browse to C:\Labfiles\VHD-Used\70411HPV.vhd, and click **Open.**

d) On the Attach Virtual Hard Disk window, click **Ok.**

e) Note the new drive letter of the mounted VHD drive. It will have a different colour - Mine appeared as drive E.

6. Add the Windows Server 2012 R2 OS to your Windows 7 boot menu:

a) Open elevated CMD using **Run As administrator** (Right-click a CMD and select **Run As administrator)**.

b) Execute the following command:

bcdboot E:\windows

(Where 'E' is the drive letter of my mounted VHD above). You should see a message **Boot files successfully created**.

      a. To confirm that Windows Server 2012 R2 has been added to the boot menu, execute:

BCDEdit

7. Configure Windows Server 2012 R2:

a) Reboot the PC and select **Windows Server 2012 R2** from the boot menu.

b) On the Settings screen, select, Country or region, App Language and Keyboard layout, then click **Next**.

c) On the next screen, click **I accept**, to the licence terms, then enter Administrator password and click **Finish.** The computer will reboot.

d) Log on with the Administrator password you set up in step (f) above. Server Manager opens.

e) If you are prompted to find PCs, devices and content on your network, click **no.**

f) Rename the computer:

i) Highlight **Server Manager** Console and click **Local Server** (On the left pane).

ii) On the **Properties** pane that opens, click the name beside **Computer name** (normally begins with **WIN-**).

iii) On the **Systems Properties** page, click **Change...**, then enter 70411HPV as the Computer name, and click **Ok**.

iv) On the Computer Name/Domain Changes prompt, click Ok, and then click Close.

v) On the Microsoft Windows prompt, click Restart Later.

g) Configure a static IPv4 address:

i) Highlight **Server Manager** Console and click **Local Server** (On the left pane).

ii) On the details pane, beside **Ethernet**, click **IPv4 address assigned by DHSCP, IPv6 enabled**, then double-click your network card.

iii) On the **Ethernet Status** screen, click **Properties**, then uncheck the box beside **Internet Protocol Version 6 (TCP/IPv6)** to disable it.

iv) Highlight **Internet Protocol Version 4 (TCP/IPv4)** and click **Properties** to open TCP/IP properties page.

v) On the **Internet Protocol Version 4 (TCP/IPv4) Properties,** click **Use the following IP address,** then enter a static IP address 192.168.0.80, and subnet mask of 255.255.255.0.

vi) Enter the IP of your router as your **Default gateway** and **Preferred DNS server,** and then click **Ok.**

vii) Close Ethernet Properties page.

Note

To obtain information about your router, run IPCONFIG /all.

h) Configure Time zone to your actual time zone and set the date and time correctly.

i) Reboot the server:

i) From **Server Manager**, on the left pane highlight **Local Server**.

ii) On the details pane, click **TASKS** drop-down and select **Shut Down Local Server.**

iii) Select **Restart,** provide a comment, and click **Ok.**

Note

70411HPV will be your Hyper-V host. All virtual servers for this study guide will be built on this Hyper-V platform. We will require the VHD file (WindowsSRV2012R2.vhd) to build all the virtual servers for this study guide. No other server role will be installed on the Hyper-V server.

8. Install Hyper-V Role:
    a) Log on to 70411HPV with admin account created in the previous section.
    b) Open Server Manager, click **Manage** and select **Add Roles and features**. The Add Roles and features Wizard opens, click **Next.**
    c) On the Installation Type screen, ensure that Role-based or feature-based installation is selected, then click Next.
    d) On the **Select destination Server** page, ensure that 70411HPV is selected, then click **Next.**
    e) On **Server Roles** page, select **Hyper-V**, click **Add features**, to the Add features for Hyper-V prompt, then click **Next** twice.
    f) On the **Hyper-V** screen, note the information and click **Next.**
    g) On the **Create Virtual Switches** page, select your primary network card (Likely displayed as **Ethernet**), and click **Next**.
    h) On the Virtual Machines Migration page, click Next.
    i) On the **Default Stores** page, enter **D:\Labfiles\VHD-Used** (Drive C:\ on the Windows 7 OS is now drive D:\) as the Default location for virtual Hard Disks. Enter **D:\Labfiles\VHD-Used\Config** as Default location for virtual machine configuration files. Click **Next.**
    j) On the **Confirm installation selections** page, review your selections, check the box Restart the destination server automatically if required, respond Yes then click **Install**.
9. Rename your Virtual Switch:
    a) Log on to 70411HPV and open Hyper-V Manager (Server Manager, Tools).
    b) On the left pane, click 70411HPV and on the **Actions** menu (top right), click **Virtual Switch Manager**.
    c) On the **Virtual Switch Manager for 70411HPV** console, beneath **Virtual Switches,** click your network card name and on the details pane, complete the following tasks:
        i) On the **name** field, enter **VLAN1.**
        ii) Confirm that **External network** is selected and on the drop-down list, that your network card is selected as well.
        iii) Confirm that Allow management operating system to share this network adapter is checked.
        iv) Click **Ok** to save your changes.

10. Enable Enhanced Session Mode Policy:
   a) Still on Hyper-V Manager, right-click 70411HPV and select **Hyper-V Settings.**
   b) On the Hyper-V Settings for 70411HPV, on the left pane, click **Enable Enhanced Session Mode Policy**.
   c) On the details pane, check the box beside **Allow Enhanced Session Mode** and click **Ok**.

Note

All VMs will be connected to VLAN1Virtual switch.

11. Create Virtual Machines:
   a) Copy WindowsSRV2012R2.vhd from **D:\Labfiles\VHD** (It was drive C:\ when you logged on to your Windows 7 PC but from Windows Server 2012 R2, it will appear as drive D:\) to **D:\Labfiles\VHD-Used** and rename to **70411SRV**.
   b) Repeat step a) above for 70411SRV1, 70411SRV2, 70411SRV3, 70411SRV4, 70411SRV5 and 70411RODC (You should have 7 VHD files).
   c) Open a PowerShell console and run the commands below to create each VM (Run one command before you the next from 70411HPV):

```
New-VM -Generation 1 -MemoryStartupBytes 768MB -Name '70411SRV' -
Path 'D:\Labfiles\VHD-Used\Config' -SwitchName 'VLAN1' -VHDPath
'D:\Labfiles\VHD-Used\70411SRV.vhd'
Set-VM -Name '70411SRV' -DynamicMemory
New-VM -Generation 1 -MemoryStartupBytes 768MB -Name '70411SRV1' -
Path 'D:\Labfiles\VHD-Used\Config' -SwitchName 'VLAN1' -VHDPath
'D:\Labfiles\VHD-Used\70411SRV1.vhd'

Set-VM -Name '70411SRV1' -DynamicMemory
New-VM -Generation 1 -MemoryStartupBytes 768MB -Name '70411SRV2' -
Path 'D:\Labfiles\VHD-Used\Config' -SwitchName 'VLAN1' -VHDPath
'D:\Labfiles\VHD-Used\70411SRV2.vhd'

Set-VM -Name '70411SRV2' -DynamicMemory

New-VM -Generation 1 -MemoryStartupBytes 768MB -Name '70411SRV3' -
Path 'D:\Labfiles\VHD-Used\Config' -SwitchName 'VLAN1' -VHDPath
'D:\Labfiles\VHD-Used\70411SRV3.vhd'

Set-VM -Name '70411SRV3' -DynamicMemory
```

```
New-VM -Generation 1 -MemoryStartupBytes 768MB -Name '70411SRV4' -
Path 'D:\Labfiles\VHD-Used\Config' -SwitchName 'VLAN1' -VHDPath
'D:\Labfiles\VHD-Used\70411SRV4.vhd'

Set-VM -Name '70411SRV4' -DynamicMemory

New-VM -Generation 1 -MemoryStartupBytes 768MB -Name '70411SRV5' -
Path 'D:\Labfiles\VHD-Used\Config' -SwitchName 'VLAN1' -VHDPath
'D:\Labfiles\VHD-Used\70411SRV5.vhd'

Set-VM -Name '70411SRV5' -DynamicMemory

New-VM -Generation 1 -MemoryStartupBytes 768MB -Name '70411RODC'
-Path 'D:\Labfiles\VHD-Used\Config' -SwitchName 'VLAN1' -VHDPath
'D:\Labfiles\VHD-Used\70411RODC.vhd'

Set-VM -Name '70411RODC' -DynamicMemory
```

    d) Create a second virtual Hard disk for all the VMs, except 70411RODC - Run the following PowerShell commands from a PowerShell console in 70411HPV:

```
New-VHD -Path 'D:\Labfiles\VHD-Used\70411SRV_1.vhd' -Dynamic -
SizeBytes 50GB | ADD-VMHardDiskDrive –VMName '70411SRV' -Path
'D:\Labfiles\VHD-Used\70411SRV_1.vhd'

New-VHD -Path 'D:\Labfiles\VHD-Used\70411SRV1_1.vhd' -Dynamic -
SizeBytes 50GB | ADD-VMHardDiskDrive –VMName '70411SRV1' -Path
'D:\Labfiles\VHD-Used\70411SRV1_1.vhd'

New-VHD -Path 'D:\Labfiles\VHD-Used\70411SRV2_1.vhd' -Dynamic -
SizeBytes 50GB | ADD-VMHardDiskDrive –VMName '70411SRV2' -Path
'D:\Labfiles\VHD-Used\70411SRV2_1.vhd'

New-VHD -Path 'D:\Labfiles\VHD-Used\70411SRV3_1.vhd' -Dynamic -
SizeBytes 50GB | ADD-VMHardDiskDrive –VMName '70411SRV3' -Path
'D:\Labfiles\VHD-Used\70411SRV3_1.vhd'

New-VHD -Path 'D:\Labfiles\VHD-Used\70411SRV4_1.vhd' -Dynamic -
SizeBytes 50GB | ADD-VMHardDiskDrive –VMName '70411SRV4' -Path
'D:\Labfiles\VHD-Used\70411SRV4_1.vhd'
```

New-VHD -Path 'D:\Labfiles\VHD-Used\70411SRV5_1.vhd' -Dynamic - SizeBytes 50GB | ADD-VMHardDiskDrive –VMName '70411SRV5' -Path 'D:\Labfiles\VHD-Used\70411SRV5_1.vhd'

Note

For improved performance, power the VMs as required. 70411SRV (DC) should be powered most of the time (A Domain controller is required for most of the labs). 70411SRV2 and 70411SRV4 (also DCs) should also be powered most of the time to ensure AD sync and DB consistency. 70411SRV1 and 70411SRV3 (Member servers), can be off and powered as required.

12. Install Operating system on Virtual Machines:
    a) With Hyper-V Manager still open, right-click 70411SRV and select **start.**
    b) Right-click again and click **Connect.**
    c) When the server boots, complete installation as outlined in step 4. (a-c) above.
    d) When installation completes and server reboots, log on and complete the following tasks:
        i) Rename the computer to 70411SRV (Run the PowerShell command below):

Rename-Computer -NewName 70411SRV -Force

        ii) Configure IP with the following details:
            (1) Static IPv4 address 192.168.0.81, mask 255.255.255.0, Default Gateway 192.168.0.1.
            (2) Primary DNS Server 192.168.0.81, Alternate DNS Server: IP address of your ADSL router.
        iii) Disable IPv6
        iv) Configure Time zone and set time.
        v) To format the second hard disk for each VM, run the command below on each VM:

Initialize-Disk -Number 1 -PartitionStyle MBR

New-Partition -DiskNumber 1 -UseMaximumSize –AssignDriveLetter

Format-Volume -DriveLetter E -FileSystem NTFS -Confirm:$false

    e) Shutdown the server.
13. Complete step 12 for each VM.

a) Remember to amend computer name to the name of the server when you run the Rename-Computer command on each VM.
b) Configure static IPs for each virtual machine as outlined below:
    i) 70411SRV - 192.168.0.81
    ii) 70411SRV1 - 192.168.0.32
    iii) 70411SRV2 - 192.168.0.33
    iv) 70411SRV3 - 192.168.0.34
    v) 70411SRV4 - 192.168.0.35
    vi) 70411SRV5 - 192.168.0.37
    vii) 70411RODC - 192.168.0.36

Important

Do not join 70411SRV5 and 70411RODC to the domain. Prepare the VMs as outlined and shut them down.

14. Checklist: confirm that the following have been completed for each VM:
    a) Operating system installation completed.
    b) Computer renamed.
    c) Second hard disk created and formatted.
    d) Static IP address assigned.
    e) IPv6 disabled.
    f) Computer shutdown.
15. Install Server Roles (AD-DS, DNS and DHCP):
    a) Log On to 70411SRV, 70411SRV2 and 70411SRV4 and run the following PowerShell commands:

```
Install-WindowsFeature -Name DNS -Includemanagementtools
Install-WindowsFeature -Name AD-Domain-Services -
includeManagementTools
```

b) Log On to 70411SRV3 and run the following PowerShell commands:

```
Install-WindowsFeature -Name DNS –Includemanagementtools
Install-WindowsFeature -Name DHCP –includeManagementTools
```

c) Confirm you have installed server roles as outlined below:
    i) DNS and AD DS installed on 70411SRV, 70411SRV2 and 70411SRV4.
    ii) DNS and DHCP installed on 70411SRV3.
16. Configure DNS Server Role - Create forward and reverse lookup zones:
    a) Log on to 70411SRV and run the following PowerShell commands:

```
Add-DnsServerPrimaryZone -Name "70411Lab.com" -ZoneFile
"70411Lab.com.dns"
Add-DnsServerPrimaryZone -NetworkID 192.168.0.0/24 -ZoneFile
"0.168.192.in-addr.arpa.dns"
```

```
Add-DnsServerResourceRecordA -Name "70411SRV" -ZoneName
"70411Lab.com" -AllowUpdateAny -IPv4Address "192.168.0.81"

Add-DnsServerResourceRecordPtr -Name "81" -ZoneName "0.168.192.in-
addr.arpa" –AllowUpdateAny -PtrDomainName "70411SRV.70411Lab.com"

Add-DnsServerResourceRecordA -Name "70411HPV" -ZoneName
"70411Lab.com" -AllowUpdateAny -IPv4Address "192.168.0.80"
```

  b) Open DNS console and expand **Forward lookup zones** and right-click **70411Lab.com**, then click **Properties.**
  c) Highlight **Name Servers** Tab. 70411SRV will be highlighted with IP address **unknown.**
  d) Click **Edit**, Under Server fully qualified domain name (FQDN), type **70411SRV.70411Lab.com** and click **Resolve**. This will populate the IP address of the server. Click **Ok**, then **Apply** (Perform same task on the Reverse Lookup zone).
  e) Configure 70411SRV to forward DNS queries to your broadband router:
    i) On the DNS Manager console, right-click **70411SRV**, click **properties.**
    ii) On the **Interfaces** tab, select **Only the following IP addresses** and check the IP address for 70411SRV, Uncheck others if any.
    iii) Click **Forwarders** Tab, click **Edit**, and type the IP address of your ADSL router, then click **Ok.** .
    iv) On the properties of 70411SRV, click **Ok.**
  f) Confirm that 70411SRV can resolve host names, type nslookup on a command prompt and type an internet name like www.google.com
  g) Configure your Hyper-V server, 70411HPV to use 70411SRV (192.168.0.81) as primary DNS server.
  h) Confirm that DNS is configured for:
    i) 70411SRV
    ii) 70411HPV configured to use 70411SRV as primary DNS server.
17. Configure AD DS Server Role - Configure domains and Domain Controllers:
  a) Log on to 70411SRV and run the following PowerShell commands:

```
Install-ADDSForest -DomainName 70411Lab.com -DomainMode
Win2012R2 -ForestMode Win2012R2 -Confirm:$false
```

      Enter SafeModeAdministratorPassword when prompted. Server is promoted to a DC then reboots.
  b) Configure 70411Lab.com zone for secure dynamic update, AD-Integrated, replication to all DCs:

c) Run the following PowerShell commands from 70411SRV:

```
ConvertTo-DnsServerPrimaryZone "70411Lab.com" -ReplicationScope
"Forest" -Force
Set-DnsServerPrimaryZone -Name "70411Lab.com" -DynamicUpdate
"Secure" -PassThru
```

d) Promote 70411SRV2 as additional DCs in the 70411Lab.com domain: (Ensure that 70411SRV is online before you run the command). Run the command below from 70411SRV2.

```
Install-ADDSDomainController -DomainName "70411Lab.com" -
SkipPreChecks -Confirm:$false —Credential (Get-Credential)
```

When prompted for username and password, enter 70411lab\Administrator as user name, then enter your domain admin password. The installation will also prompt for SafeModeAdministratorPassword, enter a password and confirm it to proceed.

e) Log on to 70411SRV and complete the following tasks:
   i) Open DNS Manager console, expand **Forward Look Up Zones**, then expand **70411Lab.com** and click _tcp.
   ii) On the details pane, double-clikc _ldap properties for 70411SRV2 and set priority to 2.

f) Promote 70411SRV4 as additional DCs in the 70411Lab.com domain: (Ensure that 70411SRV is online before you run the command). Run the command below from 70411SRV4.

```
Install-ADDSDomainController -DomainName "70411Lab.com" -
SkipPreChecks -Confirm:$false —Credential (Get-Credential)
```

When prompted for username and password, enter 70411lab\Administrator as user name, then enter your domain admin password. The installation will also prompt for SafeModeAdministratorPassword, enter a password and confirm it to proceed.

g) Join 70411SRV1 and 70411SRV3 to the 70411Lab.com domain as member servers. Log on to 70411SRV1 then 70411SRV3 and run the following PowerShell commands:

```
Add-Computer -DomainName 70411Lab.com
```

Provide your domain admin credentials when prompted. Reboot each server after installation:

```
Restart-Computer
```

h) Confirm that servers have been configured as outlined below:

i)   70411SRV promoted to domain controller in the 70411Lab.com domain (Also configured as Global Catalog server).

ii) 70411SRV2 and 70411SRV4 promoted to additional domain controllers in the 70411Lab.com domain (Also configured as Global Catalog servers).

iii) 70411SRV1 and 70411SRV3 joined to the 70411Lab.com domain as member servers.

18. Configure DHCP Server Role - Create scope:

   a) Log on to 70411SRV3 and run the following commands - Authorises the DHCP server:

```
Add-DhcpServerInDC -DnsName 70411SRV3.70411Lab.com -IPAddress
192.168.0.34
```

   b) Log on to 70411SRV3 and run the following PowerShell commands - Creates a new DHCP scope and sets DNS options:

```
Add-DhcpServerv4Scope -Name 'ITechGuides' -StartRange 192.168.0.10 -
EndRange 192.168.0.20 -SubnetMask 255.255.255.0 –Confirm:$false

Set-DhcpServerv4OptionValue -OptionId 6 -value 192.168.0.81

Set-DhcpServerv4OptionValue -OptionId 3 -value 192.168.0.1
```

     Option 6 is DNS; Option 3 is router (Default gateway).

   c) Confirm that DHCP has been configured on 70411SRV3.

19. Create a Windows 8.1 Virtual Machine:

   a) Log on to 70411HPV (Your Hyper-V PC) and run the following PowerShell commands:

```
New-VHD -Path 'D:\Labfiles\VHD-Used\70411Win8.vhdx' -Dynamic -
SizeBytes 50GB

New-VHD -Path 'D:\Labfiles\VHD-Used\70411Win8_1.vhdx' -Dynamic -
SizeBytes 20GB

New-VM -Generation 2 -MemoryStartupBytes 1024MB -Name '70411Win8' -
Path 'D:\Labfiles\VHD-Used\Config' -SwitchName 'VLAN1' -VHDPath
'D:\Labfiles\VHD-Used\70411Win8.vhdx' -BootDevice CD

ADD-VMHardDiskDrive –VMName '70411Win8' -Path 'D:\Labfiles\VHD-
Used\70411Win8_1.vhdx'

Set-VM -Name '70411Win8' -DynamicMemory -MemoryMinimumBytes
1024MB
```

Set-VMDvdDrive -VMName '70411Win8' -Path 'D:\Labfiles\ISO-Used\8.1
Enterprise\Windows 8.1 Ent x64.iso'

    b) Boot the DHCP server (70411SRV3) before proceeding to the next
        tasks.

    c) Boot 70411Win8 client VM and install OS:
        i)   Right-click 70411Win8 and click **Start**. Right-click again and click
             Connect.
        ii)   Place your mouse on the screen of the VM and press any key to
             boot from CD when prompted.
        iii) On the Windows 8 screen, select your **Language to install,
             Time and currency format** and **Keyboard or input method**,
             and then click **Next.**
        iv) On the next page, click **Install now.**
        v)   On the **Licence terms** page, accept agreement and click **Next.**
        vi) On the type of installation page, select **Custom,** and on the
             install location page, ensure that the 50GB hdd is selected, then
             click **Next.**
        vii) While setup is running, proceed to step 20 (a) below.
        viii) When the installation loads the **Personalise** screen, on the **PC
             name** field, enter 70411Win8 and click **Next.**
        ix) On the **Settings** screen, select **Use express settings.**
        x)   On the **Sign in to your Microsoft account** screen, enter your
             Microsoft ID and password, and then click **Next.**
        xi) On the **Help us protect your info** screen, select the method to
             receive your code, verify your info and click **Next.**
        xii) On the **Enter the code you received** screen, enter your
             verification code and click **Next.**
        xiii) On the **OneDrive** screen, click **Next.**
        xiv) When the account setup is completed, proceed to the next step.
        xv) While Windows 8 setup is configuring settings, proceed to step
             20 (b) below.
        xvi) Reboot the computer:

Restart-Computer

    d) To join 70411Win8 to the domain, log on to the client and run the
        following PowerShell commands:

Add-Computer -DomainName 70411Lab -Credential (Get-Credential) -
Restart

Important

It is a requirement to open PowerShell with Run As Administrator. If you do not, you will receive error 'Access Denied'. Follow step e) to open Windows PowerShell before executing Add-Computer command.

    e) To open PowerShell with Administrative privileges, follow the steps below:
        i) Click on the Windows logo then click on the search tool on the top right corner of the desktop.
        ii) On the search box, enter PowerShell. Right-click **PowerShell** and select **Run as administrator**, then confirm.
        iii) Enter the domain admin logon (70411lab\administrator) and password when prompted.
    f) Shutdown 70411Win8

Important

If 70411Win8 is leasing an IP address from your router instead of your DHCP, disable the DHCP feature in your router (the router you connected your pc).

Note

If you have problems communicating between your VMs, complete the following tasks on the problematic VM, to disable Authorconfiguration:
Step 1: Open command prompt and run: **netsh interface ipv4 show inter**. Returns a result. Note the idx number of your NIC (Mine was 11).
Step 2: Run this command: netsh interface ipv4 set interface 11 dadtransmits=0 store=persistent.
Step 3: disable and then enable then network Interface.

20. Create a Windows 7 Virtual Machine:
    a) Log on to 70411HPV (Your Hyper-V PC) and run the following PowerShell commands:

```
New-VHD -Path 'D:\Labfiles\VHD-Used\70411Win7.vhdx' -Dynamic -
SizeBytes 50GB

New-VHD -Path 'D:\Labfiles\VHD-Used\70411Win7_1.vhdx' -Dynamic -
SizeBytes 20GB
```

New-VM -Generation 1 -MemoryStartupBytes 768MB -Name '70411Win7' -Path 'D:\Labfiles\VHD-Used\Config' -SwitchName 'VLAN1' -VHDPath 'D:\Labfiles\VHD-Used\70411Win7.vhdx' -BootDevice CD

ADD-VMHardDiskDrive –VMName '70411Win7' -Path 'D:\Labfiles\VHD-Used\70411Win7_1.vhdx'

Set-VM -Name '70411Win7' -DynamicMemory

Set-VMDvdDrive -VMName '70411Win7' -Path 'D:\Labfiles\ISO-Used\7 Pro\Windows 7 Pro x64.iso'

b) Boot 70411Win7 client VM and install OS:
    i) Right-click 70411Win7 and click **Start**. Right-click again and click **Connect.** The OS installation will commence.
    ii) On the Windows 7 screen, select your **Language to install, Time and currency format** and **Keyboard or input method**, and then click **Next**.
    iii) On the next page, click **Install now.**
    iv) On the **Licence terms** page, accept agreement and click **Next.**
    v) On the type of installation page, select **Custom,** and on the install location page, ensure that the 50GB hdd is selected, then click **Next.**
    vi) On the **Choose a user name..** page, enter a user name, then enter 70411Win7 as the computer name and click **Next.**
    vii) On the **Set password for your account** screen, enter a password for your account and a password hint, and then click **Next.**
    viii) On the **Type your Windows product key** page, uncheck **Automatically activate Windows when I'm online** and click **Skip.**
    ix) On the **Help protect your computer and improve Windows automatically** screen, select **Use recommended settings**.
    x) On the **Review your time and date settings** page, confirm the details and click **Next.**
    xi) On the **Select your computer's current location** page, click **Home network.**
    xii) Reboot the computer:

Restart-Computer

c) To join 70411Win7 to the domain, log on to the client and run the following PowerShell commands:

Add-Computer -DomainName 70411Lab -Credential (Get-Credential)

    d) To open PowerShell with Administrative privileges, follow the steps below:

        i) On the search box, enter PowerShell. Right-click **PowerShell** and select **Run as administrator**, then confirm.

        ii) Enter the domain admin logon (70411lab\administrator) and password when prompted.

        iii) It is a requirement to open PowerShell with **Run As Administrator**. If you do not, you will receive error 'Access Denied'.

    e) Restart computer:

```
Restart-Computer
```

    f) Shutdown 70411Win7

    g) Shutdown 70411SRV3

    h) Start up 70411SRV1

Important

Windows 7 trial runs for 30 days. To extend the trial for another 30 days (for up to 120 days), run the command **slmgr -rearm** when you receive prompt to activate windows. If you don't do this before the 30-day trial expires, you may have to rebuild your Windows 7 PC.

21. Copy Windows 7 Source files:

    a) Complete the following tasks:

        i) Log on to 70411HPV (Hyper-V server)

        ii) Navigate to D:\Labfiles\ISO-Used\7 Pro folder.

        iii) Right-click **Windows 7 Pro x64.iso** and select Mount.

        iv) The ISO image will be mounted on a drive (Note the drive letter - mine was mounted to drive H).

        v) Log on to 70411SRV1 and run the following PowerShell commands to create the required folder structure:

```
New-Item -type directory E:\Images\Install\x64
New-Item -type directory E:\Images\Install\x86
New-Item -type directory E:\Images\WDS
New-Item -type directory E:\Images\Boot
New-Item -type directory E\Downloads
New-Item -type directory E:\MountedImages
New-Item -type directory E:\Updates\WDS
New-Item -type directory E:\Updates\WSUS
New-Item -type directory 'E\Downloads\Windows Automated Installer'
New-Item -type directory E\Images\Discover
New-Item -type directory E\Downloads\AIK
```

> New-Item -type directory E:\Drivers

    vi) Share the E:\Images folder as **Images** (Grant **Everyone change** access).

        (1) Back to 70411HPV, copy Install.wim from <drive_letter>\sources\ to \\70411SRV1\Images\Install\x64.

        (2) Copy Boot.wim from <drive_letter>\sources\ to \\70411SRV1\Images\Boot\.

22. Final Lab Preparations:

    a) Log on to 70411SRV1 and complete the following tasks:

        i) Before you proceed with the following tasks, modify IE security:

            (1) Open Internet Explorer Options and select the **Security** tab.

            (2) Under **Select zone to view and change security settings**, select **Internet.**

            (3) Beneath **Security level for this zone,** click **Custom level...**

            (4) Under **Security Settings,** locate **Downloads,** and enable **File download.**

            (5) Click **Ok,** respond **Yes** and click **Apply.**

            (6) Close IE.

Note

If you experience difficulties downloading files while logged on to Windows Server 2012 R2, boot your Windows 7 and complete the downloads. Then boot your Hyper-V server and access the file.

        ii) Install .Net Framework 2.0:

            (1) Open Server Manager, click **Manager** and select **Add Roles and Features** to open the Add Roles and Features Wizard.

            (2) Click **Next** four times until you get to **Select features** page.

            (3) On the **Select features** page, Expand **.Net Framework 3.5 and** Select **.Net Framework 3.5 (includes .Net 2.0 and 3.0)** (This is a pre-requisite for AIK) and then click **Next,** then click **Install.**

    b) Still logged on to 70411SRV1 download and install Windows Automated Installer Kit (AIK):

        i) Open the URL http://www.microsoft.com/en-us/download/details.aspx?id=5753&751be11f-ede8-5a0c-058c-2ee190a24fa6=True and click the download link. To ensure you are able to download the file, add all prompted sites to the **Trusted site.**

        ii) Click **save** to save the file in your default location.

        iii) Save the file (KB3AIK_EN.iso) to E:\Downloads\AIK.

iv) Mount the ISO file and save the unpacked files to **E:\Downloads\Windows Automated Installer.**

v) Install the AIK - Open the folder and double-click **StarterCD.**

vi) Click **Windows AIK Setup** to complete the installation.

vii) Download the following MSU files (save in E:\Updates\WDS):
http://download.microsoft.com/download/A/4/6/A46A2319-FB0C-4D9C-A113-38B55170AD94/Windows6.1-KB2296199-x86.msu:
http://download.microsoft.com/download/8/C/0/8C01156B-32C6-436F-8575-DFBB8CE9F848/Windows6.1-KB2305420-x86.msu.

viii) Copy the MSU files to E:\Updates\WDS.

ix) Download the following drivers (INF files) and (unzip and save to E:\Drivers):

x) Download Driver_Win7_7073_07232013.zip from https://drive.google.com/file/d/0B3R_B2UjgcjrV3NmSTJuNXJEeDA/edit?usp=sharing.

xi) Unzip files to E:\Drivers

xii) Open the folder E:\Drivers\Driver_Win7_7073_07232013\Driver_Win7_7073_07232013 and move **WIN7** folder to E:\Drivers\Driver_Win7_7073_07232013.

xiii) Run the PowerShell scripts from the servers specified to create the required folders:

(1) Log on to 70411SRV3 and run the following PowerShell commands:

```
New-Item -type directory E:\Updates\WSUS
New-Item -type directory E:\ServerMon\DCSPerfMon
New-Item -type directory E:\ServerMon\Templates
```

(2) Log on to 70411SRV and run the following PowerShell commands:

```
New-Item -type directory E:\DFS\Namespace
New-Item -type directory E:\DFS\Replication
New-Item -type directory E:\DFS\Reptargets\Reptarget1
New-Item -type directory E:\DFS\DFSRClone
```

xiv) Share E:\DFS\Reptargets\Reptarget1 shared as **Reptarget1.**

xv) Log on to 70411SRV2 and run the following PowerShell commands:

```
New-Item -type directory E:\DFS\Namespace
New-Item -type directory E:\DFS\Replication
New-Item -type directory E:\DFS\Reptargets\Reptarget2
```

     xvi)   Share E:\DFS\Reptargets\Reptarget2 as **Reptarget2** and grant domain admins granted Full Control.

     xvii)   Log on to 70411SRV4 and run the following PowerShell commands:

```
New-Item -type directory E:\DFS\Reptargets\Reptarget1
New-Item -type directory E:\DFS\DFSRClonecopy
```

     xviii)   Share E:\DFS\DFSRClonecopy as **DFSRClonecopy** and grant domain admins granted Full Control.

     xix)   Share E:\DFS\Reptargets\Reptarget1 shared as **Reptarget1.**

     xx)   The following MSU files downloaded: "Windows6.1-KB2296199-x86.msu" and "Windows6.1-KB2305420-x86.msu" on 70411SRV1.

     xxi)   Driver INF file download and saved.

     xxii)   Installed Windows AIK on 70411SRV1.

Congratulations! You have successfully set up your lab. Welcome to a new way of preparing for Microsoft professional exams – Completely hands-on!

Chapter 1

Deploy, Manage and Maintain Servers

1.1 Deploy and manage server images

Introduction

Windows Deployment Services (WDS) provides a simplified, secure means of rapidly and remotely deploying Microsoft Operating systems to computers over the network. WDS installs and configures Microsoft Operating Systems remotely on Computers that are PXE-enabled. It replaces Remote Installation Service (RIS) and assists with the rapid adoption and deployment of Windows. The WDS MMC snap-in allows you to manage all aspects of Windows Deployment Services.

WDS also provides end-users with an experience that is consistent with Windows setup. This means that you do not have to install each operating system directly from an installation media, for example a DVD or USB drive. The benefits of WDS to organizations become immediately apparent - Saves time and speeds up Windows Operating System deployment.

In this section, we will cover following exam objectives:

1.1.0 Install the Windows Deployment Services (WDS) role
1.1.1 Configure and manage boot, install, and discover images
1.1.2 Update images with patches, hotfixes, and drivers
1.1.3 Install features for offline images
1.1.4 Configure driver groups and packages (2012 R2 Objective)

Lab Plan

We will use 70411SRV1 for this lab. WDS will be installed on this server, all configurations in this chapter performed on it.

Additional lab setup

None

1.1.0 Install the Windows Deployment Services (WDS) role

WDS can be installed as a Deployment or Transport Server, or both. These options are available when installing WDS using Server Manager.

Transport Server: This option provides a subset of the functionality of Windows Deployment Services. It contains only the core networking parts which you can use to transmit data (including operating system images) using multicasting on a stand-alone server. You can also use it if you want to have a PXE server that allows clients to PXE boot and download your own custom setup application. You should use this option if you want to use either of these scenarios, but you do not want to incorporate all of Windows Deployment Services.

Deployment Server: This option provides the full functionality of Windows Deployment Services, which you can use to configure and remotely install Windows operating systems. Deployment Server is dependent on the core parts of Transport Server.

WDS server role can be installed via Server Manager or by using Windows PowerShell. After the WDS role is installed, the server has to be configured before it can be used for automated Windows Operating system deployment. WDS can be configured as a stand-alone or Active Directory-integrated server.

Note

When you install Windows Deployment Services, it will automatically provide the option (selected by default) to install the Remote Server Administration Tools. You can also add this feature by using the Add Roles and Features Wizard and checking Remote Server Administration Tools on the Select feature page.

To install the Windows Deployment Services role with Server Manager

1. Login in to 70411SRV1 with Administrator privileges and open Server Manager.
2. From Server Manager, click **Manage** and select **Add roles and features**, the Add Roles and Features Wizard opens, click **Next.**
3. On the **Before you begin** screen, click **Next.**
4. On the Select installation type screen, click Role-based or feature-based installation, and then click **Next**.

5. On the **Select destination server** screen, ensure **70411SRV1** is selected, click **Next**.
6. On the **Select server roles** page, scroll down and then select the **Windows Deployment Services** check box. Click **Next**.
7. A screen requesting you to install **Remote Server Administration Tools** pops up, click **Add Features** and click **Next**.
8. On the **Select features** page, click **Next**.
9. On the **WDS screen**, read the information provided and click **Next**.
10. On the Select role services screen, check Deployment Server and Transport Server, and then click **Next**.
11. On the Confirm installation selections screen, click **Install**.

Note

For an Active Directory integrated configuration; the Deployment Server requires that Active Directory Domain Services, DHCP, and DNS services are available on your network. Transport Server does not require any additional roles or services. Both of these services require an NTFS partition for the file store.

To install the Windows Deployment Services role with Windows PowerShell

Run the following commands on an elevated PowerShell prompt:

```
Install-WindowsFeature –Name WDS –IncludeManagementTools
```

In Windows PowerShell, unlike in the Add Roles and Features Wizard, management tools and snap-ins for a role are not included by default. To include management tools as part of a role installation, add the -IncludeManagementTools parameter to the cmdlet.

Configuring Windows Deployment Services

As stated earlier, after you install the Windows Deployment Service role, you must configure the server. For the purposes of this guide, we will be configuring WDS integrated with Active Directory.

To configure Active Directory- Integrated WDS Server

1. Log on 70411SRV1 and open Server Manager.
2. From Server Manager, click **Tools**, and then click **Windows Deployment Services** to launch the Windows Deployment Services MMC-snap.
3. On the left pane of the Windows Deployment Services MMC snap-in, expand servers.
4. Right-click 70411SRV1.70411Lab.com and click Configure Server.
5. On the **Before you begin** screen, note the pre-requisites and click **Next**.

6. On the Install options page, choose Integrated with Active Directory and click **Next**.

7. On the **Remote Installation Folder Locations** screen, type E:\RemoteInstall (This folder must be in an NTFS partition). Click **Next.**

8. On the **PXE Server Initial Settings** screen, choose **Respond to all client computers (Known and Unknown)**, leave box below unchecked (This will complete the configuration of Windows Deployment Services). click **Next.**

9. On the Operation Complete screen, uncheck Add images to server now check box and click **Finish**.

Initial Windows Deployment Services configuration may also be completed with the WDSUtil.exe command line tool. To complete the task outlined above, execute the command below:

```
WDSUtil.exe /Initialize-Server /Server:70411SRV1
/REMINST:"E:\RemoteInstall"
```

To revert changes made during the server configuration or Initialization, execute the command:

```
WDSUtil.exe /UnInitialize-Server /Server:70411SRV1
```

If the WDS server is not showing green in the Windows Deployment Services Console, highlight servers on the left pane and on the right pane, right-click the server, select All tasks then start. Click ok.

1.1.1 Configure and manage boot, install, and discover images

After configuring WDS server, images need to be added. These images include a boot image (which is the bootable environment that you initially boot the computer into), and an install images (which are the actual operating system images that you deploy). At least one boot and one install image must be added for clients to boot to the Windows Deployment Services server.

Boot images: Boot images are Windows PE images that you boot a client computer into to perform an operating system installation. In most scenarios, you should use the **Boot.wim** file from the installation media. The Boot.wim file contains Windows PE and the Windows Deployment Services client.

Install images: Install images are the operating system images that you deploy to the client computer. You can also use the **Install.wim** file from the installation media.

To add a default boot image

1. Log on to 70411SRV1 and open Server Manager.

2. From **Tools** menu in Server Manager, open Windows Deployment Services MMC snap-in.

3. On the left pane of the Windows Deployment Services MMC snap-in, expand Severs, then expand **70411SRV1.70411Lab.com**.
4. Right-click the **Boot Images** node, and then click **Add Boot Image.**
5. On the **Image file** screen, browse to E:\Images\Boot\boot.wim and click **Open**, then click **Next.**
6. On the **Image Metadata** screen, enter **Windows 7 Professional setup x64** for image name and description fields and click **Next.**
7. On the Summary screen, click **Next.**
8. When task completes, click **Finish.**

Note

The default boot and install images (Boot.wim and Install.wim) are located on the Operation System installation DVD (\Sources folder).

To add a default install image

1. Still logged on to 70411SRV1 and WDS console open.
2. On the left pane of the Windows Deployment Services MMC snap-in, expand **Severs**, then expand **70411SRV1.70411Lab.com.**
3. Right-click the **Install Images** node and then click **Add Install Image.**
4. On the Create an image group name field, enter Win7OSImages and click **Next**.
5. On the **Image file** screen, browse to E:\Images\Install\x64\Install.wim and click **Open**, then click **Next.**
6. On the Available Images screen, uncheck all but Windows 7 Professional and Windows 7 Ultimate, then click Next.
7. On the **Summary** screen, click **Next.**
8. When task completes, click **Finish.**

Manage Boot and Install Image Priorities

A WDS server may contain multiple boot or install images available to client computers. If a WDS server contain multiple boot or install images, clients will be presented with a boot and an install menu that displays the selection of images to choose from. Image priorities may be set in Windows Deployment Services. This controls the order that boot and install image listings are presented to clients.

To configure menu order for boot images

1. Log on 70411SRV1 and open Server Manager.
2. From Server Manager, click **Tools**, and then click **Windows Deployment Services** to launch the Windows Deployment Services MMC-snap.
3. On the left pane of the Windows Deployment Services MMC snap-in, expand **Servers**, and then expand **70411SRV1.70411Lab.com.**

4. Click the **Boot Images** node, list of available boot images will be displayed in the details pane.
5. Right-click Windows 7 Professional setup x64 and click Properties.
6. On the **Image Properties** dialog, on the **General** tab, enter in your desired priority into the Priority text box. The items that appear first on your install image menu are the ones with the lowest value. (Default priority is 50000)
7. Click **Ok**.

To configure menu order for install images

1. Still logged on to 70411SRV1 and WDS console open.
2. On the left pane of the Windows Deployment Services MMC snap-in, expand **Severs**, expand **70411SRV1.70411Lab.com.**
3. Expand **Install Images** node, **Windows7OSImages** group is highlighted and a list of available install images will be displayed in the details pane.
4. On the details pane right-click **Windows 7 Professional** and click **Properties**.
5. On the **Image Properties** dialog, in the **General** tab, enter in your desired priority into the Priority text box. The items that appear first on your install image menu are the ones with the lowest value.
6. Click **Ok**.

Exam Tip

Note how to set the priority of boot and install images. Also note that images with lower numbers appear first on the list. To amend the Operating system order, you should amend the install image and not the boot image boot order.

Working With custom install images

If you want to customize the operating system you deploy in your environment, you may customize the default install image with the following procedure:

1. Deploy the default install image to a reference computer.
2. Install all custom applications you want in the custom install image.
3. Boot the Operating system, log on and run Sysprep, then reboot the reference computer.
4. Boot into PXE, and capture the reference computer as a .WIM file.
5. Upload the .Wim file into Windows Deployment Services console.
6. Configure and deploy the install images.

Note

Referring to Volume to capture during custom image creation, you will see only drives that contain operating systems prepared with Sysprep. If you do not run sysprep, you will not see any drives to capture when you boot the reference computer into PXE. It is very important to boot to WDS after sysprep reboot.

Creating discover images

In some circumstances, A computer might not have PXE-enabled network cards. In this situation, discover images may be created and used to install operating system on those computers. A discover image may be saved on a media (CD, DVD, or USB drive), and a client computer may then be booted with the media.

The discover image on the media locates a Windows Deployment Services server, and the server deploys the install image to the computer. Discover images may be configured to target a specific Windows Deployment Services server. This means that if there are multiple WDS servers in an enterprise, discover images may be created for each one.

Note

A discover image is created from a boot image not an install image.

To create a discover image

1. Still logged on to 70411SRV1 and WDS console open.
2. On the left pane of the Windows Deployment Services MMC snap-in, expand **Severs**, expand **70411SRV1.70411Lab.com.**
3. Click the **Boot Images** node, the list of available boot images will be displayed in the details pane.
4. Right-click Windows 7 Professional setup x64 and select Create Discover Image. The Create Discover Image Wizard opens.
5. On the **Metadata and Locations** screen, accept the default name and description then click **Next.**
6. On the **Location and file name** field, click Browse and select E\Images\Discover. Enter the name of your discover image as **Windows 7 Professional (x64).wim** and click **Open**.
7. Optionally, enter the name of your Windows Deployment Services server that you want to respond when you boot a computer into this image. Click **Next** and then **Finish.**

Additional Server and Image configurations

In this section, we will explore all WDS server and image configurations. We will explore all the tabs in the WDS server properties then Install and Boot image properties and attempt to explain each option. I will explore the most important tabs for the purposes of the exam.

Exploring The Properties Of A WDS Server

A number of options can be configured from the properties of a Windows Deployment Server. It is essential to know what to configure in each tab of the properties sheet.

To explore the properties of a Windows Deployment Services Server:

1. Log on 70411SRV1 and open Server Manager.
2. From Server Manager, click **Tools**, and then click **Windows Deployment Services** to launch the Windows Deployment Services MMC-snap.
3. On the left pane of the Windows Deployment Services MMC snap-in, expand **Servers**, and then right-click **70411SRV1.70411Lab.com** and click **Properties.**
4. Examine the following tabs:
   a) **General** tab: Contains the following - Computer name and Remote installation folder.
   b) **PXE Response** tab: On this tab, you can define which client computers the WDS server will respond to. **known clients** are clients that appear in the list of prestaged devices. You can configure **Do not respond to any computer, Respond only to known client computers** or **Respond to all client computers (known and unknown).** You can also configure the PXE response Delay in this tab.
   c) **Client** tab: Here, you can enable unattended installation, configure not to join computers to the domain and Enable client logging.
   d) **Boot** tab: In the boot tab, you can configure PXE Boot Policy for known and unknown clients, and configure default boot image by architecture.
   e) **AD DS** tab: In the AD DS tab, you can configure Client Naming Policy and Computer Account container Location in Active Directory.
   f) **Advanced** tab: The Advanced tab allows you to configure WDS to dynamically discover valid domain controllers or use specific domain controllers. You are also able to configure DHCP Authorization in DHCP.

Exam Tip

It is important to note what you can configure on each tab. Pay particular attention to PXE Response, Client and Boot tabs.

To explore the properties of a boot image

1. Still logged on to 70411SRV1 and WDS console open.
2. On the left pane of the Windows Deployment Services MMC snap-in, expand **Servers**, and then expand **70411SRV1.70411Lab.com.**
3. Highlight **Boot Images**, and in the details pane, right-click **Windows 7 Professional Setup (x64)** and click **properties**.
4. Examine the following tabs
   a) **General** tab: You can configure the boot image priority, change the name, and also description of the boot image.
   b) **Version** tab: No configurable option available on this tab.

To explore the properties of an Install image

1. Still logged on to 70411SRV1 and WDS console open.
2. In the left pane of the Windows Deployment Services MMC snap-in, expand **Servers**, and then expand **70411SRV1.70411Lab.com.**
3. Expand Install Images, then highlight **Windows7OSImages**, in the details pane, right-click **Windows 7 Professional** and click **properties**.
4. Examine the following tabs
   a) **General** tab: You can configure the install image priority, change the name, and also description. You can also configure the install image to use an answer file in unattended mode.
   b) **Version** tab: No configurable option.
   c) **Filters** tab: You can use Filters to define which clients receive a specific image for installation based on the hardware of the installing client. If you leave the Filters blank, all clients with suitable permissions will receive the image.
   d) **User Permissions** tab: Controls the ACL for the Install image.

Performing an unattended installation

WDS allows you to optionally automate the entire installation of an Operating System deployment. To do this, you use two different unattend files: one for the Windows Deployment Services UI screens, and one for the latter phases of Setup. You can associate an unattend file by install image or associate one to the WDS server.

To associate a client unattend file by Image

1. Still logged on to 70411SRV1 and WDS console open.
2. In the left pane of the Windows Deployment Services MMC snap-in, expand **Servers**, and then expand **70411SRV1.70411Lab.com.**
3. Expand **Install   Images** node,   **Windows7OSImages**   group   is highlighted, and a list of available install images will be displayed in the details pane.
4. Right-click **Windows 7 Professional** install image and click **Properties.**

5. On the **General** tab, check the box **Allow image to install in unattended mode** then click **Select File**, Browse to the .xml file, click **Ok**.

6. Click **Ok** to close the Properties of the image.

To associate Client unattend to WDS server

1. Still logged on to 70411SRV1 and WDS console open.
2. On the left pane of the Windows Deployment Services MMC snap-in, expand **Servers**, and then right-click **70411SRV1.70411Lab.com** and select **properties.**
3. On the **Clients** tab, check the box **Enable Unattended installation**, on the architecture you wish to configure, browse to the location of the .xml file and then click **Open**.

Exam Tip

Note the procedure above, especially the tab to click to associate an answer file to the WDS server and to an image. To associate an answer file to an image, do it from the General tab, to associate to an image, it is done from the Clients tab. Also note that you can only associate by architecture on the server level via the Clients tab.

1.1.2 Update images with patches, hotfixes, and drivers

Deployment Image Servicing and Management (DISM) tool is used to mount an offline Windows image (WIM, VHD or VHDX file). DISM installs, removes, or updates Windows packages provided as cabinet (.cab) or Windows Update Stand-alone Installer (.msu) files to a mounted WIM, VHD or VHDX file. Packages are used by Microsoft to distribute software updates, service packs, and language packs. Packages can also contain Windows features.

DISM servicing commands may also be used to enable or disable a Windows features on an offline image or on a running Windows installation. DISM supports one servicing command per command line. If servicing a running Operating System, use the /online switch instead of specifying the location of the mounted Windows Image.

Note

Windows AIK (Installed during Lab preparation) is a requirement for the DISM commands in this section to work.

The following operating system package-servicing options are available for an offline image:

DISM.exe /Image:<path_to_image_directory>

DISM /image switches for servicing an offline image are detailed below:

Mount-Image: Mounts an image from a .wim, .vhd or .vhdx file to the specified directory so that it is available for servicing.

Commit-Image: Applies the changes that you have made to the mounted image. The image remains mounted until the /Unmount-Image option is used.

Unmount-Image: Unmounts the .wim, .vhd or .vhdx file and either commits or discards the changes that were made when the image was mounted.

Get-Packages: Displays basic information about all packages in the image

Get-PackageInfo: Displays detailed information about a package provided as a .cab file. Only .cab files can be specified.

Add-Package: Installs a specified .cab or .msu package in the image.

Remove-Package: Removes a specified .cab file package from the image. Only .cab files can be specified.

Get-Features: Displays basic information about all features (operating system components that include optional Windows foundation features) in a package.

Get-FeatureInfo: Displays detailed information about a feature. You must use /**FeatureName** switch. Feature names are case sensitive if you are servicing a Windows image other than Windows 8. You can use the /Get-Features option to find the name of the feature in the image.

Enable-Feature: Enables or updates the specified feature in the image. The /FeatureName option must be specified.

Disable-Feature: Disables the specified feature in the image. The /FeatureName option must be specified.

Cleanup-Image: Performs cleanup or recovery operations on the image.

The following operating system package-servicing options are available for a running operating system: DISM.exe /Online

DISM /online switches for servicing an online operating system are the same for an offline image. Obviously, you cannot use Mount-Image, Commit-Image and Unmount-Image for an online or a running operating system.

Note

The difference between servicing an offline image and a running operating system are the switches /Online and /Image. Do not use the /Image or /WinDir option when using /Online option to specify a running Operating system.

The following DISM driver servicing options are available for an offline image: DISM.exe /image

DISM driver servicing switches for an offline image are detailed below:

Get-Drivers: Displays basic information about driver packages in the online or offline image.

Get-DriverInfo: Displays detailed information about a specific driver package.

Add-Driver: Adds third-party driver packages to an offline Windows image.
Remove-Driver: Removes third-party drivers from an offline image.
Export-Driver: Exports all third-party driver packages from a Windows image to a destination path. The exported drivers can then be injected to an offline image by running the DISM Add-Driver command. This command is new for Windows 8.1 Update.

DISM driver servicing for an online or running operating system, DISM.exe /Online has only three applicable switches: Get-Drivers, Get-DriverInfo and Export-Driver

In the next section, you will add the package "Windows6.1-KB2305420-x86.msu"to "Windows 7 PROFESSIONAL x86" image file located in E:\Images\Install\x86 folder.

To add a package (.MSU file) to an offline image

1. Log on to 70411SRV1, and open an elevated command prompt.
2. Run the DISM /Get-ImageInfo command to retrieve the name or index number for the image that you want to update:

Dism /Get-ImageInfo /ImageFile:E:\Images\Install\x86\Install.wim

The index number for "Windows 7 PROFESSIONAL" is 4. You will need to specify this index number in step 3 since the image file contains more than one image.

3. Mount the Windows image:

Dism /Mount-Image /ImageFile:E:\Images\Install\x86\install.wim /Index:4 /MountDir:E:\MountedImages

Image will take a while to mount. When completed, proceed to step 4

4. In this step, you will add "Windows6.1-KB2305420-x86.msu" package to the mounted Windows image:

Dism /Image:E:\MountedImages /Add-Package /PackagePath:E:\Updates\WDS\Windows6.1-KB2305420-x86.msu

When completed, proceed to step 5

5. The last stage will be to commit the changes:

Dism /Commit-Image /MountDir:E:\MountedImages

The changes will take a while to commit. In the next task, you will remove the package we just added from the image.

To remove a package (.MSU file) from an offline image

Review the packages that have been installed in your image, and then remove a specific package from the image.

1. Find the names of the packages that are in your image:

```
Dism /Image:E:\MountedImages /Get-Packages
```

This returns a long list of package files. To make it easier to view, add >E:\PackageList.txt to output the result in the text file:

```
Dism /Image:E:\MountedImages /Get-Packages >E:\PackageList.txt
```

When the command completes, open the text file and search for the package with the number KB2305420 and install time as today's date. Note the package identity of the package:
Package_for_KB2305420~31bf3856ad364e35~x86~~6.1.1.3

2. Specify the package identity of a package and remove it from the mounted image:

```
Dism /Image:E:\MountedImages /Remove-Package
/PackageName:Package_for_KB2305420~31bf3856ad364e35~x86~~6.1.1.3
```

3. The final stage will be to commit the changes and unmount the image:

```
Dism /Unmount-Image /MountDir:E:\MountedImages /Commit
```

Note

You can also use DISM to upgrade editions of windows in the offline image:First list the editions that are available for the upgrade using the /Get-TargetEditions switch; then specify the edition that you want to upgrade to with the /Set-Edition:<edition_name> switch.

To add a Driver (.INF file) to an offline image

1. Using the same Image index from previous task (step 3), mount the Windows image:

```
Dism /Mount-Image /ImageFile:E:\Images\Install\x86\install.wim /Index:4
/MountDir:E:\MountedImages
```

When the action completes successfully, proceed to step 2

2. Add   driver   (.INF   file)   in
    E:\Drivers\Driver_Win7_7073_07232013\WIN7\32   to   the   image
    mounted in E:\MountedImages:

```
Dism /Image: E:\MountedImages /Add-Driver /Driver:
E:\Drivers\Driver_Win7_7073_07232013\WIN7\32\rt86win7.inf
```

DISM will return message "Found 1 driver package(s) to install", performs the installation and return a success message. Move to step 3 when completed.

Multiple drivers can be added on one command line if you specify a folder instead of an .inf file. To install all of the drivers in a folder and all its subfolders, use the /recurse option. For example:

Dism /Image:E:\MountedImages /Add-Driver /Driver:E:\Drivers /Recurse

To install an unsigned driver, use /ForceUnsigned to override the requirement that drivers installed on X64-based computers must have a digital signature. For example:

Dism /Image:E:\MountedImages /Add-Driver /Driver:
E:\Drivers\Driver_Win7_7073_07232013\WIN7\32\rt86win7.inf
/ForceUnsigned

3. Review the list of third-party driver (.inf) files in the Windows image. Drivers added to the Windows image are named Oem*.inf. This is to guarantee unique naming for new drivers added to the computer. For example, the files rt86win7.inf is renamed Oem0.inf ; a second driver is renamed Oem1.inf.:

Dism /Image:E:\MountedImages /Get-Drivers >E:\driverlist.txt

Open E:\driverlist.txt for the list of drivers installed in your current image. The driver you installed in step 3 will display as Published Name: oem2.inf; Original File Name : rt86win7.inf. It will also display other information about the driver.

4. The final stage will be to commit the changes and unmount the image:

Dism /Unmount-Image /MountDir:E:\MountedImages /Commit

The driver servicing command supports only .inf files. Windows Installer or other driver package types (such as .exe files) are not supported. Drivers are installed in the order that they are listed in the command line. In the following example, rt86win7.inf,rt86win8.inf, and rt86win9.inf will be installed in the order that they are listed in the command line.

Dism /Image:
E:\MountedImages /Add-Driver /Driver:
E:\Drivers\Driver_Win7_7073_07232013\WIN7\32\rt86win7.inf/Driver:
E:\Drivers\Driver_Win7_7073_07232013\WIN7\32\rt86win8.inf/Driver:
E:\Drivers\Driver_Win7_7073_07232013\WIN7\32\rt86win9.inf

1.1.3 Install features for offline images

Windows Operating System has a number of features that will only become available after you have installed or enabled them. For example, Indexing

Services, SNMP or Telnet. Most Administrators are used to enabling these features on an operating system, but may not be familiar with enabling the features in an offline image. In this section, we will examine how to use DISM to install or remove features from an offline image.

To install a feature to an offline image

1. Log on to 70411SRV1, and open an elevated command prompt.
2. Run the DISM /Get-ImageInfo command to retrieve the name or index number for the image that you want to update:

Dism /Get-ImageInfo /ImageFile: E:\Images\Install\x86\Install.wim

The image we want to work on displays Name: Windows 7 PROFESSIONAL, Index: 4. In our previous example, we mounted with index number, in this task, we will mount with Name: "Windows 7 PROFESSIONAL"

3. Mount the Windows image:

Dism /Mount-Image /ImageFile:E:\Images\Install\x86\install.wim /Name:"Windows 7 PROFESSIONAL"/MountDir:E:\MountedImages

Image will take a while to mount. When completed, proceed to step 4

4. The next step will be to list all of the features available in our image:

Dism /Image:E:\MountedImages/Get-Features>E:\imagefeatures.txt

Open E:\imagefeatures.txt for a list of all available features in our image. As you can imagine, it is a fairly long list; exactly why we piped it to a text file for easy reading. The command also displays the status of each feature as "Enabled", "Disabled", "Enable Pending" or "Disable Pending".

5. Use /Get-FeatureInfo to list information about a specific feature you are interested in, for example:

Dism /Image:E:\MountedImages/Get-FeatureInfo /FeatureName:TFTP

In the next step, you will enable the TFTP features, currently disabled.

6. Enable a specific feature in the image. You can use the /All argument to enable all of the parent features in the same command. For example:

Dism /Image:E:\MountedImages/Enable-Feature /FeatureName:TFTP

7. Now get the status of the TFTP feature you have enabled:

Dism /Image:E:\MountedImages/Get-FeatureInfo /FeatureName:TFTP

The status is "Enable Pending", you must boot the image in order to enable the feature entirely.

8. Finally, unmount the image and commit the changes:

Dism /Unmount-Image /MountDir:E:\MountedImages /commit

You may also:

9. Disable a specific feature in the image:

Dism /online /Disable-Feature /FeatureName:TFTP or Dism
/Image:E:\MountedImages /Disable-Feature /FeatureName:TFTP

10. Enable or disable Windows features by using DISM and an answer file:

Dism /online /Apply-Unattend:C:\test\answerfiles\myunattend.xml or Dism
/Image:C:\test\offline /Apply-
Unattend:C:\test\answerfiles\myunattend.xml.

The /Unmount switch must be followed by the /commit or /disregard
switch.

1.1.4 Configure driver groups and packages (2012 R2 Objective)

Windows Deployment Services Server console has a **Drivers** node. From this
node, you can perform the following tasks:
Add Driver Package: Defines which client computers will install drivers in a
package using a Drivers Group. You can also add driver packages to boot
images. To add a driver package, the package must be extracted. It cannot be
.msi or .exe. You have option to select a package from an .INF file or select
all driver packages from a folder.
Add Driver Group: A Driver Group is a collection of Driver Packages that
are available to a select group of client computers. You can also **Enable**,
Disable or **Delete** Driver Packages.

To Add a Driver Package

1. Log on 70411SRV1 and open Server Manager.
2. From Server Manager, click **Tools**, and then click **Windows Deployment Services** to launch the Windows Deployment Services MMC-snap.
3. On the left pane of the Windows Deployment Services MMC snap-in, expand **Servers**, and then expand **70411SRV1.70411Lab.com.**
4. Right-click **Drives** node and select **Add Driver Package**.
5. On the **Driver Package Location** screen, select the option "Select driver packages from an .inf file", then Browse to
6. "E:\Drivers\Driver_Win7_7073_07232013\WIN7\32\rt86win7.inf", then click **Next.**

7. On the **Available Driver Packages** screen, confirm that rt86win7(x86) is checked, click **Next.**
8. On the **Summary** screen, click **Next.**
9. When the task completes, click Next, then select the option Do not put the driver packages in a drivers group at this time and click Next then Finish.

To Add a Driver Group

1. Right-click **Drives** node and select **Add Driver Group.**
2. In the **Driver Group Name** field, type **NICDrivers,** and click **Next.**
3. On the Client Hardware Filter screen, click Add, on the Add Filter screen under Filter Type, select Model; under Operator, select Equal To, then type Microsoft Corporation Virtual Machine and click Add, then click Ok.
4. On the Client Hardware Filter screen, click Next.
5. On the **Install image Filters** screen, click **Add**, and on the **Add Filter** screen, under **Filter Type,** select **OS Edition**; under **Operator,** select **Equal To**, then type **ULTIMATE** click **Add**, and click **Ok.**
6. On the Install image Filters screen, click Next.
7. On the Packages to install page, select Install only the driver packages that match a client's hardware, click Next, then Finish.

To Add a Driver Package to a Driver Group

1. Expand **Drives** node, then highlight **All Packages.**
2. On the details pane, right-click **rt86win7 [x86]** and select **Properties.**
3. On the Properties page of rt86win7 [x86], click **Group Membership** tab then select **NICDrivers** Driver Group and click the > button. Click **Apply,** then **Ok.**
4. Now if you highlight **NICDrivers**, rt86win7 [x86] will be displayed as a member.

The task above can be performed from either the properties of the Driver package or by right-clicking the **NICDrivers** driver group. To complete the task from the driver group, right-click **NICDrivers** driver group and select **Add Driver Packages to this Group**. The properties page of a driver group does not have the option. The only configurable option from a driver group's properties sheet is the Filters tab.

To Add A driver package to a boot image

1. Log on 70411SRV1 and open Server Manager.
2. From Server Manager, click **Tools**, and then click **Windows Deployment Services** to launch the Windows Deployment Services MMC-snap.
3. In the left pane of the Windows Deployment Services MMC snap-in, expand **Servers**, and then expand **70411SRV1.70411Lab.com.**

4. Highlight **Boot Images,** then in the details pane, right-click "Windows 7 Professional Setup (x64)" and select **Add Driver Package to Image,** then click **Next.**

5. On the **Select Driver Packages** screen, no package is displayed because we do not have a driver package for x64 architecture. But you get the message!

6. Cancel the Add Driver Package to a Boot Image wizard.

1.2 Implement Patch Management

Introduction

Windows Server Update Service (WSUS) server allows Network administrators to specify the Microsoft updates that should be installed, create separate groups of computers, and get reports on the compliance levels of the computers and updates that must be installed.

In addition, a WSUS server can be the update source for other WSUS servers within the organization. The WSUS server that acts as an update source is called an upstream server; other WSUS servers that connect to the upstream server are called downstream servers. In a WSUS implementation, at least one WSUS server in the network must connect to Microsoft Update to get available update information. The administrator can determine, based on network security and configuration, how many other servers connect directly to Microsoft Update.

In this section, we will cover following exam objectives:

1.2.0 Install and configure the Windows Server Update Services (WSUS) role;

1.2.1 Configure group policies for updates

1.2.2 Configure client-side targeting

1.2.3 Configure WSUS synchronization

1.2.4 Configure WSUS groups

1.2.5 Manage patch management in mixed environments (2012 R2 Objective)

Lab Plan

We will use 70411SRV1 as our upstream server, 70411SRV3 as our downstream server. 70411Win8 as our client.

Additional Lap setup

Create a folder called **WSUSFiles** on 70411SRV1, drive E:\

1.2.0 Install and Configure the Windows Server Update Services (WSUS) role

In this section, we will consider the requirements for WSUS installation and install the role on two servers, 70411SRV1 (Our upstream server connects to Microsoft update) and 70411SRV3 (Our downstream server connects to 70411SRV1). After installing WSUS role on both servers, we will perform post-installation configurations.

WSUS Installation system requirements

Before you enable the WSUS server role, confirm that the server meets the system requirements and confirm that you have the necessary permissions to complete the installation by adhering to the following guidelines:

1. Server hardware requirements to enable WSUS role. The minimum hardware configuration for WSUS are listed below:
   a) Processor: 1.4 gigahertz (GHz) x64 processor (2Ghz or faster is recommended)]
   b) Memory: WSUS requires an additional 1.5GB of RAM - above and beyond what is required by Windows Server 2012 R2 or Windows Server 2012.
   c) Available disk space: 10 GB (40GB or greater is recommended)
   d) Network adapter: 100 megabits per second (Mbps) or greater.
2. If you install roles or software updates that require you to restart the server when installation is complete, restart the server before you enable the WSUS server role.
3. Microsoft .NET Framework 4.5must be installed on the server where the WSUS server role will be installed.
4. The NT Authority\Network Service account must have Full Control permissions for the following folders so that the WSUS Administration snap-in displays correctly:

%windir%\Microsoft.NET\Framework\v4.0.30319\Temporary   ASP.NET Files and %windir%\Temp folder. This path might not exist prior to installing a Web Server Role that contains Internet Information Services (IIS).

5. Confirm the account you plan to use to install WSUS as a member of the Local Administrators group.
6. During the installation process, WSUS will install the following by default:
   a) .NET API and Windows PowerShell cmdlets
   b) Windows Internal Database (WID), which is used by WSUS
   c) Services used by WSUS, which are:
      i)   Update Service
      ii) Reporting Web Service
      iii) Client Web Service

iv) Simple Web Authentication Web Service
v)   Server Synchronization Service
vi) DSS Authentication Web Service

WSUS database requirements

WSUS requires one of the following databases:

1. Windows Internal Database (WID).
2. Microsoft SQL Server 2012 Standard Edition.
3. Microsoft SQL Server 2012 Enterprise Edition.
4. Microsoft SQL Server 2012 Express Edition.
5. Microsoft SQL Server 2008 R2 SP1 Standard Edition.
6. Microsoft SQL Server 2008 R2 SP1 Enterprise Edition.
7. Microsoft SQL Server 2008 R2 SP1 Express Edition.

SQL Server Express 2008 R2 has a database size limitation of 10 GB. This database size is likely to be sufficient for WSUS, although there is no appreciable benefit to using this database instead of WID. WID database has a minimum RAM memory requirement of 2 GB.

You can install the WSUS role on a computer that is separate from the database server computer. In this case, the following additional criteria apply:

1. The database server cannot be configured as a domain controller.
2. The WSUS server cannot run Remote Desktop Services.
3. The database server must be in the same Active Directory domain as the WSUS server, or it must have a trust relationship with the Active Directory domain of the WSUS server.
4. The WSUS server and the database server must be in the same time zone or be synchronized to the same Coordinated Universal Time (Greenwich Mean Time) source.

Perform pre-installation tasks

Perform the following WSUS pre-installation actions in 70411SRV1 and 70411SRV3

1. Add the domain admin account as member of the Local Administrators group of both servers: Server Manager – Tools – Computer Management.
2. Confirm that Microsoft .NET Framework 4.5 is installed. If not, install it via Server Manager – Add Roles or Features – Features.
3. Confirm that the Network Service account have Full Control permissions to:
    a)   C\Windows\Microsoft.NET\Framework64\v4.0.30319\ folder
    b)   To complete this task, take ownership of the folder C\Temp folder.
4. Confirm that your servers meet the minimum hardware requirements:

a) Processor: 1.4 gigahertz (GHz) x64 processor (2 Ghz or faster is recommended)
b) Memory: WSUS requires an additional 1.5 GB of RAM - above and beyond what is required by Windows Server 2012 R2 or Windows Server 2012.
c) Available disk space: 10 GB (40 GB or greater is recommended)
d) Network adapter: 100 megabits per second (Mbps) or greater.

To install the WSUS server role

1. Log on to 70411SRV1 and open Server Manager.
2. In Server Manager, click **Manage**, and then click **Add roles and features.**
3. On the Before you begin page, click Next.
4. In the Select installation type screen, confirm that Role-based or feature-based installation option is selected and click **Next.**
5. On the Select **destination server** page, select **70411SRV1**, and then click **Next.**
6. On the Select server roles screen, select Windows Server Update Services and click Next.
7. In the **Add Roles and Features** Wizard dialog box, click **Add Features**, and then click **Next.**
8. On the **Select features** screen, leave the default selections, and then click **Next.**

Note

WSUS only requires the default Web Server role configuration. If you are prompted for additional Web Server role configuration while setting up WSUS you can safely accept the default values and continue setting up WSUS.

9. On the **Windows Server Update Services** page, note the following:
   a) At least one WSUS server in the network must be able to download updates from Microsoft Updates.
   b) WSUS server-to-server and server-to-client communication should be setup to use the Secure Sockets layer (SSL), click **Next**.
10. On the **Select Role Services** screen, leave the default selections, and then click **Next.**
11. On the Content location selection screen, check the box **Store Updates in the following location** and type E:\Updates\WSUS (Updates will be stored here), and then click **Next.**
12. On the **Web Server Role services** screen, note the information and click **Next.**
13. On the **Role Services** screen, accept the defaults and click **Next.**

14. On the **Confirm installation selections** screen, review the selected options, and then click **Install.**
15. On the Installation progress screen, click **Close.**
16. In Server Manager, verify if a notification appears to inform you that a restart is required. If a restart is prompted, restart the server to complete the installation.

While the installation on 70411SRV1 is running, install WSUS on 70411SRV3 using Windows PowerShell.

To install the WSUS using Windows PowerShell:

Log on to 70411SRV3 as administrator and run the following command:

```
Install-WindowsFeature -Name UpdateServices -IncludeManagementTools
```

Configure WSUS by using the WSUS Configuration Wizard

After installing the WSUS server role on 70411SRV1 and 70411SRV3, you need to properly configure them. The following sections describe the steps required to perform the initial configuration for your WSUS servers.

Note

By default, in Windows Server 2012, WSUS 4.0 uses port 8530. However, WSUS 3.0 uses port 80, by default.

To configure 70411SRV1 as an upstream server

1. Log on to 70411SRV1 and open Server Manager.
2. In the Server Manager Navigation pane, click Tools, and then click Windows Server Update Services.
3. In the **Before You Begin** screen, click **Next.**
4. On the Join the Microsoft Update Improvement Program, uncheck Yes, I would like to Join the Microsoft Update Improvement Program and click **Next.**
5. On the Choose Upstream Server screen, select Synchronize from Microsoft Update and click **Next.**
6. On the Specify Proxy Server screen, click **Next.**
7. On the **Connect to Upstream Server screen**, Click **Start Connecting,** (This will take a while, to connect). When it connects, click **Next** to proceed.
8. On the Choose Languages screen, Select Download updates in these Languages, then select English and click **Next.**

Note

You have the option to select the languages from which WSUS will receive updates. There is an option to select All languages or a subset of languages. Selecting a subset of languages will save disk space, but it is important to choose all of the languages that are needed by all the clients of your WSUS server. If you select the option Download updates only in these languages, and the upstream server has downstream WSUS servers connected to it, all the downstream servers will be forced to also use only the selected languages.

9. On the **Choose Products** screen, to make download faster, check Windows 7, Windows 8, and Windows Server 2012 R2 and uncheck all others and click **Next.**

10. On the **Choose Classifications** screen, take note how the updates are classified. In particular, note the defaults selected: **Critical, Definition** and **Security** updates. Accept the defaults and click **Next.**

11. On the **Set Sync Schedule** screen, you have the option whether to perform synchronization manually or automatically. Information on available options are discussed below:

    a) If you choose **Synchronize manually**, you must start the synchronization process from the WSUS Administration Console.

    b) If you choose **Synchronize automatically**, the WSUS server will synchronize at set intervals.

    c) Set the time for the First synchronization and specify the number of Synchronizations per day that you want the server to perform. For example, if you specify that there should be four synchronizations per day, starting at 3:00 A.M., synchronizations will occur at 3:00 A.M., 9:00 A.M., 3:00 P.M., and 9:00 P.M.

12. On the Set Sync Schedule screen, select Synchronize manually and click Next.

13. On the Finished page, ensure that Begin initial synchronization box is UNCHECKED, then click Finish.

14. When you click **Finish**, Windows Server Update Services Console opens.

15. Click 70411SRV1 and on the details pane, under **Synchronization status**, click **Synchronize now.**

16. While initial synchronization is running on 70411SRV1, configure 70411SRV3 as a downstream server.

To configure 70411SRV3 as a downstream server

1. Log on to 70411SRV3 as administrator and open Server Manager.

2. In the Server Manager Navigation pane, click **Tools**, and then click **Windows Server Update Services**.

3. On the Complete WSUS Installation wizard, check the box **Store updates locally**, and enter the path E:\Updates\WSUS in Current directory path, then click **Run**.
4. When the Post-Installation task completes, click **Close**. Windows Server Update Services Opens.
5. On the **Before You Begin** screen, click **Next**.
6. On the Join the Microsoft Update Improvement Program, uncheck Yes, I would like to Join the Microsoft Update Improvement Program, and click **Next**.
7. On the Choose Upstream Server screen, select Synchronize from another Windows Server Update Services server, and on the Server Name field, enter 70411SRV1 (Note the default port number - 8530), check the box This is a replica of the upstream server (A replica server mirrors update approvals settings, computers, and groups from the parent. Updates can be approved only on the upstream server) then click **Next**.
8. On the Specify Proxy Server screen, click **Next**.
9. On the **Connect to Upstream Server** screen, **Click Start Connecting**, (This will take a while, to connect). When it connects, click **Next** to proceed.
10. On the **Choose Languages screen**, Select **Download updates in these Languages**, then select English (English is the only Language option available because this was what we configured on the upstream server) then click **Next**.
11. On the **Choose Products** screen check Windows 7, Windows 8, and Windows Server 2012 R2, **uncheck** all others and click **Next**.
12. On the Choose Classifications screen, click **Next**
13. On the **Set Sync Schedule** screen, you have the option whether to perform synchronization manually or automatically. Chose Manual Synchronize manually and click **Next**.
14. On the **Finished** page, ensure that **Begin initial synchronization** box is **UNCHECKED**, then click **Finish**. Windows Server Update Services Console opens.
15. Click 70411SRV3, and on the details pane, under **Synchronization status, click Synchronize now**.

Configure WSUS Options

After initial post-installation configuration of WSUS, you may still want to perform additional configurations or reconfigure the WSUS server. In this section, we will review the available configurable options in Windows Server Update Service. The options to configure for an upstream server may differ from a downstream server.

Configure Options for an Upstream Server

Log on to 70411SRV1 and open Windows Server Update Services from Server Manager. Click **Options**. From the details pane, you can configure the following:

1. **Update Source and Proxy Server**: This allows you to configure whether the WSUS server synchronizes from Microsoft Update or from an upstream server. To review the options available, click on the hyper-link **Update Source and Proxy Server** and click the following:
   a) **Update Source** Tab: Used to configure synchronization.
   b) **Proxy Server** tab: Used to configure proxy server that WSUS may use to connect to the internet.
2. **Products and Classification**: This node has two tabs:
   a) **Products** tab: You can specify the products for which you want to synchronize updates. For example, Active Directory, Exchange, etc.
   b) **Classifications** tab: Allows you to specify class of updates. The following classes are selected by default: Critical updates, Definition Updates and Security Updates. Other classifications are: Drivers, Feature Packs, Service Packs, Tools, Update Rollups and Updates.

Note

Note the class of updates that are checked by default: **Critical** updates, **Definition** Updates and **Security** Updates.

---

   c) **Update Files and Languages**: Specify where to store updates. There are two tabs:
      i) **Update Files** tab - Has two options:
         (1) Store Update files Locally on this server and Do not store updates update files Locally; computers install from Microsoft Update.
         (2) Under Store Update files Locally on this server, there are two check boxes:
            (a) Download update files to this server only when updates are approved.
            (b) Download express installation files.

Note

The express installation files feature identifies the exact bytes between versions, creates and distributes updates of only those differences, and then merges the existing file with the updated bytes. Express installation files setting is used to limit the bandwidth consumed on the local network. However, this is at the cost of additional bandwidth on the Internet connection and additional local disk space. By default, WSUS does not use express installation files. If you require this feature, it must be enabled on the WSUS server.

      ii) **Update Languages** tab: This is the second tab under Update Files and languages. On this tab, you can decide which Languages to download.

3. **Synchronization Schedule**: This option configures how WSUS server synchronizes with an upstream server. Manual or scheduled synchronize is supported. We will configure synchronization in sections 1.2.3 and 1.2.2. It is important to note that you can configure up to 24 synchronizations per day. When synchronizing from Microsoft update, the synchronization start time will have a random offset of up to 30 minutes after the specified time.

4. **Automatic Approvals**: Allows you to specify how to automatically approve automated installation of updates for selected groups and define how to approve revisions for existing updates. There are two tabs on this node:

    a) **Update Rules** tab: Specify Rules for automatically approving updates when they are synchronized. You can edit the Default Automatic Approval Rule or create a new rule. To create a new rule click **New Rule** and complete the following:

      i) **Under Step 1: Select Properties**, Select any of the following:

        (1) When an update is in a specific classification.

        (2) When an update is in a specific product.

        (3) Set a deadline for approval.

      ii) **Under Step 2: Edit the properties**. You can configure this depending on the options you checked in step 1.

        (1) If you selected **When an update is in a specific classification,** then you can configure: When an update is in a specified classification, approve updates for a specified computer group.

        (2) If you selected **When an update is in a specific product,** then you can configure: When an update is in a specified product, approve updates for a specified computer group.

        (3) If you selected **Set a deadline for approval,** then you can configure: approve updates for a specified computer group

and then set a deadline after **X** number of days after the approval at **Y** hours.

iii) **Under Step 3: Specify a name**; enter a name for the Automatic Approval Rule.

b) **Advanced** tab: This is the second tab on the properties of Automatic Approvals node. You can check the check boxes Automatically approve updates to the WSUS product itself and Automatically Approve new revision updates that are already approved.

5. **Computers**: The Computers node allows you to specify how to assign computers to groups. Two options are available:

a) **Use Update Services Console**: New computers will automatically be placed in the **Unassigned** Computers group.

b) **Use Group Policy or Registry settings on computers**: Select this option. We will be configuring Group Policy settings for WSUS in the next section.

6. **Server Clean Up Wizard**: With WSUS server cleanup wizard, you can free up old computers, updates and update files from the WSUS server.

7. **Reporting Rollup**: Gives you the option to allow or deny a replica downstream server rollup computer and update status to the Upstream WSUS server.

Exam Tip

Reporting Rollup can only be configured from the upstream server when the downstream server is configured as a replica server. As you will see when we configure our downstream server, this option is greyed out.

8. **Email Notification**: WSUS can send email notifications of new updates and status reports. There are two tabs:

a) **General** tab: Configure email recipients and status report frequency and Language

b) **Email Server** tab: Configure your email server settings.

9. **Microsoft Update Improvement program**: Gives you the option to join the program.

10. **Personalization**: In Personalization, you can chose how downstream roll up data is displayed, which items are shown in the To Do List, and how validation errors are displayed. This node has two tabs:

a) **General** tab: In this tab, you configure how replica downstream data is displayed. If you roll up data from your replica downstream servers, you can choose whether to include that information when viewing computers and status.

b) **To Do list** tab: Determine which items in the To Do list of the WSUS server.

11. **WSUS Server Configuration Wizard**: This wizard allows you to configure the basic Windows Server Update Services settings. Each of the settings that can be configured using this wizard can be configured using all the tools already discussed above.

Exam Tip

Once you have performed the initial post-installation configuration using the WSUS Server Configuration wizard, you do not need to re-run the wizard to configure any of the options above. It is recommended to use the configuration options in the WSUS server console.

To Configure a Downstream Server

The options for the downstream server are very similar to that of the upstream server with a few exceptions. I have highlighted the options where the downstream server differs from the upstream server.

Log on to 70411SRV3 and open Windows Server Update Services. Click **Options** and from the details pane, review the following:

1. **Update Source and Proxy Server**: The downstream server synchronizes from the upstream server 70411SRV1. There are two nodes in this option:

    a) **Update Source** tab: This tab allows you to configure 70411SRV3 to synchronize with 70411SRV1. You can also configure whether the downstream server is a replica of the upstream server. When a server is configured as a replica server, an option to download updates directly from Microsoft is greyed out. Finally, the Update Source tab has a box where you can specify the port number of the upstream server and a check box to configure the downstream server to use SSL during synchronization.

    b) **Proxy Server** tab: Allows you to configure proxy server that WSUS may use to connect to the internet. This option is valid only when the downstream server is not configured as a replica server.

2. Products and Classification: All options here are disabled as this server is a replica of the upstream server.

3. **Update Files and Languages**: The two tabs are available for configuration. The only difference is the Update Languages tab. As this is a downstream server, the only languages available are the Languages configured in the Upstream server.

4. **Synchronization Schedule**: This option can be configured on the downstream server.

5. Automatic Approvals: This option is disabled as this is a replica server.

6. **Computers**: You can configure this option. Select Use Group Policy or Registry settings on computers.

7. **Server Clean Up Wizard**: You can use the WSUS server clean up wizard on the downstream server
8. Reporting Rollup: This option is disabled because 70411SRV3 is a replica server.
9. **Email Notification**: This option is fully available for configuration on the downstream server.
10. Microsoft Update Improvement program: This is disabled in a downstream server that is configured as a replica server.
11. **Personalization**: Personalization can be configured on a downstream server.
12. **WSUS Server Configuration Wizard**: Most part of the wizard is disabled except the following:
    a) **Chose Upstream server**: You can also deselect to configure the downstream server as a replica of the upstream server.
    b) **Specify Proxy**: You are able to configure proxy for the downstream server.

Exam Tip

It is very important to note the WSUS options that are not available for configuration when the downstream server is configured as a replica of an upstream server. I intentionally left them in red above. When you configure the downstream server as a non-replica, all the options become available for configuration except Product and Classification.

1.2.1 Configure group policies for updates

Group Policy settings can configure multiple WSUS clients simultaneously. Creating a new GPO containing only WSUS settings is recommended. The Active Directory container that a WSUS GPO is linked depends on the environment. In a simple environment, a single WSUS GPO might be linked to the domain. In a more complex environment, multiple WSUS GPOs might be linked to several organizational units (OUs). This enables administrators to apply different WSUS policy settings to different types of computers.
In the task below, you will copy the Default Domain Policy, name it WSUS Policy, edit the WSUS GPO and link it to the 70411Lab.com domain.

To enable WSUS through a domain GPO

1. Log on to 70411SRV and Open Group Policy Management Console.
2. On the Group Policy Management Console (GPMC), expand **Forests: 704011Lab.com**, expand **Domains**, and beneath Domains, expand **704011Lab.com**. Finally expand **Group Policy Objects** container.
3. To make a copy of **Default Domain Policy**, drag and drop it to the Group Policy Objects container. On the **Copy GPO** dialogue, select **Use**

the default permissions for new GPO and click **Ok.** When the copy completes, click **Ok.**

4. A new GPO, named **Copy of Default Domain Policy** appears in the Group Policy Objects container. Right-click the new GPO and select rename, then type **WSUS Policy** as the new name. In the next step, you will edit the GPO and configure WSUS settings.

5. Right-click **WSUS Policy** GPO and select **edit**. The Group Policy Management Editor Opens **WSUS Policy** GPO for editing.

6. Navigate to Computer Configuration\Policies\Administrative Templates\Windows Components, and then click **Windows Update**.

7. In the details pane, double-click **Configure Automatic Updates**, click **Enabled**, and then click one of the following options under the **Configure automatic updating** setting: (Note the following but accept the default, in red):

   a) **Notify for download and notify for install**: This option notifies a logged-on administrative user to the logged on user can download and install the updates.

   b) Auto download and notify for install (Default selection): This option automatically begins downloading updates and then notifies a logged-on administrative user before installing the updates.

   c) **Auto download and schedule the install:** This option automatically begins downloading updates and then installs the updates on the day and time that you specify.

   d) **Allow local admin to choose setting**: This option lets local administrators to use Automatic Updates in Control Panel to select a configuration option. For example, they can choose a scheduled installation time. Local administrators cannot disable Automatic Updates.

   e) On the **Schedule install day**, select **Friday** from the drop down, and on the **schedule install time** select **3pm**.

   f) On the Configure Automatic Updates, click **Ok**.

8. In the Windows Update details pane, double-click the policy Specify intranet Microsoft update service location. Click Enabled, and check the Set the intranet update service for detecting updates.

9. In the **Set the intranet statistics server** boxes, enter http://70411SRV1:8530 on both boxes and then click **Ok**.

Note

When you type the intranet address of your WSUS server make sure to specify which port is going to be used. By default WSUS will use port 8530 for HTTP and 8531 for HTTPS.

To link the WSUS Policy GPO to the domain

1. Log on to 70411SRV and Open Group Policy Management Console.
2. In the Group Policy Management Console (GPMC), expand **Forests: 704011Lab.com**, expand **Domains**, and beneath Domains, expand **704011Lab.com**. Finally expand **Group Policy Objects** container.
3. Drag the **WSUS Policy** GPO from the **Group Policy Objects** container to the root of the 70411Lab.com domain.
4. Respond Ok to the dialogue box Do you want to link the GPOs that you have selected to this Domain?
5. **WSUS Policy** GPO will now appear under the 70411Lab.com domain.

All computers in the domain are expected to accept the configuration in the GPO as specified above. After a client computer updates WSUS configuration via group policy, it will take several minutes before the computer appears on the Computers page in the WSUS Administration Console.

For client computers that are configured with a domain-based Group Policy Object, it can take about 20 minutes for Group Policy to apply the new policy settings to the client computer. By default, Group Policy updates in the background every 90 minutes, with a random offset of 0-30 minutes. To update Group Policy sooner, open a Command Prompt on the client computer and type **gpupdate /force**.

For client computers configured using the Local Group Policy Editor, the GPO is applied immediately, and the update takes about 20 minutes. If you begin detection manually, you do not have to wait 20 minutes for the client computer to contact WSUS. For WSUS detection to start immediately, run the **wuauclt.exe /detectnow** command from the client computer.

1.2.2 Configure client-side targeting

Client-side targeting is configured via group policy and specifies the target group name or names in WSUS that should be used to receive updates from an intranet Microsoft update service. The **Enable Client-side targeting** policy configures client computers to add themselves to target computer groups on the WSUS server, when Automatic Updates is redirected to a WSUS server. If the status of this policy is set to **Enabled**, a client computer will identify itself as a member of a particular WSUS computer group when it sends information to the WSUS server; the WSUS server uses the information received from the client to determine which updates are deployed to the client computer. The WSUS computer group must be created on the WSUS server. Domain-member computers group should be added as members of this group.

If the status of the policy is set to **Disabled** or **Not Configured**, no target group information will be sent to the intranet Microsoft update service. If the intranet Microsoft update service supports multiple target groups, this policy can specify multiple group names separated by semicolons. Otherwise, a single group must be specified.

Note

The **Enable Client-side targeting** policy applies only when the intranet Microsoft update service is configured to support client-side targeting. If the **Specify intranet Microsoft update service location** policy is **Disabled** or **Not Configured**, the policy has no effect. In simple terms, before client-side targeting will work, the **Specify intranet Microsoft update service location** GPO must be configured. You must create the group on the WSUS server, and add domain-member computers to that group. Client-side targeting configuration can be performed using domain-based or Local GPO.

To configure client-side targeting using Domain GPO

Open the **WSUS Policy** GPO created in the previous section for editing, and complete the following tasks:

1. Navigate to Computer Configuration\Policies\Administrative Templates\Windows Components, and then click Windows Update.
2. In the details pane, click **Enable Client-side targeting** Policy and select **Enabled**.
3. On the **Target Group Name for this Computer** enter **WSUS Computers** (This group will be created in WSUS in section 1.2.4).
4. Click **Ok** to close Enable Client-side targeting Policy.

To View the WSUS Policy GPO Configuration

1. Log on to 70411SRV2 and Open Group Policy Management Console.
2. In the Group Policy Management Console (GPMC), expand **Forests: 704011Lab.com**, expand **Domains**, and beneath Domains, expand **704011Lab.com**. Finally expand **Group Policy Objects** container.
3. Highlight **WSUS Policy** GPO and click the **Settings** tab, after a while, the GPO settings will be generated.
4. Under **Computer Configuration (Enabled),** click **Show**, then **Show Policies**, Administrative Templates, Windows Component / Windows update. You can now view all the configurations we enabled.

1.2.3 Configure WSUS synchronization

We have configured synchronization when we performed post-installation configuration on both the upstream and downstream servers. For the purpose of clarity, the elements of this task are:

1. Specify a proxy server: Necessary if you connect to the internet via a proxy server.

2. Specify WSUS Languages: Refer to point number 3: Update Files and Languages under Configure Options for an Upstream Server treated earlier in this chapter.
3. Synchronize WSUS Server: This has also been covered. Under Options, on the Update Server Console, select Synchronization Schedule: This option allows you to configure how you want your WSUS server to synchronize with the upstream server. You can synchronize manually of schedule synchronization.

By default, WSUS is configured to use Microsoft Update as the location from which to obtain updates. If you have a proxy server on the network, you can configure WSUS to use the proxy server. If there is a corporate firewall between WSUS and the Internet, you might have to configure the firewall to ensure that WSUS can obtain updates.

Note

Although Internet connectivity is required to download updates from Microsoft Update, WSUS offers you the ability to import updates to a server is not connected to the Internet.

1.2.4 Configure WSUS groups

Computer groups are an important part of Windows Server Update Services (WSUS) deployments. Computer groups permit the testing and targeting updates to specific computers. There are two default computer groups: **All Computers** and **Unassigned Computers**. By default, when each client computer first contacts the WSUS server, the server adds the client computer to both groups.

WSUS allows you to create as many custom computer groups as you need to manage updates in your organization. It is recommended to create at least one computer group to test updates before you deploy them to other computers in your organization. Assignment of computer groups is determined by the option selected on the **Computers** node. As explained when we reviewed this option in the previous section, you can either configure the **Use update services console** or **Use Group Policy or registry settings on the computers**. We selected the second option and have configured group policy to manage the placement of computers.

Plan WSUS computer groups

WSUS allows you to target updates to groups of client computers, so you can ensure that specific computers always get the right updates at the most convenient times. For example, if all the computers in one department (such as the IT team) have a specific configuration, you can set up a computer group for that team, decide which updates their computers need and what time they should be installed, and then use WSUS reports to evaluate the updates for the team.

Note

If a WSUS server is running in replica mode, computer groups cannot be created on that server. All the computer groups that are needed for client computers of the replica server must be created on the WSUS server that is the root of the WSUS server hierarchy. To confirm this, log on to 70411SRV3, navigate to **Computers**, when you right-click **All Computers**, the **Add Computer Group** Option is disabled.

Computers are always assigned to the **All Computers** group, and they remain assigned to the **Unassigned Computers** group until you assign them to another group. Computers can belong to more than one group.

Computer groups can be set up in hierarchies. For example, if two computer groups, **First Line Support** and **Second Line Support** are both below another computer group called **IT Support** Group, updates approved for the higher group (**IT Support**) will automatically be deployed to the lower groups (**First Line Support** and **Second Line Support** groups), in addition to the higher group (**IT Support**). In this example, if you approve **Update1** for the **IT Support** group, the update will be deployed to all the computers in the **IT Support** group and all the computers in the **First Line Support** group, and the **Second Line Support** group.

It is possible for a single update to be approved more than once for the same computer (because computers can be assigned to multiple groups). However, the update will be deployed only once, and any conflicts will be resolved by the WSUS server. To continue with the example in the previous paragraph, if **ComputerA** is assigned to the **First Line Support** group and **Second Line Support** group, and **Update1** is approved for both groups, it will be deployed only once.

You can assign computers to computer groups by using server-side or client-side targeting.

Server-side targeting: Deploys manual assignment of one or more client computers to multiple groups simultaneously.

Client-side targeting: Deploys Group Policy or registry settings on client computers to enable those computers to automatically add themselves into previously created computer groups.

Targeting is configured under Computers (Options node) in WSUS update console. Selecting Use update services console, configures Server-side targeting. Selecting Use Group Policy or registry settings on the computers, configures WSUS for Client-side-targeting. Client-side-targeting requires group policy configuration to manage the placement of computers in WSUS.

Note

Selecting "Use Group Policy or registry settings on the computers" in the Computer configuration option requires two more configurations to complete client-side-targeting configuration:
1. Create a computer group in WSUS console.
2. Configure group policies: Enable Client-side targeting and specify intranet Microsoft update service location GPOs must be configured.

Conflict Resolution

WSUS server applies the following rules to resolve conflicts and determine the resultant action on clients: Priority, Install/Uninstall and Deadline.

Priority

The actions associated with the group of the highest priority override the actions of other groups. The deeper a group appears within the hierarchy of groups, the higher its priority. Priority is assigned only based on depth; all branches have equal priority. Figure 1.2.0 illustrates a sample Update Services console hierarchy pane, for a WSUS server named 70411SRV1. Computer groups named **Desktop Computers** and **Servers** have been added to the default **All Computers** group. Both the **Desktop Computers** and **Servers** groups are at the same hierarchical level.

- Update Services
  - 70411SRV1 (WSUS Server)
    - Updates
    - Computers
      - All Computers
        - Unassigned Computers
        - Desktop Computers
          - 70411Cli1-L1
            - 70411Cli2-L2
        - Servers
          - 70411SRV3-L1
    - Downstream Servers
    - Synchronizations
    - Reports
    - Options

Figure 1.2.0 – WSUS priority by dept.

In this example, the group two levels beneath the **Desktop Computers** branch (70411Cli2-L2) have a higher priority than the group one level beneath the **Server** branch (70411SRV3-L1). Accordingly, for a computer that has membership in both the 70411Cli2-L2 and the 70411SRV3-L1 groups, all actions for the 70411Cli2-L2 group take priority over actions specified for the 70411SRV3-L1 group.

Install/Uninstall

Install actions override uninstall actions. Required installs override optional installs. Optional installs are only available through the API and changing an approval for an update using the WSUS Administration Console will clear all optional approvals.

Deadline

Actions that have a deadline override those with no deadline. Actions with earlier deadlines override those with later deadlines.

Plan WSUS performance considerations

There are some areas that should be carefully planned before deploying WSUS to optimize performance. The key areas are:

1. Network setup
2. Deferred download
3. Filters
4. Installation
5. Large update deployments
6. Background Intelligent Transfer Service (BITS)
7. Antivirus integration

To create a computer group for client-side-targeting

1. Log on to 70411SRV1 and open Server Manager.
2. In the Server Manager Navigation pane, click **Tools**, and then click **Windows Server Update Services.**
3. On the WSUS Administration Console, expand **Computers**, right-click **All Computers**, and then click **Add Computer Group.**
4. On the **Add Computer Group** dialog box, in the **Name** field type **WSUS Computers**, then click then **Add.**

To test WSUS Configuration

1. Boot the client computer, 70411Win8 and log on to the domain.
2. Log on to the WSUS server 70411SRV1; navigate to the **WSUS Computers** group.
3. Confirm that 70411Win8, 70411SRV1 and 70411SRV3 appear on this group. If not log on to each of the computers and perform the following tasks:
   a) Run Gpupdate.exe /force

    b)   Run wuauclt.exe /detectnow

4.   Log back to the WSUS server 70411SRV1 and open WSUS console.

5.   On the WSUS console, right-click **WSUS Computers** group and click **refresh.**

6.   Both WSUS servers 70411SRV1 and 70411SRV3 as well as 70411Win8 should now appear under the **WSUS Computers** group.

Explore WSUS Console

In this section; we will explore the different nodes in the WSUS console and what you can accomplish on each node. Log on to 70411SRV1 (the upstream WSUS server). Open Windows Server Update Services from Server Manager and expand 70411SRV1. Now, let's explore the various nodes:

1.   **Updates** node: Highlight **Updates** node, and in the details pane view the summary of the status of all updates by Update View.

2.   Expand **Updates** to view the following: **All Updates, Critical Updates, Security Updates** and **WSUS Updates.** You recall that these were the only categories we selected to download during the WSUS post-installation configuration.

3.   Highlight **All Updates** and review the information at the details pane. This displays all updates currently downloaded by WSUS server. You can sort updates by **Approval** with the following options: **Unaproved, Approved, Declined or Any Except Declined**. You can also sort updates by **Status** with the following options: **Failed or Needed, Installed/Not Applicable or No Status, Failed, Needed, Installed/Not Applicable, No Status** or **Any.**

4.   Still on the details pane with the **All Updates** highlighted, you can:

    a)   Right-click a particular update to:

        i)   Approve, or Decline, the update.

        ii)   View Revision History, File Information, and Status Report of the update

        iii)   Group the update by Title, Classification, MSRC Severity, Approval and Decline.

        iv)   When you click **Approve**, you have to select the Computer Group you are approving the update for.

        v)   Beside the group, click the grey circle. This presents three choices: **Approve for install, Approve for removal** or **Not approved**.

        vi)   Select Approve for install and click Ok.

    b)   Highlight multiple updates and right-click them to perform the above tasks except view Revision History, File Information.

    c)   Refresh the content of the **All Updates**.

Note

If you do have internet connection, you may import updates into WSUS by right-clicking Updates view, and selecting Import Updates.

The **All Updates** view also provides other sub-category views, depending on the categories you downloaded. When you right-click **Updates** node, you have the following options: Search, New Updates View, and Import Updates.

5. **Computers** node: When you highlight the Computers node a summary of the status of all computers by Computer Group will be displayed. To drill down, expand **Computers** and Highlight **All Computers** node. On the details pane, all computers in the WSUS server are displayed.

   a) Right-click **All Computers** node to perform the following tasks:
      i) **Search**: Allows you to search by Updates or Computers
      ii) **Add Computer Group**: Add a new group to the **All Computers** node. This is where you start defining your computer hierarchy.

   b) Highlight the **All Computers** node to view by status or refresh the node

   c) Expand the **All Computers** node reveals the following:
      i) **Unassigned Computers** group: Used to place unassigned computers if you are using Server-side-targeting as against client-side-targeting.
      ii) Displays any other group under the **All Computers** group.

Note

You can only create a new computer group under the All Computers node or any other group you create beneath the All Computers node. There is no option to add a new group under the Unassigned Computers group.

6. **Downstream Servers** Node: Displays all downstream servers connected to the upstream server. At the details pane, right-click a downstream server to:
   a) Add the server to Console
   b) Delete the server

7. **Synchronization** Node: Highlighting the **Synchronization** Node displays all synchronizations performed by this server. It will also display the number of New Updates downloaded during the synchronization, and number of Revised and Expired updates. To the far right, you can perform additional tasks:
   a) Synchronize now: Synchronizes the server immediately with the upstream server.
   b) Configure Synchronization: opens the Options Node where you can configure synchronization schedule.

8. **Reports** Node: You can view Updates, synchronization or Computer Reports. To view reports, The Microsoft Report Viewer 2008 Redistributable is required.
9. **Options** Node: We covered this node in section 1.2.0.

1.2.5 Manage patch management in mixed environments (2012 R2 Objective)

Most enterprise environments are likely to be running a mix of Windows operating systems versions. In this situation, WSUS will be configured to deliver updates to different versions of Windows Operating systems.

In this section, we will examine how to configure WSUS in a mix Windows Operating system environment to ensure that you are delivering the right patch to the right Operating system. To configure WSUS to manage patches in a mixed Operating System environment, we will require Active Directory OUs, Group Policies, WSUS Computer Groups, and WSUS Auto approval Policies.

High-level plan

1. Enable Client-Side-targeting.
2. Create WSUS Computer Groups by OS version.
3. Create Organisational Units to mimic WSUS Computer groups.
4. Move computers to the right OU by OS version.
5. Create Group Policies to mimic Organisational Units.
6. Apply group policies to specific Organisational Units.
7. Configure client side targeting in Group policy to drop computers in the right WSUS Computer group.
8. Enforce the new policy and update WSUS Server.
9. Configure WSUS Auto approval Policy.

To configure WSUS in a mixed Windows Operating System Environment

1. Log on to 70411SRV1 and open WSUS console, complete the following tasks:
   a) To Enable Client-Side-targeting:
      i) Navigate to **Options** and on the details pane, Click **Computers**. Ensure that **Use Group Policy or registry settings on Computers** is selected.
      ii) Click **Ok**.
   b) To Create Computer Groups by OS version:
      i) Right-click **WSUS Computers**, (created in a previous section), and select **Delete**.

      ii)   Select **Remove the Computers from this group** and click **Remove**. Notice that all the computers will be moved to the **Unassigned Computers** group

     iii)   Create two new Computer Groups **WINSRV2012R2** and **WIN8PRO** under **All Computers** group.

2. Log on to 70411SRV and open **Active Directory Users and Computers**. Then complete the following tasks:

   a)   To Create Organisational Units to mimic WSUS Computer groups:

      i)   Right-click 70411Lab.com domain, point to New, then select **Organisational Unit**. Enter **WINSRV2012R2** in the name field and click **Ok.**

      ii)   Repeat task and create a second OU called **WIN8PRO.**

   b)   To Move computers to the right OU by OS version, highlight the **Computers** container and perform the following tasks:

      i)   In the details pane, select 70411SRV1 and 70411SRV3, right-click both and select Move, the select **WINSRV2012R2** and click **Ok.**

      ii)   Right-click 70411WIN8, select Move, the select **WIN8PRO** and click **Ok.**

   c)   To Create Group Policies to mimic Organisational Units, Open Group Policy Management Console and complete the following tasks:

      i)   Navigate to **Group Policy Objects** and highlight it. At the details pane, right-click **WSUS Policy** (Created in previous section), and rename it as **WINSRV2012R2.**

      ii)   Expand **Group Policy Objects** and drag **WINSRV2012R2** into **Group Policy Objects** container. At the dialogue box, select **Preserve the existing permissions**, and click **Ok.** When the copy completes, click **Ok.**

     iii)   Right-click **Copy of WINSRV2012R2**, and rename it as **WIN8PRO.**

     iv)   To ensure that WINSRV2012R2 is not linked to the domain, delete the copy beneath 70411Lab.com domain.

   d)   To Apply group policies to specific Organisational Units, complete the following tasks:

      i)   Drag **WIN8PRO** under **Group Policy Objects** container and drop it in **WIN8PRO** OU (Created earlier under 70411Lab.com domain). Respond **Ok** to link the GPO to the OU.

      ii)   Drag **WINSRV2012R2** under **Group Policy Objects** container and drop it in **WINSRV2012R2** OU. Respond **Ok** to link the GPO to the OU.

     iii)   Confirm that you have the right policy under the right OU.

   e)   To Configure **Enable client-side-targeting** in the group policies, perform the following tasks:

    i) Right-click **WINSRV2012R2** Policy and select **Edit**. GPM editor opens

    ii) Navigate to Computer Configuration\Policies\Administrative Template\ Windows Component, and highlight Windows Update.

    iii) Double-click **Enable client-side-targeting** policy and on the left pane of the policy, change the **Target group name for this computer** to **WINSRV2012R2** then click **Ok** and close GPM editor.

    iv) Back to GPMC, right-click **WIN8PRO** Policy and click **Edit,** GPM editor opens.

    v) Navigate to Computer Configuration\Policies\Administrative Template\ Windows Component, and highlight Windows Update.

    vi) Double-click **Enable client-side-targeting** policy and on the left pane of the policy, change the **Target group name for this computer** to **WIN8PRO** then click **Ok.**

3. To Enforce the new policy and update WSUS Server, complete the task:
   a) Log on to 70411SRV1, 70411SRV3 and 70411WIN8 and run the following commands:

```
gpupdate /force
wuauclt.exe /detectnow
```

4. Log on to 70411SRV1 and open WSUS console, complete the following tasks:
   a) Confirm that the computers are now on the right Computer Group (You may need to refresh the Computer Groups).
   b) To Configure WSUS Auto approval Policy, complete the following tasks:
      i) Navigate to **Options** and on the details pane click **Automatic Approval.**
      ii) On the Automatic Approval windows, Update Rules tab, click New Rule.
      iii) In Step 1: Select Properties, select When an update is in a specific product.
      iv) In **In Step 2: Edit the properties** (click an underline value), click **Any product.** On the **Choose product** dialogue, deselect **All Products.** Scroll down to **Windows,** locate **Windows Server 2012 R2** and check the box beside it. Click **Ok.**
      v) On the **Add Rule** window, click **All computers,** uncheck **All computers** and check **WINSRV2012R2,** click **Ok.**
      vi) On the Add Rule window Step 3: Specify name, type WINSRV2012R2 and click Ok

vii) On the Automatic Approval window, Update Rules tab, click New Rule.

viii) In Step 1: Select Properties, select When an update is in a specific product

ix) In **Step 2: Edit the properties** (click an underline value), click **Any product**, On the **Choose product** dialogue, deselect **All Products**. Scroll down to **Windows**, locate **Windows 8** and check the box beside it. Click **Ok.**

x) On the **Add Rule** window, click **All computers**, uncheck **All computers** and check WIN8PRO, click **Ok.**

xi) On the Add Rule window Step 3: Specify name, type WIN8PRO and click Ok.

xii) On the **Automatic Approval** window, note the two new rules (You may click **Run Now**, to run the rules) and click **Ok.**

Managing WSUS with Command lines and Windows PowerShell

Before we move on, it is important to examine some important command line and cmdlets used to manage WSUS. This is particularly important for the exam, but also useful for administering your WSUS server infrastructure.

Managing WSUS from the Command Line

WSUSutil.exe is a tool that you can use to manage your WSUS server from the command line. This utility is located in the **%drive%\Program Files\Update Services\Tools** folder on your WSUS server. The syntax for WSUSutil.exe commands are summarized below:

Export: The first of the two parts that make up the export/import process. The export command enables you to export update metadata to an export package file. You cannot use this parameter to export update files, update approvals, or server settings.

Import: This is the second of the two parts that make up the export/import process. The import command imports update metadata to a server from an export package file created on another WSUS server. This synchronizes the destination WSUS server without using a network connection.

Migratesus: This command migrates update approvals from a SUS 1.0 server to a WSUS server.

Movecontent: Changes the file system location where the WSUS server stores update files, and optionally copies any update files from the old location to the new location.

Reset: Checks that every update metadata row in the database has corresponding update files stored in the file system. If update files are missing or have been corrupted, WSUS downloads the update files again.

Deleteunneededrevisions: Purges the update metadata for unnecessary update revisions from the database.

Listinactiveapprovals: Returns a list of update titles with approvals that are in a permanently inactive state because of a change in server language settings.

Removeinactiveapprovals: Removes approvals for updates that are in a permanently inactive state because of a change in WSUS server language settings.

Managing WSUS with Windows PowerShell

As you would expect, WSUS can be managed with Windows PowerShell. The descriptions and syntax of all Windows Server Update Services (WSUS) administration-specific cmdlets are detailed below:

Add-WsusComputer: Adds a specified client computer to a specified target group.

Approve-WsusUpdate: Approves an update to be applied to clients.

Deny-WsusUpdate: Declines the update for deployment.

Get-WsusClassification: Get the list of all Windows Server Update Services (WSUS) classifications currently available in the system.

Get-WsusComputer: Gets the Windows Server Update Services (WSUS) computer object that represents the client computer.

Get-WsusProduct: Get the list of all products currently available on Windows Server Update Services (WSUS) by category.

Get-WsusServer: Gets the value of the Windows Server Update Services (WSUS) update server object.

Get-WsusUpdate: Gets the Windows Server Update Services (WSUS) update object with details about the update.

Invoke-WsusServerCleanup: Performs the process of cleanup on a specified Windows Server Update Services (WSUS) server.

Set-WsusClassification: Sets whether the classifications of updates that Windows Server Update Services (WSUS) synchronizes are enabled or disabled.

Set-WsusProduct: Sets whether the product representing the category of updates to synchronize is enabled or disabled.

Set-WsusServerSynchronization: Sets whether the Windows Server Update Services (WSUS) server synchronizes from Microsoft Update, or an upstream server and the upstream server properties.

Exam Tip

Note the following WSUS commands and cmdlets: **WSUSutil.exe movecontent**, and **Set-WsusServerSynchronization.** Very important to understand these commands.

WSUS Command Examples

Perform the following tasks on 70411SRV1, except the last which should be performed from 70411SRV3. Updates on 70411SRV1 are currently stored in E:\Updates\WSUS. If you receive an error message, copy WSUSutil.exe from C:\Program Files\Update Services\Tools to %windir%\system32.

1. To change the file system location where the WSUS server stores update files to E:\WSUSFiles, and log file location, run the command:

```
WSUSutil.exe movecontent E:\WSUSFiles E:\logfile.log
```

Note

In the previous command, both the location of the files and log MUST be specified. The command also copies the current content to the new location. To skip copying the current, specify the -skipcopy switch.

2. To specify that the local WSUS Server is to synchronize from Microsoft Update, run the cmdlet:

```
Set-WsusServerSynchronization –SyncFromMU
```

3. To specify that 70411SRV3 WSUS Server is to synchronize from another server named 70411SRV1 using port number 42 and the SSL protocol, run the following cmdlet:

```
Set-WsusServerSynchronization -UssServerName 70411SRV1 -PortNumber 42 -UseSSL
```

1.3 Monitor servers

Introduction

Windows Performance Monitor is a Microsoft Management Console (MMC) snap-in that provides tools for analyzing system performance. From a single console, you can monitor application and hardware performance in real-time, customize what data you want to collect in logs, define thresholds for alerts and automatic actions, generate reports, and view past performance data in a variety of ways.

Windows Performance Monitor combines the functionality of previous stand-alone tools including Performance Logs and Alerts (PLA), Server Performance Advisor (SPA), and System Monitor. It provides a graphical interface for the customization of Data Collector Sets and Event Trace Sessions. Windows Performance Monitor performs data collection and logging using Data Collector Sets. Performance counters are measurements of system state or activity. They can be included in the operating system or can be part of individual applications. Windows Performance Monitor requests the current value of performance counters at specified time intervals.

Event trace data is collected from trace providers, which are components of the operating system or of individual applications that report actions or events. Output from multiple trace providers can be combined into a trace session. Configuration information is collected from key values in the Windows registry. Windows Performance Monitor can record the value of a registry key at a specified time or interval as part of a log file.

Resource Monitor lets you view detailed real-time information about hardware resources (CPU, disk, network and memory) and system resources (including handles and modules) in use by the operating system, services and running application. In addition, you can use Resources Monitor to stop processes, start and stop services, analyze process deadlocks, view thread wait chains and identify processes locking files.

In this section, we will cover the following exam objectives:

1.3.0 Configure Data Collector Sets (DCS)
1.3.1 Configure alerts
1.3.2 Monitor real-time performance
1.3.3 Monitor virtual machines (VMs)
1.3.4 Monitor events
1.3.5 Configure event subscriptions
1.3.6 Configure network monitoring
1.3.7 Schedule performance monitoring (Server 2012 R2 Objective)

Lab Plan

We will use 70411SRV3 and 70411HPV (To configure VM monitoring).

Additional Lab Setup

None

1.3.0 Configure Data Collector Sets (DCS)

A Data Collector Set (DCS) is the building block of performance monitoring and reporting in Windows Performance Monitor. It organizes multiple data collection points into a single component that can be used to review or log performance. A Data Collector Set can be created and then recorded individually, grouped with other Data Collector Sets and incorporated into logs, viewed in Performance Monitor, configured to generate alerts when thresholds are reached, or used by other non-Microsoft applications. It can be associated with rules of scheduling for data collection at specific times. Windows Management Interface (WMI) tasks can be configured to run upon the completion of Data Collector Set collection.

Data Collector Sets in Windows Server 2012 R2 can contain the following types of data collectors: **Performance counter**, **Event trace**, **Configuration** and **Performance counter alerts**. You can create a Data Collector Set from a template, from an existing set of Data Collectors in a Performance Monitor view, or by selecting individual Data Collectors and setting each individual option in the Data Collector Set properties.

In this section, we will examine the following: Create a Data Collector Set from Performance Monitor, Create a Data Collector Set from a Template and Create a Data Collector Set Manually.

Create a Data Collector Set from Performance Monitor

You can create a Data Collector Set from counters in the current Performance Monitor display. Membership in the local Performance Log Users or Administrators group, or equivalent, is the minimum required to complete this procedure.

Note

The Performance Log Users group must be assigned the Log on as a batch user right, as described in Enable Logging for Performance Log Users Group Members.

To create a Data Collector Set from Performance Monitor

1. Log on to 70411SRV3 and open Server Manager. From **Tools** Menu, open **Performance Monitor.**
2. Expand Monitoring Tools, then right-click Performance Monitor, point to New, select Data Collector Set. The Create new Data Collector Set wizard opens.
3. In the **Name** box, type **DCSPerfMon** and click **Next.**
4. On the Where you would like the data collector set saved, in Root directory enter, E:\ServerMon\DCSPerfMon and click **Next.**

5. On the final page, click **Finish.**

The Data Collector Set created will contain all of the data collectors selected in the current Performance Monitor view.

To confirm that the DCS created contain DCs in current PerMon View

1. Expand Monitoring Tools, then right-click Performance Monitor and select Properties.
2. Click the **Data** tab. Note that under Counters,
3. \Processor Information(_Total)\%Processor Time is the only counter present.
4. Click **Cancel** to close the properties of Performance Monitor.
5. Expand **Data Collector Sets**, then expand **User Defined**, and highlight **DCSPerfMon** data collector set.
6. In the details pane, right-click **System Monitor Log** and click **Properties.**
7. On the Performance counters tab, notice also that the only listed counter is **\Processor Information(_Total)\%Processor Time.**
8. On the System Monitor Log Properties, click **Cancel.**

Note

If you are a member of the Performance Log Users group, you must configure Data Collector Sets you create to run under your own credentials. Data Collector Sets, by default execute as the System user. As a security best practice, you should accept this default value unless you have a compelling reason to change it.

Create a Data Collector Set from a Template

The recommended way to create a new Data Collector Set is via the wizard in Windows Performance Monitor. Windows Server 2012 R2 includes several templates that focus on general system diagnosis information or collect performance data specific to server roles or applications. In addition, you can import templates created on other computers and save Data Collector Set you create for use elsewhere.

In the task below, you will modify DCSPerfMon data collector set and export it as a template.

To modify and export DCS as a Templates

1. To modify **DCSPerfMon** data collector set:
    a) Expand Data Collector Sets, then expand User Defined
    b) Highlight **DCSPerfMon** data collector set, in the details pane, right-click **System Monitor Log** and click **Properties.**

    c)   On the Performance counters tab beneath performance counters, click **Add.**

    d)   On the **Select Counters from computer,** ensure that **<Local computer>** is in the box. Scroll down to view counters you can monitor on 70411SRV3. (Available counters will depend on the Roles installed on the server).

    e)   Locate and expand **PhysicalDisk,** highlight **% Disk Read Time** and **% Disk Time** and beneath **Instance of selected object**, highlight **_Total**, click **Add**, then click **Ok.**

    f)   At the Properties of System Monitor Log, notice that we now have two more counters – \PhysicalDisks(_Total)\% Disk Read Time and \PhysicalDisks(_Total)\% Disk Time.

    g)   To apply the changes and close **System Monitor Log**, click **Ok.**

2.   To export DCSPerfMon data collector set as a Templates:

    a)   Right-click **DCSPerfMon** data collector set, and click **Save Template.**

    b)   On the **Save As** window, type E:\ServerMon\Templates\DCSPerfMontemplate and click **Save.**

To create a Data Collector Set from an exported template

1. In the Windows Performance Monitor navigation pane, expand **Data Collector Sets**, then right-click **User Defined** point to **New**, and click **Data Collector Set.** The Create new Data Collector Set Wizard opens.

2. In the name field, type **DCSTemplate**, ensure that **Create from template (Recommended)** is selected, and then click **Next.**

3. In the template selection window, under **Template Data Collector Set**, (Note the template types - details below) and click **Browse**, then Browse to E:\ServerMon\Templates\, select **DCSPerfMontemplate** and click **Open.**

4. DCSPerMon will now appear under **Template Data Collector Set**, click **Finish.**

5. To change the location to store data for the DCSTemplate DCS:

    a)   Create a folder called **DCSTemplate** in E\ServerMon.

    b)   Right-click **DCSTemplate** and click **Properties**, click **Directory** tab, type E\ServerMon\DCSTemplate, and click **Ok.**

Types of Template Data Collector Sets

From the previous task, we see that there are four types of Template Data Collector Sets. You can create DCSs using these templates.

Basic

This creates a basic DCS. You can add or remove counters and change the scheduling options by editing the DCS properties.

System Diagnostics

Data Collector Set created from this template generates a report detailing the status of local hardware resources, system response times, and processes on the local computer along with system information configuration data. This report includes suggestions for ways to maximize performance and streamline system operation.

System Performance

This generates a report detailing the status of local hardware resources, system response times, and processes on the local computer. This is useful to identify possible causes of performance issues.

WDAC Diagnostics

Used to trace detailed debug information for WDAC components with BidTrace.

Note

Note the difference between System Diagnostics and System Performance Data Collector SetTemplates: Both "generate a report detailing the status of local hardware resources, system response times, and processes on the local computer" but System Diagnostics includes system information configuration data and suggestions for ways to maximize performance and streamline system operation.

To create a Data Collector Set from a system template

1. In the Windows Performance Monitor navigation pane, expand **Data Collector Sets**, then right-click **User Defined** point to **New**, and click **Data Collector Set**. The **Create new Data Collector Set** Wizard opens.
2. In the **Name** field, type **DCSTemplateSys**, ensure that **Create from template (Recommended)** is selected, and then click **Next**.
3. In the template selection window, under **Template Data Collector Set**, select. **System Diagnostics** and click **Next**.

4. On the **Root Directory** click **Browse**, and browse to E:\ServerMon\DCSTemplate (Be sure to create the folder), then click **Next.**
5. Accept the default **Run As** values and click **Finish.**
6. Review DCSTemplateSys DCS:
   a) Highlight **DCSTemplateSys** DCS and in the details pane, note the Data Collectors included from the **System Diagnostics** template.
   b) Right-click **DCSTemplateSys** DCS and click **Properties.** Notice the description. We will explorer in details, the properties of a DCS and what you can configure later in this section.

Create a Data Collector Set Manually

You can build a Data Collector Set from a custom combination of Data Collectors. These Data Collectors can include Performance Counters, Configuration data, or data from Trace Providers.

To create a Data Collector Set manually

1. In the Windows Performance Monitor navigation pane, expand **Data Collector Sets**, then right-click **User Defined** point to **New**, and click **Data Collector Set**. The **Create new Data Collector Set** Wizard opens.
2. In the **Name** field, type **DCSManual**, ensure that **Create Manually (Advanced)** is selected then click **Next.**
3. In the next page, select **Create data logs**, then check all the boxes under it and click **Next.**
   a) **Performance counters** provide metric data about the system's performance
   b) **Event trace data** provides information about activities and system events
   c) **System configuration information** allows you to record the state of, and changes to, registry keys.
4. Because we selected all three data logs, we will be presented with dialogs to add Data Collectors to the Data Collector Set. Complete the tasks below to add Data Collectors:
   a) In the **Performance counters** screen, click **Add** to open the Add Counters dialog box. Beneath **Available** counters, expand **Server**, and highlight **Errors Access Permissions** and click **Add**, then click **Ok.** In the Create **Data Collector Set** Wizard, click **Next.**
   b) In the **Event Trace Providers** screen, click **Add** to select from a list of available Event Trace Providers, select **Active Directory Services: SAM,** and then click **Ok.** In the **Create Data Collector Set** Wizard, click **Next.** (You can select multiple providers by holding down the

Control key and highlighting. Event Trace Providers can be installed with the operating system or part of a non-Microsoft application.).

c) In the **Registry keys** screen, click **Add**, and enter the value **HKEY_LOCAL_MACHINE\SOFTWARE\Microsoft\DFS** (Record system configuration information by entering Registry keys you want to track. You must know the exact key you want to include in the Data Collector Set). Click **Next**.

5. In the **Create Data Collector Set** Wizard, Save the DCS in E:\ServerMon\DCSManual (Be sure to create the folder path) and click **Next.**

6. Accept the defaults in the **Run As** page and click **Finish.**

Exploring the Properties of a Data Collector Set

To explore the properties of a DCS, right-click **DCSPerfMon** and select **Properties**. Below, I will explore the various tabs and provide more information about what can be configured:

1. **General** tab: Includes the description and keywords associated with the Data Collector Set. Data Collector Sets created from a templates that had a description and keywords, will be included here. For custom Data Collector Set, you can add data here to help identify it later, or to provide more information to others if you export it as a template. You can change what user the Data Collector Set will **Run As** by clicking **Change...** and entering a user name and password.

Note

The Data Collector Set must run as a user with administrative credentials or as a member of the Performance Log Users group. If you configure the Data Collector Set to run as a user with a higher level credentials than the currently logged on user, you will be prompted to enter the user name and password of the account the Data Collector Set is configured to run as when you change its properties.

2. **Directory** tab: In addition to defining a root directory for storing Data Collector Set data, you can specify a single Subdirectory or create a Subdirectory name format by clicking the arrow to the right of the text entry field. The Example directory at the bottom of the page provides a real-time sample of the directory and/or subdirectory where the Data Collector Set data will be stored.

3. **Security** tab: You can change the permissions of groups or users for the Data Collector Set by selecting the Group or User name and then selecting the Allow or Deny check boxes for each permission type. To add, remove, or change permission types, click the Advanced button.

4. **Schedule** tab: The schedule tab includes options for configuring when data collection begins. Use the Stop Condition tab to configure stopping data collection.

5. **Stop Condition** tab: A single stop condition, or a combination of multiple criteria, can be used to automatically to halt or restart the collection of data from a Data Collector Set. Select the check boxes to choose one or all of the stop conditions you want to apply to the Data Collector Set. If no stop conditions are selected on this tab, the Data Collector Set will collect data from the time it is started (either manually or automatically) until it is manually stopped. You can check the Overall duration and limits check boxes. Details below:

    a) **Overall duration** causes the Data Collector Set to stop collecting data when the configured time has elapsed. The overall duration setting takes precedence over any settings defined as limits.

    b) **Limits** can be used instead of, or in addition to, the overall duration stop condition.

Exam Tip

Take a close look at the Stop Condition tab.

To automatically restart collection of the Data Collector Set when limits for duration, size, or both are reached, select the check box **Restart the data collector set at limits**. When used in combination with the overall duration stop condition, configuring automatic restarts will cause the data to be collected in separate log files for each specified time period or size until the overall duration stop condition is met.

6. **Task** tab: You can run a Windows Management Instrumentation (WMI) task upon completion of the Data Collector Set collection by entering the command in the Run this task when the data collector set stops box. Refer to WMI task documentation for options.

Manage Data in Windows Performance Monitor

Data Collector Sets create a raw log data file, in addition to optional report files. With Data Management, you can configure how log data, reports, and compressed data are stored for each Data Collector Set. Below we explore the various options available in the Data Manager Properties of a Data Collector Set.

Exploring the Data Manager Properties of a Data Collector Set

To explore the Data Manager Properties of a Data Collector Set, right-click **DCSPerfMon** and click **Data Manager**.

1. **Data Manager** tab: The following options can be configured in the Data Manager tab:
    a) **Minimum free disk:** The amount of disk space that must be available on the drive where log data is stored. If selected, previous data will be deleted according to the Resource policy that you choose when the limit is reached.
    b) **Maximum folders:** The number of subfolders that can be in the Data Collector Set data directory. If selected, previous data will be deleted according to the Resource policy that you choose when the limit is reached.
    c) **Resource policy:** Specifies whether to delete the oldest or largest log file or directory when limits are reached.
    d) **Maximum root path size:** The maximum size of the data directory for the Data Collector Set, including all subfolders. If selected, this maximum path size overrides the Minimum free disk and Maximum folders limits, and previous data will be deleted according to the Resource policy that you choose when the limit is reached.
2. **Actions** tab: To configure a Folder action, click Add. The options available for a folder action are:
    a) **Age**: The age in days or weeks of the data file. If the value is 0, the criterion is not used.
    b) **Size:** The size in megabytes (MB) of the folder where log data is stored. If the value is 0, the criterion is not used.
    c) **Cab:** A cabinet file, which is an archive file format. Cab files can be created from raw log data and extracted later when needed. Choose create or delete can files to take action based on the age or size criteria.
    d) **Data:** Raw log data collected by the Data Collector Set. Log data can be deleted after a cab file is created to save disk space while still retaining a backup of the original data. You can choose to delete data files when configuring a folder action.
    e) **Report:** The report file generated by Windows Performance Monitor from raw log data. Report files can be retained even after the raw data or cab file has been deleted.

Note

Folder actions allow you to choose how data is archived before it is permanently deleted. You may decide to disable the Data Manager limits in favour of managing all data according to these folder action rules.

1.3.1 Configure alerts

Alerts are actions triggered when a performance counter reaches a configured threshold. A threshold could be below or above a value set. Once the alert is triggered, it is expected to perform an action, for example **Log an entry in the application event log** or **Start a Data collector set**. You may also want the alert to run a task for example, delete a log file, etc. To configure an alert, we first create a Data Collector Set with performance counter alert data collector. You can also add a performance counter alert data collector to an existing DCS.

A reasonable threshold will depend on the environment, what is monitored and a good understanding of the counter.

To Create a DCS with Performance counter alerts Data Collector

1. Log on to 70411SRV3 and open Server Manager. From **Tools** Menu, open **Performance Monitor.**
2. Expand Data Collector Sets, then right-click User Defined, point to **New** and select **Data Collector Set**.
3. On the How would you want to create this new data collector set screen, on the Name field, enter PhysicalDiskAlert, then select Create Manually (Advanced), and click Next.
4. On the What type of data do you want to include, select Performance Counter Alert, and click Next.
5. Under **Performance counter**, click **Add**, then in the available counters, highlight **PhysicalDisk**, and under **Instances of selected object**, click **_Total**, click **Add** and click **Ok**.
6. In the Create new data Collector wizard, click Next.
7. In the **Create data Collector?** screen, select **save** and **close** then click **finish**.

To configure alert actions

1. Expand Data Collector Sets, expand User Defined and highlight PhysicalDiskAlert DCS.
2. At the details pane, right-click **DataCollector01** (Or whatever name yours is called) Alert and click **Properties.**
3. From the **alerts** tab, performance counters displays all the PhsicalDisk counters we added in step 5 above. To configure an alert, complete the following tasks:
   a) Under **performance counters**, select \PhysicalDisk_Total\% Disk Time.
   b) Under **Alert When** select **Above** from the drop down.
   c) And in the **limit** box type 20 (This is an arbitrary number).

4. Click **Alert action** tab. This tab allows you to set an action to perform when the alert is triggered – That is when select \PhysicalDisk_Total\% Disk Time goes above 20%:
   a) Check Log an entry in the application event log.
   b) Beneath the Start a data collector set drop down, select PhysicalDiskAlert.
5. Click **Alert Task** tab to add an Alert task as required, then click **Ok.**

1.3.2 Monitor real-time performance

Real-Time performance monitoring in Windows Server 2012 and Windows Server 2012 R2 is achieved using Task Manager and Windows Resource Monitor. Task Manager has been around in Windows Operating systems for a while. Task Manager in Windows Server 2012 R2 has five tabs: Processes, Performance, Users, Details and Services.

Our interest is the **Performance** tab. If you can't find these tabs when you open Task Manager, click **More Details** beneath it. The Performance tab gives you a quick overview of your CPU, Memory and Ethernet (NIC) performance. Later in this section, you will see that Resource Monitor provides more detailed information about these three resources, including Disks performance which is not included in Task Manager.

To examine details of the task manager tabs, click on each tab for more information:

CPU: Displays your processor utilization, type and speed including Maximum speed, Threads, Handles and Uptime. You can also view information about Number of sockets, Cores, Logical Processors, Virtualization status (Enabled or disabled), and information about your Process Cache.

Memory: Displays your memory usage (in %). You will be able to see the total memory installed on your system, the memory type (DDR3 for example). You will also be able to see Memory in use, available, committed, cached, Paged Pool, and non-paged pool. Finally, Memory Speed, Slots used, Form Factor (SODIMM, for example) and Hardware Reserved are displayed.

Ethernet: Displays Throughput, type, speed, sent and received data, Adapter name, connection type (For example Ethernet), and IPv4 and IPv6 address. If any of these system resources is degrading your system performance, task manager gives you a quick overview of where the problem might be.

For a more detailed analysis of the root cause of the problem, click **open Resource Monitor**. As an example, I am concerned that my memory usage is currently at 88%! I want to know what is causing this and deal with it in time before it causes further damage like my system becoming completely unresponsive.

Note

Disk Utilization information is not available in Task Manager. Resource Manager provides this additional information.

Windows Resource Monitor

Introduced in Windows 7 and Windows Server 2008, Windows Resource Monitor is a powerful tool for understanding how your system resources are used by processes and services. In addition to monitoring resource usage in real-time, Resource Monitor can help you analyze unresponsive processes; identify which applications are using files, and control processes and services.

How to access Resource Monitor

In Windows Server 2012 and Windows Server 2012 R2, resource Monitor can be accessed in four ways: From **Tools** menu in **Server Manager**, from the **Performance** node of Performance Monitor, from **performance** tab of Task Manager or by typing **resmon.exe** in command prompt.

Resource Monitor Elements and Features

Windows Resource Monitor includes the following elements and features:

Tabs: Resource Monitor includes five tabs: Overview, CPU, Memory, Disk, and Network. The Overview tab displays basic system resource usage information; the other tabs display information about each specific resource. Switch between tabs by clicking on the tab titles.

If you have filtered results on one tab, only resources used by the selected processes or services will be displayed on the other tabs. Filtered results are denoted by an orange bar below the title bar of each table. To stop filtering results while viewing the current tab, in the key table, clear the check box next to Image. We will perform a task later in this section to demonstrate filtering.

Tables: Each tab in Resource Monitor includes multiple tables that provide detailed information about the resource featured on that tab.

1. The first table displayed is always the key table, and it always contains a complete list of processes using the resource included on that tab. The key table on the Overview tab contains a complete list of processes running on the system.

2. To add or hide data columns in a table, right-click any column label (For example, in the Overview tab, expand CPU and right-click image or PID column label), and then click Select Columns. Select or clear the check boxes for the columns you want displayed. Not all columns are displayed by default.

3. If you have filtered results, tables other than the key table will only display data for the selected processes or services.
4. A process that is no longer running, but that is included in the current displayed data, will appear as a grey entry in a table until the data expires.

Chart pane: Each tab in Resource Monitor includes a chart pane on the right side of the window that displays graphs of the resources included on that tab.

1. You can change the size of the graphs by clicking the Views button and selecting a different graph size.
2. You can hide the chart pane by clicking the arrow at the top of the pane.
3. If you have filtered results, the resources used by the selected processes or services will be shown in the graphs as an orange line.
4. If you have multiple logical processors, you can choose which ones are displayed in the chart pane. On the CPU tab, click Monitor, and then click Select Processors. In the Select Processors dialog box, clear the All CPUs check box, and then select the check boxes for the logical processors you want to display.

Resource Monitor displays one graph for each logical processor. For example, a computer with a single processor that has two cores will have two processor graphs in the chart pane on the CPU tab. For computers with multiple processors organized into NUMA nodes, you can use the **Select NUMA** nodes menu option to configure Resource Monitor to display all of the logical processors in a selected NUMA node.

Performing basic tasks in Resource Monitor

From the **File** menu of Resource Monitor, you can **Save Settings As**, **Load Settings**, and **Restore Default Settings**. From the Monitor menu, you can Start or Stop Monitoring, and Auto-Fit Columns in Window.
Resource Monitor always starts in the same location and with the same display options as the previous session. However, at any time you can save your display state including window size, column widths, optional columns, expanded tables, and the active tab. You can then open the configuration file to use the saved settings.

Analyse real-time performance with Resource Monitor

In this section, we will dig deep into Resource Monitor to identify resource consumers, filter data in RM, troubleshoot unresponsive applications and View "handles and modules".

Identify Resource Consumers

In Windows Resource Monitor; you can sort table data by any column to help you identify which processes are using which resources. The following procedures describe how to complete some common troubleshooting tasks using Resource Monitor.

To identify the process with the highest current CPU usage

1. Log on to 70411HPV (Hyper-V Host) and open **Resource Monitor**
2. Click the **CPU** tab.
3. In **Processes**, click on **CPU** to sort processes by current CPU resource consumption.
4. The first process name in the **Image** column, which will also have the highest value in CPU, is the process using the most CPU.
5. To view service CPU usage by process:
   a) Click the **CPU** tab.
   b) Beneath the **Image** column, select the check box next to **Performon.exe** to see usage details. You can select multiple services. Selected services are moved to the top of the column.
   c) Click the title bar of **Services** to expand the table.
   d) Review the data in Services to see the list of processes hosted by the selected services, and to view their CPU usage.

To identify the process that is using a file

1. Click the **CPU** tab, and then click the title bar of **Associated Handles** to expand the table.
2. Click in the **Search Handles** box, and type the name of the file you want to search for, and then click the search button.

Note

The search string is not case-sensitive, and wildcard characters are not supported. You can type all or part of the file name or path in the search box. For example, searching for c:\windows will return all files with c:\windows as part of the file path.

3. Review the results to identify the process using the file

Exam Tip

The only portion of Resource Monitor that supports search string is CPU tab, Associated Handles. Any question related to identifying the process that is using a file should be linked to Associated Handles. Note also that wildcard characters, for example * are not supported.

To identify the network address that a process is connected to

1. Click the **Network** tab, and then click the title bar of **TCP Connections** to expand the table.
2. Locate the process whose network connection you want to identify. If there are a large number of entries in the table, you can click **Image** to sort by executable file name.
3. Review the **Remote Address** and **Remote Port** columns to see which network address and port the process are connected to. You may use **nslookup** to resolve the Remote Address to name for easy identification.

To view available space on all storage devices

Click the **Disk** tab, and then click the title bar of **Storage** to expand the table. The **Available Space** column displays the amount of free space, in megabytes (MB), for each physical disk on the system, Active Time (%) and Disk Queue Length.

To view the amount of memory available to programs

1. Click the **Memory** tab.
2. In **Physical Memory**, review the **Available to Programs** value. Available memory is the combined total of **standby memory** and **free memory**. Free memory includes zero page memory.

Filter Resource Monitor data

We are still reviewing how to use Resource Monitor to analyze real-time performance. We have looked at how to Identify Resource Consumers. In this section, we want to look at how to filter data in Resource Monitor.

Resource Monitor displays real-time information about all of the processes running on your system. If you want to view only the data related to selected processes, you can filter the detailed results.

To filter data by one or more processes

1. Click the **CPU** tab.
2. Expand **Processes**, in the **Image** column; select the check box next to **perfmon.exe** and **svchost.exe**. Selected processes are moved to the top of the column.

Note

After you have selected at least one process for filtering, the Associated Handles and Associated Modules tables on the CPU tab will contain data related to your selection.

3. Filtering applies to all tabs. To see additional resource usage data for your selection, you can click another tab. Tables that contain only filtered results include an orange information bar below the title bar of the table.

Note

If the selected process is not using any of the resources displayed on the current tab, the process name will not appear in the key table. To make changes to your selection, return to the original tab.

4. To stop filtering for a single process or service, clear its check box. To stop filtering altogether, in the key table, clear the check box next to Image.

Troubleshoot unresponsive applications

Applications that are not responding might be waiting for other processes to finish, or for system resources to become available, before they can continue. Windows Resource Monitor allows you to view a **process wait chain**, and to end processes that are preventing a program from working properly.

A process that is not responding will appear as a red entry in the **CPU** table of the **Overview** tab, and in the Processes table of the **CPU** tab.

Note

You should use Resource Monitor to end a process only if you are unable to close the program by normal means. If an open program is associated with the process, it will close immediately and you will lose any unsaved data. Ending a system process might result in system instability and data loss.

To analyse a process using Resource Monitor

1. Click the **CPU** tab.
2. In the key table (The first table displayed is always the key table), in the **Image** column, right-click **performon.exe** to analyse it, and then click **Analyse Wait Chain.**
3. If the process is running normally and is not waiting for any other processes, no wait chain information will be displayed. If the process is waiting for another process, a tree organized by dependency on other processes will be displayed. On top of the **Analyse Wait Chain** window, a status message will be displayed - processX.exe is waiting for another process (processY.exe).

Note

Many system processes depend on other processes and services for normal operation. Resource Monitor will display wait chain information for any process. If a process entry in the table is not red, if the process status is **Running**, and if the program is operating normally, no user action should be required.

4. If a wait chain tree is displayed, you can end one or more of the processes in the tree by selecting the check boxes next to the process names and clicking **End process.**

View handles and modules

This is the last sub-section in analyzing real-time performance. Windows Resource Monitor can show you which handles and modules are in use by a selected process.

1. Handles are pointers that refer to system elements including (but not limited to) files, registry keys, events, or directories.
2. Modules are helper files or programs including (but not limited to) dynamic-link library (DLL) files.

To view all handles and modules associated with a process

1. On the **CPU** tab, in the **Image** column of the **Processes** table, select the check box next to **perfmon.exe** and **svchost.exe** to see their **associated handles and modules.**
2. Click the title bars of the **Associated   Handles** and **Associated Modules** tables to expand them. An orange bar below the title bar of each table shows the processes you have selected.
3. Review the results in the detail tables. To refine the results, you can use the procedure in the next task to search for specific handles in the Associated Handles table.

To identify applications using a handle

1. In the title bar of the **Associated Handles** table, click in the **Search Handles** box and type the name of the handle you want to search for. Results will be displayed as soon as you stop typing in the field.
2. To refine your search results, in the Processes table, you can select the check box next to the name of a process after searching. The results will then be filtered by the selected process or processes.

Note

The results table is not dynamically updated. If you think that the system state has changed, click the search button again to refresh the results.

1.3.3 Monitor virtual machines (VMs)

In monitoring the performance of Virtual Machines, I guess the first question would be "where do I monitor resources, the root or guest Operating System?" To answer this question and set a baseline for our discussion in this section, I will do a quick overview of the Hyper-V architecture. Don't worry; I will not bore you with unnecessary details!

Overview of Hyper-V Architecture

Hyper-V implements isolation of virtual machines in terms of a partition. A partition is a logical unit of isolation, supported by the hypervisor, in which each guest operating system executes. A hypervisor instance has to have at least one parent partition, running a supported version of Windows Server (2008, 2008 R2, 2012 or 2012 R2). The virtualization stack runs in the parent partition and has direct access to the hardware devices. The parent partition then creates the child partitions which host the guest Operating Systems. A parent partition creates child partitions using the hypercall API, which is the application programming interface exposed by Hyper-V. Child partitions do not have direct access to hardware resources, but instead have a virtual view of the resources; in terms of virtual devices. Hyper-V has three main components – the virtstack, devices, and hypervisor.

Windows Server (Host) boots the system and launches the virtstack and hypervisor. The virtstack is responsible for handling emulated devices, managing VM's, servicing I/O, and more. The hypervisor is responsible for scheduling Virtual Processors, managing interrupts, servicing timers, and controlling other chip-level functions. It does not understand devices or I/O (that is, there are no hypervisor drivers). The devices are part of the root and are also installed in guests as part of the Integration Services. Since the root has a full view of the system and controls the VM's, it is also responsible for providing monitoring information via WMI and Performance Counters. With the above basic overview of Hyper-V architecture, it is obvious that the right performance information will be received from the host – The Hyper-V machine.

What to Monitor

After you have determined where to monitor performance; the next question would be what do I monitor? What you monitor depends on what you want to achieve. The top level performance counters to monitor are listed below:

1. Overall health:

    a)   Hyper-V Virtual Machine Health Summary.
    b)   Hyper-V Hypervisor.
2. Processor:
    a)   Processor.
    b)   Hyper-V Hypervisor Logical Processor.
    c)   Hyper-V Hypervisor Root Virtual Processor.
    d)   Hyper-V Hypervisor Virtual Processor.
3. Memory:
    a)   Memory.
    b)   Hyper-V Hypervisor Partition.
    c)   Hyper-V Root Partition.
    d)   Hyper-V VM Vid Partition.
4. Networking:
    a)   Network Interface.
    b)   Hyper-V Virtual Switch.
    c)   Hyper-V Legacy Network Adapter.
    d)   Hyper-V Virtual Network Adapter.
5. Storage:
    a)   Physical Disk.
    b)   Hyper-V Virtual Storage Device.
    c)   Hyper-V Virtual IDE Controller (emulated).

Now that we have identified components to monitor, we will configure performance monitoring for Overall health, Processor, Memory, Networking and Storage.

To configure Monitoring for Hyper-V

1. Log on to 70411HPV (your Hyper-V host) and open **Performance Monitor.**
2. Expand Data Collector Sets, then right-click User Defined point to New and select Data Collector Set, the Create New Data Collector Set wizard opens
3. In the **name** field, type **VMMonitor**, click **Next.**
4. Under **Create Data Log**, check the box beside **Performance counter** and click **Next.**
5. In the Performance Counters to Log screen, click Add, then locate Hyper-V Virtual Machine Health Summary, click Add; also locate Hyper-V Hypervisor and click **Add.**
6. Locate each subcomponent listed above, Processor, Memory, Networking (In Network Interface, select the active network interface), and Storage, click **Add.**
7. When you finish click **Ok.**
8. Back to the Performance Counters to Log screen, click **Next.**

9. In the where to save data screen, select a drive other than drive C;\ - Preferably, save in D:\PerfLogs\Admin\VMMonitor, click **Next.**
10. In the Create the data collector screen, accept defaults and click **Finish.**

Note

When you select Hyper-V Virtual Network Adapter in the available counters dialogue, Instances of selected objects will list your physical network adapter, your Hyper-V virtual LAN and the network adapter for each Virtual Machine created in your current Hyper-V host. Each network adapter will have a unique GUID beside it. To monitor all network adapters listed select <All Instances>, to monitor a specific network adapter, select it and click Add.

Measuring Performance of Hyper-V

The information provided in this section is a general guideline on how to use some of the counters added in the previous section to measure, analyze and improve the performance of your Hyper-V host and the guest VMs.

Measuring Memory Performance

Use the following performance monitor counters to measure the impact of available memory on the performance of a guest operating system installed on a Hyper-V virtual machine:

1. **Measure available memory on the Hyper-V host operating system:** The amount of physical memory available to the Hyper-V host operating system can be determined by monitoring the **\Memory\Available MBytes** performance monitor counter on the physical computer. This counter reports the amount of free physical memory available to the host operating system. Use the following rules of thumb when evaluating physical memory available to the host operating system:
2. **\Memory\Available Mbytes:** Available MBytes measures the amount of physical memory available to processes running on the computer, as a percentage of physical memory installed on the computer
3. **\Memory\Pages/sec:** This performance monitor counter measures the rate at which pages are read from or written to disk to resolve hard page faults. To resolve hard page faults, the operating system must swap the contents of memory to disk, which negatively impacts performance. A high number of pages per second in correlation with low available physical memory may indicate a lack of physical memory.
4. **Measure available memory on the guest operating system:** Memory that is available to the guest operating systems can be measured with the same performance monitor counters used to measure memory available to the Hyper-V host operating system.

Measuring Network Performance

Hyper-V allows guest computers to share the same physical network adapter. While this helps to consolidate hardware, take care not to saturate the physical adapter. Use the following methods to ensure the health of the network used by the Hyper-V virtual machines:

1. **Test network latency:** Ping each virtual machine to ensure adequate network latency. On local area networks, expect to receive less than 1ms response times.

2. **Test for packet loss:** Use the **pathping.exe** utility to test packet loss between virtual machines. Pathping.exe measures packet loss on the network and is available with all versions of Windows Server since Windows Server 2000. Pathping.exe sends out a burst of 100 ping requests to each network node and calculates how many pings are returned. On local area networks there should be no loss of ping requests from the pathping.exe utility.

3. **Test network file transfers:** Copy a 100MB file between virtual machines and measure the length of time required to complete the copy. On a healthy 100Mbit (megabit) network, a 100MB (megabyte) file should copy in 10 to 20 seconds. On a healthy 1Gbit network, a 100MB file should copy in about 3 to 5 seconds. Copy times outside these parameters are indicative of a network problem. One common cause of poor network transfers occurs when the network adapter has **auto detected** a 10MB half-duplex network which prevents the network adapter from taking full advantage of available bandwidth.

4. **Measure network utilization on the Hyper-V host operating system:** Use the following performance monitor counters to measure network utilization on the Hyper-V host operating system:

   a) **\Network Interface(*)\Bytes Total/sec:** The percentage of network utilization is calculated by multiplying **Bytes Total/sec** by 8 to convert it to bits, multiply the result by 100, then divide by the network adapter's current bandwidth.

   b) **\Network Interface(*)\Output Queue Length:** The output queue length measures the number of threads waiting on the network adapter. If there are more than 2 threads waiting on the network adapter, then the network may be a bottleneck. Common causes of this are poor network latency and/or high collision rates on the network.

Ensure that the network adapters for all computers (physical and virtual) in your solution are configured to use the same value for maximum transmission unit (MTU). If an output queue length of 2 or more is measured, consider adding one or more physical network adapters to the physical computer that hosts the virtual machines and bind the network adapters used by the guest operating systems to these physical network adapters.

5. **Measure network utilization on the guest operating systems:** If a network adapter on the Hyper-V root partition is busy as indicated by the performance monitor counters mentioned above, then consider using the **\Hyper-V Virtual Network Adapter(*)\Bytes/sec** performance monitor counter to identify which virtual network adapters are consuming the most network utilization.

Measuring Processor Performance

The following considerations apply when evaluating processor performance on a guest operating system installed on a Hyper-V virtual machine:

1. **Guest operating system processors do not have a set affinity to physical processors/cores:** The hypervisor determines how physical resources are used. In the case of processor utilization, the hypervisor schedules the guest processor time to physical processor in the form of threads. This means the processor load of virtual machines will be spread across the processors of the physical computer. Furthermore, virtual machines cannot exceed the processor utilization of the configured number of logical processors, for example if a single virtual machine is configured to run with 2 logical processors on a physical computer with 8 processors/cores, then the virtual machine cannot exceed the processor capacity of the number of configured logical processors (in this case 2 processors).

2. **Measure guest operating system processor utilization:** Traditionally, processor performance can be measured using the **\Processor(*)\% Processor Time** performance monitor counter. This is not an accurate counter for evaluating processor utilization of a guest operating system though because Hyper-V measures and reports this value relative to the number of processors allocated to the virtual machine. If more processors are allocated to running virtual machines than are actually present on the physical computer, the value returned by each guest operating system for the **\Processor(*)\% Processor Time** performance monitor counter will be low, even if in fact processor utilization is a bottleneck. This occurs because the virtual processors utilize the physical processors in a round-robin fashion. Each virtual processor will try and allocate itself a share of overall system resources, so in a 4 physical processor system, each virtual processor will by default try to utilize 25% of the system resources. If 8 virtual processors are created this means that collectively the virtual processors will attempt to utilize 200% of the server CPU capacity. In this case, each virtual processor will report a low utilization as measured by the **\Processor(*)\% Processor Time** performance

monitor counter (relative to the level it expects) and the excessive context switching between the virtual processors will result in poor performance for each virtual machine. In this scenario, consider reducing the number of virtual processors allocated to Hyper-V virtual machines on the host operating system.

Hyper-V provides hypervisor performance objects to monitor the performance of both logical and virtual processors. A logical processor correlates directly to the number of processors or cores that are installed on the physical computer. For example, 2 quad core processors installed on the physical computer would correlate to 8 logical processors. Virtual processors are what the virtual machines actually use, and all execution in the root and child partitions occurs in virtual processors. To accurately measure the processor utilization of a guest operating system, use the **\Hyper-V Hypervisor Logical Processor(_Total)\% Total Run Time** performance monitor counter on the Hyper-V host operating system.

To troubleshoot processor performance of guest operating systems on a Hyper-V environment, it is best to strive for a balance between the values reported by the host operating system for **\Hyper-V Hypervisor Logical Processor(_Total)\% Total Run Time** (LPTR) and **\Hyper-V Hypervisor Virtual Processor(_Total)\% Total Run Time** (VPTR). If **LPTR** is high and **VPTR** is low then verify that there are not more processors allocated to virtual machines than are physically available on the physical computer. Use the **\Hyper-V Hypervisor Virtual Processor(*)\%Guest Run Time** counters to determine which virtual Processors are consuming CPU and de-allocate virtual processors from virtual machines as appropriate to configure a one to one mapping of virtual processors to logical processors. If **VPTR** is high and **LPTR** is low then consider allocating additional processors to virtual machines if there are available logical processors and if additional processors are supported by the guest operating system.

In the case where VPTR is high, LPTR is low, there are available logical processors to allocate, but additional processors are not supported by the guest operating system, consider scaling out by adding additional virtual machines to the physical computer and allocating available processors to these virtual machines. In the case where both VPTR and LPTR are high, the configuration is pushing the limits of the physical computer and should consider scaling out by adding another physical computer and additional Hyper-V virtual machines to the environment.

3. **Measure overall processor utilization of the Hyper-V environment using Hyper-V performance monitor counters**: For purposes of measuring processor utilization, the host operating system is logically viewed as just another guest operating system. Therefore, the

\Processor(*)\% Processor Time monitor counter measures the processor utilization of the host operating system only. To measure total physical processor utilization of the host operating system and all guest operating systems, use the **\Hyper-V Hypervisor Logical Processor(_Total)\% Total Run Time** performance monitor counter. This counter measures the total percentage of time spent by the processor running the host operating system and all guest operating systems.

Note

To measure processor utilization of guest VMs in your Hyper-V host, use the "\Hyper-V Hypervisor Logical Processor(_Total)\% Total Run Time" not the "\Processor(*)\% Processor Time" performance monitor counter.

1.3.4 Monitor events

Performance Monitor has a node called **Event Trace Sessions**. This is under Data Collector Sets. There is also a second node called **Startup Event Trace Sessions**. Event tracing sessions record events from one or more providers that a controller enables. The session is also responsible for managing and flushing the buffers. The controller defines the session, which typically includes specifying the session and log file name, type of log file to use, and the resolution of the time stamp used to record the events. If a data collector set (trace type) under Startup Event Trace Sessions is enabled, its trace session will show under Event Trace Sessions.

Note

A trace type Data collector Set can only be Enabled when it is under the Startup Event Trace Sessions. Any trace DCS created outside this node will have the enable button greyed. Enable a trace DCS from **Properties**, on the **Trace session** tab.

An Alert type DCS can be configured to log an entry in the application events log and start your trace type DCS. To illustrate this, you will configure an event trace using Micorsoft-IE event provider. You will then configure a Memory Alert to start this event trace when triggered and log an entry to the event log. Finally, you will locate the log entry in the applications event log.

To Configure Event Trace to Monitor Events

1. Log on to 70411SRV3 and open **Performance Monitor.**
2. Expand Data Collector Sets, then right-click User Defined, point to **New** and select **Data Collector Set**. The Create New Data Collector Set wizard opens.
3. At the Name field, type MicrosoftIETrace, select Create Manually (Advance) then click **Next.**

4. On the Data to include screen, select **Event trace data**, click **Next.**
5. Under **Providers**, click **Add**, select **Microsoft-IE** as your Event Trace Provider, click **Ok**, and then click **Next.**
6. Accept default location to save file and click **Next**, then at the final page, click **Finish.**

To Configure an alert to log events

1. Again right-click User Defined, point to **New** and select **Data Collector Set**. The Create New Data Collector Set wizard opens.
2. At the Name field, type Memory Alert, select Create Manually (Advance) then click **Next.**
3. On the Data to include screen, select **Performance Counter Alert**, click **Next**
4. Under Performance Counters, click Add. Expand Memory, select Available MBytes and click Add, then Ok.
5. Under **Alert When**, select **Below** from the drop-down, then on the **Limit** box, type 350 (This is an arbitrary figure), click **Next**, then **finish.**
6. Expand **User Defined** and highlight **Memory Alert** DCS, in the details pane, right-click **DataCollector01** and select **Properties**, click the **Alert Action** tab
7. Check the box, **Log an entry in the application event Log**, then under start a data collector set, from the drop-down, select **MicrosoftIETrace**.

What you have configured is for the alert to start when available memory on your server is below 350MB, it will log an entry in the application event log then run the trace DTS **MicrosoftIETrace**. When the memory alert starts your MicrosoftIETrace event trace, you can use the information provided to troubleshoot the cause of the memory alert. You may compare the information provided in the application event log with what is provided in the trace report. For your event trace to log entries in Reports on Performance Monitor, you need to enable it to do so.

To enable reporting on a Data Collector Set

1. Right-click **MicrosoftIETrace** DCS, and select **Data Manager**. The Data Manager properties of MicrosoftIETrace DCS opens.
2. Click the check box Enable data management and report generation, then click Ok
3. Right-click **Memory Alert** DCS and select **Start**. You will notice that the **MicrosoftIETrace** DCS will start as well.

To view event trace reports and log entry.

1. Right-click **MicrosoftIETrace** and click **stop.**
2. Expand **Reports** in Performance Monitor, then expand **MicrosoftIETrace**.

3. Highlight the report under MicrosoftIETrace. It will take a while to load the report.
4. To view the Event Log entries, open Event Viewer (Server Manager - Tools menu).
5. Navigate to: Event Viewer – Applications and Services Logs – Microsoft – Windows – Diagnosis-PLA – Operational.
6. Highlight Operational and in the details pane, review the log entries.

The log entry in event log will have the following information - Log name: "Microsoft-Windows-Diagnosis-PLA/Operational". Details: "Performance counter \Memory\Available MBytes has tripped its alert threshold. The counter value of 279.000000 is under the limit value of 350.000000. 350.000000 is the alert threshold value."

1.3.5 Configure event subscriptions

In Windows Server 2012 and Windows Server 2012 R2, you can collect copies of events from multiple remote computers and store them locally. To specify which events to collect, you create an event subscription. Among other details, the subscription specifies exactly which events will be collected and in which log they will be stored locally. Once a subscription is active and events are being collected, you can view and manipulate these forwarded events as you would any other locally stored events. One importance of this approach may be to collect all events on a single server, then build a PowerShell script to monitor a particular event information. This way, your script will monitor a single computer instead of multiple computers.

Event collecting feature requires the configuration of the forwarding and the collecting computers. The functionality depends on the **Windows Remote Management (WinRM)** service and the **Windows Event Collector (Wecsvc)** service. These services must be running on computers participating in the forwarding and collecting process.

In this section, you will configure the server 70411SRV3 to receive event logs from the domain controllers, 70411SRV and 70411SRV2.

To configure event forwarding and collection

1. Log on to 70411SRV and 70411SRV2 (source computers) with domain administrator account and type the command:

```
winrm quickconfig
```

2. Log on to 70411SRV3 (collector computer) with domain administrator account and type the command:

```
wecutil qc
```

3. On the wecutil dialogue, respond Y, to configure **Windows Event Collector Service**

4. Add the computer account 70411SRV3 (collector computer) to the Domain Admins group (check "Computers" object in the "select this object type" to be able to add a computer to a group).

The collector computer account, 70411SRV3 was added to the domain admins group because the source computers (70411SRV and 70411SRV2) are domain controllers. If the source computers were member servers, collector computer account would have been added to the local Administrators group on each of 70411SRV and 70411SRV2. The computers are now configured to forward and collect events. In the next section, you will configure event subscription on 70411SRV3 (collector computer).

To Create a New Subscription

1. Log on to 70411SRV3 (collector computer) with domain administrator account.
2. From Server Manager, Tools Menu, open Event Viewer.
3. Click **Subscriptions** in the console tree.
4. On the Actions menu, click Create Subscription.
5. In the Subscription Name box , type ADComputers .
6. In the **Destination Log** box, **ForwardedEvents (Default)** is selected as the log file where collected events are to be stored.
7. Under **Subscription types and source computers**, select **Collector Initiated** and click **Select Computers,** to select the computers from which events are to be collected.
8. In the **Computers** dialogue, click **Add Domain Computers**. Then Add 70411SRV and 70411SRV2.
9. Select each source computer and click **Test**, to confirm connectivity. If connectivity is successful, click **Ok**.

You can configure two types of subscriptions:

Collector Initiated: The collector computer contacts the source computers and provides subscription.

Source Computer Initiated: Source Computers in the selected groups must be configured through group policy or local configuration to contact the collector computer and receive subscriptions. Group policy configuration settings is located in: Computer Configuration\Policies\Administrative Tools\Windows Components\Event Forwarding. Name of policy is **Configure target Subscription Manager**.

1. Beside **Events to collect**, click **Select Events**, to display the Query Filter dialog box.
2. On the **Filter** tab, complete the following tasks:
   a) Beside Logged, select Last 12 Hours.
   b) On Event Level, check Critical and Error.

   c) Select **By Log**, and on the **Events Log** drop down, Select **Windows Logs**, expand **Application and service** logs, then select **DNS Server.**
   d) On the **Query Filter** dialogue, click **Ok.**
   e) On the Properties of **ADComputers** subscription, click **Advanced**, Select **Specific User**, then enter the domain password for your domain account.
   f) Click **Ok** on the **Subscription Properties** dialog box. The subscription will be added to the Subscriptions pane and, if the operation was successful, the Status of the subscription will be **Active.**

On **the Events to collect** Query Filter, you can filter by Time logged, Event Level (Critical, warning, Verbose, Error or Information). You can also filter further by Event Logs or Event Source. On an event subscription Properties, you can configure additional options:

User account: Machine account or a specific user account (Default is Machine account). If you decide to change to a selected user, the user must have read access to the source logs. Using and Active Directory account is recommended.

Event Delivery Optimization: Normal, Maximize Bandwidth, Maximize Latency.

Protocol: HTTP (Port 5985), HTTPS (Port 5986).

1.3.6 Configure network monitoring

A system's network interface card(s) needs to be monitored for performance and possible bottlenecks. To monitor network performance on a Windows Server 2012 or Windows Server 2012 R2, we use performance counters as with any other resource. As with other resources as well, you can configure alerts and event traces to log events. At the minimum, you should consider configuring the following performance counters:

1. **Network capacity Counters**: \Network Interface(*)\Output Queue Length:
   a) **High Network I/O**: More than 1 thread waiting on network I/O (If the output queue length is greater than 1. If so, the system's network is nearing capacity. Consider analysing network traffic to determine why network I/O is nearing capacity such as *chatty* network services and/or large data transfers).
   b) **Very high network I/O**: More than 2 threads waiting on network I/O (if the output queue length is greater than 2. If so, this system's network is over capacity. Consider analysing network traffic to determine why network I/O is nearing capacity such as *chatty* network services and/or large data transfers).

2. Network Utilization Analysis:
    a) \Network Interface(*)\Bytes Total/sec.
    b) **\Network Interface(*)\Current Bandwidth**: Bytes Total/sec is the rate at which bytes are sent and received over each network adapter, including framing characters. Network Interface\Bytes Received/sec is a sum of Network Interface\Bytes Received/sec and Network Interface\Bytes Sent/sec. This counter indicates the rate at which bytes are sent and received over each network adapter. This counter helps you know whether the traffic at your network adapter is saturated and if you need to add another network adapter. How quickly you can identify a problem depends on the type of network you have as well as whether you share bandwidth with other applications.
    c) Network Utilization Thresholds:
        i)   High average network utilization – more than 50%
        ii) Very high average network utilization – more than 80%
3. **Server\Bytes Total/sec**: This counter indicates the number of bytes sent and received over the network. Higher values indicate network bandwidth as the bottleneck. If the sum of Bytes Total/sec for all servers is roughly equal to the maximum transfer rates of your network, you may need to segment the network.
    a) **Server\Bytes Total/Sec Thresholds**: Not be more than 50 percent of network capacity.

To Configure network monitoring

1. Log on to 70411HPV (Your Hyper-V host) and open **Performance Monitor.**
2. Expand Data Collector Sets, right-click User Defined, point to New and select Data Collector Set.
3. In the Name field, enter Network Monitor, then select Create manually (Advanced), and click Next.
4. On the **what data to collect..** screen, check Performance Counter, then click Next.
5. On the Which performance counters... screen, under Performance counters, click Add.
6. Select the following counters (For each counter select **<All Instances>**, if present and add):
    a) \Network Interface\ Output Queue Length
    b) \Network Interface\Current Bandwidth
    c) \Network Interface\Bytes Total/sec
    d) Server\Bytes Total/sec
7. When you finish adding the performance counters, click **Ok.**
8. On the Which performance counters... screen, click **Finish**.

1.3.7 Schedule performance monitoring (2012 R2 Objective)

Windows Performance Monitor uses a consistent scheduling method for all data collection. To configure scheduling, configure a **Start Condition** (from Schedule tab) and **Stop condition** (from Stop Condition tab).

To Schedule a start condition

1. Log on to 70411SRV3 and open Performance Monitor.
2. Expand Data Collection Sets, then expand User Defined.
3. Right-click **PhysicalDiskAler** DTS and click **Properties**, then Click the **Schedule** tab.
4. Click **Add**, on the **Beginning Date**, enter today's date; on the **Expiry Date**, enter a date after today's date; on the **Start time**, set 10 minutes from now (These settings will allow you to test).
5. On the Folder Actions dialogue, click **Ok.**

If you do not want to collect new data after a certain date, select **Expiration date** and choose a date from the calendar.

Note

Selecting an expiration date will not stop data collection in progress on that date. It will prevent new instances of data collection from starting after the expiration date. You must use the Stop Condition tab to configure how data collection is stopped.

To schedule the Stop condition for a Data Collector Set

1. From the Properties of **PhysicalDiskAler** DTS Click the **Stop Condition** tab.
2. To stop collecting data after a period of time, check **overall duration** then enter **1** and under **units**, select **hours**.
3. Use Limits to segment data collection into separate logs by selecting **Restart the data collector set at limits.** If both limit types are selected, data collection will stop or restart when the first limit is reached.
   a) Select **Duration** to configure a time period for data collection to write to a single log file.
   b) Select **Maximum Size** to restart the Data Collector Set or to stop collecting data when the log file reaches the limit.

Note

Your **overall duration** must be longer than the interval at which data is sampled in order to see any data in the report. Do not select an **Overall duration** if you want to collect data indefinitely. If an overall duration is configured, it will override Limits.

If you have configured an overall duration, you can select **Stop when all data collectors have finished** to let all data collectors finish recording the most recent values before the Data Collector Set is stopped.

4. When finished, click **Ok.**

Chapter 2

Configure File and Print Services

2.1 Configure Distributed File System (DFS)

Introduction

DFS Namespaces enables you to group shared folders that are located on different servers into one or more logically structured namespaces. Each namespace appears to users as a single shared folder with a series of subfolders. However, the underlying structure of the namespace can consist of numerous shared folders that are located on different servers and in multiple sites.

This structure increases availability and automatically connects users to shared folders in the same AD DS site, when available; instead of routing them over wide area network (WAN) connections. A namespace is a virtual view of shared folders in an organization. The path to a namespace is similar to a Universal Naming Convention (UNC) path to a shared folder, such as \\Server1\Public\Software\Tools.

If you want to give users a single place to locate data, but you want to host data on different servers for availability and performance purposes, you can deploy a namespace similar to the one shown in figure 2.1.0. In this example, the shared folder **Public** and its subfolders **Software** and **Tools** are all hosted on **Server1**.

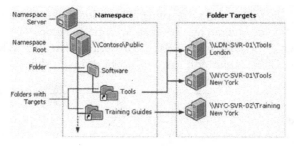

Figure 2.1.0 - Namespace Folder Targets (Microsoft TechNet)

Elements of a Namespece

The elements of a namespace are described below:

Namespace server: A namespace server hosts a namespace. The namespace server can be a member server or a domain controller.

Namespace root: The namespace root is the starting point of the namespace. In the previous figure, the name of the root is **Public**, and the namespace path is **\\Contoso\Public**. This type of namespace is a domain-based namespace because it begins with a domain name (for example, Contoso) and its metadata is stored in Active Directory Domain Services (AD DS). Although a single namespace server is shown in the previous figure, a domain-based namespace can be hosted on multiple namespace servers (including domain member servers) to increase the availability of the namespace.

Folder: Folders without folder targets add structure and hierarchy to the namespace, and folders with folder targets provide users with actual content. When users browse a folder that has folder targets in the namespace, the client computer receives a referral that transparently redirects the client computer to one of the folder targets.

Folder targets: A folder target is the UNC path of a shared folder or another namespace that is associated with a folder in a namespace. The folder target is where data and content is stored. In the previous figure, the folder named **Tools** has two folder targets, one in **London** and one in **New York;** and the folder named **Training Guides** has a single folder target in **New York**. A user who browses to **\\Contoso\Public\Software\Tools** is transparently redirected to the shared folder **\\LDN-SVR-01\Tools or \\NYC-SVR-01\Tools**, depending on which site the user is currently located in.

Note

Folders can contain folder targets or other DFS folders, but not both at the same level in the folder hierarchy. You can administer namespaces by using DFS Management, the DfsUtil command, or scripts that call WMI. DFS Namespaces and DFS Replication are role services in the File and Storage Services role.

DFS Replication: Enables you to efficiently replicate folders (including those referred to by a DFS namespace path), across multiple servers and sites. DFS Replication uses a compression algorithm known as **remote differential compression** (RDC). RDC detects changes to the data in a file, and it enables

DFS Replication to replicate only the changed file blocks instead of the entire file.

DFS Replication is an efficient, multiple-master replication engine that you can use to keep folders synchronized between servers across limited bandwidth network connections. It replaces the **File Replication Service (FRS)** as the replication engine for DFS Namespaces, as well as for replicating the Active Directory Domain Services (AD DS) SYSVOL folder in domains that use the Windows Server 2008 domain functional level.

To use DFS Replication, you must create replication groups and add replicated folders to the groups. Replication groups, replicated folders, and members are illustrated in the following figure.

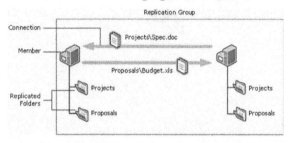

Figure 2.1.1 - DFS Replication Group (Microsoft TechNet)

Figure 2.1.1 shows that a replication group is a set of servers, known as members, which participates in the replication of one or more replicated folders. A replicated folder is a folder that stays synchronized on each member. In the figure, there are two replicated folders: **Projects** and **Proposals**. As data change in each replicated folder, the changes are replicated across connections between the members of the replication group. The connections between all members form the replication topology.

Creating multiple replicated folders in a single replication group simplifies the process of deploying replicated folders because the topology, schedule, and bandwidth throttling for the replication group are applied to each replicated folder. To deploy additional replicated folders, you can use **Dfsradmin.exe** or follow the instructions in a wizard to define the local path and permissions for the new replicated folder.

Each replicated folder has unique settings, such as file and subfolder filters, so that you can filter out different files and subfolders for each replicated folder. The replicated folders stored on each member can be located on different volumes in the member, and the replicated folders do not need to be shared folders or part of a namespace. However, the DFS Management snap-in makes it easy to share replicated folders and optionally publishes them in an existing namespace.

In this section, we will cover the following exam objectives:

2.1.0 Install and configure DFS namespaces
2.1.1 Configure DFS Replication Targets
2.1.2 Configure Replication Scheduling
2.1.3 Configure Remote Differential Compression settings
2.1.4 Configure staging
2.1.5 Configure fault tolerance
2.1.6 Optimize DFS replication (2012 R2 Objective)
2.1.7 Clone a DFS database (2012 R2 Objective)
2.1.6 Recover DFS databases (2012 R2 Objective)

Lab Plan

We will be using 70411SRV, 70411SRV2, 70411SRV3 and 70411SRV4 in this chapter. DFS Namespace, DFS replication and Management tools will be installed on the servers listed.

Additional lab setup

Open Active Directory Users and Computers and create an AD user called **DFSUser**, with only group membership as **Domain Users**.

2.1.0 Install and configure DFS namespaces

DFS Namespaces and DFS Replication are a part of the File and Storage Services role. The management tools for DFS, DFS Management, the DFS Namespaces module for Windows PowerShell, and command-line tools are installed separately as part of the Remote Server Administration Tools.

Requirements for running DFS Management

There are no additional hardware or software requirements for running DFS Management or using DFS Namespaces. Before you can deploy DFS Replication, you must configure your servers as follows:

1. Ensure that all servers in a replication group are located in the same forest. You cannot enable replication across servers in different forests.
2. Install DFS Replication on all servers that will act as members of a replication group.
3. Contact your antivirus software vendor to check that your antivirus software is compatible with DFS Replication.
4. Locate any folders that you want to replicate on volumes formatted with the NTFS file system. DFS Replication does not support the Resilient File System (ReFS) or the FAT file system. DFS Replication also does not support replicating content stored on Cluster Shared Volumes.

To Install DFS Using Server Manager

1. Log on to 70411SRV and open Server Manager.
2. Click **Manage**, and then click **Add Roles and Features,** The Add Roles and Features Wizard opens.
3. On the **Before you Begin** screen, click **Next.**
4. On the **Installation type** screen click **Next**.
5. On the **Server Selection** screen, ensure that 70411SRV is highlighted, click **Next.**
6. On the Select Server Roles screen, expand File and Storage Services, then expand File and iSCSI services, and select DFS Namespaces and DFS Replication, click add features when prompted, and click Next.
7. On the **Features** screen, expand Remote Server Administration Tools, then expand **File Services Tools**, and confirm that **DFS Management Tools** is selected, click **Next.**

Note

DFS Management Tools installs the DFS Management snap-in, the DFS Namespaces module for Windows PowerShell, and command-line tools, but it does not install any DFS services on the server.

8. At the **confirmation** screen, click **Install.**

To Install DFS Using PowerShell

1. Log on to 70411SRV2 and open a Windows PowerShell session with elevated user rights.
2. Execute the command below to install DFS-Namespace, DFS-Replication and DFS Management Tools:

Install-WindowsFeature FS-DFS-Namespace, FS-DFS-Replication, RSAT-DFS-Mgmt-Con

3. Log on to 70411SRV3 and 70411SRV4 then repeat the above command.

The PowerShell feature name for each Role service or feature is listed below:
DFS Namespaces: FS-DFS-Namespace
DFS Replication: FS-DFS-Replication
DFS Management Tools: RSAT-DFS-Mgmt-Con

Note

DFS Replication can also be used to replicate the SYSVOL folder in Active Directory Domain Services (AD DS) in domains that are on the Windows Server 2012 R2, Windows Server 2012, Windows Server 2008 R2, or Windows Server 2008 domain functional levels.

Configure DFS Namespaces

DFS Namespace can be configured as a stand-alone or Server Hosting Domain-Based Namespaces.

To create a DFS Namespace

1. Log on to 70411SRV and open Server Manager.
2. Click **Tools** and select **DFS Management**.
3. In the console tree, right-click the **Namespaces** node, and then click **New Namespace.**
4. Follow the steps below to create a domain-based Namespace:
   a) On the **Server** field, enter **70411SRV** and click **Next.**
   b) On the Enter a name for the namespace, type 70411DFS, click Edit settings
   c) On the Local path, enter **E:\DFS\Namespace\70411DFS**.
   d) Under Shared Folder Permission, select Administrators have full access, Other users Read-Only permissions and click **Ok.**
   e) On the Namespace Name and Settings screen, click **Next.**
   f) On the Namespace Type screen, select Domain-based namespace, then check box Enable Windows Server 2008 mode, click **Next.**
   g) On the **Review** screen, click **create.**
   h) When the wizard returns a **Success** status, click **close.**

Note

Do not attempt to create a domain-based namespace using the Windows Server 2008 mode unless the forest functional level is Windows Server 2003 or higher. Doing so can result in a namespace for which you cannot delete DFS folders, yielding the following error message: "The folder cannot be deleted. Cannot complete this function." When a Domain-based DFS namespace is created in Windows Server 2008 mode, the namespace supports increased scalability and access-based enumeration.

2.1.1 Configure DFS Replication Targets

A folder target is the UNC path of a shared folder or another namespace that is associated with a folder in a namespace. The folder target is where data and content is stored. In this section, you will add folders to the namespace created in the previous section and add folder targets. You will then configure DFS Replication for the folder targets.

To create folders and add folder targets

1. Log on to 70411SRV and open Server Manager.
2. Click **Tools**, click **DFS Management**, DFS Management Console opens.
3. Expand **Namespaces**, then right-click \\70411Lab.com\70411DFS and select **New Folder**.
4. In the **New Folder** screen, type **DFSFolder1** on the **name** field. Beneath **Folder targets**, click **Add**.
5. On the **Add Folder target** dialogue, on the Path to folder target, type **\\70411SRV\Reptarget1**, click **Ok**. Click Add again, on the Path to folder target, type **\\70411SRV2\Reptarget2**, click **Ok.**
6. Respond No to the Create Replication Group Query.

Note

From the task you completed above, you should understand the difference between a folder and a folder target. A Folder without folder targets adds structure and hierarchy to the namespace while a folder target is the UNC path of a shared folder.

To configure DFS Replication Target

1. Highlight **DFSFolder1** under the **\\70411Lab.com\70411DFS** namespace and in the details pane, click **Replication** tab.
2. Click the hyperlink **Replicate folder Wizard**. The Wizard opens.
3. On the Replication Group and Replication Folder Name screen, on the Replication Group Name field, type DFSFolder1Replication. On the Replicated folder name field, accept the suggested name as DFSFolder1, click **Next**.
4. On the Replication Eligibility screen, click **Next**.
5. On **Primary Member** screen, Select **70411SRV** from the drop-down and click **Next**.
6. On the **Topology Selection** screen, Select **Full Mesh** then click **Next**.
7. On the **Replication Group and Bandwidth** screen, accept the defaults and Click **Next**.
8. On the **Review** screen, review your options and click **Create**.
9. On the **Confirmation** screen, click **Close**.
10. Note the Replication Delay warning and click **Ok**.

DFS Replication Groups

There are two types of replication groups:

Multipurpose replication group: Configures replication between two or more servers for

publication, content sharing and other scenarios.

Replication group for data collection: Configures replication between servers, such that as a branch server and a hub (destination) server. This allows you to collect data at a hub server. You can then use backup software to back up the data on the hub server.

There are three Types of Topology for a Replication Group:

Hub and spoke: Requires three or more members in the replication group. In this topology, spoke members are connected to one or more hub members. This topology works well in publication scenarios where data originates from the hub member and replicates out to the spoke members.

Full mesh: Each member replicates with all other members of the replication group. This

Topology works well when there are ten or fewer members in the group.

No topology: Select this option if you want to create a custom topology. No replication will take place.

2.1.2 Configure Replication Scheduling

To edit the replication schedule or bandwidth for a replication group or connection, or to force replication with a specific member of a replication group, use the following procedures.

To edit the replication schedule and bandwidth

1. Log on to 70411SRV and open DFS Management Console via Server Manager.
2. Expand Replication node, right-click DFSFolder1Replication, then click Edit Replication Group Schedule.
3. On the **Edit Schedule configuration** screen, note the following configurable options:
   a) **Base schedule on**: Determines what time replication should be based. Available options:
      i) Local time of receiving member.
      ii) Universal Coordinated Time (UTC).
   b) **Schedule Time Scale**: 24-hour format, 0, 2, 4, …24.
   c) **Bandwidth Usage**: Configure Bandwidth usage for specific replication schedule. Available options:
      i) Full, No replication.
      ii) Then starts from 16 Kbps, 64 Kbps..then multiples of 2.
      iii) Maximum configurable Bandwidth is 256 Mbps.
   d) **Details** option. Expand the details option to:
      i) View currently configured schedule.
      ii) Add custom schedule.
4. On the **Edit Schedule configuration** screen, configure the following:
   a) **Base schedule on**: Universal Coordinated Time (UTC).
   b) Schedule Time:
      i) Under "0", click on the "All". This will highlight Monday to Sunday, under "0".
      ii) Beside **Bandwidth Usage**, select "No replication" from the drop-down. You notice that column 0 becomes white.
   c) Click **Details** button, notice that all replication schedule starts from 1.00. This is because we set all the column under 0.00 to "No replication"
      i) To add a custom schedule, click **Add**,
      ii) Configure schedule as follows - Start Time: 00.00, End time: 02:00, Days: check Monday, Bandwidth usage: 64 Mbps, Click **Ok.**
      iii) Notice now that on column 0, Monday is now blue, other days are still white.
5. On the Edit Schedule configuration screen, click **Ok.**
6. On the Properties of DFSFolder1Replication, click **Ok.**

Facts about DFS Replication schedule configuration

Each box represents an hour, Periods configured for full bandwidth replication will appear as complete blue box, while periods configured for replication using any other bandwidth, will appear as blue box with tiny white boxes.

Replication configuration changes are not applied immediately to all members. The new configuration must be replicated to all domain controllers, and each member in the replication group must poll its closest domain controller to obtain the changes. The amount of time this takes depends on AD DS replication latency and the long polling interval (60 minutes) on each member. To poll immediately for configuration changes, open a command prompt window and then type the following command once for each member of the replication group:

dfsrdiag.exe PollAD /Member:DOMAIN\ServerName

The **Update-DfsrConfigurationFromAD** PowerShell cmdlet will accomplish the same task. Update-DfsrConfigurationFromAD cdmlet was introduced in Windows Server 2012 R2.

To force replication immediately

1. Expand Replication node and highlight DFSFolder1Replication.
2. In the details pane, click **Connections** tab.
3. Right-click on **70411SRV** and click **Replicate Now**. The **Replicate Now** dialogue opens, click **Ok.**
4. Repeat step 3 and 4 for 70411SRV2.
5. To disable replication on any of the members, right click the server name and select Disable.

Enable or Disable Replication on a Specific Member

You can enable or disable replication with specific members of a replication group. However, it is important to understand the ramifications of doing so. After a disabled member is enabled, the member must complete an initial replication of the replicated folder. Initial replication will cause about 1 KB of data to be transferred for each file or folder in the replicated folder, and any updated or new files present on the member will be moved to the DfsrPrivate\PreExisting folder on the member, and replaced with authoritative files from another member.

If all members are disabled for a replicated folder, then the first member that is enabled will automatically be made the primary member. If the discretionary access control list (DACL) on the local path for this member contains any inherited access-control entries (ACE), these ACEs will be converted to explicit ACEs with the same permissions so that all members will have the same DACL on the replicated folder root.

To enable or disable replicating a replicated folder to a specific member

1. Expand Replication node, highlight DFSFolder1Replication, and click Memberships tab.
2. Select a replicated folder on a specific member, and then do one of the following:
    a) To disable the replicated folder on the member, right-click the replicated folder, and then click **Disable**.
    b) To enable the replicated folder on the member, right-click the replicated folder, and then click **Enable**.

2.1.3 Configure Remote Differential Compression settings

Remote Differential Compression (RDC) detects changes to the data in a file, and it enables DFS Replication to replicate only the changed file blocks instead of the entire file. RDC is configured on the properties page of each individual member of a DFS Replication Group.

To configure RDC

1. Expand Replication node, Highlight **DFSFolder1Replication**, and click **Connections** tab.
2. Right-click any of the replication members and click **Properties.**
3. From the **General** tab, you can enable of disable **Remote Differential Compression**.

Exam Tip

Remote Differential Compression is configured on replication member basis, not from the replication group. It is configured from the Properties page, General tab of the replication group member. By default, each member will use the replication schedule configured at the Replication Group level, but from the schedule tab of the Properties page of a replication member, you can customize the replication schedule for that member. This may be useful in situations where a server is in a location with lower bandwidth.

2.1.4 Configure Staging

In the preceding section, we reviewed and configured the properties of DFS replication group members. We will now examine the properties of replicated folders in the DFS replication group. You can configure Replicated folders from the memberships tab of a DFS replication group. We will examine the **Staging** and **ConflictAndDeleted** properties of a replicated folder.

Staging Folders

DFS Replication uses staging folders to act as caches for new and changed files to be replicated from sending members to receiving members. The sending member begins staging a file when it receives a request from the receiving member. The process involves reading the file from the replicated folder and building a compressed representation of the file in the staging folder. This is the **staged file**. After being constructed, the staged file is sent to the receiving member; if remote differential compression [RDC] is used, only a fraction of the staging file might be replicated. The receiving member downloads the data and builds the file in its staging folder. After the file has completed downloading on the receiving member, DFS Replication decompresses the file and installs it into the replicated folder.

Each replicated folder has its own staging folder, which by default is located under the local path of the replicated folder in the **DfsrPrivate\Staging** folder. The default size of each staging folder is **4,096 MB**. This is not a hard limit, however. It is only a quota that is used to govern cleanup and excessive usage based on high and low watermarks (90% and 60% of staging folder size, respectively). For example, when the staging folder reaches 90% of the configured quota, the oldest staged files are purged until the staging folder reaches 60% of the configured quota.

If a staging folder quota is too small, DFS Replication might consume additional CPU and disk resources, and replication might slow down or even stop. When a file is modified on two or more members, before the changes can be replicated the most recently updated file "wins" the conflict and DFS Replication moves the "losing" file or files to the Conflict and Deleted folder. The losing file or files are stored in the DfsrPrivate\ConflictandDeleted folder under the local path of the replicated folder on the member that resolves the conflict. The Conflict and Deleted folder is also used to store files that are deleted from replicated folders. The files in the Conflict and Deleted folder are renamed and are accessible only by members of the local Administrators group. The access control lists (ACLs) on the conflict files are preserved to help ensure security. You can view a log of conflict files and their original file names by viewing the ConflictandDeletedManifest.xml file in the DfsrPrivate folder.

Conflict and Deleted folders

DFS Replication uses a "last-writer wins" method for determining which version of a file to keep when a file is modified on two or more members. As stated in our preceding discussion, the losing file is stored in the Conflict and Deleted folder on the member that resolves the conflict. This member might not be the member where the changes originated.

Each replicated folder has its own Conflict and Deleted folder, which is located under the local path of the replicated folder in the **DfsrPrivate\ConflictandDeleted** folder. The quota size of the Conflict and Deleted folder is **660 MB** by default. Like the staging folder, the Conflict and Deleted folder has high and low watermarks (90% and 60% of Conflict and Deleted folder quota, respectively) that govern cleanup and excessive usage of the folder. The size of each Conflict and Deleted folder on a member is cumulative per volume.

The Conflict and Deleted folder can also be used to store files that are deleted from replicated folders. You can configure this option by viewing the properties of a member. Deleted files are treated like conflict files in that they are purged when the Conflict and Deleted folder reaches 90% of the configured quota. They are also renamed and listed in the ConflictandDeletedManifest.xml file.

Note

When a conflict exists between two replicating members, the member with the latest copy of the file or folder causing the conflict "Wins". The losing file is stored in the Conflict and Deleted folder on the member that resolves the conflict. This member might not be the member where the changes originated.

To edit the quota size or location of the staging folder and Conflict and Deleted folder

1. Expand **Replication** node and highlight **DFSFolder1Replication**, then click the **Memberships** tab.
2. Right-click any of the available replicated folders and click **Properties.**
3. On the **Staging** tab, adjust the staging folder quota and path as necessary.
4. On the **Advanced** tab, adjust the Conflict and Deleted folder quota as necessary.

Optimize the size of staging folders

Optimizing the size of the staging folder can improve performance and reduce the likelihood of replication failing. When adjusting the size of the staging folder, consider the following factors:

1. If a staging folder quota is configured to be too small, DFS Replication might consume additional CPU and disk resources to regenerate the staged files. Replication might also slow down, or even stop because the lack of staging space can effectively limit the number of concurrent transfers with partners.
2. Increase the staging folder quota when you must replicate multiple large files that change frequently.

3. If possible, increase the staging folder quota on hub members that have many replication partners.
4. If free disk space is a concern, you might need to configure the staging quota to be lower than the default quota when several replicated folders share staging space on the same volume.
5. In normal operation, if the event that indicates the staging quota (event ID 4208 in the DFS Replication event log) is over its configured size and is logged multiple times in an hour, increase the staging quota by 20 %.
6. To improve input/output (I/O) throughput, locate staging folders and replicated folders on different physical disks. This can be done by editing the path of the staging folder.

For the initial replication of existing data on the primary member, the staging folder quota must be large enough so that replication can continue even if multiple large files remain in the staging folder because partners cannot promptly download the files.

To properly size the staging folder for initial replication, you must take into account the size of the files to be replicated. At a minimum, the staging folder quota for servers running Windows Server 2012, Windows Server 2008 R2 or Windows Server 2008 should be at least the size of the 32 largest files in the replicated folder, or the 16 largest files for read-only replicated folders. To improve performance, set the size of the staging folder quota as close as possible to the size of the replicated folder. You can relocate the Staging folder, but not the ConflictAndResolution folder.

Exam Tip

If there is any question relating to high CPU and disk resources, the answer will relate to increasing the size of the staging folder; any question relating to high disk I/O will require locating the staging folders and replicated folders on different physical disks.

Determine the quota size of your Staging Folder

You can estimate the quota your staging folder using Windows Explorer or Windows PowerShell.

To determine the size of your Staging Folder Using Windows Explorer

1. Using Windows Explorer and open the replicated folder.
2. Sort the contents of the replicated folder by size.
3. Add the 32 largest file sizes (16 if it's a read-only replicated folder).

Configure the quota size of your staging folder to the minimum size of the value in stage 3 above.

To determine the size of your Staging Folder Using Windows PowerShell

To get the recommended minimum staging folder size (Bytes) from a Windows PowerShell command prompt, use this Windows PowerShell command:

Get-ChildItem –Path E:\DFS\Reptargets\Reptarget1 -recurse | Sort-Object length -descending | select-object -first 32 | measure-object -property length –sum

---

The above command returned a value of 5817110 Bytes. So the minimum quota size of my Staging folder will be 5.54 MB. The **length** attribute of the **measure-object** cdmlet returns value in Bytes. You can easily convert using google search converter.

Note

The staging quota for DFS Replication is not a hard limit, and it can grow over its configured size, unlike the staging quota for FRS. When the quota is reached, DFS Replication deletes old files from the staging folder to reduce the disk usage under the quota. The staging folder does not reserve hard disk space, and it only consumes as much disk space as is currently needed. The value returned by the PowerShell command let above is in Bytes. You must have some files and folders in the replicating folder for a value to be returned. Set-DfsrMembership cmdlet, introduced in Windows Server 2012 R2 can also be used to edit the staging folder quotas. To list all the cmdlets that are available, use the Get-Command –Module DFSN cmdlet.

Edit the Replication Filters for a Replicated Folder

File and subfolder filters can be configured to prevent specific files and subfolders from replicating. Both types of filters are set on a per-replicated folder basis. Subfolders can be excluded by specifying their name or by using the asterisk (*) wildcard character. Files can be also be excluded by specifying their name or by using the asterisk (*) wildcard character to specify file names and extensions.

By default, no subfolders are excluded. The default file filters exclude the following files from replication:

1. File names starting with a tilde (~) character.
2. Files with .bak or .tmp extensions.

Regardless of which filters are set, the following types of files are always excluded from replication:

1. NTFS volume mount points.

2. Files that are encrypted by using the encrypting file system (EFS).
3. Any reparse points except those associated with DFS Namespaces (If a file has a reparse point that is used for Hierarchical Storage Management (HSM) or Single Instance Store (SIS), DFS Replication replicates the underlying file, but not the reparse point).
4. Files on which the temporary attribute has been set.

To edit the replication filters for a replicated folder

1. Expand Replication node and highlight DFSFolder1Replication, then click Replicated Folders tab.
2. On the **Replicated Folders** tab, right-click **DFSFolder1**, and click **Properties.**
3. On the **General** tab, edit the existing filters or add new filters, paying attention to the following restrictions:
   a) You cannot create file or subfolder filters by specifying a full path, such as C:\Replicatedfolder\Temp or C:\Replicatedfolder\file.dat.
   b) You cannot use a comma in a filter because commas are used as delimiters.

When a member detects a new filter, the member scans its database and removes the file records of files that match the filter. Since the files are no longer listed in the database, future changes to the files are ignored. After a member detects that a filter has been removed, the member scans the file system, adds records for all files that match the removed filter, and replicates the files.

2.1.5 Configure fault tolerance

Availability of a domain-based namespace can be increase by specifying additional namespace servers to host the namespace. To increase the availability of a stand-alone namespace, specify a failover cluster as the namespace server in the New Namespace Wizard.

To add a namespace server to a domain-based namespace

1. Log on to 70411SRV and open Server Manager.
2. From Server Manager click **Tools** and select **DFS Management.**
3. Expand **Namespaces** node, right-click \\70411Lab.com\70411DFS, and then click **Add Namespace Server**.
4. Click **Browse** on the window that opens and type 70411SRV3, click **Check Names**, and then click **Ok.**
5. On the Add Namespace Server page, click Edit Settings, change the Local Path to E:\DFS\Reptargets\Reptarget3 and under shared folder permissions, select Administrators have full access; other users have Read-Only permissions, then click Ok.

6. On the Add **Namespace Server** page, click **Ok.**

Note

Stand-alone namespaces support only a single namespace server. The only way to configure fault tolerance is to specify a failover cluster as the namespace server in the New Namespace Wizard. Domain member servers and domain controllers can act as Namespace Servers in a domain-based DFS namespace.

2.1.6 Optimize DFS replication (2012 R2 Objective)

Performance of a DFS Namespace can be greatly improved by configuring the following:

1. Configure folder access:
    a) Enable Access-Based Enumeration on the Namespace:
        Access-based enumeration hides files and folders that users do not have permission to access. By default, this feature is not enabled for DFS namespaces.
    b) Configure Inherited Permissions:
        By default, the permissions used for a DFS folder are inherited from the local file system of the namespace server. The permissions are inherited from the root directory of the system drive and grant the DOMAIN\Users group Read permissions. As a result, even after enabling access-based enumeration, all folders in the namespace remain visible to all domain users. There are two primary benefits to using inherited permissions to control which users can view folders in a DFS namespace:
        i)   You can quickly apply inherited permissions to many folders without having to use scripts.
        ii) You can apply inherited permissions to namespace roots and folders without targets.
    c) You could also set explicit view permissions on the DFS folder. When you configure this option in DFS folders, those users that do not have access to the DFS folder will not be displayed for them.
2. Configure Client Referrals:
    A referral is an ordered list of servers that a client computer receives from a domain controller or namespace server when the user accesses a namespace root or DFS folder with targets. After the computer receives the referral, the computer attempts to access the first server in the list. If the server is not available, the client computer attempts to access the next server. To improve DFS replication performance, consider the following:
    a) Enable or Disable Referrals and Client Failback:
        If a server becomes unavailable, you can configure clients to fail back to the preferred server after it becomes available.

b) Change the Amount of time that Clients Cache Referrals:
    You can adjust how long clients cache a referral before requesting a new one. You can also specify the order that targets should be referred to clients.

c) Set Target Priority to Override Referral Ordering:
    Each target in a referral is ordered according to the ordering method for the namespace root or folder. To refine how targets are ordered, you can set priority on individual targets. For example, you can specify that the target is first among all targets, last among all targets, or first (or last) among all targets of equal cost. The three ordering methods are:

    i) **Random order**: Targets are ordered as follows:
        (1) Targets in the same AD DS site as the client are listed in random order at the top of the referral.
        (2) Targets outside of the client's site are listed in random order.

    ii) **Lowest cost**: Targets are ordered as follows:
        (1) Targets in the same site as the client are listed in random order at the top of the referral.
        (2) Targets outside of the client's site are listed in order of lowest cost to highest cost. Referrals with the same cost are grouped together, and the targets are listed in random order within each group.

    iii) **Exclude targets outside of the client's site**: In this method, the referral contains only the targets that are in the same site as the client. These same-site targets are listed in random order. If no same-site targets exist, the client does not receive a referral and cannot access that portion of the namespace.

Note

Targets that have target priority set to "First among all targets" or "Last among all targets" are still listed in the referral, even if the ordering method is set to **Exclude targets outside the client's site**. Site link costs are not shown in the DFS Management snap-in. To view site link costs, use the Active Directory Sites and Services snap-in.

3. Override referral ordering:
    Referral ordering can be overridden at the shared folder level. When you set a folder target to override referral ordering, you can set the following options:
    a) First among All targets.
    b) Last among all targets.
    c) First among targets of equal cost.
    d) Last among targets of equal cost.

4. Configure Namespace Polling:
    To maintain a consistent domain-based namespace across namespace servers, namespace servers to periodically poll Active Directory Domain Services (AD DS) to obtain the most current namespace data. Polling can optimise for consistency or scalability.
    a) **Optimize for consistency**: Namespace servers pool the Primary Domain Controller (PDC) emulator each time the namespace changes.
    b) **Optimize for scalability**: Each namespace server pools its closest domain controller at regular intervals.

When you enable Access-Based enumeration on a DFS namespace, you have to set explicit view permissions on the DFS folder for Access-Based enumeration to take effect.

If permissions used for a DFS folder are inherited from the local file system of the namespace server (Use inherited permissions from the local file system), the permissions are inherited from the root directory of the system drive and grant the DOMAIN\Users group Read permissions. As a result, even after enabling access-based enumeration, all folders in the namespace remain visible to all domain users.

Optimize DFS replication Performance

To optimize the performance of DFS replication, complete the following tasks:

1. Configure folder access:
    a) Log on to 70411SRV and open **DFS Management.**
    b) Expand **Namespaces** and right-click \\70411Lab.com\70411DFS then select **Properties.**
    c) To enable Access Based Enumeration:
        i)   Click **Advanced** and check the box **Enable Access-Based Enumeration** on a Namespace.
        ii) Click **Ok** to Apply your change and close the properties page of \\70411Lab.com\70411DFS.
2. Configure Inherited Permissions:
    a) Expand \\70411Lab.com\70411DFS DFS namespace
    b) Right-click **DFSFolder1** and select **Properties.**
    c) Click Advanced tab and select Set explicit view permission on this DFS folder, then click Configure View Permission.
    d) On the **Permissions** screen, add **Domain Admins** group, click **Ok.**
    e) On the **DFSFolder1** Properties page, click **Ok.**
    f) To confirm that access based enumeration works:
        i)   Log on to 70411SRV1 as **DFSUser.**
        ii) From Windows Explorer, type \\70411Lab.com\70411DFS.

iii) No folder will be visible to this user. Access based enumeration is working!

Note

Referrals behaviour is configured at the DFS namespace or folder level

3. Configure Referrals for a DFS namespace:
   a) Right-click \\70411Lab.com\70411DFS and click Properties
   b) Click **Referrals** tab. Configure the following:
      i) Catche Duration (In seconds): Default is 300 seconds (5 Minutes).
      ii) Ordering Method: Default is Low cost.
      iii) Click the check box Clients Failback to preferred target
      iv) Click Ok.
4. Configure referrals for a DFS folder:
   a) Right-click DFSFolder1 and click Properties.
   b) Click Referrals tab and Configure the following:
      i) Catche Duration (In seconds): Default is 1800 seconds (30 Minutes).
      ii) Note that effective referral ordering is set to Low cost (Same settings at the DFS namespace root). Referral ordering at the DFS folder can only be configured to Exclude targets outside of the client's site. Once this option is checked, referral inheritance is disabled.
      iii) Configure client fail back to preferred targets. This can also be configured. to overrides the settings at the root DFS namespace.
      iv) Click Ok to save and close.
   c) To override referral ordering for a specific folder target:
      i) Highlight **DFSFolder1** and at the details pane, click **Folder Targets** tab.
      ii) Right-click any of the shared folder targets and select **Properties**.
      iii) Click **Advanced** tab and check the box, **Override referral ordering**, chose one of the options and click **Ok.**

There are three referral ordering methods: Random order, Lowest cost, Exclude targets outside of the client's site. For all three methods - Targets in the same site as the client are listed in random order at the top of the referral. Referrals configuration at the DFS namespace root is inherited by all DFS folders except **Catche Duration**. Default Cache Duration at the DFS namespace root is 300 seconds, and 1800 seconds at DFS folders level. Inheritable referrals configuration at DFS Folder level can be configured to override the inherited configuration. **Low cost** and **Random referral** ordering cannot be configured at the DFS folder level.

5. Configure Namespace Polling:

a) Right-click \\70411Lab.com\70411DFS and click Properties.
b) Click Advanced tab and Configure the following:
   i)   Optimize for consistency.
   ii) Optimize for scalability.
c) Click Ok to save your settings.

2.1.7 Clone a DFS database (2012 R2 Objective)

Distributed File System Replication synchronizes files between two or more servers. When you set up replication, the initial synchronization time drops significantly if, DFS Replication can use files already in place on the destination volume.

Cloning a DFS Replication database is a new capability introduced in Windows Server 2012 R2. With this capability, you can remove the need for members of a replication group to exchange files or metadata during replication setup by preseeding a replicated folder and exporting a clone of the database. This can reduce the initial synchronization time by up to 99% under ideal circumstances, and it's useful when you configure replication for the first time, add new replication partners, replace server hardware, or recover from loss or corruption of the DFS Replication database.

DFS Replication Preseed Stage: DFS Replication is a state-based, multi-master file replication service that uses a database and the NTFS USN journal to track file changes. In its simplest configuration, two servers communicate with each other bi-directionally (writable) or unidirectionally (Read-only). For an individual file update operation, each server can operate in an upstream or downstream fashion.
When configuring replication on the second – and subsequent – servers, DFS Replication completes a two-phase process:

Phase 1: Initial build: DFS Replication scans all existing files and folders in the replicated folder and adds a record for each one to the database.

Phase 2: Initial sync: DFS Replication exchanges replicated file metadata - such as each file hash, unique identifier, and global version sequence number – with its partner server. Inbound, the downstream (destination) server replicates any missing files or files that have a different hash from the file on the upstream (source) server. If DFS Replication finds any files that have a matching hash on the same relative path on both servers, the file is not replicated downstream.
When you preseed file data on the downstream server, DFS Replication does not have to replicate those files inbound during initial synchronization. For larger data sets, this can save significant setup time and allow DFS Replication

faster entry into the normal replication state, in which only new, changed, or modified files are replicated between servers.

For preseeding to work, however, you must copy files from the upstream servers to the downstream servers without changing their file hashes. A file hash created by DFS Replication incorporates the data stream, the alternate data stream, and the access control list (ACL) applied directly to that file. This will ensure that any aspect of file changes replicates to all other nodes. Incorrectly preseeding files on a downstream server leads to slower replication than not preseeding, because DFS Replication takes the additional step of verifying every existing file, but then must discard and replicate each file.

The following tools can be used to preseed files: Robocopy, Windows Server Backup or Windows NTBackup.

Robocopy: Can be used to preseed files from Windows Server 2003 R2 and later, through Windows Server 2012 R2. Cannot copy files with exclusive locks. To effectively preseed, you must stabilize files on the source computer before copying begins.

Windows Server Backup: Copies files with exclusive locks. Cannot be used to preseed files from Windows Server 2003 R2. On a source server running Windows Server 2008, Windows Server Backup can only back up volumes, not individual folders. However, individual folders can be restored.

Windows NTBackup: Copies files with exclusive locks. Preseeds files from Windows Server 2003 R2 for DFS Replication in Windows Server 2008 R2 or Windows Server 2008. Cannot be used to preseed files for DFS Replication in Windows Server 2012 R2 or Windows Server 2012.

Requirements for DFS database cloning

Requirements for both source server and the destination server:
The DFS Replication role service must be installed and running.
You can perform only one cloning operation at a time per server.
You must be signed in as a member of the Domain Administrators security group or the Enterprise Administrators security group, or you must have delegated permissions to create replication groups
Specific requirements for the source server from which you want to export a database clone:

1. The DFS Replication database must be on a volume that contains at least one Read-write replicated folder. This is because SYSVOL and Read-only replicated folders are not included in the database export process.

2. The volume you are exporting must contain replicated folders that are in the Normal state. The replicated folders in that database cannot be in initial sync, initial building, or recovery states.
3. Use only approved preseeding techniques to copy files in replicated folders to the destination server.
4. Confirm that the preseeding worked properly by using the Get-DfsrFileHash cmdlet.
5. To maximize cloning performance and data fidelity, prevent all user changes to files on the source server during the cloning operation. The more changes that occur during cloning, the more DFS Replication must update the destination server.
6. Export a database clone only when it is acceptable that replication will pause. Cloning takes the DFS Replication volume manager offline, which prevents any replication from running on that volume during cloning. When cloning completes, DFS Replication automatically resumes replication.

Specific requirements for the destination server on which you want to import a database clone:

1. The destination volume cannot have a replicated folder on it.
2. If the destination volume previously contained a replicated folder, delete the following hidden folder on the volume: <volume>:\system and volume information\dfsr\database_<string>.
3. To export database clones to a hub server with numerous replication partners, you might have to use NTFS volume mount points on the hub server to create a separate volume for each imported database. This is because each volume can only host one DFS Replication database, and cloning can't merge an existing database with an imported database.
4. Prevent all Write access to existing file shares on the destination replication folders by changing the share permissions to Read-only for all users. Don't create any new file shares for the folders until cloning and the post-cloning initial sync processing finishes. As an alternative to changing file share permissions, you can note and remove the file shares. As with any initial sync, users shouldn't use a destination server until all the files are available.

How to Clone a DFS Replication database

Cloning a DFS Replication database is a two-step process:
Step 1 is to export a clone of a DFS Replication database.
Step 2 involves importing the clone of a DFS Replication database.
In this section, our source server is 70411SRV and our destination server is 70411SRV4. Before you perform the following tasks, copy some folders into the replicated folders E:\DFS\Reptargets\ Reptarget1 and

E:\DFS\Reptargets\ Reptarget2 on 70411SRV and 70411SRV2. Ensure they have been replicated before you proceed.

To export a clone of a DFS Replication database

1. Log on to 70411SRV.
2. Before exporting the DFS Replication Database, run the following PowerShell commands to validate the state of all replicated folders:

```
Get-WmiObject -Namespace "root\Microsoft\Windows\DFSR" -Class
msft_dfsrreplicatedfolderinfo -ComputerName 70411SRV | ft
replicatedfoldername,state -auto - wrap
```

All replicated folders listed for that computer will show state **4** (that is, **Normal**) if they have completed the initial build or initial sync, and they are ready to clone.

You may also validate the state of the DFS replication folders by examining the DFS Replication event log to ensure that all replicated folders have a 4112 or 4104 events or by running the WMIC command:

```
wmic /namespace:\\root\microsoftdfs path dfsrreplicatedfolderinfo get
replicatedfoldername, state
```

There are five possible replication states:

0: Uninitialized
1: Initialized
2: Initial Sync
3: Auto Recovery
4: Normal
5: In Error

3. To export the database and create a clone run the following sample command:

```
Export-DfsrClone -Volume E: -Path "E:\DFS\DFRSClone"
```

Respond "Y" to confirm the cloning operation.

When the command completes, note the hints provided by Export-DfsrClone:

```
"CloneFolderPath : E:\DFS\DFSRClone
CopyHint : Robocopy.exe "E:\DFS\DFSRClone" "<destination path>" /B
RootFolderPath : E:\DFS\Reptargets\Reptarget1
PreseedingHint     :     Robocopy.exe     "E:\DFS\Reptargets\Reptarget1"
"<destination   path>"   /E   /B   /COPYALL   /R:6   /W:5   /MT:64   /XD
DfsrPrivate /TEE /LOG+:preseed.log"
```

4. Open E:\DFS\DFSRClone to review the contents. The following files
    will be on E:\DFS\DFSRClone:
    a) config.xml – volume configuration XML
    b) dfsr.db.clone – DFS Replication clone file

To Import a clone of a DFS Replication database

1. Still logged on to 70411SRV and open a command prompt with elevated
    privileges.
    a) To preseed the destination server with the contents of the replicated
        folders from the source server, run the Robocopy command below:

```
Robocopy.exe "E:\DFS\Reptargets\Reptarget1"
"\\70411SRV4\E$\DFS\Reptargets\Reptarget1" /E /B /COPYALL /R:6
/W:5 /MT:64 /XD DfsrPrivate /TEE /LOG+:preseed.log
```

    b) To copy the exported dfsr.db.clone database and config.xml files that
        you created, to the destination server, run this command:

```
Robocopy.exe "E:\DFS\DFSRClone"
"\\70411SRV4\E$\DFS\DFSRClonecopy" /B
```

    c) Confirm that the preseeding worked properly by using the **Get-
        DfsrFileHash** cmdlet below:
        i)   Log on to 70411SRV and execute the PowerShell cdmlet:

```
Get-DfsrFileHash -path "E:\DFS\Reptargets\Reptarget1"
```

        ii) Log on to 70411SRV4 and execute the PowerShell cdmlet:

```
Get-DfsrFileHash -path "E:\DFS\Reptargets\Reptarget1"
```

        iii) If preseeding was successful, the file hashes returned by both
             Get-DfsrFileHash commands should be the same value.
2. Log on to 70411SRV4 and complete the import process
    a) To Import the cloned DFSR database, run the cdmlet:

```
Import-DfsrClone -Volume E: -Path "E:\DFS\DFSRClonecopy"
```

Respond "Y" to the clone query

    b) Run the **Get-DfsrCloneState** cmdlet to confirm the import. The
        command should returns **Ready** when completed

Note

For the **Import-DfsrClone** cdmlet to run successfully, the DFSR path on the source server MUST be the same as the destination server. In the example above since the path to the DFS folder on 70411SRV is E:\DFS\Reptargets\Reptarget1, you must create E:\DFS\Reptargets\Reptarget1 directory on 70411SRV4 and preseed the contents of the source server to the destination server on this location. If you do not have the same folder structure, **Import-DfsrClone** will fail with the following error: *"Import-DfsrClone : Could not import the database clone. Error code: 0x000023EE".*

Although the Import-DfsrClone cmdlet does not return any output until cloning completes, you can safely close the Windows PowerShell session after running the command. The DFS Replication service performs the processing while the command synchronously waits for the result. If you close the Windows PowerShell console or exit the command, you can continue to see progress by examining the DFS Replication event log, the **DFS Replication debug logs**, or by using the **Get-DfsrCloneState** cmdlet. Event log will show DFSR event with ID 2404, when the operation completes.

3. Log on to 70411SRV and add 70411SRV4 to the replication group:
   a) Open **DFS Management**, expand **Namespaces**, right-click **DFSFolder1Replication** replication group then select **New Member.** The New Member wizard opens.
   b) On the **server name** field, type **70411SRV4** and click **Next.**
   c) On the **Connections** screen, high-light 70411SRV and 70411SRV2, click **Add**, then click **Next.**
   d) On the **Replication** Schedule screen, click **Next.**
   e) On the Local Path of Replicated Folders, highlight DFSFolder1, and click Edit. Edit page opens.
   f) On the **Edit** screen, select **Enabled,** on the **Local path folder** field, type: E:\DFS\Reptargets, click **Ok.**
   g) Back on the Local Path of Replicated Folders screen, click **Next.**
   h) On the Share Replicated Folders screen, highlight DFSFolder1, and click Edit. Edit Share page opens.
   i) On the **Edit Share** page, accept the default share name; on the Shared folder permissions for new shared folder, select **Administrator: full access; other users: read-only permissions** then click **Ok**
   j) Back on the Share Replicated Folders screen, click **Next**
   k) On the Review Settings and Create Member screen, click Create
   l) On the **Confirmation** screen, click **Close,** then respond **Ok** to the **Replication Delay** notification.

2.1.8 Recover DFS databases (2012 R2 Objective)

In the event of DFS Replication database corruption, caused by hardware issues (such as abrupt power loss), you can save time by cloning the database from another server rather than waiting for the automatic nonauthoritative recovery to complete.

To perform a database recovery by using cloning, follow the procedures to export a database clone and import a database clone, but skip preseeding the replicated folder. Also, prior to running the **Import-DfsrClone** cmdlet, to import a clone of a DFS Replication database, remove the server(s) affected by the corruption from the replicated folder membership. This prevents DFS Replication from attempting to rebuild the database. As a guide, below is a high-level procedure to recover a corrupt DFS database. Use same commands or PowerShell cdmlet used in the preceding section.

Steps to recover a corrupt DFS database

1. Validate the state of all replicated folders:
    a) Run the Get-WmiObject -Namespace cdmlet.
    b) State must return a value of 4 (Normal) to proceed.
2. Export the DFS Replication database and create a clone
    a) Use the Export-DfsrClone cdmlet.
    b) Returns two files:
        i) config.xml – volume configuration XML.
        ii) dfsr.db.clone – DFS Replication clone file.
3. Skip the step to preseed the destination server with the contents of the replicated folders from the source server.
4. To copy the exported **dfsr.db.clone** database and **config.xml** files that you created, to the destination server, execute:

Robocopy /B command

5. Remove the servers that are affected by the corruption, from the replicated folder memberships. This prevents DFS Replication from attempting to rebuild the database.
    a) Open DFS Management console.
    b) Highlight replication group and click **Memberships** tab.
    c) Right-click the member and select **Delete Member.**
    d) Select the option Delete the member and remove the member as a target in the namespace, then click **Ok.**

To complete the task in step 5 using Windows PowerSehll, run the cdmlet:

Remove-DfsrMember –GroupName <Replication group name> – ComputerName <Replication member server name>

6. To Import the cloned DFSR database, run the cdmlet: Import-DfsrClone.

7. The final step is to add the previously corrupt member back to the replication group.

If you remove a replication group member from a replication group, all of its memberships are affected. Only perform step 5 if all the server's memberships exist only on the volume with the corrupt database. If there are volumes without corrupt databases, you should use the DFSRADMIN command instead. For usage and syntax, run the command DFSRADMIN /help.

Exam Tip

Recovering a corrupt DFS Replication database does not require preseeding of the destination server.

Restoring an FRS-Replicated SYSVOL Folder

The System Volume (SYSVOL) folder provides a standard location to store important elements of Group Policy objects and scripts. A copy of the SYSVOL folder exists on each domain controller in a domain. The SYSVOL folder is replicated by either Distributed File System Replication (DFSR) or the File Replication Service (FRS). Windows 2000 Server and Windows Server 2003 use File Replication Service (FRS) to replicate SYSVOL, whereas Windows Server 2008 and beyond use the newer DFS Replication service when in domains that use the Windows Server 2008 domain functional level.

To perform a nonauthoritative restore of SYSVOL folder

1. Stop the FRS service.
2. Restore the backed-up data to the SYSVOL folder.
3. Configure the BurFlags registry key by setting the value of the following registry key to the DWORD value D2.
4. HKEY_LOCAL_MACHINE\System\CurrentControlSet\Services\NtF rs\Parameters\Backup/Restore\Process at Startup\BurFlags.
5. Restart the FRS service.

Exam Tip

Note the procedure for performing a nonauthoritative restore of SYSVOL folder. There might be questions relating to operating in a mixed environment and domain functional level still at Windows Server 2003. If this is the case, SYSVOL replication is performed with FRS, not DFSR. The above procedure applies.

2.2 Configure File Server Resource Manager (FSRM)

Introduction

File Server Resource Manager is a suite of tools that allows administrators to understand, control, and manage the quantity and type of data stored on their servers. File Server Resource Manager enables administrators to place quotas on volumes, actively screen files and folders, and generate comprehensive storage reports. This set of advanced instruments, not only help the administrator to efficiently monitor existing storage resources, but it also aids in the planning and implementation of future policy changes. With FSRM, you can schedule file management tasks and storage reports, classify files and folders, configure folder quotas and define file screening policies.

In this section, we will cover following exam objectives:

2.2.0 Install the FSRM role2.2.1 Configure quotas
2.2.2 Configure file screens2.2.3 Configure reports
2.2.4 Configure file management tasks (2012 R2 Objective)

Lab Plan

We will use 70411SRV3 and 70411SRV in this section.

Additional Lab setup:

Perform the following additional task to get the lab for this section ready:

1. Log on to 70411SRV3
2. Create a folder called **Quotas** in drive E.
3. Open E:\Quotas and create two folders: **Sharequotas** and **Userquotas.**
4. Share these folders and grant Domain users **Read**; domain admins **Full Control.**
5. Create a folder path: E:\Quotas\Exceptions\Userquotas.
6. Share **Userquotas** folder in E:\Quotas\Exceptions as **ExceptionUsers:** grant Domain users **Read**; domain admins **Full Control**.
7. Create the following Folder structures:
   a) E:\StorageReports\Incident.
   b) E:\StorageReports\Scheduled.
   c) E:\StorageReports\Interactive.
   d) E:\Users\Expiry.
8. Log on to 70411SRV, open Active Directory Users and Computers.
9. Under the Users container, create a user with the following details:
   a) First Name: Quota, Last Name: User, User Name: QuotaUser.

    b)   Set a password and check **Password Never expires.**

10. Ensure that the only group membership for this user is Domain Users.

2.2.0 Install the FSRM role

FSRM can be installed using Server Manager or Windows PowerShell

To Install File Server Resource Manager Using Server Manager

1. Log on to 70411SRV3 and open Server Manager.
2. From Manage, click Add Roles and Features.
3. On the Before you begin screen, click **Next.**
4. On the Select installation type screen, select Role-based or feature-based then click Next.
5. On the **Select destination server** screen, ensure that 70411SRV3 is selected then click **Next.**
6. On the **Select Server roles** screen, expand **File and storage services**, expand **File and iSCSI Services**, then check the box beside **File Server Resource Manager**, click **Add Features**, to the prompt for additional features and click **Next.**
7. On the **Features** screen, click **Next.**
8. On the **Confirmation** screen, click **Install.**

To Install File Server Resource Manager Using Windows PowerShell

Open PowerShell with elevated privileges and type the following PowerShell command:

```
Install-WindowsFeature -Name FS-Resource-Manager, RSAT-FSRM-Mgmt
```

File Server Resource Manager Features

File Server Resource Manager includes the following features:

1. **File Classification Infrastructure**: Provides insight into your data by automating classification processes so that you can manage your data more effectively. You can classify files and apply policies based on this classification. Example policies include dynamic access control for restricting access to files, file encryption, and file expiration. Files can be classified automatically by using file classification rules or manually by modifying the properties of a selected file or folder.
2. **File Management Tasks**: File Management Tasks enables you to apply a conditional policy or action to files based on their classification. The conditions of a file management task include the file location, the classification properties, the date the file was created, the last modified date of the file, or the last time the file was accessed. The actions that a

file management task can take include the ability to expire files, encrypt files, or run a custom command.

3. **Quota management**: Quotas allow you to limit the space that is allowed for a volume or folder, and they can be automatically applied to new folders that are created on a volume. You can also define quota templates that can be applied to new volumes or folders.

4. **File screening management**: File screens help you control the types of files that users can store on a file server. You can limit the extension that can be stored on your shares. For example, you can create a file screen that does not allow files with an MP3 extension to be stored in personal shared folders on a file server.

5. **Storage reports**: To identify trends in disk usage and how your data is classified. You can also monitor a selected group of users for attempts to save unauthorized files.

How to configure the General FSRM Options

To send e-mail notifications and configure the storage reports with parameters that are appropriate for your server environment, you must first set the general File Server Resource Manager options. To prepare the environment for the tasks you will perform in this section, first configure FSRM options.

To configure the General FSRM Options

1. Log on to 70411SRV3 and open **File Server Resource Manager** from Server Manager.

2. Highlight **File Server Resource Manager (Local)** then click **Actions** and select **Configure Options**. The File Server Resource Manager Options page opens.

3. Review the following tabs and what you can configure:

   a) **Email Notifications**: Specify your SMTP server and other default email   settings.
   The **Default administrator recipients** can be used in other areas of FSRM as a variable. If you need to customize who receives which notifications (for example, one person receives quota notices and another receives storage reports), you will be able to configure that later.

   b) **Notification Limits:** Allows you to limit how often notifications are generated. The defaults (60 minutes for all notifications frequency), is recommended.

   c) **Storage Reports**: Allows you to customize default parameters on the various storage reports FSRM generates. These defaults can be overridden, but using them as baselines is recommended before you start making changes to a particular file server.

d) **Report Locations:** Here, you can configure the location where reports generated by FSRM are stored. The default of storing them on the C:\StorageReports but is recommended to save the reports in another drive. Change the location of the storage reports to E:\StorageReports\Incident,   E:\StorageReports\Scheduled   and E:\StorageReports\Interactive.

e) **File Screen Audit**: Allows you to record file screening activity in an auditing database which may be viewed be later by running a file screen auditing reports. You will configure file screening in section **2.2.2 Configure file screens.**

f) **Automatic Classification**: Allows you to set a schedule for your file classifications to run.

g) **Access-Denied Assistance**: This is a new feature in Windows Server 2012. Clients accessing the file server can receive customized pop-up messages to help them when they receive **access denied** messages. This feature also requires that the clients are running Windows 8.

4. To configure Access-Denied Assistance, complete the following tasks:
   a) Check the box beside Enable access-Denied Assistance.
   b) To configure email requests click **Configure email requests**.
   c) In the text field enter the following sample message:

"You may not have the rights to view this resource. If you require access to this resource, contact the ServiceDesk at: desk@xyz.com or call 0208 xxx xxx", click **Preview** to preview the message. "

Note

Enabling **access-denied assistance** adds the **Access-Denied Assistance Users** group to the **Remote Management Users group**, which by default contains the Authenticated Users group. This allows all authenticated users to obtain assistance. The inbound Windows Firewall rule, **Windows Remote Management (HTTP-In),** must be enabled for access-denied assistance to work. This rule is enabled by default.

5. On the File Server Resource Manager Options page, click **Ok** to save your changes.
6. Confirm access-denied configuration by performing the following actions:
   a) Still logged on to 70411SRV3.
   b) From Server Manager, click Tools and open Firewall with advanced security.
   c) Click **Inbound Rules** and on the details pane, locate **Windows Remote Management (HTTP-In),** and ensure that it is enabled.

Exam Tip

It is very important to note that access-denied assistance is configured in File Server Resource Manager, access-denied assistance tab of File Server Resource Manager, not Distributed File System.

2.2.1 Configure quotas

There are two kinds of quotas in FSRM- **soft quotas** and **hard quotas**. A soft quota means that the disk space quota limits are not enforced. A user will be allowed to go over the quota and will not be prevented from adding additional data. Soft quotas are good for monitoring usage and generating notifications. A hard quota enforces disk space limits. A user will not be allowed to store data beyond what has been allowed in the quota. Hard quotas are used for controlling disk space usage especially in SLA situations where customers pay for set blocks of storage. Quotas can be applied to a single share or to all sub-folders in a shared folder using Auto Apply Quotas.

Quota Templates

A quota template defines a space limit, the type of quota (hard or soft), and a set of notifications to be generated when the quota limit approaches or is exceeded. Quota templates simplify the creation and maintenance of quotas:

1. By using a quota template, you can apply a standard storage limit and a standard set of notification thresholds to many volumes and folders on servers throughout your organization.
2. If you base your quotas on a template, you can automatically update all quotas that are based on a specific template by editing that template. This feature simplifies the process of updating the properties of quotas by providing one central point where all changes can be made.

For example, you can create a **User Quota** template that you use to place a 200 MB limit on the personal folder of each user. For each user, you would then create a quota based on the User Quota template and assign it to the user's folder. If you later decide to allow each user additional space on the server, you simply change the space limit in the User Quota template and choose to automatically update each quota that is based on that quota template.

File Server Resource Manager provides several quota templates. To review the various templates that ship with FSRM in Windows Server 2012 R2, from the left pane of FSRM, expand **Quota Management,** highlight **Quota templates,** and **double-click** each to view their properties in the details pane as discussed below:

1. **100 MB Limit** has the following settings:
    a) 100 MB hard quota limit.

b) Send e-mail notification to user at 85% usage.

c) Send e-mail notification to user at 95% usage, log an entry in the event log.

d) Send e-mail notification to user and Administrator at 100% usage, log an entry in the event log.

2. 200 MB Limit Reports to User has the following settings:

a) 200 MB hard quota limit.

b) Send e-mail notification to user at 85% usage.

c) Send e-mail notification to user at 95% usage, log an entry in the event log.

d) Send e-mail notification to user and Administrator at 100% usage, log an entry in the event log, generate a report and send to the user who exceeded threshold.

3. **200 MB Limit with 50 MB Extension** has the following settings:

a) 200 MB hard quota limit.

b) Send e-mail notification to user at 85% usage.

c) Send e-mail notification to user at 95% usage, log an entry in the event log.

d) Send e-mail notification to user and Administrator at 100% usage, log an entry in the event log, **DOES NOT** generate a report and send to the user who exceeded threshold.

e) Runs a command to extend quota by 50 MB when user reaches 100%.

4. **250 MB Extended Limit** has the following settings:

a) 250 MB hard quota limit.

b) Send e-mail notification to user at 85% usage.

c) Send e-mail notification to user at 95% usage, log an entry in the event log.

d) Send e-mail notification to user and Administrator at 100% usage, log an entry in the event log.

5. **Monitor 500 MB Share** has the following settings:

a) 500 MB soft quota limit on the share.

b) Send e-mail notification to administrator at 80% share usage.

c) Send e-mail notification to administrator at 100% share usage, log an entry in the event log.

d) Send e-mail notification to administrator at 120% share usage, log an entry in the event log.

6. **Monitor 200 GB Volume Usage** has the following settings:

a) 200 GB soft quota on the volume.

b) Send e-mail notification to administrator at 70% and 80% Volume usage.

c) Send e-mail notification to administrator at 90% Volume usage, log an entry in the event log.

d) Send e-mail notification to administrator at 100% Volume usage, log an entry in the event log.

Note

You can run the dirquota.exe command to extend a quota limit at a specific threshold. The dirquota.exe command line tool is depreciated and may be removed in future release of Windows.

Exam Tip

It is important to understand default available quotas that ship with FSRM. There might be question relating to quota scenarios, a specific template used and whether you need to edit the quota or use default properties. Questions are likely to be based on quota template applications rather than the actual properties of the quota templates.

To create a quota for shares

1. Log on to 70411SRV3 and open Server Manager.
2. From Server Manager, Tools and select File Server Resource Manager.
3. Expand **Quota Management**, right-click **Quotas** and select **Create Quota**. The **Create Quota** dialogue opens.
4. On the **Quota Path**, enter E:\Quotas\Sharequotas and ensure that **Create a quota on path** is selected.
5. Under Quota Properties, select Derive quota from this quota template (Recommended), from the drop down, select 100 MB Limit and click Create, to create the quota.
6. To explore the properties of the quota:
   a) Right-click E:\Quotas\Sharequotas and select **Edit Quota Properties**
   b) Review the Properties of the quota:
   c) Under **Copy properties from a quota template (optional),** you can select another quota template to apply.
   d) You can add a custom description
   e) Under **Space Limit,** you can customize a space limit (You can set size in KB, MB, GB or TB).
   f) Define whether it is Hard quota (Do not allow users to exceed limit) or Soft quota (Allow users to exceed limit (use for monitoring)).
   g) Under **Notification thresholds,** note current notifications, thresholds. You may add, edit or remove notifications.
   h) Under Notification thresholds, high-light warning (85%), and click edit.
   i) Note notification options you can configure: You will complete this task in the next section.
   j) Below **notification threshold**, you can disable the quota.

    k)   On the 85% threshold properties click cancel.

7.   On the quota properties for E:\Quotas\Sharequotas, click **cancel.**

If you do not want to base your quota on a template, or if you want to edit the properties copied from a template, in the **Create Quota** dialog box you can choose **Define custom quota properties**, and then click **Custom Properties**. Note that if you create a quota with custom properties, you have the option of saving a quota template with the custom quota settings when you save the new quota. If you choose that option, a new template is saved, and then the template is applied to the new quota so that a link is maintained between the quota and the template.

Microsoft recommends using quota templates for generating quotas rather than setting everything manually every time.

Auto Apply Quotas

Auto apply quotas allow you to assign a quota template to a volume or folder and specify that quotas based on that template will be automatically generated and applied to the existing subfolders, as well as to any new subfolders created in the future.

As seen in the next section, every time a new subfolder is created, a new quota entry is automatically generated for that subfolder, using the template defined in the auto apply quota profile of its parent folder. These automatically generated quota entries can then be viewed in the Results pane, under the **Quotas** node, as individually created quotas, which can be edited and modified separately. This is particularly useful if you create home folders for your users and want to automatically apply quotas to the individual user's folders when created.

To create a quota for User folders

1.   Log on to 70411SRV3 with domain administrator account, and open Server Manager.

2.   From Server Manager, click Tools, and then click File Server Resource Manager.

3.   Expand **Quota Management**, right-click **Quotas** and select **Create** Quota. The **Create Quota** dialogue opens.

4.   On the Quota Path, enter E:\Quotas\Userquotas and set the Auto apply template and create quotas on existing and new subfolders option.

5.   Leave all other defaults and click **Create**, to create the quota.

6.   To show all quotas, on the left pane, right-click **Quotas**, and click **Refresh**

7.   If the last quota created does not show, do the following:

    a)   On the top of the FSRM console details pane, click the **Filters** hyperlink.

b)   On the **Quota Filter** dialogue, select **All** for quota type and **quota path**, then click **Ok.**

All new user folders created under E:\Quotas\Userquotas, will be given the same quota template that you specified above.

8.   To test this and bring it to real-life use, assuming you create Home folders for all users on the share \\70411SRV3\Userquotas, perform the following:

   a)   Log on to 70411SRV with domain admin privileges and open AD Users and Computers.

   b)   Navigate to the **Users** container and open the properties of **Quota User** created on the **Additional Lab Preparation** section. Click **Profile** tab.

   c)   Under **Home Folder,** click **connect** then select **H** from the drop down, type \\70411SRV3\Userquotas\%Username% on the **To:** field. Click **Ok.**

   d)   Log on to 70411SRV3 and confirm that **QuotaUser** has been created under E:\Quotas\Userquotas\.

9.   The **QuotaUser** folder will automatically inherit the quota applied to E:\Quotas\Userquotas\.

10. To confirm point 9, refresh **Quotas**, in FSRM console, you will notice that E:\Quotas\Userquotas\QuotaUser folder will show up with the properties of the 100 MB hard quota limit template.

11. To Modify how Auto Apply Quotas are applied, perform the task below:

   a)   Right-click E:\Quotas\Userquotas Auto Apply Quota and select **Edit Quota Properties**, the **Edit Auto Apply Quota properties** window opens.

   b)   Click Ok, the Update quotas derived from Auto Apply Quotas configuration page opens.

   c)   Note the options you can configure:

      i)   **Apply auto apply quota only to derived quotas that match the original auto apply quota**: All existing quotas are changed to the new quota unless they have been changed. (This means any users/folders that you've given more quota space will not receive new quotas.) All new folders created will have the new quota applied.

      ii) **Apply auto apply quota to all derived quotas**: All existing quotas are changed to the new quota. (This includes any individual or one-off changes you may have made to individual folders/users.) All new folders created will have the new quota applied.

iii) **Do not apply auto apply quota to derived quotas**: Existing quotas are not changed. All new folders created will have the new quota applied.

d) When you finish your review, click **Ok**

Note

Auto Apply Quotas is used to apply quotas to new folders created under the original folder. As seen when we created user quota, when new user folders are created (either manually or via Active Directory), quotas are automatically applied.

Creating a Quota Template

Quota templates can be created either from existing quotas or templates. Templates cannot be created from existing Auto Apply Quotas.

To create a quota template

1. Log on to 70411SRV3 and open File Server Resource Manager.
2. Expand Quota Management, and click the Quota Templates node.
3. Right-click **Quota Templates**, and then click **Create Quota Template** (or click Create Quota Template in the Actions pane).
4. You could copy the properties of an existing template to use as a base for your new template, or create an entirely new template.
5. To copy from an existing template:
    a) Select a template from the drop-down and click **Copy.**
    b) Then complete the following actions:
        i)   In the **Template Name** field, enter a name for the new template.
        ii) In the **Label** text box, enter an optional descriptive label that will appear next to any quotas derived from the template.
        iii) Under **Space Limit,** complete the following tasks:
            (1) In the **Limit text** box, enter a number and choose a unit (KB, MB, GB, or TB) to specify the space limit for the quota.
            (2) Click the **Hard quota or Soft quota** option. (A hard quota prevents users from saving files after the space limit is reached and generates notifications when the volume of data reaches each configured threshold. A soft quota does not enforce the quota limit, but it generates all configured notifications.)
    c) You can configure one or more optional threshold notifications for your quota template, as described in the previous section.
6. After you have reviewed all the quota template properties as outlined above, click **Cancel.**

Note

Quota templates can be created either from existing quotas or templates. Templates cannot be created from Auto Apply Quotas, only share quotas. You cannot edit the configuration of an Auto Apply Quota. To change the configuration of an Auto Apply Quota configuration, make changes to the template from which you created the Auto Apply Quota. However, you can edit how the Auto Apply Quota is applied to existing or new folders.

Monitoring Quota Use

In the section **create a quota for shares**; we saw that information about quota usage can be received by configuring notifications. Another way to find out about quota usage is to generate a **Quota Usage report**, or create soft quotas for the purpose of monitoring overall disk usage.

To viewing quota usage information

Click **Quota Management**, and then click **Quotas**. In the details pane, complete the following tasks:

1. In the Results pane, you can quickly find out the quota limit, the percentage of the limit that is used, whether the quota is hard or soft, and Volume information.
2. Click **Filter** at the top of the Results pane to limit the display to quotas that affect a specific path.

2.2.2 Configure file screens

File screens are created to block files that belong to particular file groups from being saved on a volume or in a folder tree. A file screen affects all folders in the designated path. For example, you might create a file screen to prevent users from storing audio and video files in their personal folders on the file server. File Server Resource Manager can be configured to generate e-mail or other notifications when a file screening event occurs. A file screen can be either active or passive:

1. Active screening prevents users from saving unauthorized file types on the server.
2. Passive screening monitors users saving specific file types and generates any configured notifications, but does not prevent users from saving files.

A file screen does not prevent users and applications from accessing files that were saved to the path before the file screen was created, regardless of whether the files are members of blocked file groups.

Working with File Groups

Before working with file screens, it is important to understand the role of file groups in determining files that are screened. A **file group** is used to define a namespace for a file screen or a file screen exception; or to generate a **Files by File Group** storage report. A file group consists of a set of file name patterns, which are grouped into files to include and files to exclude:

1. Files to include: files that belong in the group.
2. Files to exclude: files that do not belong in the group.

For example, an Audio Files file group might include the following file name patterns:

1. Files to include:*.mp*: includes all audio files created in current and future MPEG formats (MP2, MP3, and so forth).
2. Files to exclude:*.mpp: excludes files created in Microsoft Project (.mpp files), which would otherwise be included by the *.mp* inclusion rule.

File Server Resource Manager provides several default file groups. These file groups can be accessed in **File Screening Management** by clicking the **File Groups** node. New file groups can be defined and existing ones can be modified to change the files to include and exclude. Any changes made to a file group affect all existing file screens, templates, and reports to which the file group has been added.

Note

For convenience, you can modify file groups when you edit the properties of a file screen, file screen exception, file screen template, or the Files by File Group report. Note that any changes that you make to a file group from these property sheets will affect all items that use that file group.

Default File Groups

The following default file groups are available in Windows Server 2012 R2. To view these file groups, open FSRM console, click **File screening Management**, then highlight **File Groups**. The file extension beside each file group is an example of file types in a file group.

1. Audio and Video Files: *.aac
2. Backup Files: *.bak
3. Compressed Files: *.rar
4. E-mail Files: *.msg
5. Executable Files: *.bat, *.cmd
6. Image Files: *.bmp,
7. Office Files: *.doc,
8. System Files: *.dll

9. Temporary Files: *.temp
10. Text Files: *.txt
11. Web Page Files: *.asp

Even with 9 default file groups in FSRM, you might still want to create file groups to me your specific needs.

Exam Tip

For exam 70-411, it is important to clearly understand how file screening works. Pay particular attention to file types, as well as file inclusion and file exclusion.

To create a file group

1. Expand File Screening Management, and click the File Groups node.
2. In the **Actions** pane, click **Create File Group**. This opens the **Create File Group Properties** dialog box. (Alternatively, while you edit the properties of a file screen, file screen exception, file screen template, or Files by File Group report, under **Maintain file groups**, click Create.)
3. In the **Create File Group** Properties dialog box, enter **None Business Files**.
4. Add files to include and files to exclude as outlined below:
    a) In **Files to include**, type a file name pattern, and then click **Add**. (Include *.jpg)
    b) For each set of files that you want to exclude from the file group, under **Files to exclude**, type a file name pattern, and then click **Add**. (Exclude *.gif. Note that standard wildcard rules apply - for example, ***.exe** selects all executable files.)
5. When you finish with your changes, click **Ok**.

File screen templates

Like Quota Management, Microsoft recommends using templates for setting up File Screens. You can use pre-defined templates in FSRM or create yours.

Creating a File Screen

In the following procedure, you will create a new file screen, and in the process save a file screen template based on the custom file screen properties that you defined. The new template will be applied to the file screen so that a link is maintained between the file screen and the template. In a similar way, you can save a new quota template based on the custom properties of a quota you create.

To create a file screen

1. Expand File Screening Management, and click the **File Screens** node.

2. Right-click **File Screens**, and click **Create File Screen** (or click Create File Screen in the Actions pane). This opens the **Create File Screen** dialog box.

3. Under **File screen path**, type E:\Quotas\Userquotas. The file screen will apply to the selected folder and all of its subfolders.

4. Under How do you want to configure file screen properties, click Define custom file screen properties, and then click Custom Properties. This opens the File Screen Properties dialog box.

5. To copy the properties of an existing template to use as a base for the new file screen, select **Block Image files** from the **Copy properties from template** drop-down list. Then click **Copy**. This populates the new file screen with the properties of the copied file screen.

6. Under **Screening type**, click the **Active screening** option. Active screening prevents users from saving files that are members of blocked file groups, and generates notifications when users try to save unauthorized files. Passive screening sends configured notifications, but it does not prevent users from saving files.

7. Under **File groups**, note that **Images file** file group is already selected.

8. Under **maintain file groups**, click **Edit** to edit the file group selected, or to create to create a new file group. For this task, accept the defaults.

9. Click **Email Messages** tab: You can configure File Server Resource Manager to generate one or more notifications by setting the following options on the E-mail Messages tab - Event Log, Command, and Report tabs - Very similar to the Quota notification configuration.

10. When you are done reviewing notification configurations, click **Ok**

11. In the **Create File Screen** dialog box, click **Create** to save the file screen. This opens the **Save Custom Properties as a Template** dialog box. (Respond **Yes** to any SMTP configuration message.)

12. To save a template that is based on these customized properties, click **Save the custom properties as a template** and type **None Business Files** as the template name. This option will apply the template to the new file screen, and you can use the template to create additional file screens in the future.

13. When you finish making your changes, click **Ok.**

Creating a File Screen Exception

Occasionally, you will need to allow exceptions to file screening. For example, you might want to block video files from a file server, but you need to allow your training group to save the video files for their computer-based training. To allow files that other file screens are blocking, create a **file screen exception**.

A file screen exception is a special type of file screen that overrides any file screening that would otherwise apply to a folder, and all its subfolders, in a designated exception path. That is, it creates an exception to any rules derived from a parent folder. To determine which file types the exception will allow, file groups are assigned.

To create a file screen exception

1. In File Screening Management node, click the **File Screens**.
2. Right-click **File Screens**, and click **Create File Screen Exception** (or click Create File Screen Exception in the Actions pane). This opens the **Create File Screen Exception** dialog box.
3. In the **Exception path** text box, type E:\Quotas\Exceptions\Userquotas - The exception will apply to the selected folder and all of its subfolders. In a real world situation, any user you want the file screen exception to apply to, you should then create their home folder in this path.
4. To specify which files to exclude from file screening:
    a) Under File groups, select None Business Files.
    b) To create a new file group, click **Create**.
5. When you finish making your changes, click **Ok.**

Note

Like Quota management, you can view information about a file screen by highlighting it; the details are displayed beneath. You can also filter file screen view by clicking filters.

File screens and file content

File Screening blocks files based on file extension, not the content of the file. So, if you block "Audio and Video Files", File Screening will not block **.mp3** files that have their extension changed to **.exe**

2.2.3 Configure reports

File Server Resource Manager can generate reports that will help you understand file usage on the file server. You can use the storage reports to monitor disk usage patterns (by file type or user), identify duplicate files and dormant files, track quota usage, and audit file screening.

By default, reports are stored in C:\StorageReports\, but can be saved in other locations (In section 2.2.0, under **Set the General FSRM Options**, we changed the default location to E:\StorageReports\). Reports can also be emailed to a server administrator when they are generated.

Unfortunately, the built-in reports cannot be edited but most have parameters that can be configured, but the report itself cannot be changed much. FSRM reports support five different formats: DHTML, HTML, XML, CSV, and text.

Configuring Report Parameters

In Windows Server 2012, except for the Duplicate Files report, all reports have configurable report parameters, which determine the content that the report includes. However, in Windows Server 2012 R2, all reports including Duplicate Files report, have configurable parameters. The parameters vary with the type of report. For some reports, report parameters can be used to select the volumes and folders on which to report, set a minimum file size to include, or restrict a report to files owned by specific users. We already covered default reports configuration in 2.2.0, under Set the General FSRM Options.

To configure the default parameters for storage reports

1. Open File Server Resource Manager console from Server Manager.
2. Right-click File Server Resource Manager, and then click Configure Options.
3. Click **Storage Reports** tab and under **Configure default parameters**, select the type of report that you want to modify. The default parameters are used in the incident reports that are generated automatically during quota and file screen notifications. You can override the default parameters for scheduled reports and reports generated on demand.

Saving reports

Regardless of how you generate a report, or whether you choose to view the report immediately, the report is saved on disk. Incident reports are saved in Dynamic HTML (DHTML) format. You can save scheduled and on-demand reports in DHTML, HTML, XML, CSV, and text formats.

Scheduled reports, on-demand reports, and incident reports are saved in separate folders within a designated report repository. By default, the reports are stored in subdirectories of the **%Systemdrive%\StorageReports** folder. To change the default report locations, in the **File Server Resource Manager Options** dialog box, on the **Report Locations** tab, specify where to save each type of storage report.

Scheduling a Set of Reports

To generate a set of reports on a regular schedule, you schedule a **report task.** The report task specifies which reports to generate and what parameters to use. It also includes which volumes and folders to report on, how often to generate the reports, and which file formats to save them in.

When you schedule a set of reports, the reports are saved in the report repository. You also have the option of e-mailing the reports to a group of administrators.

To schedule a report task

1. Click the Storage Reports Management node.
2. Right-click **Storage Reports Management**, and then click **Schedule a New Report Task** (or click Schedule a New Report Task in the Actions pane). This opens the Storage Reports Task Properties dialog box.
3. In the **Storage Reports Task Properties** dialog box complete the following tasks:
   a) In the **Settings** tab:
      i) Under the Report Name field, type **Monthly Report**.
      ii) Under **Report Data,** you can check the reports to generate. You can also edit the parameters for each report. (Leave defaults).
      iii) Under **Report format,** select different report formats.
   b) In the **Scope** tab, you can:
      i) Include folders by data type stored.
      ii) Include specific volumes or folders.
   c) In the **Delivery** tab:
      i) Specify which Administrators will receive the report via email.
      ii) Scheduled reports are stored in the default location specified in **Storage Reports** tab in the FSRM **options** page.
   d) In the **Schedule** tab: Specify when the report will run, options:
      i) Specify time.
      ii) Select **weekly** then day(s) of week.
      iii) Select **Monthly** then select day (s) of the month to run the report.
      iv) Specify **Limit** in hours.
4. To save the report task, click **Ok.**

Note

To minimize the impact of report processing on server performance, generate multiple reports on the same schedule so that the data is only gathered once. To quickly add reports to existing report tasks, under **Storage Reports Management**, click Add or Remove Reports for a Report Task in the Actions pane. This action allows you to add or remove reports from all existing report tasks and to edit the report parameters. To change schedules or delivery addresses, you must edit individual report tasks.

Generating Reports on Demand

During daily operations, you may want to generate reports on demand to analyze different aspects of current disk usage on the server. Before the reports are generated, current data is gathered. When you generate reports on demand, the reports are saved in the report repository, but no report task is created for later use. You can optionally view the reports immediately after they are generated or e-mail the reports to a group of administrators.

To generate reports on demand

1. Click the Storage Reports Management node.
2. Right-click Storage Reports Management, and then click Generate Reports Now (or click Generate Reports Now in the Actions pane). This opens the Storage Reports Task Properties dialog box.
3. Navigate to different tabs and configure the report just like a scheduled report.
4. When you finish click Ok.

Note

Unlike a scheduled report, you do not schedule On Demand reports, so the Schedule tab is not available.

File Screening Audit report

File Screening Audit report is used to identify individuals or applications that violate your file screening policy. This is one of the standard reports available in FSRM, but before you run a **File Screening Audit report**, in the **File Server Resource Manager Options** page, on the **File Screen Audit** tab, verify that the **Record file screening activity in auditing database** check box is selected.

2.2.4 Configure file management tasks (2012 R2 Objective)

File Management Tasks in FSRM allow you to archive files, encrypt files, or run custom commands based on file classifications, timestamps associated with a file (last accessed, last modified), and file location. File management tasks are based on file classifications. Before we dive into file management tasks configuration, we will first examine classification management.

Classification Management

Files typically have attributes like author, last saved, company, owner, etc. File Classification allows you to supplement those attributes with additional information that may be industry or organization specific based on classifications you perform manually or automatically.

To classify files

1. Expand **Classification Management**, right-click **Classification properties** and select **Create Local Property** (You may also do this from the Actions Menu).
2. On the **Name** field type **Contains NI Numbers**. In the Description field, type a description - or leave the description field blank.
3. From the **Property Type drop-down** select **Yes/No**. Select each property type to examine the details:
   a) **Yes/No**: A Yes value provided by other classification rules or file content will override a No value.
   b) **Date-time**: A simple date/time property. When combining multiple values during classification or from file content, conflicting values will prevent re-classification.
   c) **Number**: A simple number property. When combining multiple values during classification or from file content, conflicting values will prevent re-classification.
   d) **Multiple-choice-list**: A list of fixed values. Multiple values can be assigned to a property at a time. When combining multiple values during classification or from file content, a value with all selected items will be used.
   e) **Ordered-list**: In the list below, top values take precedence over lower values during classification. Lower values may be overridden by more important values provided by other classification rules or file content.
   f) **Single-choice**: A single choice value from the possible values specified below. When combining multiple values during classification, conflicting values will prevent re-classification.
   g) **String**: A simple string property. When combining multiple values during classification or from file content, conflicting values will prevent re-classification.
   h) **Multi-string:** A list of strings. Multiple values can be assigned to a property at a time. When combining multiple values during classification or from file content, a value containing all strings will be produced.
4. When you finish reviewing, click **Ok.**
5. To see the effect of classification:
   a) Open any file on 70411SRV3 (FSRM Server), and examine the properties of the file.
   b) The **classification** tab will have the attribute **Contains NI Numbers,** with values Yes, No or None.

Note

Any file you view from the File server (Even files on other servers) will have a classification tab and you can set the attribute value configured in FSRM.

Create Classification Rule

The file classification created in the previous section, can be configured to apply to files automatically via a schedule or on an ongoing basis. Automatic classification schedule can be configured from the FSRM Options page, **automatic classification** tab.

To create a Classification Rule

1. Expand **Classification Management**, right-click **Classification Rules** and select **Create Classification Rule** (You may also do this from the Actions Menu.
2. On the **Name** field, type File **Contains NI Number**, ensure that the **Enabled** box is checked.
3. Click **Scope** tab, click the boxes beside **Group Files** and **Users Files** (sets the type of data and folders that will be scanned).
4. Under **The following folders are included in this scope**, click **Add**, select drive E and click **Ok**. (Note that you can also set folder management properties here - skip for now).
5. Click Classification tab, Under Classification method, on the Chose a method to assign a property to files, drop-down, select Content Classifier. Note other methods of classification:
   a) **Content Classifier:** Searches for strings and regular expression patterns in files.
   b) **Folder Classifier:** Classifies all files in folders included in the scope of this rule
   c) **Windows PowerShell Classifier:** Classifies files using Windows PowerShell scripts.
6. Still on **Classification** tab, Under **Property**, on the **Chose a property to assign files** drop-down, select a classification property (Only one available, **Contains NI Numbers** created in the previous section). Complete the following as well:
   a) Under **Specify a Value**, select **Yes** from the drop-down.
   b) Under Parameters, click **configure**.
7. On the **Classification Properties** page (I used arbitrary values below):
   a) Expression type: select **Regular expression**
   b) Expression: Type **SK** (A possible content of NI Number in the United Kingdom).
   c) Minimum Occurrences: type **1.**
   d) Minimum Occurrences: type **5.**
   e) File name pattern (Optional): <Leave blank>.
   f) Click **Ok** to save and close the **classification Properties** page.
8. Click **Evaluation Type** tab, check the box **re-evaluate existing property values** (Determine how the rule handles conflict between new and existing value). You can then chose one of the following:

a) **Aggregate the values** (This is the default): For **Yes/No** and **Ordered List** property types, the value with the higher priority is selected. For **Multi-Choice** and **Multi-String** property types, the values are combined. **Date-time**, **String**, and **Number** property types produce an error when different values are aggregated but do not prevent other files from being classified.

b) **Overwrite the existing value**: This provide two check boxes:

   i) **Clear Automatically Classified Property**: Once selected this will enable classification to clear the previous system defined property value if it no longer applies to the updated file.

   ii) **Clear User Classified Property**: Once selected this will enable classification to clear the previous user defined property value if it no longer applies to the updated file.

Note

When you create a new classification rule, by default, property values that have already been set are ignored during classification. To enable this rule to re-evaluate existing property values, check the box **re-evaluate existing property values**. This can be found in the **Evaluation Type** tab.

9. Still on the **Evaluation Type** tab, select **Aggregate the values** and click **Ok**

Configure Classification Schedule

You have created a classification property and created a classification rule based on that property. You may run the classification manually or set a regular schedule to run this rule. In section 2.2.0, under **Set the General FSRM Options** section, we examined the **Automatic classifications** tab briefly. We will now examine this in detail below.

To Configure Classification Schedule

1. Expand **Classification Management**, right-click **Classification Rules** and select **Configure Classification Schedule** (You may also do this from the Actions Menu. This opens the **Automatic classifications** tab of the FSRM options page.

2. To configure Automatic classification, check the box **Enable fixed schedule** and configure the following:

   a) Run at: set 04:00:00 (Better to run off-peak hours).
   b) Select **Weekly** and check **Sunday.**
   c) On the **Generate log file** and **Generate Report**: Note the type of logs and location of report: Select **Log, Error** and **Audit.**
   d) Reports will be saved in E:\StorageReports\Scheduled (All scheduled reports are saved here (Change location in the Reports Location tab).

e) When you finish, click **Ok.**

Classifying folders

In File Server Resource Manager, classification can be configured for files as well as folders. The following properties can be set for folders:

Access-Denied Assistance Message: Allows you to configure a custom message an end user sees when he/she is denied access to a file or folder. Rather than getting a generic **access denied** message, the user will receive a custom message. Only clients using Windows Server 2012 or Windows 8 can access this feature. Users denied access to folders that do not have a custom message configured, are referred to the **Access-Denied Assistance Message** specified in File Server Resource Manager options page.

Folder Owner Email: Setting this property allows you to present a user that requires access to the folder, with the owner's email address so that they can seek access approval before contacting IT for example. This feature also requires at least Windows 8/Server 2012.

Folder Usage: Used when running classification and file management tasks. Folders can be classified as Application Files, Backup & Archival Files, Group Files, and User Files. This allows you to run different classification rules against different types of files which enable you eliminate areas like archives or software shares from your file classification schedules since those files, most likely, do not need to be scanned.

Exam Tip

General **Access-Denied Assistance Message** can be set in the Options page of FSRM. This message is shown to users that access all folders in the file server. To set Access-Denied Assistance Message for specific folders, you configure this in folder management, classification properties. You can also configure access-denied assistance for all file servers within a domain by using Group Policy - Computer Configuration\Policies\Administrative Templates\System, and then click **Access-Denied Assistance**.

To Classifying folders

1. Expand Classification Management, then right-click Classification properties and select Set folder management properties.
2. Under **Property**, select **Access-Denied Assistance Message** from the drop-down. Under Folders with the selected property, click Add.
3. On the **Add value dialogue**, click Browse, select E:\Quotas. Under value field type the following " You do not have the right to view this folder. Please contact IT for more information.", click **Ok.**

4. Back to Property, select Folder Owner Email from the drop-down. Under Folders with the selected property, click Add.
5. On the **Add value** dialogue, click Browse, select E:\Quotas. Under value **field** type: valid emails, for example testemail@xyz.com, click **Ok** when done.
6. Back to Property, select **Folder Usage** from the drop-down. Under **Folders** with the **selected property**, click **Add**.
7. On the **Add** value dialogue, click Browse, select E:\Quotas. Under value field select the following: **Application files, Backup and archive files**, then click **Ok**.
8. When you finish, click close to the Set Folder Management Properties page.

Configure file management tasks

Now that you have configured file and folder classification, configured classification rule and automatic classification schedule, you are ready to configure file management tasks. In this section, you will configure the following file management tasks: **File Expiration, Encrypting Files with RMS** and **Custom Action Types**.

To configure file management task for File Expiration

1. Highlight File Management Tasks and on the Actions pane, click Create File Management Task.
2. On the **General** tab, in the **Name** field type **User File Archiving**, ensure that **Enabled** is selected.
3. Click **Scope** tab. On the **Include all folders that store the following kinds of data**, check the boxes **User files**, and under **The following folders are included in this scope**, click **Add**, then select E:\Quotas. You can also set folder management properties in the scope tab.
4. Click **Actions** tab, Under Type, click **File Expiry** from the drop down, click browse beside **expiry** directory and select E:\Users\Expiry.
5. Click **Notification** tab, click **Add**. You can configure the following notifications:
   a) Advanced notification (In Days) - Default is 15 days.
   b) Email Messages (To administrators and to the affected user).
   c) Run specific commands.
   d) Click **Cancel** to exit Notifications.
6. Click **Reports** tab. You can:
   a) Log entries in the log file.
   b) Generate reports (As expected, Reports will be saved in the E:\StorageReports\Scheduled folder).
   c) Send reports to administrators.

7. Click **Condition** tab (determine what rules will control which files are archived):
   a) Under **Property conditions** click Add. Available options:
      i) Property (Only one file property available): Contains NI Numbers.
      ii) Operator: Equal, Not Equal, Exists, Not Exists - Select Not Equal.
      iii) Value: Select values based on Property and Operator set. - Select Yes
      iv) Click **Ok**.
   b) Still on **Property conditions**, you can set the following conditions:
      i) Days since file was created.
      ii) Days since file was last modified.
      iii) Days since file was last accessed.
      iv) File Name patterns.
8. Click Schedule tab. Configure schedule and click **Ok**.

To create file management task for Encrypting Files with RMS or Custom, select the type of task from the **Actions** tab. Custom actions allow you to run scripts to perform actions specific to your environment.

2.3 Configure file and disk encryption

Introduction

BitLocker Drive Encryption protects data on lost, stolen, or inappropriately decommissioned computers by encrypting the entire volume and checking the integrity of early boot components. Encrypted data will be decrypted only if those components are successfully verified and the encrypted drive is located in the original computer. Integrity checking requires a compactible Trusted Platform Module (TPM). BitLocker provides the most protection when used with a Trusted Platform Module (TPM) version 1.2 or later. The TPM is a hardware component installed in many newer computers by the computer manufacturers. It works with BitLocker to help protect user data and to ensure that a computer has not been tampered with while the system was offline.

On computers that do not have a TPM version 1.2 or later, you can still use BitLocker to encrypt the Windows operating system drive. However, this implementation will require the user to insert a USB startup key to start the computer or resume from hibernation. In Windows 8, using an operating system volume password is another option to protect the operating system volume on a computer without TPM. Both options do not provide the pre-startup system integrity verification offered by BitLocker with a TPM.

In addition to the TPM, BitLocker offers the option to lock the normal startup process until the user supplies a personal identification number (PIN) or inserts a removable device, such as a USB flash drive that contains a startup key. These additional security measures provide multifactor authentication and assurance that the computer will not start or resume from hibernation until the correct PIN or startup key is presented.

BitLocker hardware requirements

For BitLocker to use the system integrity check provided by a Trusted Platform Module (TPM), the computer must have TPM 1.2 or TPM 2.0. A computer with a TPM must also have a Trusted Computing Group (TCG)-compliant BIOS or UEFI firmware. The BIOS or UEFI firmware establishes a chain of trust for the pre-operating system startup, and it must include support for TCG-specified Static Root of Trust Measurement. A computer without a TPM does not require TCG-compliant firmware.

The system BIOS or UEFI firmware (for TPM and non-TPM computers) must support the USB mass storage device class; including reading small files on a USB flash drive in the pre-operating system environment. The core requirements for BitLocker are listed below:

1. The hard disk must be partitioned with at least two drives:
    a) The operating system drive (or boot drive) contains the operating system and its support files. It must be formatted with the NTFS file system.
    b) The system drive contains the files needed to load Windows after the firmware has prepared the system hardware. BitLocker is not enabled on the system drive. For BitLocker to work, the system drive must not be encrypted, must differ from the operating system drive, and must be formatted with the FAT32 file system on computers that use UEFI-based firmware or with the NTFS file system on computers that use BIOS firmware. Microsoft recommends that system drive be approximately 350 MB in size. After BitLocker is turned on, it should have approximately 250 MB of free space.
2. Supported operating systems:
    a) Windows 8 - Professional or Enterprise edition.
    b) Windows 7 - Enterprise or Ultimate edition.

In this section, we will cover following exam objectives:

2.3.0 Configure BitLocker encryption
2.3.1 Configure the Network Unlock feature
2.3.2 Configure BitLocker Policies
2.3.3 Configure the EFS recovery agent
2.3.4 Manage EFS and BitLocker certificates including backup and restore

Lab Plan

We will use 70411SRV (Configure group policies), 70411SRV1 (WDS and Network Unlock Server), 70411SRV3 (DHCP and Certificate Authority Server) and 70411Win8 (BitLocker Client).

Additional Lab setup

1. Log on to 70411Win8 with Admin privileges, and perform the following tasks:
    a) Click Start and then click on the Windows Logo.
    b) Click the Arrow key pointing downwards to open Apps.
    c) Scroll (Via the task bar) towards the right to locate Control Panel.
    d) Change Control Panel view to Large or Small icons.
    e) Locate and open Administrative Tools, when Administrative Tools opens, click Computer Management.
    f) Click Disk Management, then click **Ok** to the **initialize Disk** message.

g) Right-click **Disk 0,** create a new **Simple Volume** and perform a quick format (NTFS, drive E).

h) Change Control Panel to Category View.

2. Create the following folder structure:

   a) In 70411SRV - E:\BitLocker\LocalRecovery

   b) In 70411SRV1 E:\BitLocker\NetworkRecovery

3. Install Active Directory Certificate services on 70411SRV3

   a) Log on to 70411SRV3 with domain admin privileges and open Server Manager.

   b) From Server Manager, click **Manage**, then **Add roles and features**. The Add roles and features wizard opens, click Next thrice, until you get **Select Server Roles.**

   c) Check the box beside **Active Directory Certificate Services,** when prompted to add additional features, click **Add features.**

   d) On the **Select Server roles** screen, click **Next** thrice until you get to **Role services.**

   e) On the **Role services** screen, ensure that **Certificate Authority** is selected, click **Next.**

   f) On the **Confirmation** screen, click **Install.**

   g) When installation completes, click **Close.**

4. Configure Active Directory Certificate services on 70411SRV3

   a) Still logged on to 70411SRV3 with domain admin privileges.

   b) On Server Manager, click on the yellow triangle with a black exclamation and click on **Configure Active Directory Certificate Services on the destination server. AD CS Configuration** wizard opens.

   c) On the **Credentials** screen, ensure your domain account is specified, click **Next.**

   d) On the Role Services screen, check Certificate Authority, click **Next.**

   e) On the **Specify Type** screen, select **Enterprise CA**, click **Next.**

   f) On the **CA Type**, select **Root CA**, click **Next.**

   g) On the Private Key screen, select create a new private key, click **Next**.

   h) On Cryptography, CA Name, Validity Period, and Certificate Database accept the defaults.

   i) On the **Confirmation** screen, click **Configure.**

   j) Click **Close** on the **Result** screen.

2.3.0 Configure BitLocker encryption

When BitLocker is enabled, a personal identification number (PIN) is created. The PIN is required every time the computer starts up. A recovery key is also generated. The recovery key may be used to gain access to the computer if the password is forgotten. After the recovery key is generated, the computer will prompt a restart. The encryption process starts when the computer restarts.

To Configure BitLocker encryption

1. Log on to 70411Win8 with an account with domain administrator privileges.
2. Configure Local Security Policy for BitLocker without TPM Support(This is required since we are using a VM without TPM support):
   a) Open command prompt and type **gpedit.msc.**
   b) Navigate to Local Computer Policy\Computer Configuration\Administrative Templates\Windows Components\BitLocker Drive Encryption\Operating System.
   c) On the details pane, click on the policy Require additional authentication at startup.
   d) On the policy page, click Enable. Ensure that the check box beside Allow BitLocker without a compactible TPM (requires a password or a startup key on a USB flash drive) is checked. Accept all defaults, and then click **Ok.**
3. To Enable BitLocker Drive Encryption on 70411Win8:
   a) Open Control Panel and click **System and Security.**
   b) Under System and Security, click BitLocker Drive Encryption.
   c) Beside Drive C: BitLocker Off, click **Enable BitLocker.**
   d) Under Chose how to unlock your drive at startup, select Enter a password.
   e) On the **Create a password to unlock this drive**, enter a strong password and click **Next.**
   f) On the How do you want to back up your recovery key, select Save to a file.
   g) On the **Save BitLocker recovery key as** dialogue box, enter \\70411SRV\E$\Localrecovery and save the recovery key in that location.
   h) On the How do you want to back up your recovery key, click Next.
   i) On the next page, click **Continue.**
   j) Restart the computer.
   k) When the computer reboots, it will require a BitLocker password.
4. After the reboot, drive C will have a Key beside it. Encryption will continue on the background.

2.3.1 Configure the Network Unlock feature

BitLocker Network Unlock enables a network-based key protector to be used to automatically unlock BitLocker-protected operating systems drives in a domain-joined computer. This is beneficial if you are doing maintenance operations on computers during non-working hours that require the computer to restart to complete an operation. Network Unlock requires a Windows Server 2012 running Windows Deployment Services (WDS) in the environment where the feature will be utilized. Configuration of the WDS installation is not required; however, the WDS service needs to be running on the server.

The network key for BitLocker Network Unlock is stored on the system drive along with an AES 256 session key, and encrypted with the 2048-bit RSA public key of the unlock server's certificate. The network key is decrypted with the help of a provider on a Windows Server 2012 WDS server and returned encrypted with its corresponding session key.

Network Unlock Core Requirements

Network Unlock must meet mandatory hardware and software requirements before the feature can automatically unlock domain joined systems. These requirements include:

1. Computers running Windows 8 or Windows Server 2012 with UEFI DHCP drivers can be Network Unlock clients.
2. BitLocker Network Unlock optional feature installed on Windows Server 2012.
3. A separate Windows Server 2012 server running the Windows Deployment Services (WDS) role.
4. A DHCP server, separate from the WDS server.
5. Properly configured public/private key pairing.
6. Network Unlock Group Policy settings configured.

To properly support DHCP within UEFI, the UEFI-based system should be in native mode without a compatibility support module (CSM) enabled. For Network Unlock to work reliably, the first network interface card (NIC) on the computer, usually the on-board NIC, must be configured to support DHCP and used for Network Unlock. This is especially worth noting when there are multiple NICs, and one is configured without DHCP, such as for a lights-out management protocol. This configuration is necessary because Network Unlock will stop enumerating NICs when it reaches one with a DHCP port failure for any reason. Thus, if the first enumerated NIC does not support DHCP, is not plugged into the network, or fails to report availability of the DHCP port for any reason, then Network Unlock will fail.

Configure Network Unlock

High-level configuration steps:

1. Setup DHCP server
2. Setup WDS Server:
   a) Install WDS BitLocker Network Unlock feature.
   b) Create the Network Unlock self-signed certificate.
   c) Deploy the private key and certificate to the WDS server.
3. Configure Group Policy settings for Network Unlock .
4. Verify 'manage-bde-status' output protector lists has "Network (Certificate based)".
5. Verify Network Unlock works.
   a) Restart the machine.
   b) Verify if OS boots directly to Windows Logon, Network Unlock works.
   c) If prompted for BitLocker PIN, IPv6 and IPv4, Network Unlock failed.

To create Network Unlock

1. Setup DHCP: DHCP is already installed and configured on 70411SRV3.
2. Setup WDS Server to support Network Unlock.
   a) To install BitLocker Network Unlock: Log on to 70411SRV1 and run the command:

```
Install-WindowsFeature BitLocker-NetworkUnlock
```

   b) Create a self-signed Network Unlock certificate: Create an empty text file with .inf extension: Open a command prompt and execute the command:

```
notepad.exe E:\BitLocker\NetworkRecovery\BitLocker-NetworkUnlock.inf
```

   c) Respond yes to create the new file, the .INF file opens.
   d) Enter the information below into the text:

```
[NewRequest]
Subject="CN=BitLocker Network Unlock certificate"
Exportable=true
RequestType=Cert
KeyLength=2048

[Extensions]
1.3.6.1.4.1.311.21.10 = "(text)"
_continue_ = "OID=1.3.6.1.4.1.311.67.1.1"

2.5.29.37 = "(text)"
_continue_= "1.3.6.1.4.1.311.67.1.1"
```

Figure 2.3.0 – self-signed certificate

e) Use the certreq tool to create a new certificate using the following command:

```
certreq –new E:\BitLocker\NetworkRecovery\BitLocker-NetworkUnlock.inf
BitLocker-NetworkUnlock.cer
```

Wait until it returns "CertReq: Certificate Created and Installed"

f) Still logged on to 70411SRV1, create a private key:
   i) Launch the Certificate Manager by running **certmgr.msc.**
   ii) Navigate to the **Certificates - Current User,** then expand **Personal** and highlight **Certificates.**
   iii) In the details pane, right-click **BitLocker-NetworkUnlock Certificate** point to **All Tasks,** then point to **Export.**
   iv) On the **Welcome to Certificate export wizard,** click **Next.**
   v) On the **Export private key** screen, select **Yes, export private key** and click **Next.**
   vi) On the **Export File format page,** check the boxes **Include all certificates in the certificate part if possible** and **export all extended properties,** click **Next.**
   vii) On the **security** screen, click **password** and provide a password to protect the private key. Click **Next.**
   viii) On the **file to export** screen, **Name** field, click **Browse** and select the path E:\BitLocker\NetworkRecovery, type **BitLocker-NetworkUnlock** as the file name and click **Save.**
   ix) Back to the **file to export** screen, click **Next.**
   x) On the Summary screen, click **Finish.**

g) Repeat the certificate export to export a .CER file:
   i) In the details pane, right-click **BitLocker-NetworkUnlock Certificate,** point to **All Tasks,** then point to **Export.**
   ii) On the **Welcome to Certificate export wizard,** click **Next.**
   iii) On the **Export private key** screen, select **No, do not export the private key** and click **Next.**
   iv) On the **Export File format page,** select **DER encoded binary X.509 (.CER)** and click **Next.**
   v) On the **file to export** screen, **Name** field, click **Browse** and select the path E:\BitLocker\NetworkRecovery, type **BitLocker-NetworkUnlock** as the file name and click **Save.**
   vi) Back to the **file to export** screen, click **Next.**
   vii) On the Summary screen, click **Finish.**

h) Deploy the private key and certificate to the WDS server:
   i) Still logged on to 70411SRV1 (WSUS server), open an mmc console.
   ii) Add the certificates snap-in. Select the **Computer account** and local computer when given the options.

iii) Right-click **BitLocker Drive Encryption Network Unlock item,** point to **All tasks,** then point to **import.** The **Certificate import wizard** opens. click **Next.**

iv) On the **file to import** screen, beside the **Name** field, click **Browse** and select the path E:\BitLocker\NetworkRecovery\BitLocker-NetworkUnlock.pfx (If the file is not shown, select **Personal Information exchange (.pfx, .p12).** Click **Next.**

v) On the **private key protection** screen, type the password you used when you created the private key. Check the boxes **Mark this key as exportable. This will allow you to back up or export your keys at a later stage** and **include all extended properties.** Click **Next.**

vi) On the **Certificate store,** note default store, click **Next.**

vii) On the final screen, click **Finish.** The certificate will be imported.

i) Enable Use of self-signed certificates:

   i) Open Registry editor.

   ii) Navigate to **HKLM\Software\Policies\Microsoft\FVE,** and set the DWORD value **SelfSignedCertificates** to **1.**

   iii) If the key FVE does not exist, create it and then create the DWORD SelfSignedCertificates with value 1.

Note

Use of self-signed certificates is disabled by default. You must modify the registry to enable the use of self-signed certificates. To do this, open the Registry Editor, navigate to the key HKLM\Software\Policies\Microsoft\FVE, and set the DWORD value SelfSignedCertificates to 1.

3. Configure Group Policy settings for Network Unlock: With certificate and key deployed to the WDS server for Network Unlock, the final step is to use Group Policy settings to deploy the public key certificate to computers that you want to be able to unlock using the Network Unlock key. To deploy the required Group Policy setting:

   a) Log on to 70411SRV (DC) and open Group Policy Management Console.

   b) Expand Forest: 70411Lab.com, expand Domains, then expand 70411Lab.com

   c) Right-click Default Domain Policy and click **Edit.**

   d) To deploy the public certificate to clients:

      i) Navigate to Computer Configuration\Policies\Windows Settings\Security Settings\Public Key Policies\.

ii) Right-click BitLocker Drive Encryption Network Unlock Certificate and click Add Network Unlock Certificate. The Add Network Unlock Certificate Wizard opens.

iii) On the Welcome screen, click **Next.**

iv) On the **Select Network Unlock Certificate** screen, click **Browse   Folders**,   and   enter   the   path \\70411SRV1\E$\BitLocker\NetworkRecovery,   highlight **BitLocker-NetworkUnlock.CER** and click Open. If you get a Certificate Revocation warning, respond **Yes.**

v) Back on the Select Network Unlock Certificate screen, click Next.

vi) On the final page, click **Finish.**

e) Configure Group Policy for BitLocker without TPM Support and allow Network Unlock:

i) Open the Default Domain Policy with Group policy management editor.

ii) Navigate to \Computer Configuration\Administrative Templates\Windows Components\BitLocker Drive Encryption\Operating System.

iii) On the details pane, click on the policy Require additional authentication at startup.

iv) On the policy page, click Enable. Ensure that the check box beside Allow BitLocker without a compactible TPM (requires a password or a startup key on a USB flash drive) is ticked. Accept all defaults, and then click Ok.

4. To enforce group policy immediately on 70411Win8 - Log on to 70411Win8 and run execute the command:

```
gpupdate /force
```

Note

The policy configured in **Computer Configuration\Policies\Windows Settings\Security Settings\Public Key Policies\,** to Add Network Unlock Certificate can only work with Computers with compatible TPMs. This unlock method uses the TPM on the computer, so computers that do not have a TPM cannot create Network Key Protectors to automatically unlock with Network Unlock.

Turning off Network Unlock

To turn off the unlock server, the PXE provider can be unregistered from the WDS server or uninstalled altogether. However, to stop clients from creating Network Unlock protectors the **Allow Network Unlock at startup** Group Policy setting should be disabled. When this policy setting is updated to

disabled on client computers, any Network Unlock key protectors on the computer will be deleted. Alternatively, the BitLocker Network Unlock certificate policy can be deleted on the domain controller to accomplish the same task for an entire domain.

Note

Removing the FVENKP certificate store that contains the Network Unlock certificate and key on the WDS server will also effectively disable the server's ability to respond to unlock requests for that certificate. However, this is seen as an error condition and is not a supported or recommended method for turning off the Network Unlock server.

Manage-bde command line tool

Manage-bde is a command-line tool that can be used for scripting BitLocker operations. The tool offers additional options not displayed in the BitLocker control panel. Managed-bde can be used to manage operating systems volumes as well as data volumes. I have listed some examples and applications of the Manage-bde command line tool below.

To determine the status of the volume, run the command:

```
manage-bde -status
```

The command returns the volumes on the target, current encryption status and volume type (operating system or data) for each volume.

To enable BitLocker on a computer without a TPM chip:

Step 1: create the startup key needed for BitLocker and save it to the USB drive:

```
manage-bde –protectors -add C: -startupkey E:
```

Drive E represents the USB drive. When BitLocker is enabled for the operating system volume, BitLocker will need to access the USB flash drive to obtain the encryption key (Drive E in this example).

Step 2: encrypt the operating system volume:

```
manage-bde -on C
```

After the encryption is completed, the USB startup key must be inserted before the operating system can be started. An alternative to the startup key protector on non-TPM hardware is to use a password and an **ADaccountorgroup** protector to protect the operating system volume. This requires two steps as well:

Step 1: add the protectors:

```
manage-bde -protectors -add C: -pw -sid <user or group>
```

Step 2: On computers with TPM, encrypt the operating systems drive with the command:

manage-bde -on C:

Exam Tip

For the purposes of the exam, note how to create a startup key and encrypt the OS volume using manage-bde.

2.3.2 Configure BitLocker policies

To control the user experience in the BitLocker Control Panel item and to modify other configuration options, you can use Domain Group Policy or local computer policy settings. BitLocker Drive Encryption Group Policy settings can be set for specific BitLocker-protected drives (or on your local computer if your computer is not part of a domain). This gives system administrators the ability to define policies based on how the drives are used. These policy settings can be configured for:

1. **All drives**: These policy settings apply to all BitLocker-protected drives.
2. **Operating system drives**: This is the drive on the local computer on which the operating system is installed.
3. **Fixed data drives**: These are drives that are permanently installed on the local computer and cannot be removed while the computer is running.
4. **Removable data drives**: These are drives that are designed to be removed from one computer and used on another computer while the computer is in use.

BitLocker Group Policy settings are located in \Computer Configuration\Administrative Templates\Windows Components\BitLocker Drive Encryption.

Policies available for Operating system, fixed data and removable drives:

Configure use of hardware-based encryption, Enforce drive encryption type, Configure use of passwords, Choose how BitLocker-protected drives can be recovered.

Policy available only for removal data drives: Control use of BitLocker on removable drives.

Policies available only for Fixed Data and Removable Data Drives: Configure use of smart cards.

2.3.3 Configure the EFS recovery agent

Data recovery agents are accounts that are able to decrypt BitLocker-protected drives by using their smart card certificates and public keys. Recovery of a BitLocker-protected drive can be accomplished by a data recovery agent that has been configured with the proper certificate. Before a data recovery agent can be configured for a drive, you must add the data recovery agent to **Public Key Policies\BitLocker Drive Encryption** in either the Domain Group Policy Management Console (GPMC) or the Local Group Policy Editor.

To configure EFS recovery agent, you must also enable and configure the **Provide the unique identifiers for your organization** policy setting to associate a unique identifier to a new drive that is enabled with BitLocker. An identification field is a string that is used to uniquely identify a business unit or organization. Identification fields are required for management of data recovery agents on BitLocker-protected drives. BitLocker will only manage and update data recovery agents when an identification field is present on a drive and is identical to the value configured on the computer.

Before you proceed with the tasks below, ensure that you install and configured Enterprise CA as specified in the **Additional lab requirement** section at the beginning of this section.

To configure BitLocker EFS recovery agent, we will follow the high level plan outlined below:

1. Issue the EFS Data Recovery Agent.
2. Export the DRA Certificate.
3. Configure the Bitlocker Data Recovery Agent in Group Policy.
4. Configure BitLocker Identification Field.
5. Enable Allow Data Recovery Agent.

To configure BitLocker EFS recovery agent

1. Issue the EFS Data Recovery Agent:
   a) Log on to 70411SRV with admin rights and open command prompt.
   b) At the command prompt type **certmgr.msc** to open the Certificates snap-in.
   c) On the Certificates snap-in, expand **Personal,** right-click **Certificates** and click on **All Tasks** and then **Request New Certificate.** Certificate Enrollment wizard opens.
   d) On the first page of the Certificate Enrollment wizard click **Next.**
   e) Select Active Directory Enrolment Policy and click **Next.**
   f) On the **Request Certificates** screen, check the **EFS Recovery Agent** policy and then click **Enroll.**
   g) When the enrollment completes successfully, click **Finish.**
   h) A new certificate will now appear under **Certificates.**
2. Export the DRA Certificate: The next step will be to export the DRA certification information to be used in the BitLocker Drive Encryption group policy in a future step:
   a) Double-click the new DRA certificate (From previous step) and click on the **Details** tab.

   b) On the **Details** tab, Click **Copy to File**. The Certificate Export Wizard opens. click **Next.**
   c) On the Export private key screen, Leave the No, do not export the private key selected and then click **Next.**
   d) On the **Export File Format** screen, verify that **DER encoded binary x.509 (.CER)** is selected, and then click **Next.**
   e) On the **File Name** field, browse to E:\BitLocker\NetworkRecovery and type **BitLockerDRA**, click **Save.**
   f) On the **File to export** screen, click **Next.**
   g) On the final page, click **Finish,** then **Ok.**
3. Configure the Bitlocker Data Recovery Agent in Group Policy: In this section we will import the Data Recover Agent certificate we exported above into group policy to apply to computers that will have DRA certification for encrypting Bitlocker drives.
   a) Still Logged on to 70411SRV, open **Group Policy Management** from **Server Manager, Tools** menu.
   b) Expand Forest: 70411lab.com, then expand Domains, finally, expand 70411Lab.com.
   c) Right-click **Default Domain Policy** and click **Edit.** The GPM Editor opens.
   d) In the console tree under Computer Configuration\ Policy \Windows Settings\Security Settings\Public Key Policies, right-click **BitLocker Drive Encryption**, and then click **Add Data Recovery Agent**, to start the Add Recovery Agent Wizard.
   e) On the Add Recovery Agent Wizard welcome screen Click Next.
   f) On the Select Recovery Agents screen, click Browse Folder.
   g) Browse to E:\BitLocker\NetworkRecovery, select **BitLockerDRA** and click **Open,** then click **Next.**

Note

The example above has USER_UNKNOWN because the DRA file was manually imported.

   h) On the **Completing the Recovery Agent** Wizard page, click **Finish** to add the data recovery agent.
4. Configure BitLocker Identification Field: The next step will be to configure the BitLocker Identification field by enabling the **provide the unique identifiers for your organization** option in group policy.
   a) Still on GPM Editor on 70411SRV, navigate to: Computer Configuration\Policies\Administrative   Templates\Windows Components\Bitlocker Drive Encryption.

b) Double-click on Provide the unique identifiers for your organization, click Enable, then type 70411Lab, in the BitLocker identification field.

c) Click **Ok** to enable and close the policy.

Note

You can add additional Bitlocker identifiers from other trusted organisations in the Allowed BitLocker identification field.

5. Enable Allow Data Recovery Agent (DRA): This group policy can be configured for Operating system, Fixed data or Removable data drives.

a) Still on group policy management editor, Navigate back one step to: Computer Configuration\Policies\Administrative Templates\Windows Components\ then expand **Bitlocker Drive Encryption**

b) To configure DRA for Operating system drives:

i) High-light Operating system drives, on the details pane, double-click the policy Choose how Bitlocker-protected Operating system drives can be recovered and click Enable.

ii) Under Options, check Allow Data Recovery Agent. Beneath it, from the drop down select Do not allow 48-digit recovery password, and Do not allow 256-bit recovery key.

iii) Check the boxes Omit recovery options from the BitLocker setup wizard and Do not enable BitLocker until recovery information is stored in AD DS for Operating systems drives.

iv) On the Configure storage of BitLocker information to AD DS, select Store recovery passwords and key packages.

6. When you complete the above tasks, click **Ok** to save your changes.

2.3.4 Manage EFS and BitLocker certificates including backup and restore

When we configured Network Unlock, we created a self-signed certificate stored in E:\BitLocker\NetworkRecovery\BitLocker-NetworkUnlock.cer. We also created a PKI stored in E:\BitLocker\NetworkRecovery\BitLocker-NetworkUnlock.pfx. In the DRA section above, we created a certificate - E:\BitLocker\NetworkRecovery\BitLockerDRA in 70411SRV.

In this section, we will walk through management tasks for these certificates including backup and recovery.

To Manage EFS and BitLocker certificates

1. Log on to 70411SRV1 and open **Certmgr.**
2. Expand **Personal** and highlight **Certificates**. In the details pane, double-click **BitLocker Network Unlock Certificate** to open it. Let's examine the properties of this certificate:
   a) Click **Details** tab. On the details tab, you can perform two actions:
      i) **Copy files**: Allows you to export the certificate to a file.
      ii) **Edit Properties**: This option allows you to edit the properties of the certificate:
   b) On the **General** tab, you can:
      i) Specify a Friendly Name.
      ii) Enable all certificate purposes, Disable all certificate purposes, or enable specific purposes.
   c) **Cross-certificates** tab: You can specify additional cross-certificate locations
   d) **OCSP** tab: here you can:
      i) Specify additional Online Certificate Status Protocol (OCSP) URLs.
      ii) Disable Certificate Revocation Lists (CRL).
   e) **Extended Validation** tab: Specify Certificate Policy OIDs to mark a root Certificate an extended Validation (EV) root Certificate.

Back Up domain EFS recovery agent

Before you back up the domain EFS recovery agent's private key, you have to export it from **Public Key Policies** in group policy management.

To export the domain EFS recovery agent's private key

1. Log on 70411SRV and open Group Policy Management from Server Manager.
2. Right-click the **Default Domain Policy,** and then click **Edit.**
3. In the console tree (on the left), navigate to Computer Configuration\Policies\Windows Settings\Security Settings\Public Key Policies, and then click **Bitlocker Drive Encryption.**
4. In the details pane, right-click the certificate you want to export.
5. Point to **All Tasks,** and then click **Export**. The **Certificate Export Wizard** starts. Click **Next.**
6. Click DER Encoded binary X.509 (.CER), Click **Next.**
7. In the **File to export**, type E:\BitLocker\NetworkRecovery\ExportedBitLockerDRA.cer, Click **Next.**
8. Verify the settings that are displayed on the **Completing the Certificate Export Wizard** page, and then click **Finish.**

It is recommended that you back up the file to a disk or to a removable media device, and then store the backup in a location where you can guarantee the physical security of the backup.

2.4 Configure Advanced Audit Policies

Introduction

Security auditing is a powerful tool to help maintain the security of an enterprise. Auditing can be used for a variety of purposes, including forensic analysis, regulatory compliance, monitoring user activity, and troubleshooting. Industry regulations in various countries or regions require enterprises to implement a strict set of rules related to data security and privacy. Security audits can help implement such policies and prove that these policies have been implemented. Also, security auditing can be used for forensic analysis, to help administrators detect anomalous behavior, to identify and mitigate gaps in security policies, and to deter irresponsible behavior by tracking critical user activities.

In this section, we will cover following exam objectives:

2.4.0 Implement auditing using Group Policy and AuditPol.exe
2.4.1 Create expression-based audit policies
2.4.2 Create removable device audit policies

Lab Plan

We will use 70411SRV for this lab

Additional Lab setup

None

2.4.0.0 Implement auditing using Group Policy

Security auditing enhancements in Windows Server 2012 R2 can help your organization audit compliance with important business-related and security-related rules by tracking precisely defined activities, such as:

1. Settings or data modifications on servers that contain critical information.
2. An employee within a defined group has accessed an important file.
3. The correct system access control list (SACL) is applied to every file and folder or registry key on a computer or file share as a verifiable safeguard against undetected access.

Creating and Verifying Advanced audit policy

The nine basic audit policies under **Computer Configuration\Policies\Windows Settings\Security Settings\Local Policies\Audit Policy** allow you to configure security audit policy settings for broad sets of behaviors, some of which generate many more audit events than others. An administrator has to review all events that are generated, whether they are of interest or not.

In Windows Server 2012 R2 and Windows 8, administrators can audit more specific aspects of client behavior on the computer or network with **Advanced Audit Policy Configuration**, thus making it easier to identify the behaviors that are of greatest interest. For example, in **Computer Configuration\Policies\Windows Settings\Security Settings\Local Policies\Audit Policy**, there is only one policy setting for logon events, **Audit logon events**. But in **Computer Configuration\Policies\Windows Settings\Security Settings\Advanced Audit Policy Configuration\Audit Policies**, you can instead choose from ten different policy settings in the **Logon/Logoff** category. This provides you with more detailed control of what aspects of logon and logoff you can track.

Below is a list of the ten audit policies available in the **Advanced Audit Policy Configuration**:

1. Account logon Policies:
   a) **Audit Credential Validation**: This security policy setting determines whether the operating system generates audit events on credentials submitted for a user account logon request.
   b) **Audit Kerberos Authentication Service**: This security policy setting allows you to generate audit events for Kerberos authentication ticket-granting ticket (TGT) requests.
   c) **Audit Kerberos Service Ticket Operations**: This security policy setting determines whether the operating system generates security audit events for Kerberos service ticket requests. Events are generated every time Kerberos is used to authenticate a user to access a protected network resource.

d) **Audit Other Account Logon Events**: This security policy setting allows you to audit events generated by responses to credential requests submitted for a user account logon that are not credential validation or Kerberos tickets.

2. Account Management Policies:

a) **Audit Application Group Management**: This security policy setting determines whether the operating system generates audit events when application group management tasks are performed, such as:
   i) An application group is created, changed, or deleted.
   ii) A member is added to or removed from an application group.

b) **Audit Computer Account Management**: This security policy setting determines whether the operating system generates audit events when a computer account is created, changed, or deleted. This policy setting is useful for tracking account-related changes to computers that are members of a domain.

c) **Audit Distribution Group Management**: This security policy setting determines whether the operating system generates audit events for the following distribution group management tasks:
   i) A distribution group is created, changed, or deleted.
   ii) A member is added to or removed from a distribution group.

d) **Audit Other Account Management Events**: This security policy setting determines whether the operating system generates user account management audit events when:
   i) The password hash of an account is accessed. This typically happens when the Active Directory Migration Tool (ADMT) is moving password data.
   ii) The Password Policy Checking application programming interface (API) is called. Calls to this function could be part of an attack from a malicious application that is testing whether password complexity policy settings are being applied.
   iii) Changes are made to domain policy here:

Computer Configuration\Windows Settings\Security Settings\Account Policies\Password Policy or Computer Configuration\Windows Settings\Security Settings\Account Policies\Account Lockout Policy.

e) **Audit Security Group Management**: This security policy setting determines whether the operating system generates audit events when any of the following security group management tasks are performed:
   i) A security group is created, changed, or deleted.
   ii) A member is added to or removed from a security group.
   iii) A group's type is changed.

f) **Audit User Account Management**: This security policy setting determines whether the operating system generates audit events when the following user account management tasks are performed:
   i)   A user account's password is set or changed.
   ii) A security identifier (SID) is added to the SID History of a user account.
   iii) The Directory Services Restore Mode password is configured.
   iv) Permissions on administrative user accounts are changed.
   v)   Credential Manager credentials are backed up or restored.

3. Detailed Tracking Policies:
   a) **Audit DPAPI Activity**: This security policy setting determines whether the operating system generates audit events when encryption or decryption calls are made into the data protection application interface (DPAPI), which is used to protect secret information such as stored passwords and key information.
   b) **Audit Process Creation**: This security policy setting determines whether the operating system generates audit events when a process is created (starts) and the name of the program or user that created it. These audit events can help you understand how a computer is being used and to track user activity.
   c) **Audit Process Termination**: This security policy setting allows you to generate audit events when an attempt is made to end a process.
   d) **Audit RPC Events**: This security policy setting determines whether the operating system generates audit events when inbound remote procedure call (RPC) connections are made.

4. DS Access Policies:
   a) **Audit Detailed Directory Service Replication**: This security policy setting can be used to generate security audit events with detailed tracking information about data replicated between domain controllers. This audit subcategory can be useful to diagnose replication issues.
   b) **Audit Directory Service Access**: This security policy setting determines whether the operating system generates events when an Active Directory Domain Services (AD DS) object is accessed.

Note

Audit events will only be generated on objects with configured system access control lists (SACLs), and only when they are accessed in a manner that matches the SACL settings.

---

   c) **Audit Directory Service Changes**: This security policy setting determines whether the operating system generates audit events when changes are made to objects in Active Directory Domain Services (AD DS). The types of changes that are reported are:

i)   Create.
ii)   Delete.
iii) Modify.
iv)   Move.
v)   Undelete.

Directory Service Changes auditing, where appropriate, indicates the old and new values of the changed properties of the objects that were changed. The note above also applies to this category.

    d) **Audit Directory Service Replication**: This security policy setting determines whether the operating system generates audit events when replication between two domain controllers begins and ends.

5. Logon/Logoff Policies:

    a) **Audit Account Lockout**: This security policy setting allows you to audit security events generated by a failed attempt to log on to an account that is locked out.

    b) If this policy setting is configured, an audit event is generated when an account cannot log on to a computer because the account is locked out. Success audits record successful attempts and failure audits record unsuccessful attempts.

    c) **User / Device Claims**: This policy allows you to audit user and device claims information in the user's logon token. Events in this subcategory are generated on the computer on which a logon session is created. For an interactive logon, the security audit event is generated on the computer that the user logged on to. For a network logon, such as accessing a shared folder on the network, the security audit event is generated on the computer hosting the resource.

    d) User claims are added to a logon token when claims are included with a user's account attributes in Active Directory.

    e) Device claims are added to the logon token when claims are included with a device's computer account attributes in Active Directory. In addition, compound identity must be enabled for the domain and on the computer where the user logged on.

    f) **Audit IPsec Extended Mode**: This security policy setting determines whether the operating system generates audit events for the results of the Internet Key Exchange (IKE) protocol and Authenticated Internet Protocol (AuthIP) during Extended Mode negotiations.

    g) **Audit IPsec Main Mode**: This security policy setting determines whether the operating system generates events for the results of the

Internet Key Exchange (IKE) protocol and Authenticated Internet Protocol (AuthIP) during Main Mode negotiations.

h) **IPsec Quick Mode**: This policy setting allows you to audit events generated by Internet Key Exchange protocol (IKE) and Authenticated Internet Protocol (AuthIP) during Quick Mode negotiations.

i) **Audit Logoff**: This security policy setting determines whether the operating system generates audit events when logon sessions are terminated. These events occur on the computer that was accessed. In the case of an interactive logon, these would be generated on the computer that was logged on to.

Note

There is no failure event in the **Audit Logoff** subcategory because failed logoffs (such as when a system abruptly shuts down) do not generate an audit record.

Logon events are essential to understanding user activity and detecting potential attacks. Logoff events are not 100 percent reliable. For example, the computer can be turned off without a proper logoff and shutdown taking place; in this case, a logoff event will not be generated.

j) **Audit Logon**: This security policy setting determines whether the operating system generates audit events when a user attempts to log on to a computer. These events are related to the creation of logon sessions and occur on the computer that was accessed. For an interactive logon, events are generated on the computer that was logged on to. For network logon, such as accessing a share, events are generated on the computer hosting the resource that was accessed. The following events are recorded:
   i) Logon success and failure.
   ii) Logon attempts by using explicit credentials. This event is generated when a process attempts to log on an account by explicitly specifying that account's credentials. This most commonly occurs in batch-type configurations such as scheduled tasks, or when using the Runas command.
   iii) Security identifiers (SIDs) are filtered.

k) **Audit Network Policy Server**: This security policy setting determines whether the operating system generates audit events for RADIUS (IAS) and Network Access Protection (NAP) activity on user access requests (Grant, Deny, Discard, Quarantine, Lock, and Unlock). NAP events can be used to understand the overall health of the network.

l) **Audit Other Logon/Logoff Events**: This security policy setting determines whether Windows generates audit events for other logon or logoff events, such as:
   i)   Terminal Services session disconnections.
   ii) New Terminal Services sessions.
   iii) Locking and unlocking a workstation.
   iv) Invoking a screen saver.
   v)   Dismissal of a screen saver.
   vi) Detection of a Kerberos replay attack, in which a Kerberos request was received twice with identical information. This condition could be caused by network misconfiguration.
   vii) A user is granted access to a wired 802.1x network. It can either be a user account or the computer account.

Logon events are essential to understanding user activity and detecting potential attacks.

m) **Audit Special Logon**: This security policy setting determines whether the operating system generates audit events when:
   i)   A special logon is used. A special logon is a logon that has administrator-equivalent privileges and can be used to elevate a process to a higher level.
   ii) A member of a special group logs on. Special Groups is a Windows feature that enables the administrator to find out when a member of a certain group has logged on. The administrator can set a list of group security identifiers (SIDs) in the registry. If any of these SIDs is added to a token during logon and this auditing subcategory is enabled, a security event is logged.

6. Object Access Policies:
   a) **Audit Application Generated**: This security policy setting determines whether the operating system generates audit events when applications attempt to use the Windows Auditing application programming interfaces (APIs). The following events can generate audit activity:
      i)   Creation, deletion, and initialization of an application client context
      ii) Application operations

Applications designed to use the Windows Auditing APIs can use this subcategory to log auditing events related to their function. The level, volume, relevance, and importance of these audit events depend on the application generating them. The operating system logs the events as they are generated by the application.

b) **Audit Certification Services**: This security policy setting determines whether the operating system generates events when Active Directory Certificate Services (AD CS) operations are performed, such as:

   i)   AD CS starts, shuts down, is backed up, or is restored.
   ii)   Certificate revocation list (CRL)-related tasks are performed.
   iii) Certificates are requested, issued, or revoked.
   iv)   Certificate manager settings for AD CS are changed.
   v)   The configuration and properties of the certification authority (CA) are changed.
   vi)   AD CS templates are modified.
   vii) Certificates are imported.
   viii) A CA certificate is published to Active Directory Domain Services.
   ix)   Security permissions for AD CS role services are modified.
   x)   Keys are archived, imported, or retrieved.
   xi)   The OCSP Responder Service is started or stopped.

Monitoring these operational events is important to ensure that AD CS role services are functioning properly.

c) **Audit Detailed File Share**: This security policy setting allows you to audit attempts to access files and folders on a shared folder. The Detailed File Share setting logs an event every time a file or folder is accessed, whereas the File Share setting only records one event for any connection established between a client computer and file share. Detailed File Share audit events include detailed information about the permissions or other criteria used to grant or deny access.

Note

There are no system access control lists (SACLs) for shared folders. If 'Audit Detailed File Share' security policy setting is enabled, access to all shared files and folders on the system is audited.

d) **Audit File Share**: This security policy setting determines whether the operating system generates audit events when a file share is accessed. Audit events are not generated when shares are created, deleted, or when share permissions change. Combined with **File System auditing**, File Share auditing allows you to track what content was accessed, the source (IP address and port) of the request, and the user account used for the access.

e) **Audit File System**: This security policy setting determines whether the operating system audits user attempts to access file system objects. Audit events are only generated for objects that have configured system access control lists (SACLs), and only if the type of access requested (such as Write, Read, or Modify) and the account making the request match the settings in the SACL.

If success auditing is enabled, an audit entry is generated each time any account successfully accesses a file system object that has a matching SACL. If failure auditing is enabled, an audit entry is generated each time any user unsuccessfully attempts to access a file system object that has a matching SACL.

These events are essential for tracking activity for file objects that are sensitive or valuable and require extra monitoring.

Note

You can set a SACL on a file system object using the Security tab in that object's Properties dialog box.

---

f) **Audit Filtering Platform Connection**: This security policy setting determines whether the operating system generates audit events when connections are allowed or blocked by the Windows Filtering Platform, such as when:

 i) The Windows Firewall service blocks an application from accepting incoming connections on the network.

 ii) The Windows Filtering Platform allows or blocks a connection.

 iii) The Windows Filtering Platform permits or blocks a bind to a local port.

 iv) The Windows Filtering Platform permits or blocks the listening of an application or service on a port for incoming connections.

g) **Audit Filtering Platform Packet Drop**: This security policy setting allows you to audit packets that are dropped by the Windows Filtering Platform. A high rate of dropped packets may indicate attempts to gain unauthorized access to computers on your network.

h) **Audit Handle Manipulation**: This security policy setting determines whether the operating system generates audit events when a handle to an object is opened or closed. Only objects with configured system access control lists (SACLs) generate these events, and only if the attempted handle operation match the SACL.

Note

Handle Manipulation events are only generated for object types where the corresponding File System or Registry Object Access subcategory is enabled.

---

i) **Audit Kernel Object**: This security policy setting allows you to audit attempts to access the system kernel, which include mutexes and semaphores. Only kernel objects with a matching system access control list (SACL) generate security audit events.

Note

The **Audit: Audit the access of global system objects** policy setting controls the default SACL of kernel objects.

The audits generated are usually only useful to developers. Typically kernel objects are given SACLs only if he **AuditBaseObjects** or **AuditBaseDirectories** auditing options are enabled.

j) **Audit Other Object Access Events**: This security policy setting determines whether the operating system generates audit events for the management of Task Scheduler jobs or COM+ objects. For scheduler jobs, the following are audited:
    i)   Job created.
    ii)   Job deleted.
    iii) Job enabled.
    iv)   Job disabled.
    v)   Job updated.

For COM+ objects, the following are audited:

     vi)   Catalog object added.
     vii) Catalog object updated.
     viii) Catalog object deleted.

k) **Audit Registry**: This security policy setting determines whether the operating system audits user attempts to access registry objects. Audit events are only generated for objects that have configured system access control lists (SACLs) specified, and only if the type of access requested (such as Write, Read, or Modify) and the account making the request match the settings in the SACL.

l) **Audit Removable storage**: This policy setting allows you to audit user attempts to access file system objects on a removable storage device. A security audit event is generated only for all objects for all types of access requested.

m) **Audit SAM**: This security policy setting allows you to audit events generated by attempts to access Security Accounts Manager (SAM) objects. SAM objects include the following:
    i)   SAM_ALIAS: A local group
    ii)   SAM_GROUP: A group that is not a local group
    iii) SAM_USER: A user account
    iv)   SAM_DOMAIN: A domain
    v)   SAM_SERVER: A computer account

If you configure this policy setting, an audit event is generated when a SAM object is accessed. Success audits record successful attempts, and failure audits record unsuccessful attempts.

Note

Only the SACL for SAM_SERVER can be modified.

Changes to user and group objects are tracked by the Account Management audit category. However, user accounts with enough privileges could potentially alter the files where the account and password information is stored in the system, bypassing any Account Management events.

n) **Audit Central Access Policy Staging**: This policy setting allows you to audit access requests where the permission granted or denied by a proposed policy differs from the current central access policy on an object.

7. Policy Change Policies:

a) **Audit Audit Policy Change**: This security policy setting determines whether the operating system generates audit events when changes are made to audit policy, including:

i)   Permissions and audit settings on the audit policy object (by using auditpol /set /sd).

ii) Changing the system audit policy.

iii) Registration and de-registration of security event sources.

iv) Changing per-user audit settings.

v)   Changing the value of **CrashOnAuditFail**.

vi) Changing audit settings on an object (for example, modifying the system access control list (SACL) for a file or registry key.)

Note

SACL change auditing is performed when a SACL for an object has changed and the Policy Change category is configured. Discretionary access control list (DACL) and owner change auditing is performed when Object Access auditing is configured and the object's SACL is set for auditing of the DACL or owner change.

vii) Changes made to the Special Groups list.

Important

Changes to the audit policy are critical security events.   a.
                                                                             b.

b) **Audit Authentication Policy Change**: This security policy setting determines whether the operating system generates audit events when changes are made to authentication policy, including:

    i)   Creation, modification, and removal of forest and domain trusts.
    ii) Changes to Kerberos policy under Computer Configuration\Windows Settings\Security Settings\Account Policies\Kerberos Policy.

Note

The audit event is logged when the policy is applied, not when settings are modified by the administrator.

    iii) When any of the following user rights are granted to a user or group:
      (1) Access this computer from the network
      (2) Allow logon locally
      (3) Allow logon through Remote Desktop
      (4) Logon as a batch job
      (5) Logon as a service
    iv) Namespace collision, such as when an added trust collides with an existing namespace name.

This setting is useful for tracking changes in domain and forest level trust and privileges granted to user accounts or groups.

c) **Audit Authorization Policy Change**: This security policy setting determines whether the operating system generates audit events when the following changes are made to the authorization policy:
    i)   Assigning or removing of user rights (privileges) such as **SeCreateTokenPrivilege**, except for the system access rights that are audited by using **the Audit Authentication Policy Change** subcategory.
    ii) Changing the Encrypting File System (EFS) policy.

d) **Audit Filtering Platform Policy Change**: This security policy setting determines whether the operating system generates audit events for:
    i)   IPsec services status.
    ii) Changes to IPsec settings.
    iii) Status and changes to the Windows Filtering Platform engine and providers.
    iv) IPsec Policy Agent service activities.

e) **Audit MPSSVC Rule-Level Policy Change**: This security policy setting determines whether the operating system generates audit events when changes are made to policy rules for the Microsoft Protection Service (MPSSVC.exe), which is used by Windows Firewall. The tracked activities include:
    i)   Active policies when the Windows Firewall service starts.

ii)   Changes to Windows Firewall rules.

iii) Changes to the Windows Firewall exception list.

iv) Changes to Windows Firewall settings.

v)   Rules ignored or not applied by the Windows Firewall service.

vi) Changes to Windows Firewall Group Policy settings.

vii) Changes to firewall rules are important to understand the security state of the computer and how well it is protected against network attacks.

f) **Audit Other Policy Change Events**: This security policy setting determines whether the operating system generates events for security policy changes that are not otherwise audited in the Policy Change category, such as the following:

i)   Trusted Platform Module (TPM) configuration changes.

ii) Kernel-mode cryptographic self tests.

iii) Cryptographic provider operations.

iv) Cryptographic context operations or modifications.

8. Privilege Use Policies:

a) **Audit Non-Sensitive Privilege Use**: This security policy setting allows you to audit events generated by the use of non-sensitive privileges (user rights). The following privileges are non-sensitive:

i)   Access Credential Manager as a trusted caller

ii)   Access this computer from the network

iii) Add workstations to domain

iv) Adjust memory quotas for a process

v)   Allow log on locally

vi) Allow log on through Terminal Services

vii) Bypass traverse checking

viii) Change the system time

ix) Create a page file

x)   Create global objects

xi) Create permanent shared objects

xii) Create symbolic links

xiii) Deny access to this computer from the network

xiv) Deny log on as a batch job

xv) Deny log on as a service

xvi) Deny log on locally

xvii)   Deny log on through Terminal Services

xviii)   Force shutdown from a remote system

xix)   Increase a process working set

xx)   Increase scheduling priority

xxi)   Lock pages in memory

xxii)   Log on as a batch job

xxiii)   Log on as a service

xxiv)   Modify an object label

xxv)   Perform volume maintenance tasks

xxvi)   Profile single process

xxvii) Profile system performance

xxviii) Remove computer from docking station

xxix)   Shut down the system

xxx)   Synchronize directory service data

b) **Audit Other Privilege Use Events**: This security policy setting is not used in Windows Server 2012 R2.

c) **Sensitive Privilege Use**: This policy setting allows you to audit events generated when sensitive privileges (user rights) are used such as the following:

i)   A privileged service is called.

ii) One of the following privileges are called:

(1) Act as part of the operating system.

(2) Back up files and directories.

(3) Create a token object.

(4) Debug programs.

(5) Enable computer and user accounts to be trusted for delegation.

(6) Generate security audits.

(7) Impersonate a client after authentication.

(8) Load and unload device drivers.

(9) Manage auditing and security log.

(10) Modify firmware environment values.

(11) Replace a process-level token.

(12) Restore files and directories.

(13) Take ownership of files or other objects.

9. System Polices:

a) **Audit IPsec Driver**: This security policy setting determines whether the operating system audits the activities of the IPsec driver and reports any of the following events:

i)   Startup and shutdown of IPsec services.

ii) Packets dropped due to integrity check failure.

iii) Packets dropped due to replay check failure.

iv) Packets dropped due to being in plaintext.

v)   Packets received with an incorrect Security Parameter Index (SPI). (This can indicate malfunctioning hardware or interoperability problems.)

vi) Failure to process IPsec filters.

A high rate of packet drops by the IPsec filter driver may indicate attempts to gain access to the network by unauthorized systems. Failure to process IPsec filters poses a potential security risk because some network interfaces may not get the protection provided by the IPsec filter.

b) **Audit Other System Events**: This security policy setting determines whether the operating system audits any of the following events:
    i)   Startup and shutdown of the Windows Firewall service and driver.
    ii) Security policy processing by the Windows Firewall service.
    iii) Cryptography key file and migration operations.

Note

Failure to start the Windows Firewall service may result in a computer that is not fully protected against network threats.

---

c) **Audit Security State Change**: This security policy setting determines whether the operating system audits changes in the security state of a system and reports any of the following events:
    i)   System startup and shutdown.
    ii) Change of system time.
    iii) System recovery from **CrashOnAuditFail**. This event is logged after a system reboots **followingCrashOnAuditFail**.

Note

Some auditable activity may not be recorded when a system reboots due to CrashOnAuditFail.

System startup and shutdown events are important to understand system usage.

d) **Audit Security System Extension**: This security policy setting determines whether the operating system audits events related to security system extensions, including any of the following events:
    i)   When a security extension code is loaded (such as an authentication, notification, or security package). A security extension code registers with the Local Security Authority and will be used and trusted to authenticate logon attempts, submit logon requests, and be notified of any account or password changes. Examples of this are Kerberos and NTLM.
    ii) When a service is installed. An audit log is generated when a service is registered with the Service Control Manager. The audit log contains information about the service name, binary, type, start type, and service account.

Note

Attempts to install or load security system extensions or services are critical system events that could indicate a security breach.

e) **Audit System Integrity**: This security policy setting determines whether the operating system audits events that violate the integrity of the security subsystem, which can include any of the following events:
   i) Audited events are lost due to a failure of the auditing system.
   ii) A process uses an invalid local procedure call (LPC) port in an attempt to impersonate a client, reply to a client address space, read to a client address space, or write from a client address space.
   iii) A remote procedure call (RPC) integrity violation is detected.
   iv) A code integrity violation with an invalid hash value of an executable file is detected.
   v) Cryptographic tasks are performed.

Note

Violations of security subsystem integrity are critical and could indicate a potential security attack.

10. Global Object Access Auditing Policies:
    a) **Registry (Global Object Access Auditing)**: This security policy setting allows you to configure a global system access control list (SACL) on the registry for a computer.
    b) If you select the Configure security check box, you can add a user or group to the global SACL. This policy setting must be used in combination with the **Registry security policy** setting under **Object Access**.
    c) **File System (Global Object Access Auditing)**: This security policy setting allows you to configure a global system access control list (SACL) on the file system for an entire computer. If both a file or folder SACL and a global SACL are configured on a computer, the effective SACL is derived from combining the file or folder SACL and the global SACL. This means that an audit event is generated if an activity matches either the file or folder SACL or the global SACL. If you select the Configure security check box, you can add a user or group to the global SACL. This policy setting must be used in combination with the **File System security policy** setting under **Object Access**.

2.4.0.1 Implement auditing using AuditPol.exe

The Auditpol.exe tool performs audit policy configuration actions from the command line. This is the only tool you can use to configure auditing on a Server Core computer or to configure directory service auditing subcategories. The basic syntax of the command is:

Auditpol command [<sub-command><options>]

The command line is helpful for automating common user management tasks. For example, configuring the auditing policies for a group of users is extremely easy at the command line. On the other hand, the command line cannot easily perform some user management tasks.

Audit user access

Auditing system activity is a necessary process in many situations. Of course, there is the obvious use of ensuring the system remains secure by thwarting any misguided user activity. However, auditing can help you do more than just check security. For example, careful auditing can often alert you to potentially damaging system activities or help you better understand why a system doesn't perform as well as it could. Checking object access can help you better define how a user interacts with a system so that you can make the system more efficient. A user's privilege use can help you locate security holes that occur when a user has more rights than required. The following sections discuss how to use the AuditPol utility to **List**, **Get** and **Set** policies.

1. **List the policies**: Before you can use audit policies, you need to know which policies are available and whom they affect. Windows applies categories of auditing policies to specific users, so you actually have two concerns when discovering the current auditing configuration. The **AuditPol /List** command makes it possible to check users, auditing categories, and auditing subcategories as described in the following sections.

    a) **List audit users:** To discover which users are audited, type the command below:

AuditPol /List /User

The output of this command provides a list of which users are audited, but not how they are being audited. To discover how the user is being audited, execute:

AuditPol /Get /User:*UserName* /Category:*

Replace UserName with a valid username in your domain. To list all users who have a defined audit policy and their associated SID, execute the command:

```
Auditpol /list /user /v
```

Note

The SID is useful for a number of purposes and ensures that you can uniquely identify the user to the system.

---

b) **List audit categories:** Many of the AuditPol commands require that you know a category. If you want information for all categories, you simply use the asterisk (*), but often the wildcard search returns far too much information to be useful unless you limit the output in some other way. Consequently, knowing the precise category you want is important in many situations.

To obtain a basic category listing, type:

```
AuditPol /List /Category
```

In most cases, the basic listing is all you need. However, if you plan to work with the category at a detailed level or want to search for its entry in the registry, you need a Globally Unique Identifier (GUID) that precisely identifies the category to the system. To obtain this information, type:

```
AuditPol /List /Category /V
```

c) **List audit subcategories:** Categories are divided into subcategories. For example, the Object Access category contains a subcategory of File System (among other subcategories). You can choose to audit a user's access to the file system, without monitoring other kinds of Object Access, by specifying a subcategory. To obtain the subcategories for **Detailed Tracking** in the **Object Access** categories, type:

```
Auditpol /list /subcategory:"Detailed Tracking","Object Access"
```

If you want to see multiple categories, simply create a list separated by commas of category names. To see all of the subcategories for every category, type

```
AuditPol /List /Subcategory:*
```

As with categories, subcategories have GUIDs. To see the GUIDs for the subcategories, add the /V command line switch.

2. **Get a policy**: Listing a policy simply tells you that the policy exists but doesn't tell you the policy setting. Getting a policy will not tell you that the policy exists - you must already know that the policy exists. However, it does tell you how the policy is configured. Even though listing and

getting may sound a lot alike, the two are completely different. The AuditPol / Get command is all about discovering the system settings.

It's also important to understand that audit policies are configured at two levels. First, you can configure an audit policy at the system level, which means that the policy affects everyone. Second, you can configure an audit policy for a specific user, which means that the policy affects only that user. The AuditPol /Get /User command tells you about specific user settings, while the AuditPol /Get /Category and AuditPol /Get /Subcategory commands tell you about system-level settings.

Some special settings affect the system directly when an audit event occurs.

For example, the CrashOnAuditFail option causes the system to crash when the auditing system fails for some reason. This is a safety feature because it ensures that no one can turn off auditing and then continue to use the system unless they use the standard methods to do so and have the proper rights. The following sections describe all of these AuditPol /Get command scenarios.

a) **Get audit users:** The AuditPol /Get /User command obtains information about a specific user. In most cases, To obtain information about a user's full rights, execute:

AuditPol /Get /User:UserName /Category:*

---

*where *UserName* is the name of the user. However, you can specify a particular category to discover information about just that category or you can use the /Subcategory command line switch to be even more selective and discover information about just one setting. The output you see contains three columns: the name of the category or subcategory, the inclusive setting, and the exclusive setting.

Note

When you set a user audit policy, it is either inclusive or exclusive. An inclusive policy is one that adds to the system-level settings. For example, if you audit the user's failure to log on to the system, it is an inclusive policy because it is in addition to any system-level settings. However, if the system normally monitors logon failures, but you don't want to check a particular user, then you would create an exclusive policy. Even though everyone else is monitored, this particular user is excluded from the policy. It is unusual to create exclusive policies - inclusive policies are far more common.

You may need to output the user settings in a form that you can import into a database. In this case, you'd add the /R command line switch to create Comma Separated Value (CSV) output. For example, if you need to retrieve the settings for user Jamal and output them in a CSV file, you will execute:

AuditPol /Get /User:Jamal /Category:* /R > c:\Jamal.CSV

---

b) **Get audit categories:** The AuditPol /Get /Category command obtains the system-wide settings for both categories and subcategories. You can choose to obtain a specific category by using the category name in place of *. For example, to obtain the Logon/Logoff category for a user, you type:

Auditpol /get /user:domain\UserName /Category:"Logon/logoff"

As with the user information, you can output the categories to CSV format using the /R command line switch.

c) **Get audit subcategories:** Use the AuditPol /Get /Subcategory command when you need to obtain the system-wide setting for a single subcategory. For example, to retrieve the status of the Logon subcategory, execute:

AuditPol /Get /Subcategory:"Logon"

Unlike the /Category command line switch, you cannot use * with the /Subcategory command line switch.

d) **Get audit options:** The AuditPol /Get /Option command sets the audit policy for the CrashOnAuditFail, FullPrivilegeAuditing, AuditBaseObjects, or AuditBaseDirectories options. The following list describes each of these options:

i) **CrashOnAuditFail:** When you enable this setting, it forces the system to crash should the auditing system become unable to log events. The advantage to this setting is that it forces everyone to use the auditing policies you set. However, the disadvantage is that an outsider could use this option to force the server to crash and cause an apparent Distributed Denial of Service (DDoS) attack. You need to use this setting with care. After this event occurs, only administrators can log on to the system. The administrator must fix whatever caused the crash before the system will allow anyone to log back on. This setting is generally useful on client systems, but not recommended for servers.

ii) **FullPrivilegeAuditing:** When you tell the system to audit privileges, it normally does so for most privileges, but it leaves out a few commonly-used privileges to keep the event log from quickly overflowing, such as the following privileges:

(1) Generate security audit (SeAuditPrivilege).

(2) Bypass traverse checking (SeChangeNotifyPrivilege) debug programs (SeDebugPrivilege).

(3) Create a token object (SeCreateTokenPrivilege).

(4) Replace   process-level   token (SeAssignPrimaryTokenPrivilege).

(5) Generate security audits (SeAuditPrivilege).

(6) Back up files and directories (SeBackupPrivilege).

(7) Restore files and directories (SeRestorePrivilege).

Enabling this setting forces the system to audit all privilege changes except SeAuditPrivilege. You can't audit the SeAuditPrivilege because it would cause an endless loop - every access to the audit system generates this privilege and therefore every entry to the log would generate another SeAuditPrivilege event.

iii) **AuditBaseObjects and AuditBaseDirectories:** Kernel objects come in two forms: container objects and base objects. The AuditBaseObjects policy affects base objects, those that can't contain objects such as semaphores and mutexes. The AuditBaseDirectories policy affects container objects, those that can contain other objects, such as directories. Many kernel objects are unnamed and rely only on a handle that's accessible to just the process that created the object for access. Unnamed kernel objects are secure, but they don't allow interprocess communication, which is often necessary in applications. Named kernel objects do allow interprocess communication, but they present security risks because another process (other than those that should use the named process) can interact with the kernel object should it discover the object's name. Setting either of these options forces the operating system to assign a System Access Control List (SACL) to the named objects so that the auditing system can monitor them. The normal use for these settings is to detect and thwart squatting attacks. A problem with these settings is that you normally must reboot the system before the changes you make take effect.

You use these options individually. For example, to obtain the status of the CrashOnAuditFail, you type the command:

```
AuditPol /Get /Option:CrashOnAuditFail
```

Unlike other audit policy settings, options are either enabled or disabled.

Note

The **Get audit options** and **Set audit options** switches are only applicable to audit policy for the **CrashOnAuditFail**, **FullPrivilegeAuditing**, **AuditBaseObjects**, or **AuditBaseDirectories** options. The /Options switch is not applicable to **Auditpol /list.** The /list /v switch displays the GUID with the category or subcategory, or when used with /user, displays the SID of each user. The **/list /r** or **/get /r** switches will display the output as a report in comma-separated value (CSV) format.

3. **Set a policy**: Setting a policy is the act of creating a new entry for the system or a particular user. When you create a new policy, the user or the system as a whole is monitored for the success or failure of certain actions. You can also enable or disable audit options that perform a task based on an audit event (such as crashing the system when someone tries to override the audit system). The following sections describe how to set an audit policy.

    a) **Set audit users:** The AuditPol /Set /User command controls settings made to a specific user. When working with users, you must remember that you can create inclusive settings that add to the system-level settings or exclusive settings that remove auditing from the system-level settings. Audits can affect failures and successes. You can also enable or disable a setting.

For example, to set a user account to add (inclusive) failure auditing to the Object Access category, execute the command:
AuditPol /Set /User:*Username*/Category:"Object Access" /Include /Failure:Enable
where Username is the name of the user.
All user-level settings follow this same pattern. You provide the username, a category or subcategory, whether the setting is inclusive or exclusive, whether the auditing is for a success or failure, and whether the setting is enabled or disabled. As another example, let's say you want to create an exclusion for a user for Logon subcategory auditing for both success and failure. In this case, execute:

AuditPol /Set /User:Username /Subcategory:"Logon" /Exclude
/Failure:Enable /Success:Enable

    b) **Set audit categories:** The AuditPol /Set /Category command controls settings made to the system as a whole. Unlike user-level settings, you simply set the policy to monitor success or failure. There isn't any concept of inclusion or exclusion. For example, to audit Account Logon failures, **execute:**

> Auditpol /set /category:"Account logon" /failure:enable

AuditPol sets all of the subcategories for the entire Account Logon category to audit failures.

    c) **Set audit subcategories:** The AuditPol /Set /Subcategory command controls settings made to the system as a whole, just like the category-level command. However, this command lets you set the individual subcategory entries, rather than an entire category. For example, you might want to failure audit the Credential Validation subcategory of the Account Logon category. To perform this task, execute:

> AuditPol /Set /Subcategory:"Credential Validation" /Failure:Enable

    d) **Set audit options:** The AuditPol /Set /Option command sets the audit policy for the CrashOnAuditFail, FullPrivilegeAuditing, AuditBaseObjects, or AuditBaseDirectories options. You either enable or disable these options. For example, to enable the CrashOnAuditFail option, execute:

> AuditPol /Set /Option:CrashOnAuditFail /Value:Enable

To confirm that CrashOnAuditFail is now enabled, execute:

> AuditPol /get /Option:CrashOnAuditFail

Auditpol command switches

I have outlined a summary of the **Auditpol** command line switches below:
Get: Displays the current auditing policy
Set: Sets the audit policy
List: Displays audit policy categories and subcategories, or lists users for whom a per-user audit policy is defined
Backup: Saves the audit policy to a specified file
Restore: Retrieves the audit policy from a specified file
Clear: Clears the audit policy
Remove: Removes per-user audit policy settings and disables system audit policy settings
Auditpol Subcommands and Options:
User:<username>: Specifies the security principal for a per-user audit. Specify the username by security identifier (SID) or by name. Requires either the /category or /subcategorysubcommand   when   used   with the /set command.
Category:<name>: One or more auditing categories separated by | and specified by name or Globally Unique Identifier (GUID).
Subcategory:<name>: One or more auditing subcategories separated by | and specified by name or GUID.

Success:enable: Enables success auditing when using the /set command.
Success:disable: Disables success auditing when using the /set command.
Failure:enable: Enables failure auditing when using the /set command.
Failure:disable: Disables failure auditing when using the /set command.
File: Specifies the file to which an audit policy is to be backed up, or from which an audit policy is to be restored.

2.4.1 Create expression-based audit policies

Dynamic Access Control (DAC) is a new feature in Windows Server 2012 that enables administrators to granularly control access to filter server resources by using expression-based logic. You can also apply conditional logic to Global Object Access Auditing policy. For instance, you can share a folder that grants access to a group of employees located in a specific region for files that are marked as high-priority. This security access method makes it easier to manage hundreds or thousands of shared folders. DAC allows you to create user and computer claims based on Active Directory schema attributes.

To create User Claims

1. Log on to 70411SRV, and open Server manager.
2. From Server Manager, Tools menu, click Active Directory Administrative Center.
3. Navigate to the Dynamic Access Control node in ADAC; you'll find the following containers:
   a) **Claim Types**: These are user and/or computer property assertions.
   b) **Resource Properties**: These are metadata tags that we apply to shared folders in our infrastructure.
   c) **Resource Property Lists**: These consist of one or more Resource Properties and are the deployable unit to your file servers.
   d) **Central Access Rules**: These are conditional statements that allow or deny access to a shared resource (the access is based upon claims).
   e) **Central Access Policies**: These consist of one or more Central Access Rules and are the deployable unit to your file servers.
4. Click **Dynamic Access Control** node, on the details pane, click **Claim Types** then on the **Task** pane, click **New**, click **Claim Type** on **filter** field, type **loca**, then select l (Lower case "L"), under **Value Type**: string, **ID**: Locality-Name. In the Display Name box, towards the right in the **Display Name** field, type **Location**.
5. Check that **Claim Type** is **User**, and then click **Ok.**
6. Repeat steps 4 and 5 for Department.
7. To specify City and Department for a specific user:
   a) Open Active Directory Users and computers and open a specific user
   b) Click **Address** tab and under City, type **London.**
   c) Click **Organization** tab, under department field, type **Marketing.**

Note

In schema mappings, l is mapped as "City" (The l attribute name is a lowercase "L" as in Locale) while Department is "department".

For full schema mapping details check the link:

http://msdn.microsoft.com/en-us/library/windows/desktop/ms677980(v=vs.85).aspx. For a user in the Marketing department, and located in London, you can apply expression-based audit policies via Dynamic Access Control (DAC). Dynamic Access Control (DAC) give you control to grant access to specific granular level.

Create expression-based audit policies

In the previous section, we created **Location** and **Department** Claim Types. In this section, we will filter audit policy based on a user that lives in London and in Marketing department.

To create expression-based audit policies

1. Log on to 70411SRV and open Server Manager.
2. In Server Manager, point to Tools, and then click Group Policy Management.
3. Expand Forest: 70411Lab.com, then expand Domains, and then expand 70411Lab.com.
4. In the console tree, right-click the **Default Domain Policy** and then click **Edit**. Group policy management editor opens.
5. Navigate to \Computer Configuration\Policies\Windows Settings\Security Settings, and expand Advanced Audit Policy Configuration, then expand **Audit Policies**, highlight **Global Object Access Auditing**, and in the details pane, double-click **File system.**
6. On the **File system Policy setting**, click **Define this policy setting**, then click **Configure**, the Advanced Security Settings for Global File SACL dialog box opens.
7. Click Add, in the Auditing Entry for Global File SACL, then click Set a principal
8. In the window that opens, type **Domain admins** and click **Ok.**
9. Click the **Type** drop-down: You can audit for Failure, All or Success, select Success.
10. Under **Permissions**, examine the permissions you can audit.
11. Click **Add Condition**, on the first drop-down; select **User**, on the next select **Department**, then select **Equals** and **Value** in the next two drop-downs. In the empty field beside **Value**, type **Marketing.**
12. Click **Add Conditions** again, select **User**, on the next select **Location**, then select **Equals** and **Value** in the next two drop-downs. In the empty field beside **Value**, type **London.**
13. When you finish, click **Ok,** twice.

2.4.2 Create removable device audit policies

If you configure this policy setting, an audit event is generated each time a user attempts to copy, move, or save a resource to a removable storage device.

To configure settings to monitor removable storage devices

1. Log on to 70411SRV and open server manager.
2. In Server Manager, point to Tools, and then click Group Policy Management.
3. Expand Forest: 70411Lab.com, then expand Domains, and then expand 70411Lab.com.
4. In the console tree, right-click the **Default Domain Policy** and then click **Edit**. Group policy management editor opens.
5. Navigate to \Computer Configuration\Policies\Windows Settings\Security Settings, and expand Advanced Audit Policy Configuration, then expand **Audit Policies**, highlight **Object Access**, and in the details pane, double-click **Audit Removable Storage.**
6. Select the **Configure the following audit events** check box, select the **Success** check box, and then click **Ok.**
7. If you selected the **Failure** check box, double-click **Audit Handle Manipulation**, select the **Configure the following audit events** check box, and then select **Failure.**
8. Click **Ok**, and then close the Group Policy Management Editor.

Exam Tip

When you enable edit removal storage policy, you have to also enable Audit Handle Manipulation

Chapter 3

Configure Network Services and Access

3.1 Configure DNS Zones

Introduction

Domain Name System (DNS) provides friendly names for computers and network services organized into a hierarchy of domains. DNS naming is used in TCP/IP networks, such as the internet, to locate computers and services with user-friendly names. When a user enters a DNS name in an application, DNS service is designed to resolve the name to other information that is associated with the name, such as an IP address.

For example, computer users prefer a friendly name, such as www.ITechguides.com to locate a computer, such as a mail or Web server, on a network. A friendly name is easier to learn and remember. However, computers communicate over a network by using numeric (IP Address) addresses. To make the use of network resources easier name systems such as DNS, maps the user-friendly name for a computer or service to the computer's numeric address.

The DNS Server role in Windows Server 2012 R2 combines support for standard DNS protocols with the benefits of integration with Active Directory Domain Services (AD DS) and other Windows networking and security features, including such advanced capabilities as secure dynamic update of DNS resource records.

In this section, we will cover following exam objectives:

3.1.0 Configure primary and secondary zones
3.1.1 Configure stub zones
3.1.2 Configure conditional forwards
3.1.3 Configure zone and conditional forward storage in Active Directory
3.1.4 Configure zone delegation
3.1.5 Configure zone transfer settings
3.1.6 Configure notify settings

Lab Plan

We will be using two domain controllers, 70411SRV and 70411SRV2 and a member server, 70411SRV3 in all tasks in this section. Secondary and Stub zone will be created on 70411SRV3. We will also require 70411SRV5 for the zone delegation section.

Additional Lab setup

None

3.1.0 Configure primary and secondary zones

A DNS namespace can be divided into zones. The zones store name information about one or more DNS domains. For each DNS domain name that is included in a zone, the zone becomes the authoritative source for information about that domain. Forward lookup zones provide name-to-address resolution. Reverse lookup zones provide address-to-name resolution. The DNS Server service provides three types of zones: Primary, Secondary and Stub zone. Primary and Secondary zones will be treated in this section. Stub zones will be discussed in section 3.1.1.

Primary zone

If a DNS server hosts a primary zone, the DNS server is the principal source for information about the zone, and it stores the master copy of the zone data in a local file or in Active Directory Domain Service (AD DS). When the zone is stored in a file, the primary zone file is named *zone_name*.dns by default and it is located in the %windir%\System32\Dns folder on the DNS server.

Secondary zone

If a DNS server hosts a secondary zone, the DNS server is a secondary source for information about the zone. The zone at local server must be obtained from a remote DNS server computer that also hosts the zone. The local DNS server must have network access to the remote DNS server that supplies it with updated information about the zone. A secondary zone cannot be stored in AD DS.

To Configure a Primary Zone

1. Log on to 70411SRV and open Server Manager.
2. From Server Manager, click **Tools**, then select **DNS**.
3. In the console tree, right-click 70411SRV, and then click New Zone to open the New Zone Wizard.
4. Follow the instructions below to create a new Primary zone:
   a) On the Welcome screen, click **Next.**
   b) On the Zone type screen, uncheck the box Store the zone in Active Directory, on the zone type, select **Primary Zone**, click **Next.**
   c) On the Forward or Reverse Lookup Zone, select Forward Lookup Zone, click Next.
   d) On the Zone Name field, type **70411primary.com** and click **Next**
   e) On the **Zone File** screen, note the default zone file name - 70411primary.com.dns, click **Next.**
   f) On the **Dynamic Updates** screen, **Do not allow dynamic updates** will be selected by default, (We will treat dynamic updates in section **3.2.4 Configure secure dynamic updates**) click **Next.**
   g) In the final page, click **Finish.**

To Configure a Secondary zone

1. Log on to 70411SRV3 and open Server Manager.
2. From Server Manager, click **Tools**, then select **DNS**.
3. In the console tree, right-click 70411SRV3, and then click **New Zone** to open the New Zone Wizard.
4. Follow the instructions below to create a new Secondary zone:
   a) On the Welcome screen, click **Next.**
   b) On the **Zone type** screen, on the zone type, select **Secondary Zone,** click **Next.**
   c) On the Forward or Reverse Lookup Zone, select Forward Lookup Zone and click Next.
   d) On the **Zone Name** field, type 70411primary.com and click **Next.**
   e) On the **Master DNS Servers type** screen, type the IP address of 70411SRV, 192.168.0.81, ensure the name resolves to **70411SRV.70411Lab.com,** click **Next.**
   f) In the final page, click **Finish.**

3.1.1 Configure stub zones

DNS servers hosting stub zones become source for information about the authoritative name servers for the zone. The DNS server hosting the stub zone must obtain updates from a remote DNS server that hosts the zone. The local DNS server must have a network access to the remote DNS server to copy the authoritative name server information about the zone. A stub zone may be stored in AD DS and may be configured in the following situations:

1. **Keep delegated zone information current**: By updating a stub zone for one of its child zones regularly, the DNS server that hosts both the parent zone and the stub zone will maintain a current list of authoritative DNS servers for the child zone.
2. **Improve name resolution**: Stub zones enable a DNS server to perform recursion using the stub zone's list of name servers, without having to query the Internet or an internal root server for the DNS namespace.
3. **Simplify DNS administration**: By using stub zones throughout your DNS infrastructure, you can distribute a list of the authoritative DNS servers for a zone without using secondary zones. However, stub zones do not serve the same purpose as secondary zones, and they are not an alternative for enhancing redundancy and load sharing.

There are two lists of DNS servers involved in the loading and maintenance of a stub zone:

1. The list of master servers from which the DNS server loads and updates a stub zone. A master server may be a primary or secondary DNS server

for the zone. In both cases, it will have a complete list of the DNS servers for the zone.

2. The list of the authoritative DNS servers for a zone. This list is contained in the stub zone using name server (NS) resource records.

When a DNS server loads a stub zone, such as **70411primary.com**, it queries the master servers, for the necessary resource records of the authoritative servers for the zone. The master server and the server hosting the stub zone may well be in different locations. The list of master servers may contain a single server or multiple servers, and it can be changed anytime.

Note

If the DNS server is also an Active Directory Domain Services (AD DS) domain controller, primary zones and stub zones can be stored in AD DS.

To Configure a stub zone

1. Log on to 70411SRV3 and open Server Manager.
2. From Server Manager, click **Tools** then select **DNS**.
3. In the console tree, right-click 70411SRV3, and then click **New Zone** to open the New Zone Wizard.
4. Follow the instructions below to create a new stub zone:
   a) On the Welcome screen, click **Next**.
   b) On the **Zone type** screen, on the zone type, select **Stub Zone,** click **Next.**
   c) On the Forward or Reverse Lookup Zone, select Forward Lookup Zone, and click **Next**.
   d) On the Zone Name field, type **70411Lab.com** and click **Next**.
   e) On the **Zone File** screen, click **Next**.
   f) On the **Master DNS Servers type** screen, type the IP address of 70411SRV, 192.168.0.81, ensure the name resolves to 70411SRV.70411Lab.com then click **Next**.
   g) In the final page, click **Finish.**
5. View details of the new zone created. Note the content of the stub zone:
   a) Name servers: 70411SRV, 70411SRV2 and 70411SRV4.
   b) Start of Authority Server: 70411SRV.70411Lab.com.
   c) Host (A) records.

Note

When creating a secondary or stub zone, the zone name MUST be the name of one of the zones on the primary server. Makes logical sense as a secondary or stub zone updates records from a primary DNS server.

3.1.2 Configure conditional forwards

A DNS server on one network may be configured to forward queries to a DNS server on another network without having to query DNS servers on the Internet. A Forwarder is another DNS server that a given DNS server may use to resolve DNS queries for records that it cannot resolve. Conditional forwarding is used to control where a DNS server forwards queries for a specific domain. Use of conditional forwarders reduces recursive DNS traffic. If a DNS server does not have the requested information when it receives a recursive query, it queries other servers until it gets the information, or until the name query fails.

Note
___
Forwarders are configured from the Properties page, Forwarders tab while Conditional Forwarders are configured from the Conditional Forwarders node of the DNS console. If Conditional Forwarders Are defined for a given domain, they will be used instead of server-level forwarders.
___

To Configure conditional forwards

1. Log on to 70411SRV and open Server Manager.
2. From Server Manager, click **Tools** then select **DNS**.
3. In the console tree, expand 70411SRV and then right-click **Conditional Forwarders** and select **New Conditional Forwarder**.
4. On the **New Conditional Forwarder** screen, complete the following:
    a) On the DNS Domain, type forward.70411Lab.com.
    b) Below IP Address of the Master Servers, type the IP address of your ADSL router.
    c) Note that you can store the Conditional Forwarder in Active Directory (We will perform this task in the next section).
    d) Also Note the default time out of 5 seconds.
    e) When you finish, click **Ok**.

3.1.3 Configure zone and conditional forward storage in Active Directory

In section 3.1.0 and 3.1.1, we discussed zone types and configured Primary, secondary and stub zones. Zones and conditional forwarders may be stored in active Directory (AD). Zones stored in AD are called Active-Directory-Integrated zones. AD-integrated zones and conditional forwarders may be configured to replicate to all domain controllers. Considering the multi-master functionality of AD, apparently this will provide some added benefits: improved security, multi-master replication, and secure dynamic update.

To Configure Active Directory Integrated Zone

1. Log on to 70411SRV and open Server Manager.

2. From Server Manager, click **Tools** then select **DNS**.
3. In the console tree, right-click 70411SRV, and then click **New Zone** to open the New Zone Wizard.
4. Follow the instructions below to create a Primary forward lookup zone:
    a) On the Welcome screen, click **Next**.
    b) On the **Zone type** screen, check the box **Store the zone in Active Directory**, and on the **Zone type**, select **Primary Zone**, then click **Next**.
    c) On the **Active Directory Zone Replication Type** screen, accept the default and click **Next**.
    d) On the Forward or Reverse Lookup Zone screen, select Forward Lookup Zone, then click Next.
    e) On the Zone Name field, type 70411ADInt.com and click **Next**.
    f) On the Dynamic Updates screen, select Allow only secure Dynamic updates (Recommended for Active Directory) and click Next.
    g) In the final page, click **Finish**.

Note

A primary zone does not have a security tab, but an AD-integrated zone does. An AD-integrated Conditional Forwarder also has a Security tab. Secure dynamic updates is available for an AD-integrated zone. This allows domain computers to dynamically update their DNS records securely.

To Configure Active Directory Integrated Conditional Forwarder

1. Log on to 70411SRV and open Server Manager.
2. From Server Manager, click **Tools** then select **DNS**.
3. In the console tree, expand 70411SRV and then right-click **Conditional Forwarders** then select **New Conditional Forwarder**. The **New Conditional Forwarder** wizard opens.
4. On the **New Conditional Forwarder** wizard, complete the following:
    a) On the DNS Domain, type 70411FWD1.com.
    b) Below IP Address of the Master Servers, type the IP address of your ADSL router.
    c) Check the box Store this Conditional Forwarder in Active Directory, and replicate as follows:
        i)   From the drop-down list, select **All DNS Servers in this domain**.
        ii) When you finish, click **Ok**.

Create a DNS Application Directory Partition

Domain Name System (DNS) zones can either be stored in a domain or an application directory partition of Active Directory Domain Services (AD DS).

A partition is a data structure in AD DS that distinguishes data for different replication purposes. When you create an application directory partition for DNS, you can control the scope of replication for the zone that is stored in that partition. For example, to store an AD-integrated DNS zone on specific Domain Controllers, you will create an application directory partition, add the DCs in the partition and replicate the zone to the application directory partition. Application directory partition is created using dnscmd command line utility or PowerShell.

To Create a DNS Application Directory Partition

1. Log on to 70411SRV and open an elevated command prompt.
2. At the command prompt, execute the command below:

```
dnscmd 70411srv2.70411lab.com /createdirectorypartition
london.70411Lab.com
```

3. To enlist a DNS server to the london.70411Lab.com application directory partition:

```
dnscmd 70411srv.70411lab.com /EnlistDirectoryPartition
london.70411Lab.com
```

Exam Tip

It is very important to note that if you need to replicate an AD-integrated zone to some and not all DNS servers, you will create an application directory partition. Also note the syntax: dnscmd <ServerName> /CreateDirectoryPartition <FQDN>. Application Directory Partition can also be created using the **Add-DnsServerDirectoryPartition** cmdlet.

3.1.4 Configure zone delegation

When you install a child domain in an existing domain, DNS delegation records point to the child DNS server as authoritative for the child zone. The zone delegation records should be created in the parent Domain Name System (DNS) zone. Delegation records transfer name resolution authority and provide correct referral to the child DNS servers and clients of the new servers that are being made authoritative for the new zone. The resource records applicable to zone delegation are listed below:

A Name Server (NS) resource record to effect the delegation. - This resource record advertises that the server named in the NS resource record is an authoritative server for the delegated subdomain.

A host (A or AAAA) resource record - also known as a glue record - must be present to resolve the name of the server that is specified in the Name Server (NS) resource record to its IP address. The process of resolving the host name in this resource record to the delegated DNS server in the name server (NS) resource record is sometimes referred to as "glue chasing."

When performing post-Active Directory installation actions, the Active Directory Domain Services Configuration Wizard can create the records specified above automatically. The wizard verifies that the appropriate records exist in the parent DNS zone after you click **Next** on the Domain Controller Options page. If the wizard cannot verify that the records exist in the parent domain, the wizard provides you with the option to create a new DNS delegation for a new domain (or update the existing delegation) automatically and continues with the new domain controller installation. Alternatively, you can create these DNS delegation records before you install DNS server.

To Configure zone delegation

1. On 70411SRV5, install Active Directory Domain Services.
2. On 70411SRV5, create a new child domain, 70411child.70411Lab.com with the steps outlined below:
   a) After installing Active Directory, from Server Manager, click the yellow triangle with black exclamation mark, and click **Promote this server to a domain controller.**
   b) On the **Deployment Configuration** screen, complete the following tasks:
      i) Under Select Deployment operation, select add a new domain to an existing forest.
      ii) Under **Select a domain type**, select **child domain** from the drop down list.
      iii) On the Parent domain name field, enter 70411Lab.com.
      iv) On the New domain name field, enter 70411child.
      v) Beside Supply the credential to perform this operation, click change and complete the following tasks:
         (1) On   the   **username**   field   type 70411lab\<your_domain_admin_account>
         (2) On the **password** filed, type your domain password
      vi) When you complete the tasks, click **Ok**.
   c) On the Deployment Configuration screen, click Next.
   d) On the **Domain Controller Options** screen, accept all defaults presentation, enter a Directory Services Restore Mode password and click **Next**.
   e) On the DNS Options screen, check Create DNS Delegation and click Next.

f)   On the **Additional Options** screen, click **Next**.

g)   On the Paths and Review Options screens, click Next.

h)   On the **Prerequisite check** screen, click **Install**. (This will take a while to complete, continue with the next section)

3.   Configure DNS on 70411SRV5 to point to 192.168.0.81.

4.   On 70411SRV, create a delegation to 70411child.70411Lab.com with 70411SRV5 as authoritative.

5.   Test that the delegation works by completing the tasks below:

a)   Open command prompt and execute:

```
nslookup 70411child.70411Lab.com
```

b)   The command should return 70411SRV5 as non-authoritative for the 70411child.70411Lab.com domain.

Review Delegation Configuration outcome

In the previous task, we deployed a child domain in the 70411Lab.com domain and made 7041SRV5 DNS server authoritative for the child domain. The active directory wizard performed the operation and created the following DNS entries:

1.   An Active Directory-Integrated DNS zone,70411child.70411Lab.com created on 70411srv5 with the following resource records:

70411child.70411Lab.com	NS	70411SRV5.70411child.70411Lab.com
70411SRV5.70411child.70411Lab.com	A	192.168.0.37

2.   A delegated DNS zone, 70411child.70411lab.com is created on 70411SRV with the following resource records:

70411child.70411Lab.com	NS	70411SRV5.70411child.70411Lab.com

3.1.5 Configure zone transfer settings

Zone Transfer is the process by which the contents of a DNS Zone file are copied from a primary DNS server to a secondary DNS server. A Zone transfer may occur in any of the following situations:

1.   When starting the DNS Service on the secondary DNS server.

2.   When a zone refresh time expires.

3.   When changes are saved to the Primary Zone file with a Notify List.

Zone Transfers are always initiated by the secondary DNS server. The primary DNS server simply answers the request for a Zone Transfer.

To Configure zone transfer settings

1.   Log on to 70411SRV3 and open DNS Manager.

2. From the console tree, expand **70411SRV3**, and expand **Forward Lookup zones**.
3. Click **70411primary.com** zone and on the details pane, confirm that the zone returns an error message.
4. Now Log on to 70411SRV and open DNS Manager.
5. From the console tree, expand **70411SRV**, and expand **Forward Lookup zones**.
6. Right-click **70411primary.com** zone and select **Properties**.
7. Click **Zone Transfers** tab and perform the following tasks:
   a) Confirm that **Allow zone transfer** is checked.
   b) Select the option **To any server.**
   c) Click **Notify** and ensure that **automatically notify** box is checked, then click **select the following servers.** On the window that opens, complete the following tasks:
      i) Enter the IP address 192.168.0.34 and ensure it resolves to 70411SRV3.
      ii) Click **Ok.**
   d) On the 70411primary.com properties, click **Ok**.
8. Log on 70411SRV3 and confirm that 70411primary.com zone loads successfully.

3.1.6 Configure notify settings

Zone **Notify setting** determines zone transfer from primary to secondary DNS servers. When zone transfer is enabled on a primary DNS server, secondary servers that need to be notified of a zone update will be listed. As noted in the previous section, zone transfer is triggered when changes are made on a Primary Zone file with **Notify List** populated. We included notify configuration in the previous section.

3.2 Configure DNS Records

Introduction

DNS zones maintain certain records about resources (such as hosts). A typical resource record consists of the name (host) of the resource record owner, information about how long the resource record can remain in the DNS cache, the resource record type (such as a host (A) resource record), and data that is specific to the record type (such as the host's address). Resource records may be added manually or automatically. Records are added automatically when a Windows-based, Dynamic Host Configuration Protocol (DHCP)-enabled client updates its IP address (dynamic update) with the DNS server. On the other hand, manual update may be done when an administrator creates a resource record for a server.

In this section, we will cover following exam objectives:

3.2.0 Create and configure DNS Resource Records (RR)
3.2.1 Configure zone scavenging
3.2.2 Configure record options including Time To Live (TTL) and weight
3.2.3 Configure round robin
3.2.4 Configure secure dynamic updates

Lab Plan

We will use the same lab plan in section 3.1

Additional Lab setup.

None

3.2.0 Create and configure DNS Resource Records (RR)

DNS Server in Windows Server 2012 R2 supports various resource records including A, AAAA, PTR, SOA, NS, SRV, CNAME, and MX records.

Configure Host (A) and Host (AAAA) records

Host (A) resource records in a zone associates DNS domain names of computers (or hosts) to their IP addresses. Host (A) resource records are added to a zone in several ways:

1. Manually create a host (A) resource record for a static TCP/IP client computer by using DNS Manager.
2. A DHCP-enabled Windows Client dynamically registers and updates its host (A) resource record when an IP configuration change occurs.

To Configure Host (A) and Host (AAAA) records

1. Log on to 70411SRV and open DNS Manager.
2. Right-click **70411Lab.com** zone point to New Host (A or AAAA), the **New Host record** window opens.
3. On the **name** field, type **HostAtest** (Note the FQDN as HostAtest.70411Lab.com)
4. On the IP address field, type 192.168.0.222 (Or any IP address you wish) - You may create a PTR record at the same time by checking the box **Create associated pointer (PTR) record**.

Note

Host (A) and Host (AAAA) records are created with the same procedure. The difference is that a Host (A) record points to an IPv4 address but a Host (AAAA) record point to an IPv6 address.

5. When you are done, click **Add Host**.
6. To test your configuration:
    a) Open command prompt and execute:

nslookup

    b) At the nslookup prompt, execute:

HostAtest

    c) Nsloopup will return Name: HostAtest.70411Lab.com, and Address: 192.168.0.222

Configure Alias (CNAME) resource record

Alias (CNAME) resource records are also sometimes called canonical name resource records. Multiple CNAMEs may be configured to point to a single host. This makes it possible to host both a File Transfer Protocol (FTP) server and a Web server on the same computer.

CNAME resource records may be used in the following scenarios:

1. When a host that is specified in a host (A) resource record in the same zone must be renamed.
2. When a generic name for a well-known server, such as www, must resolve to a group of individual computers (each with individual host (A) resource records) that provide the same service, for example, in a group of redundant Web servers.

Canonical names may also come in handy when an existing host (A) resource record in a zone is renamed. In this situation, a CNAME name resource record will be configured temporarily to allow a grace period for users and programs to switch from the old computer name to the new one, as follows:

1. For the new DNS domain name of the computer, add a new host (A) resource record to the zone.
2. For the old DNS domain name, add an alias (CNAME) resource record that points to the new host (A) resource record.
3. After the grace period, remove the original host (A) resource record for the old DNS domain name (and its associated pointer (PTR) resource record, if applicable) from the zone.

When you use an alias (CNAME) resource record for renaming a computer it is recommended to set a limit on how long the record should be used in the zone before removing it from DNS. The option to set a delete time becomes visible when the **advanced view** is enabled in DNS Management console. This is necessary because when the associated host (A) record becomes unavailable but clients still try to query the CNAME, it could lead to waste of server resources when clients try to resolve queries for a name that is no longer used on the network.

Alias (CNAME) resource record is commonly used to provide a permanent DNS aliased domain name for generic name resolution of a service-based name (such as www.targg.com) to a computer or an IP address on a Web server. The following example shows the basic syntax of an alias (CNAME) resource record:

```
alias_name IN CNAME primary_canonical_name
```

For example, if a computer named client-1.targg.com functions as both a web server named www.targg.com and as an FTP server named ftp.targg.com; to achieve the intended objective of naming the computer, add the following CNAME entries in the targg.com DNS zone:

```
client-1  IN  A          10.0.0.20
ftp       IN  CNAME      client-1
www       IN  CNAME      client-1
```

If you later decide to move the FTP service to another computer, simply change the alias (CNAME) resource record in the zone for ftp.targg.com and add an additional host (A) resource record to the zone for the new computer hosting the FTP server. If the new computer is client-2.targg.com, the new and revised host (A) and alias (CNAME) resource records appear as follows:

```
client-1  IN  A          10.0.0.20
client-2  IN  A          10.0.0.21
ftp       IN  CNAME      client-2
www       IN  CNAME      client-1
```

To configure Alias (CNAME) resource record

1. Still logged on to 70411SRV, and on DNS Management console.
2. Right-click **70411Lab.com** zone point to **New Alias (CNAME)**, the New Resource Record window opens.
3. On the **Name** field, type www (Note the FQDN appear as www.70411Lab.com)
4. On the Fully Qualified domain (FQDN) name for target host, click Browse.
5. Double-click **70411SRV**, Double-click **Forward Lookup Zones**, Double-click **70411Lab.com**, then finally highlight **70411SRV1** and click **Ok**.
6. On the New Resource Record window, click **Ok**.

Configure Mail exchanger (MX) resource record

E-mail applications use the mail exchanger (MX) resource record to locate a mail server based on a DNS domain name in the destination address for the email recipient of a message. The mail exchanger (MX) resource record shows the DNS domain name for the computer or computers that process email for a domain. If multiple mail exchanger (MX) resource records exist, the DNS Client service attempts to contact mail servers in the order of preference from lowest value number (highest priority) to highest value number (lowest priority). The following example shows the basic syntax of a mail exchanger (MX) resource record:

```
mail_domain_name IN MX preferencemailserver_host
```

For example assuming the MX resource record for 70411lab.com zone is configured as shown below, an email sent to Admin@70411lab.com is delivered to Admin@70411SRV1.70411lab.com first. If 70411SRV1 is not available, the resolver client will try to deliver the mail to Admin@70411SRV2.70411lab.com instead.

```
@    IN MX  1  70411SRV1
@    IN MX  2  70411SRV2
```

Note

The use of the "at" sign (@) in the records indicates that the mailer DNS domain name is the same as the name of origin (70411lab.com) for the zone.

To configure Mail exchanger (MX) resource record

1. Still logged on to 70411SRV, and DNS Management console
2. Right-click 70411Lab.com zone point to New Mail Exchanger (MX), the New Resource Record window opens.
3. Leave the Host or Child domain field blank
4. On the Fully Qualified domain (FQDN) name for target host field type, 70411SRV1.70411Lab.com.
5. On the Mail server priority field, type 1, click Ok, to add your record.
6. Repeat steps 2-5 to add 70411SRV2.70411Lab.com with a priority of 2

Configure Service location (SRV) resource record

Service (SRV) record allows administrators to use several servers to easily move a TCP/IP service from a host to another host. SRV records are also capable of designating some hosts as primary servers for a service and other hosts as backup servers for the same service. DNS clients that use an SRV-type query request for a specific TCP/IP service mapped to a specific DNS domain receives the names of available servers for the service queried.

Service location (SRV) resource records are required for clients to locate Active Directory domain controllers. The Active Directory Domain Services (AD DS) installation wizard, by default attempts to locate a DNS server based on the list of preferred or alternate DNS servers configured in any of the server's TCP/IP client properties, for any of the server's active network connections. During this query process, when a DNS server that accepts dynamic update of the service location (SRV) resource record is contacted, the AD DS configuration process is complete. (This is also true for other resource records that are related to registering AD DS as a service in DNS.)

Continuing with the example above, if during the installation, a DNS server that accepts updates for the DNS domain name that is used to name your directory is not found; the wizard can install a DNS server locally and automatically configure it with a zone to support the Active Directory domain. For example, if the Active Directory domain that you choose for your first domain in the forest is example.targg.com, you can add and configure a zone that is rooted at the DNS domain name of example.targg.com to use with the DNS server that is running on the new domain controller.

To configure Service location (SRV) resource record

1. Still logged on to 70411SRV, and DNS Management console,
2. Right-click 70411primary.com zone and point to **Other New records**. The **Resource Record type** window opens.
3. On the list, locate Service Location (SRV), and click Create record.
4. On the **Service** drop-down, note the different services: _finger, _ftp, _http, _kerberos, _ldap, _msdcs, _nntp, _telnet, and _whois. Select _ftp.
5. On the **Protocol** drop-down, note the protocols: _tcp or _udp, select, _tcp.
6. Set the following:
   a) Priority: 1
   b) Weight: 0
   c) Port number: accept default.
   d) Host offering this service: Enter **70411SRV3**.
7. When you finish, click **Ok**.

The **priority** field determines the precedence of use of the record's data. Clients always use the SRV record with the lowest-numbered priority value first, and fallback to other records of equal or higher value if the connection to the host with higher priority fails. If a service has multiple SRV records with the same **priority** value, clients use the **weight** field to determine which host to use.

The weight value is relevant in relation to other weight values for the service, and among records with the same priority value. The host with a higher weight will be used more in relation to other hosts. For example, if we configure two hosts, **host1** and **host2** with the same priority, but designate a weight of 60 for host1 and 40 for host2, host1 will be used 60% of the time while host2 will be used 40% of the time.

Other resource records

There are other resource records supported by Windows Server 2012 R2 DNS but used less frequently in most zones. You can add these additional types of resource records as necessary with DNS Manager.

3.2.1 Configure zone scavenging

Resource records may be configured to have time stamps. As discussed earlier, when you enable advanced view in DNS console, every zone record will show an option to enable a time stamp. When the **Delete this record when it becomes stale** is enabled and a time stamp is recorded, the record is deleted in accordance with the **Aging/Scavenging** configuration for the zone.

Aging and **Scavenging** is especially useful for preventing the accumulation of invalid records when resource records are automatically created, as with dynamic update. Scavenging can be configured at Server or zone level. For aging and scavenging to function correctly, the following prerequisites must be met:

1. Scavenging and aging must be enabled, both at the DNS server and on the zone. By default, aging and scavenging of resource records is disabled.
2. Resource records must either be dynamically added to zones or manually modified to be used in aging and scavenging operations: Typically, only those resource records that are added dynamically using the DNS dynamic update protocol are subject to aging and scavenging. You can, however, enable scavenging for other resource records that are added through non-dynamic means. For records that are added to zones in this way, either by loading a text-based zone file from another DNS server or by manually adding them to a zone, a time stamp of zero is set. This makes these records ineligible for use in aging and scavenging operations. To change this default, you can administer these records individually, to reset and permit them to use a current (nonzero) time-stamp value. This makes it possible for these records to become aged and scavenged.

To Configure scavenging for all zones

1. Log on to 70411SRV and open DNS Manager.
2. In the console tree, right-click **70411SRV** and select **Set Aging/Scavenging for all Zones**. This opens the **Server Aging/Scavenging** Properties.
3. Click **Scavenge stale records** check box and set the following:
    a) **No-refresh interval**: The time between the most recent refresh of a record timestamp and the moment when the timestamp may be refreshed again.

    b) **Refresh interval**: The time between the earliest moment when the record timestamp can be refreshed and the earliest moment when the record can be scavenged. The refresh interval must be longer than maximum record refresh period. Server default for both is 7 days.

4. When done, click **Ok**.
5. A dialogue box appears asking whether you want to apply the settings to the existing Active Directory-Integrated zones, check the box and click **Ok**.

Aging and scavenging properties configured with the procedure above act as server defaults that apply only to Active Directory Domain Services (AD DS)-integrated zones. For standard primary zones, you must set the appropriate properties at the applicable zone.

When you apply changes for server aging and scavenging settings, DNS Manager prompts you to confirm the changes. You then have the option to apply your changes to new AD DS-integrated zones only. If necessary, you can also apply your changes to existing AD DS-integrated zones. Server scavenging can also be configured from the **Advanced** tab of the **Properties** sheet of the DNS server.

To Confirm scavenging configuration of existing AD-Integrated zones

1. Log on to 70411SRV and open DNS Manager.
2. Right-click **70411Lab.com** zone, and click **Refresh**.
3. Right-click **70411Lab.com** zone, and click **Properties**.
4. Beside To set aging/scavenging properties, click Aging, click Aging. The Zone Aging/Scavenging properties opens.
5. Confirm that the check box **Scavenge stale records** is selected and click **cancel**.

To Configure scavenging for a zone

1. Log on to 70411SRV and open DNS Manager.
2. Right-click 70411primary.com zone, and click **Properties**.
3. On the General tab, click The Zone Aging/Scavenging properties opens.
4. Click **Scavenge stale records** check box and click **Ok**.
5. Respond **Yes** to the warning message.

Note

When you enable Aging on a Standard primary DNS zone, the zone transfers to secondary servers will not be affected.

To enable automatic scavenging of stale records.

1. Log on to 70411SRV and open DNS Manager.
2. Right-click 70411SRV and click Properties, on the properties sheet, click **Advanced** tab.
3. Check the check box Enable automatic scavenging of all stale records.
4. Accept the default scavenging period and click **Ok**.

Configure scavenging of zone records.

DNS zone resource records created by dynamic updates will be configured automatically for scavenging if scavenging is enabled for an AD-Integrated zone. But when you add resource records manually, it does not have a time-stamp and is not configured for automatic scavenging. This feature have to be configured manually. To configure this option, including TTL, open DNS management console, click **View,** then select **Advanced.**

To configure scavenging of zone records

1. Log on to 70411SRV and open DNS Manager.
2. Click **View** then select **Advanced** to enable advanced features.
3. Expand 70411SRV, then expand **Forward look up zones** and highlight 70411Lab.com zone.
4. In the details pane, double-click www (or any resource record created manually), in the record properties page, **General** tab, check the box **Delete this record when it becomes stale** and click **Ok**.
5. Double-click the www record and confirm that it now has a time stamp, then click **Cancel**.

3.2.2 Configure record options including Time To Live (TTL) and weight

Zone records like Host (A), NS and MX have some options like TTL and weight. All records have TTL, and scavenging options, while some records like MX and SRV have additional options like priority and weight. The following options are configured on the zone:

1. **Refresh interval**: Determines how often other DNS servers that load and host a zone must attempt to renew the zone. Default in Windows Server 2012 R2 is 15 minutes.
2. **Retry interval**: Determines how often other DNS servers that load and host a zone are to retry a request for update of the zone each time that the refresh interval occurs. Default in Windows Server 2012 R2 is 10 minutes.
3. **Expire interval**: Used by other DNS servers that are configured to load and host the zone to determine when zone data expires if it is not renewed. Default in Windows Server 2012 R2 is 1 day.

4. **Time To Live (TTL):** Time to Live is used by name servers and some DNS clients to determine the length of time that a name must be cached. This dictates how long it will be until the computer refreshes its DNS related information.

5. **Minimum (Default) TTL:** This is the minimum default TTL that all zone records will be configured to use when created.

The following options are specific to SRV records:

1. **Priority:** If more than one DNS server provides a service, it becomes necessary to specify priority in the SRV record so that clients requesting the service will know how to prioritize request. This is defined as the relative Priority of this service (range 0 - 65535). Lowest number is highest priority.

2. **Weight:** Used when more than one service with same priority exist. A value of "0" indicates no weighting should be applied. If the weight is 1 or greater it is a relative number in which the highest is most frequently delivered. For example, if two SRV records have 0 priority set, but one has a weight of 1 while other has a weight of 6, the record with weight 6 will have its RR delivered first 6 times out of 7 (85%) by the name server.

Priority and weight are used for load balancing.

Note

MX (Mail exchanger) records have priority option as well. One technique used to balance load among an array of mail servers is to configure them with the same priority.

To configure zone and Resource Record options

1. Log on to 70411SRV and open DNS Manager.
2. Expand 70411SRV, then expand **Forward look up zones**, then right-click **70411Lab.com** zone and select **Properties**.
3. Select the **Start of Authority** tab, and review the default values for **Refresh**, **Retry** and **Expire** intervals. Examine TTL and Minimum (Default) TTL as well. Click **Cancel**.
4. To configure priority for Mail Exchanger record, follow the procedure below:
   a) On the left pane, highlight 70411lab.com zone.
   b) On the details pane, double-click MX (Mail Exchanger) resource record for 70411SRV1. Confirm that the priority is 1.
   c) Perform the same task for the click MX (Mail Exchanger) resource record for 70411SRV2 and confirm that the priority is set to 2.
5. To configure priority and weight for SRV:
   a) Expand 70411primary.com zone and highlight **_tcp**.

b)   In the details pane, double-click **_ftp** on 70411SRV3 and confirm that the priority is 1 while weight is 1. Click **Cancel**.

c)   In the details pane, double-click **_ftp** on 70411SRV4 and confirm that the priority is 1 while weight is 2. Click **Cancel**.

3.2.3 Configure round robin

Round robin is a local balancing mechanism used by DNS servers to share and distribute network resource loads. You can use it to rotate all resource record types contained in a query answer if multiple resource records are found.

By default, DNS uses round robin to rotate the order of resource record data returned in query answers where multiple resource records of the same type exist for a queried DNS domain name. This feature provides a simple method to load-balance client use of Web servers and other frequently queried multi-homed computers.

If round robin is disabled for a DNS server, the order of the response for these queries is based on a static ordering of resource records in the answer list stored in the zone file or Active Directory.

To Configure Round Robin

1.   Log on to 70411SRV and open DNS Manager.
2.   Right-click 70411SRV and click Properties.
3.   Click **Advanced** tab and confirm **that Enable round robin** box is checked.

Restrict Round Robin rotation for selected RR types

DNS will complete round-robin rotation for all resource record types by default. However, certain resource record types may be excluded from round-robin rotation. This setting is configured in the registry. The registry entry is called **DoNotRoundRobinTypes** (REG_SZ) with a string value containing a list of resource record types.

Round-robin rotation for specific resource record types is turned off by modifying the **DoNotRoundRobinTypes** registry entry. For example, to prevent round-robin rotation for A, PTR, SRV, and NS record types, you should enter the following value for the **DoNotRoundRobinTypes** registry entry: **A PTR SRV NS.**

In the next task, you will configure this option for all domain controllers via group policy. In the first part of the task, you will create two registry keys:

DoNotRoundRobinTypes (REG_SZ): This registry key contains the list of resource records to be prevented from round robin rotation.

RoundRobin (REG_DWORD): If this key is set to 1, round robin rotation will be enabled for all resource record types excluding those listed in the **DoNotRoundRobinTypes** registry entry.

To Restrict Round Robin rotation for selected RR types

1. Log on to 70411SRV and open registry editor.
2. Navigate to Navigate to:
   KEY_LOCAL_MACHINE\System\CurrentControlSet\Services\DNS\
   Parameters and complete the following:
   a) Right-click **Parameters**, point to **New**, select **QWORD** (64-bit) value. Rename the QWORD to **RoundRobin**.
   b) Double-click **RoundRobin** key, and under value **data**, enter 1 then click **Ok**.
   c) Right-click **Parameters**, point to **New**, select **String Value**. Rename the new string value to **DoNotRoundRobinTypes**. Double-click **DoNotRoundRobinTypes** and enter the values **A PTR**
3. Still logged on to 70411SRV, open Group Policy Management.
4. Navigate to the **Default Domain Controllers** container and expand it.
5. Right-click **Default Domain Controllers Policy** and select **Edit**. The Group policy management editor opens.
6. Navigate Computer Configuration\Preferences\Windows Settings\, then right-click **Registry**, point to **New** and select **Registry wizard**. The Registry Browser opens, select **Local Computer** and click **Next**.
7. Navigate to:
   HKEY_LOCAL_MACHINE\System\CurrentControlSet\Services\DNS\, highlight Parameters, on the details pane, below check **RoundRobin** and **DoNotRoundRobinTypes** and click **Finish**.
8. Log on to 70411SRV2 and complete the following tasks:
9. Open a command prompt and type **gpupdate /force** to update group policy.
10. Navigate to:
    HKEY_LOCAL_MACHINE\System\CurrentControlSet\Services\DNS\, highlight Parameters, on the details pane, and confirm that **RoundRobin** and **DoNotRoundRobinTypes** registry values exist.

3.2.4 Configure secure dynamic updates

Domain Name System (DNS) client computers may use dynamic update to register and dynamically update their resource records with a DNS server whenever changes occur. This reduces the need for manual administration of zone records, especially for clients that frequently move or change locations and use Dynamic Host Configuration Protocol (DHCP) to obtain an IP address.

DNS update security is available only for zones that are integrated into AD DS. When you directory-integrate a zone, access control list (ACL) editing feature becomes available in DNS Manager so that you can add or remove users or groups from the ACL for a specified zone or resource record. Dynamic update security for DNS servers and clients can be handled as follows:

1. DNS clients attempt to use unsecured dynamic update first. If an unsecured update is refused, clients try to use secure update. Also, clients use a default update policy that permits them to attempt to overwrite a previously registered resource record, unless they are specifically blocked by update security.
2. After a zone become AD DS-integrated, DNS servers running Windows Server 2012 R2 default to allowing only secure dynamic updates. When you use standard zone storage, the default for the DNS Server service is to not allow dynamic updates on its zones. For zones that are either directory-integrated or that use standard file-based storage, you can change the zone to allow all dynamic updates. This permits all updates to be accepted.

To configure secure dynamic updates

1. Log on to 70411SRV and open DNS Manager.
2. In the console tree, expand **70411SRV**, then expand **Forward Lookup Zones,**
3. To confirm that you cannot configure **Secure dynamic update** for non-AD-integrated zone:
    a) Right-click **70411primary.com** zone and select **Properties.**
    b) In **Dynamic Updates** drop down, confirm that only **Nonsecure** option is available.
    c) Click **Cancel**.
4. To configure Secure Dynamic update for an AD-integrated zone:
    a) Right-click **70411Lab.com** zone and select **Properties.**
    b) In **Dynamic Updates** drop down, confirm that **Secure only** and **Nonsecure** options are available.
    c) Select **Secure only** if it is not selected and click **Ok.**

3.3 Configure VPN and Routing

Introduction

A router is a device that manages the flow of data among network segments, or subnets. A router directs incoming and outgoing packets based on the information about the state of the router's own network interfaces and a list of possible sources and destinations for network traffic. Network traffic and routing needs may be determined based on the number and types of hardware devices and applications used in your environment. When you have decided your Network traffic and routing needs, you can better decide whether to use a dedicated hardware router, a software-based router, or a combination of both. Generally, dedicated hardware routers handle heavier routing demands best, and less expensive software-based routers handle lighter routing loads.

A software-based routing solution, such as RRAS in Windows Server 2012 R2, could be ideal on a small, segmented network with relatively light traffic between subnets. Enterprise network environments that have many network segments and a wide range of performance requirements might need a variety of hardware-based routers to perform different roles throughout the network.

When you configure Remote Access on a server, the server can act as a remote access server that accepts connections from remote or mobile workers to your organization's networks. Remote users can work as if their computers are directly connected to the network. All services typically available to a directly connected user (including file and printer sharing, Web server access, and messaging) are enabled with the remote access connection.

For example, on a Remote Access server, clients can use File Explorer to make drive connections and to connect to printers. Since drive letters and universal naming convention (UNC) names are fully supported by remote access, most commercial and custom applications work without modification. A Remote Access server provides two different types of remote access connectivity:

1. **Virtual private networking**: A virtual private network (VPN) is a secured, point-to-point connection across a public network, such as the Internet. A VPN client uses special TCP/IP-based protocols called tunneling protocols to make a connection to a port on a remote VPN server. The VPN server accepts the connection, authenticates the connecting user and computer, and then transfers data between the VPN client and the corporate network. It is important to encrypt data sent over the connection to ensure privacy because the data traverses a public network.

2. **Dial-up networking**: In dial-up networking, a remote access client makes a dial-up telephone connection to a physical port on a remote access server by using the service of a telecommunications provider, such as analog telephone or ISDN. Dial-up networking over an analog phone or ISDN is a direct physical connection between the dial-up networking client and the dial-up networking server. Data sent over the connection may be encrypted, but it is not required because the phone line is typically considered secure.

In this section, we will cover following exam objectives:

3.3.0 Install and configure the Remote Access role

3.3.1 Implement Network Address Translation (NAT)

3.3.2 Configure VPN settings

3.3.3 Configure remote dial-in settings for users

3.3.4 Configure routing

3.3.5 Configure Web Application proxy in pass-through mode (2012 R2 Objective)

Lab Plan

We will use 70411SRV3 for this lab. This server will be used in the Network Policy Server section as a Network Access Server (NAS). It is very important that you complete this section.

Additional Lab setup.

Create a second Virtual switch

1. From Hyper-V Manager, rename the current Virtual Switch to "InternetLAN" (The External VLAN with access to the internet).
2. Create a second Virtual Switch, "InternalLAN", (This VLAN will be internal only with no access to the internet).
3. Create a second NIC on 70411SRV3, ensure that the first NIC is connected to "InternetLAN" (the External VLAN) and the second NIC is connected to "InternalLAN".
4. Boot 70411SRV3 and rename the NICs "Ethernet" to "InternetLAN" and "Ethernet 2 " to "InternalLAN". Follow the steps below to complete the task:
   a) Open Control Panel
   b) Under Network and Internet, click View network status and tasks. Network and Sharing Center window opens.
   c) On the left pane of Network and Sharing Center, click Change adapter settings.
5. Configure a static IP for "InternalLAN" – 192.168.0.38, Leave Default gateway blank, DNS server: 192.168.0.81, disable IPv6.

Create a Service Account for Active Directory Federation Service:

1. Log on to 70411SRV and open Active Directory Users and Computers.
2. Expand 70411Lab.com and right-click the **Users** node then point to **New** and select **User**.
3. On the new user wizard, enter the following information:
   a) First name: ADFS
   b) Last name: Service
   c) User log on name: ADFSService
4. On the new user wizard click **Next**.
5. Uncheck User must change password at next logon and check Password never expires, then enter a valid password, click **Next**.
6. Click **Finish**.

3.3.0 Install and configure the Remote Access role

Remote Access role in Windows Server 2012 R2 provides seamless connectivity through **DirectAccess**, **VPN**, and **Web Application Proxy**. DirectAccess provides an "Always On" and "Always Managed" experience. RAS provides traditional VPN services, including site-to-site (branch-office or cloud-based) connectivity. Web Application proxy enables the publishing of selected HTTP- and HTTPS-based applications from a corporate network to client devices outside of the corporate network. Routing provides traditional routing capabilities, including NAT and other connectivity options. RAS and Routing can be deployed in single-tenant or multi-tenant mode.

To install the Remote Access role

1. Log on to 70411SRV3. From Server Manager main window, click **Manage**, and click **Add Roles and Features**.
2. On the Add Roles and Features Wizard, click **Next**.
3. On the Select Installation Type, ensure that Role-based or feature-based installation is selected then click **Next**.
4. On the Select Destination server screen, select 70411SRV3 and click **Next**.
5. Under Select Server Roles, check Remote Access box and click **Next**.
6. On the **Select features** window click **Next**.
7. On the **Remote Access** screen, note the information about DirectAccess, VPN and Web Application Proxy then click **Next**.
8. On the **Select role services** screen, select all the Role Services (DirectAcces and VPN (RAS), Routing and Web Application proxy). If the Add features dialogue appears, click ok then click **Next** when you are done.
9. Under Confirm Installation page, click **Install**.
10. When installation is completed, click **Close**.

To Configure Remote Access Role

1. Log on to 70411SRV (DC) and open Active Directory Users and Computers.
2. Search for **RAS and IAS Servers** security group, open the group and click **Members** tab.
3. On the Members tab, click **Add**, the AD search box opens.
4. On the **Select this object type**, click Object types and check the box beside **Computers** then click **Ok**.
5. On the Search box, type 70411SRV3 and click **Check Names**, this should resolve 70411SRV3 then click **Ok**.
6. On the Properties sheet of RAS and IAS Servers security group click **Ok**.
7. Log on to 70411SRV3 and from Server manager click Tools then select **Routing and Remote access**. Notice that 70411SRV3 is not enabled for Routing and Remote Access.
8. To enable Routing and Remote Access, complete the steps below:
   a) Right-click 70411SRV3 and select **Configure and Enable Routing and Remote Access**. This opens the RAS configuration wizard.
   b) On the Welcome screen, click **Next**.
   c) On the Configuration screen, select Custom Configuration then click **Next**.
   d) Click **Finish**.
   e) On the Start the service dialogue, click **Start service**.

3.3.1 Implement Network Address Translation (NAT)

NAT allow internal clients to connect to the internet using a single public IP address.

To configure Network Address Translation (NAT)

1. Still logged on to 70411SRV3 and **Routing and Remote Access** console open.
2. On the Routing and Remote Access console, expand **70411SRV3**, and then expand **IPv4**.
3. Under **IPv4**, right-click **NAT** and select **New Interface**.
4. On the **New Interface** page, select **InternalLAN** and click **Ok**.
5. On the Network Address Translation Properties, ensure that **Private interface connected to private network** is selected, and then click **Ok**.
6. Right-click NAT again and select New Interface.
7. On the **New Interface** page, select **InternetLAN** and click **Ok**.
8. On the Network Address Translation Properties, select Public interface connected to the internet, click Enable NAT on this interface and click Ok. Selecting Public interface connected to the internet option enables two tabs on the NAT tab:

a) **Address Pool**: If your Internet service provider (ISP) provides you with a range of public IP addresses instead of a single address, use this tab to configure the addresses on the public NAT-enabled interface.

b) **Services and Ports**: Use this tab to create, modify, and activate mappings between public IP addresses and ports, and services running on hosts on the private network at specified IP addresses and ports. The list shows currently configured services. You are able to perform the tasks listed below:

   i) To configure one of the predefined services and activate the mapping, select the box next to the service in the list. The Edit Service dialog box is displayed. You must complete or confirm the mapping configuration before you can activate the service mapping.

   ii) To configure one of the predefined services and activate the mapping, select the service in the list, and then click Edit to display the Edit Service dialog box.

   iii) To define a new service and activate the mapping, click Add to display the Add Service dialog box.

9. When you finish, click **Ok**.
10. To configure DHCP Relay Agent, complete the task below:
   a) Under IPv4 right-click DHCP Relay Agent and select New Interface.
   b) On the **New Interface** page, select **InternalLAN** and click **Ok**, then click **Ok** to the **DHCP Relay Agent** Properties.
   c) Under **IPv4**, right-click **DHCP Relay Agent** and click **Properties**.
   d) Under **Server address**, type the IP address of the DHCP server (192.168.0.38) and click **Add**.
   e) Click **Ok**, to save your changes and close DHCP Relay Agent Properties.
11. To confirm that NAT is working, complete the task below:
   a) Ping 192.168.0.34 continuously (with –t switch)
   b) While the continuous ping is ongoing, refresh the **NAT** node in the Routing and Remote Access console.
   c) Notice that the InternetLAN values under **Inbound packets transmitted** and **Outbound packets transmitted** keeps increasing.
   d) Pinging 192.168.0.38 (The IP address of the InternalLAN) and notice that, it does not provide the same result.

3.3.2 Configure VPN settings

In the previous section, we configured 70411SRV3 as a Virtual Private Network (VPN) Access and NAT server. In this section, we will review the VPN settings and configuration options.

To configure VPN settings

1. Log on to 70411SRV3 and open **Routing and Remote Access** from Server Manager, **Tools** Menu.
2. On the **Routing and Remote Access Management** Console, on the left pane, right-click **70411SRV3** and click **Properties**.
3. Review the following settings and tabs:
    a) **General** tab: The General tab gives you two options. First, you can choose to enable your server as a router. If you select this option, you can choose to allow only **local LAN routing**, or you can choose to allow **LAN and demand-dial routing**. Next, you can choose to enable your server as a remote access server. These options simply enable you to use your server as both a routing server and a remote access server.
    b) **Security** tab: On the Security tab, you can select the security and accounting provider. You can select either **Windows authentication and accounting** or **RADIUS authentication and accounting**. If you choose to implement RADIUS, click **Configure** to connect to a RADIUS server. Note the Windows Authentication Methods:
        i) **Extensible authentication protocol (EAP)**: Allows the use of third-party authentication software and is also used for smart-card logon. It is recommended to use EAP if you have Network Access Protection (NAP) and use NPS to configure all other NAP settings.
        ii) **Microsoft encryption authentication version 2 (MS-CHAP V2)**: Generates encryption keys during RRAS authentication negotiation.
        iii) **Encryption authentication (CHAP)**: An earlier version of CHAP that provides secure logon.
        iv) Unencrypted password (PAP): No encryption required.
        v) Allow machine certificate authentication for IKEv2
        vi) **Unauthenticated access**: Allow remote systems to connect without authentication.
        vii) After reviewing the various authentication methods, click **Cancel.**

Note

It is recommended to use Extensible authentication protocol (EAP) if you have Network Access Protection (NAP). With NAP configuration, it is also recommended to use Network Policy Server (NPS) to configure all other NAP settings. More on this later.

Exam Tip

It is important to understand the various Windows Authentication methods described above, especially EAP.

c) Other information on the **Security** tab include:
   i) **Allow custom IPSec policy for L2TP/IKEv2 connection**: The custom IPSec policy specifies a preshared key for L2TP/IKEv2 connections. The Routing and Remote Access service should be started to set this option. IKEv2 initiators configured to authenticate the current server using certificates will not be able to connect.
   ii) **SSL Certificate Binding**: Allows you to specific a certificate that the Secure Socket Tunnelling Protocol (SSTP) server should use to bind with SSL (Web Listener). If you check the box **Use HTTP,** certificate binding will be disabled.
d) **IPv4 & IPv6 tabs**: On the **IP** tab, you can enable IPv4 routing and allow **IP-based remote access and demand-dial** connections. You can choose to implement DHCP IP leases for remote clients or you can enter a static IP address pool. These are the same options you configure with the RRAS Setup wizard, but you can use this tab to make changes as necessary. The IPv6 tab gives similar options but also supports **Default Route Advertisement**.
e) **IKEv2** tab: Allows you to configure IKEv2 client connection controls and Security Association (SA) expiration control. Options available on these tab are listed below:
   i) Idle time-out (minutes)
   ii) Network Outage Time (minutes)
   iii) Security Association expiration time (minutes)
   iv) Security Association data size limit (MB)
f) **PPP** tab: The PPP tab gives you three main check boxes for Point to Point Protocol features you can enable (Remote access policies determine which settings are used for individual connection):
   i) Multilink connections: May also configure Dynamic bandwidth protocol using BAP or BACP
   ii) Link control protocol (LCP) extensions
   iii) Software compression.
g) **Logging** tab: The Logging tab provides an effective way to monitor your remote access server through the use of log files. The following types of logging are available:
   i) Log errors only
   ii) Log errors and warnings (default)
   iii) Log all events
   iv) Do not log any events

You can also Log additional Routing and Remote Access information (Used for debugging). Log information can be viewed in the %WINDIR%\Tracing directory

4.   When you finish click **Ok** to save your changes.

3.3.3 Configure remote dial-in settings for users

In Windows Server 2012 and 2012 R2, user or computer accounts are managed either using the Security Accounts Manager (SAM) database for a stand-alone server or using an Active Directory Domain Services (AD DS) for a domain controller. Each user or computer account has a set of dial-in properties that are considered when allowing or denying a connection attempt made by a user or computer. For a stand-alone server, the dial-in properties are available on the Dial-in tab of the user or computer object in the Local Users and Groups Microsoft Management Console (MMC) snap-in. For an AD DS-based server, the dial-in properties are available on the Dial-in tab of the user or computer account in the Active Directory Users and Computers snap-in.

The dial-in properties for a user account in Active Directory are discussed below:

1. **Network Access Permission**: Use this property to set whether network access is explicitly allowed, denied, or determined by Network Policy Server (NPS) network policies. If access is explicitly allowed, network policy conditions or other account properties can override the setting.

Note

On a Windows Server 2012 or 2012 R2 domain, the built-in Administrator or Guest accounts by default are configured to Control access through NPS Network Policy.

2. **Verify Caller ID**: When Caller ID is enabled, the server verifies the caller's phone number. Caller ID must be supported by the caller, the phone system between the caller and the remote access server, and the remote access server. On a computer running the Routing and Remote Access service, caller ID support consists of call answering equipment that provides caller ID information and the appropriate Windows driver to pass the information to the Routing and Remote Access service. The connection attempt is denied if:
    a) The caller's phone number does not match the configured phone number.
    b) The caller ID phone number is configured for a user, but passing of caller ID information from the caller to the Routing and Remote Access service is not supported.
3. **Callback Options**: If this property is enabled, the server calls the caller back during the connection establishment at a phone number set by the caller or a specific phone number set by the administrator. The following sun-categories are available:
    a) No Callback.

    b)   Set by Caller (Routing and Remote Access Service only).

    c)   Always Callback to:

4. **Assign a Static IP Address**: If this property is enabled, the administrator assigns a specific IP address to the user when the connection is made.

5. **Apply Static Routes**: If this property is enabled, the administrator defines a series of static IP routes that are added to the routing table of the remote access server when a connection is made.

Note

You can configure NPS network policy to ignore the dial-in properties of user and computer accounts by selecting or clearing the **Ignore user account dial-in properties** check box on the **Overview** tab of a network policy.

3.3.4 Configure routing

The Routing and Remote Access service (RRAS) in Windows Server 2012 R2 provides multiprotocol LAN-to-LAN, LAN-to-WAN, virtual private network (VPN), and network address translation (NAT) routing services.

To enable LAN and WAN routing

1. Log on to 70411SRV3 and open **Routing and Remote Access** from Server Manager, Tools Menu.

2. On the Routing and Remote Access Management Console, on the left pane, right-click **70411SRV3** and click **Properties**.

3. On the **General** tab, select the **IPv4 Router** or **IPv6 Router** check boxes, and then under each one that you enable, complete one of the following:

    a)   To enable only LAN routing without support for demand-dial connections, click **Local area network (LAN) routing only**.

    b)   To enable both LAN routing and WAN routing by using demand-dial connections, click **LAN and demand-dial routing**.

3.3.5 Configure Web Application proxy in pass-through mode (2012 R2 Objective)

Web Application Proxy is a new Remote Access role service in Windows Server 2012 R2. It is a Remote Access Service used to publish web applications that end users can interact with from any device. It also provides proxy functionality for Active Directory Federation Services (AD FS) to help systems Administrators provide secure access to AD FS server. Web Application Proxy allows systems Administrators to choose how end users should authenticate themselves to a web application and that users are authorized to use a web application.

When Web Application Proxy is used in conjunction with Active Directory Federation Services (AD FS), it is possible to manage the risk of exposing your applications to the internet by configuring features provided by AD FS. These features include Workplace Join, Multifactor Authentication (MFA), and Multifactor Access Control.

Web Application Proxy provides the following options to publish applications: AD FS Preauthentication, Client Certificate Preauthentication or Pass-through Preauthentication. For the purposes of the exam, we will be covering Pass-through Preauthentication. Before we proceed to publish applications using Web Application proxy, we have to first complete initial configuration.

To Configure Web Application proxy

We will follow the following High-level plan:

1. Install Active Directory Federation Service (AD FS).
2. Configure AD FS.
3. Install and Configure a Server authentication certificate in the certificate authority.
4. Configure Web Application Proxy.

Detailed procedure of the above plan is outlined below:

1. To Install Active Directory Federation Service (AD FS):
   a) Log on to 70411SRV and Server Manager.
   b) From Server Manager, click **Manage** and select **Add Roles and features**.
   c) Click **Next** thrice until you get to **Server Roles.**
   d) On the Server Roles screen, click Active Directory Federation Services then click Next.
   e) On the **Features** screen, click **Next** twice.
   f) On the **Confirmation** screen, click **Install**.
   g) When installation completes, click **Close.**
2. To Configure AD FS:
   a) Open Server Manager in 70411SRV and click on the yellow notification triangle, and then click **Configure the Active Directory Federation service on this computer**.
   b) On the Welcome screen ensure that Create the first federation server in a federation server farm is selected then click **Next**.
   c) On the **Connect to AD DS** screen, click **Next**.
   d) On the Specify Service Properties screen, beside SSL Certificate, select 70411SRV.70411Lab.com and on the Federal Service Display Name field, type 70411ADFS then click Next.

e) On the **Specify Service Account** screen, click **Select** (Beside Account Name).

f) On the AD Search box, type **ADFSService**, click **Check Names** then click **Ok.**

g) On the **Specify Service Account** screen, enter the AD password for **ADFSService** account and click **Next.**

h) On the Specify Database, ensure that the Create a database on this server using Windows Internal Database option is selected then click **Next.**

i) On the **Review Options** screen, click **Next.**

j) After Pre-requisite Checks completes, click **Configure**.

k) On the **Results** screen, click **Close.**

3. Install and Configure a Server authentication certificate in the certificate authority:

a) To import Certificate into the Certificate Authority.

   i) Log on to 70411SRV3 and Open MMC.

   ii) On the File menu of the new MMC console, click **Add/Remove Snap-in**.

   iii) On the **Available snap-ins** list, select **Certificates**, and then click **Add**. The **Certificates Snap-in** Wizard starts.

   iv) Select Computer Account then click Next.

   v) Select Local computer: (the computer this console is running on), and then click Finish, then click Ok.

   vi) Navigate to (Expand) Console Root\Certificates (Local Computer)\Personal\Certificates.

   vii) Right-click Certificates then click All Tasks, click Advanced Operations, then select Create Custom Request.

   viii) On the Before You Begin screen, click Next.

   ix) On the Select Certificate Enrollment Policy screen, select Proceed without Enrollment Policy and click Next.

   x) On the Custom request screen, for Template select (No template) CNG Key and for Request Format, select PKCS #10, then click Next.

   xi) On the Certificate Information screen, click Details and then Properties.

   xii) On the **General** tab, complete the following tasks:

     (1) On the Friendly name field, type Web Proxy Certificate.

     (2) On the Description field, type Certificate issued to 70411SRV.70411Lab.com AD FS.

   xiii) On the **Subject** tab, complete the following tasks:

     (1) Under **Subject name** select **Common name** from the drop down, and on the **Value** field enter **70411SRV.70411Lab.com** then click **Add.**

      (2) Under **Alternative Name,** below **Type** drop-down, select **DNS** and on the **Value** field enter **70411SRV.70411Lab.com** then click **Add.**

   xiv) On the **Extensions** tab, complete the following tasks:

      (1) Click Extended Key Usage (application policies).

      (2) On the Available options, select Server Authentication and click Add.

   xv) On the **Private Key** tab, complete the following tasks:

      (1) Expand Key Options and check the box Make private key exportable.

   xvi) Click **Ok** to save your changes and close **Certificate Properties.**

   xvii)   On the Certificate Information screen click Next.

   xviii)   On the **Where do you want to save the offline request?** screen, save the file to E:\ServerMon\Templates\ADFS.req, select **Base 64** as the file format then click **Finish.**

  b) To export the certificate and import into Personal Certificate:

    i) Expand Certificate Enrollment Requests and highlight Certificates.

    ii) On the details pane, right-click **70411SRV.70411Lab.com**, select **All Tasks** then select **Export**.

    iii) On the **Welcome** screen, click **Next**.

    iv) On the **Export Private Key** screen select **Yes**, export the private key then click **Next**.

    v) On the Export File Format, check the box Export all extended properties and click Next.

    vi) On the **Security** screen, check the box beside **Password** then enter a password and confirmation, then click **Next**.

    vii) Save file in location E:\Certificates\70411SRV.pfx, click **Next**, then click **Finish**.

    viii) Expand **Personal**, right-click **Certificates**, point to **All Tasks** and select **Import**.

    ix) On the **Welcome** screen, click **Next**.

    x) Select E:\Certificates\70411SRV.pfx and click **Next**.

    xi) On the **Private key protection** screen, enter the password you used during export process, then check the box, **Mark this key as exportable**, click **Next**.

    xii) On the Certificate Store, select Place all certificates in the following store, and on the Certificate store field, ensure that Personal is selected then click Next and click Finish.

4. To Configure Web Application Proxy:

  a) Log on to 70411SRV3 and open **Remote Access** from Server Manager.

b) On the Remote Access Management console, click Web Application Proxy.

c) On the details pane, click Run the Web Application Proxy Configuration Wizard.

d) On the Welcome screen, click **Next**.

e) On the Federation Server screen, enter 70411SRV.70411Lab.com as the Federation service name. On the **enter the credentials of a local Administrator account on the federation servers** fields, enter a domain admin account and password and click **Next**.

f) On the **AD FS Proxy Certificate** screen, select **70411SRV.70411Lab.com** as the certificate and click **Next**.

g) On the **Confirmation** screen, click **Configure**.

h) On the **Results** screen, click **Close.**

To install AD FS to use with Web Application Proxy, the following conditions must be met:

1. The AD FS server must be joined to the domain
2. The Web Application Proxy server cannot be installed on the same computer as the Federation service server.

And the certificate must meet the following requirements:

3. Must have a Server Authentication option as an applicable policies
4. Must have private key
5. Must have a subject with the server name in FQDN format

To Configure Web Application proxy in passthrough mode

1. Log on to 70411SRV3 and open **Remote Access** from Server Manager.
2. On the Remote Access Management console, click **Web Application Proxy**.
3. Under **Tasks** (Far right corner), below **General**, click **Publish**. The **Publish New Application Wizard** opens.
4. On the **Welcome** screen click **Next**.
5. On the **Preauthentication** screen, select **Pass-through**, click **Next**.
6. On the **Publishing Settings** screen, enter the following:
   a) On the **Name** field, enter **TestpassthroughApp**.
   b) On the **External URL** Field, enter https://www.targeapps.com.
   c) On the External certificate, select 70411SRV.70411Lab.com.
7. When you finish, click **Next**.
8. On the **Confirmation** screen, click **Publish**.
9. On the Results screen, click **Close**.

3.4 Configure DirectAccess

Introduction

DirectAccess offers users the experience of being seamlessly connected to their corporate network any time they have internet access. With DirectAccess, mobile computers can be managed any time the computer has internet connectivity, ensuring mobile users stay up-to-date with security and system health policies. Both DirectAccess and RRAS implement security features to protect the server from hostile inbound traffic. Previously these security feature settings conflicted with each other if both services attempt to run on the same server, preventing either DirectAccess or RRAS from functioning as expected.

In this section, we will cover following exam objectives:

3.4.0 Implement server requirements for DirectAccess

3.4.1 Implement client configuration

3.4.2 Configure DNS for DirectAccess

3.4.3 Configure certificates for DirectAccess

Lab Plan

We will use70411SRV3 (DirectAccess Server) and 70411SRV (DNS Configuration) for this lab.

Additional Lab setup.

Disable (InternalLAN) the second NIC on 70411SRV3:

1. Shutdown 70411SRV3.
2. Disable the NIC:
    a) Open Hyper-V Manager.
    b) Right click **70411SRV3**, select **Settings**.
    c) High-light the second Network Adapter, and in the details, pane, select **Not connected** from the **Virtual switch** drop down list then click **Ok.**
3. Boot 70411SRV3.

Delete unwanted Local Certificates on 70411SRV3:

1. Log on to 70411SRV3 and Open MMC.
2. On the File menu of the new MMC console, click **Add/Remove Snap-in**.
3. In the **Available** snap-ins list, select **Certificates**, and then click **Add**. The Certificates Snap-in Wizard starts.
4. Select **Computer Account** and click **Next**.

5. Select Local computer: (the computer this console is running on), click Finish then click Ok.
6. Navigate to (Expand) Console Root\Certificates (Local Computer)\Personal\.
7. Highlight **Certificates** and on the details pane delete all certificates listed except **70411SRV.70411Lab.com**.

3.4.0 Implement server requirements for DirectAccess

The following are required to configure DirectAccess in Windows Server 2012 R2:

1. One or more DirectAccess servers running Windows Server 2012 with one or more network adapters.
2. At least one Domain Controller (DC) and Domain Name System (DNS) server running Windows Server 2008 SP2 or Windows Server 2008 R2.
3. DirectAccess clients running Windows 7 or Windows 8 "Enterprise" edition.
4. A Public Key Infrastructure for Windows 7 clients; A Public Key Infrastructure is not required for Windows 8 Clients.

In this section, we will configure the requirements to implement DirectAccess using the high level tasks listed below:

1. Create a Security Group for DirectAccess client computers
2. Configure Windows Firewall and Networking
3. Enable and Configure DirectAccess

To implement server requirements for DirectAccess

1. Create a Security Group for DirectACcess client computers:
   a) Log on to 70411SRV (Domain controller) and open Active Directory Users and Computers.
   b) In the Active Directory Users and Computers console tree, navigate to **Users** container, then right-click **Users**, point to **New**, and click **Group**.
   c) In the New Object - Group dialog box, under Group name, type the group DirectAccessClients-win8.
   d) Under **Group   scope**, choose **Global**, under **Group   type**, choose **Security**, and then click **Ok**.
   e) Open the properties sheet of **DirectAccessClients-win8** group, on the **Members** tab, add 70411WIN8 as a member of the group.
   f) Repeat the procedure above to create a group called **DirectAccessClients-win7**, then add 70411WIN7 as a member of the DirectAccessClients-win7 group.
2. Configure Windows Firewall and Networking:
   a) Log on to 70411SRV3 and open Windows Firewall with Advanced Security.
   b) Create an Inbound and Outbound rule to allow port 443:
      i) On the left pane, right-click **Inbound Rules** node and click **New Rule**, the **New Inbound Rule Wizard** Opens.

        ii) On the Rule Type screen, on the Predefined drop down list, select Secure World Wide Web Services (HTTPS) then click Next.

        iii) On the Predefined Rules screen, check World Wide Web Services (HTTPS Traffice-In) and click Next.

        iv) On the Action screen, click Allow the connection and click Finish.

  c) Enable IPv6 on the public-facing adapter:

        i) Log on to 70411SRV3 and open Server Manager.

        ii) On the Server Manager console, left pane, click **Local Server.**

        iii) Beside **InternetLAN**, click 192.168.0.34. The Network Connection page opens.

        iv) Right-click **InternetLAN** and click **properties.**

        v) On the InternetLAN NIC **properties,** check **Internet Protocol Version 6 (TCP/IPv6)** if it is not checked and click **Ok.**

  d) Configure Your Home hub to forward Port 443 to 70411SRV3 (Varies for different providers).

3. Configure Public IP on InternetLAN NIC:

  a) Log on to 70411SRV3 and determine your public IP address: open google and type **what is my public IP.** Note the IP.

  b) Open the Properties of **InternetLAN NIC,**

  c) On the InternetLAN NIC properties, highlight Internet Protocol Version 4 (TCP/IPv4) and click Properties.

  d) On the TCP/IP properties, click **Advanced,**

  e) On the **Advanced TCP/IP Settings,** click **Add,** then enter your public IP address and the equivalent subnet mask, click **Add** when you finish, click **Ok** twice, and **Close.**

4. Enable and Configure DirectAccess:

  a) Log on to 70411SRV3 and Launch **Server Manager**,

  b) Click Tools and open Remote Access Management.

  c) In the **Remote Access Management** Console, on the left pane click **VPN**.

  d) On the top right corner of the console, below **Tasks,** under **General** click **Enable DirectAccess. The Enable DirectAccess Wizard** opens.

  e) On the Welcome screen, click **Next.** The Wizard will check prerequisites and return a result.

  f) On the DirectAccess Client Setup screen, click Add. The Select Groups search box opens.

  g) Enter DirectAccessClients-win8 and click Ok. Check the box beside Allow Windows 7 clients to use Direct Access.

  h) On the DirectAccess Client Setup screen, click Next.

i)   On the **Network Topology** screen, review available topology types, explained below:
    i)   **Edge**: In this topology, the Remote Access Server is deployed at the edge of the internal corporate network and is configured with two adapters. One adapter is connected to the internal network. The other is connected to the internet.
    ii) **Behind an edge device (with two network adapters)**: In this topology, the Remote Access Server is deployed behind an edge firewall or device, and is configured with two adapters. One adapter is connected to the internal network. The second is connected to the perimeter network.
    iii) **Behind an edge device (with a single network adapter)**: In this topology, the Remote Access Server is deployed with a single network adapter connected to the internal network.

j)   On the **Network Topology** screen, Chose the option **Behind an edge device (With single network adapter)** Accept the default value of 70411SRV.70411Lab.com supplied in the **Public name or IPv4 address**, then click **Next.**

k)   On the DNS Suffix search list screen, click **Next**.

l)   On the **GPO Configuration** screen, review the GPOs that will be applied to the client computer security group and the DirectAccess server in the relevant domains. They are:
    i)   **DirectAccess client GPO**: Contains DirectAccess client settings - Default name supplied - **DirectAccess Client Settings**.
    ii) **DirectAccess Server GPO**: Contains DirectAccess Server settings - Default name supplied - **DirectAccess Server Settings**.
    iii) When you finish reviewing the GPO settings, click **Next.**

m)   On the **Summary** screen, click **Finish.**

n)   When the DirectAccess configuration is completed, click **Close.**

3.4.1 Implement client configuration

For a client computer to be provisioned to use DirectAccess it must belong to the right DirectAccess security group. After DirectAccess is configured, client computers in the security group are provisioned to receive the DirectAccess group policy. You can also configure the deployment scenario, which allows you to configure DirectAccess for client access and remote management or for remote management only. This section will cover configuration of DirectAccess client settings and will be treated under the following high-level plan:

1.   Configure Client Deployment Scenario.
2.   Configure the Teredo client.
3.   Configure the public IPv4 address of the 6to4 relay.

4. Enable the IP-HTTPS client and configure the IP-HTTPS URL.

To Implement Client Configuration for DirectAccess

1. Configure Client Deployment Scenario:
    a) Log on to 70411SRV3 and open **Remote Access Management.**
    b) In left pane of the Remote Access Management console, in the **Step 1 Remote Clients** area, click **Edit**.
    c) In the **DirectAccess Client Setup** wizard, on the **Deployment Scenario** page, note the deployment scenarios:
        i) **Deploy full DirectAccess for client access and remote management**: This option configures DirectAccess client computers located on the internet to connect to internet network via Remote Access server. Administrators can remotely manage clients. Selecting this option enables all DirectAccess features, including client access and remote client management, force tunnelling, strong authentication, and NAP compliance.
        ii) **Deploy DirectAccess for remote management only**: If this option is selected, Administrators can remotely manage DirectAccess client computers located on the internet. DirectAccess is not deployed for client access to internal network. Selecting this option enables remote client management, and disables some DirectAccess features, including client access to internal network, force tunneling, strong authentication, and NAP compliance.
    d) Select Deploy Full DirectAccess for client access and remote management option and click **Next**.
    e) On the **Select Groups** screen, click **Add**, the Select Groups search box opens. Enter **DirectAccessClients-win7** and click **Ok**. Review all available options outlined below:
        i) **Enable DirectAccess for mobile computers only:** With this setting enabled, all mobile computers in the specified security groups will be enabled as DirectAccess clients.
        ii) **Use force tunneling:** DirectAccess clients connect to the internal network and to the internet via the Remote Access server.
    f) When you finish, click **Next.**

If the security group is located in a different forest than the Remote Access server, then after you have completed the Remote Access Setup Wizard click Refresh Management Servers in the Tasks pane to discover the domain controllers and System Center Configuration Manager servers in the new forest.

Exam Tip

Note the options available in step 1(p) above, especially force tunneling.

   g)   On the **Network Connectivity Assistant** screen, complete the following tasks:

       i)   In the table, add resources that will be used to determine connectivity to the internal network. A default web probe is created automatically if no other resources are configured. When configuring the web probe locations for determining connectivity to the Enterprise network, ensure that you have at least one HTTP based probe configured. Configuring a PING probe only is not sufficient, and could lead to inaccurate determination of connectivity status. This is because ping is exempted from IPsec, and as a result does not ensure that the IPsec tunnels are properly established.

       ii)   Add a helpdesk email address to allow users to send information if they experience connectivity issues.

       iii)   Provide a friendly name for the DirectAccess connection. This name appears in the network list when users click the network icon in the notification area.

       iv)   Select the Allow DirectAccess clients to use local name resolution check box if required.

   h)   When you finish, click **Finish.**

Note

When local name resolution is enabled, users running the Network Connectivity Assistant can select to resolve names using DNS servers configured on the DirectAccess client computer.

2.   Configure the Teredo client as an enterprise client and configure the Internet Protocol version 4 (IPv4) address of the Teredo server:

   a)   Log on to 70411SRV (DC) and open **Group Policy Management (GPMC)**.

   b)   On the left pane of GPMC, expand nodes until you reach the GPO **DirectAccess Client Settings** below **70411Lab.com** domain, right-click the GPO and click **Edit.**

   c)   To Configure the Teredo client as an enterprise client, complete the tasks below:

       i)   On the Group Policy management Editor console, navigate to Computer Configuration\Policies\Administrative Templates\Network\TCPIP Settings\IPv6 Transition Technologies\ and double-click the policy **Set Teredo State.**

      ii)   On the **Set Toredo State** policy setting, click **Enable** and note available options:

          (1) Default State: The default state is "Client."

          (2) Disabled State: No Teredo interfaces are present on the host.

          (3) Client: The Teredo interface is present only when the host is not on a network that includes a domain controller.

          (4) Enterprise Client: The Teredo interface is always present, even if the host is on a network that includes a domain controller.

    d)   Select **Enterprise Client** option and click **Ok**.

Note

Teredo is an address assignment and automatic tunneling technology that provides unicast IPv6 connectivity across the IPv4 Internet. IP-HTTPS is a tunneling technology that uses the HTTPS protocol to provide IP connectivity to a remote network.

    e)   To configure the Internet Protocol version 4 (IPv4) address of the Teredo server:

      i)   On the Group Policy management Editor console, navigate to Computer Configuration\Policies\Administrative Templates\Network\TCPIP Settings\Ipv6 transition Technologies\ and double-click the policy **Set Teredo Server Name**.

      ii)   On the **Set Teredo Server Name** policy setting, click **Enable** and on the Enter a Toredo server name field, enter *FirstPublicIPv4AddressOfDirectAccessServer*.

      iii) Click **Ok**.

3.   Configure the public IPv4 address of the 6to4 relay:

    a)   On the Group Policy management Editor console, navigate to Computer Configuration\Policies\Administrative Templates\Network\TCPIP Settings\Ipv6 transition Technologies\, double-click the policy **Set 6to4 Relay Name**.

    b)   On the **Set 6to4 Relay Name** policy setting, click **Enable** and on the Enter a router or relay name field, enter the *FirstPublicIPv4AddressOfDirectAccessServer*.

    c)   Click **Ok**.

4.   Enable the IP-HTTPS client and configure the IP-HTTPS Uniform Resource Locator (URL):

    a)   On the Group Policy management Editor console, navigate to Computer Configuration\Policies\Administrative Templates\Network\TCPIP Settings\Ipv6 transition Technologies\ and double-click **Set IP-HTTPS State**.

b) On the **Set IP-HTTPS State** policy setting, click **Enable** and on the **IP-HTTPS URL,** enter *<https://SubjectOfIP-HPPTSCertificate:443/IPHTTPS>* - replace the settings in italics with your actual values. No further action required here.

c) On the Select Interface state from the following options, note the available options:

   i) Default State: The IP-HTTPS interface is used when there are no other connectivity options.

   ii) Enabled State: The IP-HTTPS interface is always present, even if the host has other connectivity options.

   iii) Disabled State: No IP-HTTPS interfaces are present on the host.

d) When you finish, click **Ok.**

Note

A third tunneling technology, can be configured for client connectivity - Intra-Site Automatic Tunnel Addressing Protocol (ISATAP) is an address-to-router and host-to-host, host-to-router and router-to-host automatic tunneling technology that is used to provide unicast IPv6 connectivity between IPv6 hosts across an IPv4 intranet.

3.4.2 Configure DNS for DirectAccess

The design of your Domain Name System (DNS) infrastructure may influence DirectAccess configuration. The biggest design aspect of your DNS infrastructure is whether you use split-brain DNS. Split-brain DNS is the use of the same DNS domain to provide access to internet and intranet resources. For example, assuming Northern Ark Limited is using split brain DNS; NorthernArk.com is the domain name for intranet resources and internet resources. Internet users use http://www.NorthernArk.com to access Northern Ark's public website and Northern Ark employees on the Northern Ark intranet use http://www.NorthernArk.com to access the intranet website.

In this section, we will examine and configure DNS for DirectAccess considering the following:

1. DNS server requirements for ISATAP.
2. AAA records for servers that do not perform DNS dynamic update.
3. Local name resolution behaviour for DirectAccess clients.
4. Name Resolution Policy Table (NRPT) rules.
5. DNS server querying behaviour for DirectAccess clients.
6. Unqualified, single-label names and DNS search suffixes.
7. External DNS.

DNS server requirements for ISATAP

If you are using Intra-Site Automatic Tunnel Addressing Protocol (ISATAP) for IPv6 connectivity on your intranet, DNS servers used by DirectAccess clients must meet the following requirements:

1. DNS servers that run Windows Server 2008 R2 or later. The DNS Server service in these versions of Windows supports processing DNS traffic on ISATAP interfaces.
2. Non-Microsoft DNS servers that are capable of processing DNS traffic on ISATAP interfaces.

By default, the DNS Server service in Windows Server 2008 and later blocks name resolution for the name ISATAP through the DNS Global Query Block List. To use ISATAP on your intranet, you must remove the ISATAP name from the list for all DNS servers running Windows Server 2008 and later.

To remove ISATAP from the DNS global query block list on the DNS server

1. Log on to 70411SRV (DNS server) and open **regedit.exe**.
2. In the console tree, navigate to:
   Computer\HKEY_LOCAL_MACHINE\SYSTEM\CurrentControlSet\Services\DNS\Parameters.
3. In the contents pane, double-click the **GlobalQueryBlockList** value.
4. In the **Edit Multi-String** dialog box, remove the name **ISATAP** from the list, and then click **Ok**.
5. Restart the DNS Service: **net stop dns** then **net start dns.**

Note

In a production environment, you can use group policy to edit and apply the above registry changes to more than one DNS server.

AAA records for servers that do not perform DNS dynamic update

For servers running IPv6-capable non-Windows operating systems that do not support DNS dynamic update for IPv6 addresses, AAAA records for the names and IPv6 addresses of these servers will have to be added manually. For details of how to manually add resource records, revisit section 3.2.0.

Local name resolution behaviour for DirectAccess clients

If a name cannot be resolved with DNS, the DNS Client service in Windows 8.1 and Windows Server 2012 R2 can perform local name resolution with the Link-Local Multicast Name Resolution (LLMNR) and NetBIOS over TCP/IP protocols.

Local name resolution is typically needed for peer-to-peer connectivity when the computer is located on private networks, such as single subnet home networks. When the DNS Client service performs local name resolution for intranet server names and the computer is connected to a shared subnet on the internet, malicious users can capture LLMNR and NetBIOS over TCP/IP messages to determine intranet server names.

Step 3 of the DirectAccess Setup Wizard provides the option to configure the local name resolution behavior for DirectAccess clients based on the responses received from intranet DNS servers. Available options are detailed below:

1. **Use local name resolution if the name does not exist in DNS (most restrictive)**: This option is the most restrictive and most secure because the DirectAccess client will only perform local name resolution for server names that cannot be resolved by intranet DNS servers. If the intranet DNS servers can be reached, the names of intranet servers will be resolved. If the intranet DNS servers cannot be reached or if there are other types of DNS errors, the intranet server names will not be leaked to the subnet through local name resolution.

2. **Use local name resolution if the name does not exist or if the internal network DNS servers are not reachable (recommended)**: This option is moderately secure because it allows the use of local name resolution on a private network when the intranet DNS servers are unreachable.

3. **Use local name resolution for any kind of DNS resolution error (least restrictive)**: This is the least restrictive and least secure option because the names of intranet network servers can be leaked to the local subnet through local name resolution.

DirectAccess clients may also be enabled to use local name resolution in step 1 of the DirectAccess setup wizard. This task may be completed in the Network Connectivity Assistant section.

To enable Local name resolution for DirectAccess clients

1. Log on to 70411SRV3 and open Remote Access management.
2. To enable DirectAccess clients to use local name resolution:

a) On **Step 1 Remote Clients**, click **Edit**. The DirectAccess client Setup opens

b) On the **Deployment Scenario** screen, click **Next**.

c) On the **Select Groups** screen, click **Next**.

d) On the Network Connectivity Assistant, screen, check Allow DirectAccess clients use local name resolution and click Finish.

3. To configure the local name resolution behaviour:

a) On **Step 3 Infrastructure Servers**, click **Edit**. The Infrastructure Server Setup opens.

b) On the Network Location Server screen, click **Next**.

c) On the DNS screen, check the **required local name resolution** option. These options were described in the introductory part of this section.

Name Resolution Policy Table (NRPT) rules

NRPT rules are internal table used by the DNS Client service to determine where to send DNS name queries. NRPT rules are configured in step 3 of the DirectAccess Setup Wizard. The DirectAccess Setup Wizard automatically creates two rules for DirectAccess clients:

1. A namespace rule for the domain name of the DirectAccess server and the IPv6 addresses corresponding to the intranet DNS servers configured on the DirectAccess server. For example, if the DirectAccess server is a member of the blog.ITechGuides.com domain, the DirectAccess Setup Wizard creates a namespace rule for the .blog.MiniVigil.com DNS suffix.

2. An exemption rule for the FQDN of the network location server. For example, if the network location server URL is https://nls.blog.ITechGuides.com, the DirectAccess Setup Wizard creates an exemption rule for the FQDN nls.blog.MiniVigil.com.

In some circumstances, it might be necessary to configure additional NRPT rules in step 3 of the DirectAccess Setup Wizard:

1. If the FDQN of your intranet and internet Certificate Revocation List (CRL) distribution points are based on your intranet namespace, you must add exemption rules for the FQDNs of your internet and intranet CRL distribution points.

2. If you have a split-brain DNS environment, you must add exemption rules for the names of resources for which you want DirectAccess clients located on the Internet to access the public (internet) version, rather than the intranet version.

3. If you are redirecting traffic to an external Web site through your intranet Web proxy servers, the external Web site is only available from the intranet, and the external Web site is using the addresses of your Web proxy servers to permit the inbound requests, then you must add an

exemption rule for the FQDN of the external Web site and specify that the rule use your intranet Web proxy server, rather than the IPv6 addresses of intranet DNS servers.

Note

CRL distribution points are locations, typically URLs, which are added to a certificate in its CRL distribution point extension. These points can be used by an application or service to retrieve a CRL. CRL distribution points are contacted when an application or service must determine whether a certificate has been revoked before its validity period has expired.

You can also configure NRPT rules from Computer Configuration\Policies\Windows Settings\Name Resolution Policy in the Group Policy object for DirectAccess clients

To configure NRPT rules Using the DirectAccess Setup Wizard

1. Log on to 70411SRV3 and open Remote Access management.
2. Highlight **DirectAccess and VPN** and on the details pane, click **Edit** under **Step 3 Infrastructure Servers**. The Infrastructure Server Setup opens.
3. On the Network Locator Server screen, click **Next**.
4. On the **DNS** screen, review the information, add name suffixes as required and the corresponding DNS Server Address then click **Next**.
5. On the **DNS Suffix Search List** screen provides the option to configure DirectAccess clients with DNS suffix search list, click **Next**.
6. On the **Management** screen, click **Finish**.

To configure NRPT rules from Group Policy

1. Log on to 70411SRV and open Group Policy management.
2. **Open DirectAccess Client Settings** GPO with group policy management editor
3. Navigate to Computer Configuration\Policies\Windows Settings\
4. Highlight **Name Resolution Policy** and on the details pane, click **DNS Settings for DirectAccess**. Configure the following:
   a) Check the box Enable DNS settings for DirectAccess in this rule.
   b) Beside DNS Servers (Optional), click **Add**.
   c) On the **DNS Server** dialogue, type 70411SRV and click **Add**.
   d) You may also configure to use Web proxy and IPSec.
5. Click **Advanced Global Policy Settings** and review available options:
   a) Network Location Dependency: This allows you to configure roaming options:

        i)   Let Network ID (NID) determine when DirectAccess settings are to be used.

        ii) Always use DirectAccess settings on the NRPT.

        iii) Never use DirectAccess settings on the NRPT.

    b) Query Failure: This allows you to configure query failure options:

        i)   Only use Link-Local Multicast Name Resolution (LLMNR) and NetBIOS if the name does not exist in DNS (most secure).

        ii) Always fall back to Link-Local Multicast Name Resolution (LLMNR) and NetBIOS if the name does not exist in DNS or if the DNS servers are unreachable when on a private network (moderate secure).

        iii) Always fall back to Link-Local Multicast Name Resolution (LLMNR) and NetBIOS for any kind of name resolution error (least secure).

    c) Query Resolution: This allows you to configure query resolution options:

        i)   Resolve only IPv6 addresses for name resolution (recommended).

        ii) Resolve both IPv4 and IPv6 addresses for names.

6. When you finish, click **Apply** to save changes made to the name resolution policy.

Note

The Name Resolution Policy Table (NRPT) stores configuration settings for DNS security (DNSSEC) and DirectAccess on DNS client computers. When you configure any part of the Direct Access steps, there will be a warning below the diagram "Some configuration changes have not been applied". Click Finish to apply the changes.

3.4.3 Configure certificates for DirectAccess

A DirectAccess deployment needs a public key infrastructure (PKI) to issue certificates to DirectAccess clients, the DirectAccess server, selected servers, and the network location server. Windows 8 and Windows 8.1 clients do not require a certificate to connect to a DirectAccess network, Windows 7 clients do.

In this section, we will cover certificate configuration for DirectAccess clients and servers under the following:

1. Configure Computer Certificate Autoenrollment for windows 7 clients.

2. Grant full permissions to Authenticated users for the web server's certificate template in the certification authority.

3. Enroll a certificate for the network location server with a common name that is unresolvable from the external network.

To Configure Certificate for DirectAccess

1. Configure Computer Certificate Autoenrollment for windows 7 clients:
   a) Log on to 70411SRV and open **Group Policy management**.
   b) Open **DirectAccess Client Settings** GPO with group policy management editor.
   c) Navigate to Computer Configuration\Policies\Windows Settings\Security Settings\ and highlight **Public Key Policies**.
   d) In the details pane, right-click Automatic Certificate Request Settings and point to New, then click Automatic Certificate Request.
   e) On the Automatic Certificate Request Wizard, click **Next**.
   f) On the **Certificate Template** page, click **Computer**, click **Next**, and then click **Finish**.
2. Grant full permissions to authenticate users for the web server's certificate template in the certification authority:
   a) Log on to 70411SRV3 (Certificate Authority) and open **certsrv.msc** (from command prompt).
   b) In the Certification Authority (Local) console, expand 70411Lab-70411SRV3-CA, right-click Certificate Templates, then click Manage.
   c) In the Certification Templates (70411SRV3.70411Lab.com) console, right-click **Web Server**, and then click **Properties**.
   d) In the Web Server **Properties** box, on the **Security** tab, click **Authenticated Users**, select **Full Control**, and then click **Ok**.
   e) Restart Active Directory Certificate Services.
3. Enroll a certificate for the network location server with a common name that is unresolvable from the external network:
   a) Log on to 70411SRV3 and Open MMC,
   b) On the File menu of the new MMC console, click **Add/Remove Snap-in**.
   c) In the **Available snap-ins list**, select **Certificates**, and then click **Add**. The Certificates Snap-in Wizard starts.
   d) Select **Computer Account** then click **Next**.
   e) Select Local computer: (the computer this console is running on), and then click Finish.
   f) Click **Ok**.
   g) Expand Console Root\Certificates (Local Computer)\Personal\Certificates.
   h) Right-click **Certificates**, click **All Tasks**, and then click **Request New Certificate**. The Certificate Enrollment Wizard opens. Click **Next**.
   i) On the Select Enrollment Policy page, click Next.
   j) On the Request Certificate screen, click Web Server, and then click More information is required to enroll this certificate.
   k) In the **Certificate Properties** box, enter the following settings:

     i)   For Subject name, select Common Name.

     ii)   For **Value**, type **DirectAccess-NLS.70411Lab.com** (the name of the network location server), and then click **Add**.

     iii)   In the **Certificate Properties**, click **Ok** to save your changes.

  l)   On the Request Certificate screen click enroll.

  m) When the certificate installs successfully, click **Finish**.

Note from the Author

Well done on covering this much ground! I am confident that at this stage you have already picked up relevant hands-on skills. You are also on your way to accomplishing your goal of passing exam 70-411 in one shot. I would like to make two requests:

1. Think of ways in which you can apply the skills gained so far on your job.
2. Please visit Amazon's website to provide a review.

Chapter 4

Configure a Network Policy Server Infrastructure

4.1 Configure Network Policy Server

Introduction

Network Policy Server (NPS) provides the platform to create and enforce organization-wide network access policies for client health, connection request authentication and connection request authorization. NPS can also be configured as a Network Access Protection (NAP), a client health policy creation, enforcement and remediation technology.

NPS is the Microsoft implementation of the Remote Authentication Dial-In User Service (RADIUS) protocol, and can be configured to act as a RADIUS server or RADIUS proxy, providing centralized network access management. When you configure NPS as a RADIUS server, network access servers that are configured as RADIUS clients in NPS, forward connection requests to NPS for authentication and authorization. When you configure NPS as a RADIUS proxy, NPS forwards authentication and accounting requests to RADIUS servers in a remote RADIUS server group. Wireless access points, virtual private network (VPN) servers, 802.1X authenticating switches, Terminal Services Gateway (TS Gateway) servers, and dial-up servers may act as RADIUS clients.

Network Access Protection (NAP) has been around for quite some time. It was introduced with Windows Server 2008 to provide a built-in policy-based technology similar to Cisco's Network Access Control (NAC). Windows Server 2012 R2 added functionality and features.

Role Services of NPAS Server

The Network Policy and Access Services include the following role services:
Network Policy Server (NPS): Allows you to create and enforce organization-wide network access policies for client health, connection request authentication and connection request authorization).
Health Registration Authority (HRA): Issues certificates to NAP-Client computers that are compliant with network health requirement.
Host Credential Authorization Protocol (HCAP): Allows integration of Microsoft's Network Access Protection Solution with Cisco's Network Access

Control. When you deploy HCAP with Network Policy Server (NPS) and Network Access Protection (NAP), NPS can perform the authorization of Cisco Network Access Control clients.

In this section, we will cover following exam objectives:

4.1.0 Configure multiple RADIUS server infrastructures
4.1.1 Configure RADIUS clients4.1.2 Manage RADIUS templates
4.1.3 Configure RADIUS accounting
4.1.4 Configure certificates
4.1.5 Configure a RADIUS server and RADIUS proxy (2012 R2 Objective)
4.1.6 Configure NPS Templates (2012 R2 Objective)

Lab Plan

We will configure 70411SRV1 as NPS server and use 70411SRV3 (The server configured as VPN server in the previous section) as our RADIUS server. 70411SRV1 will forward connection requests to 70411SRV3. 70411SRV4 – Used in section 4.1.0 (Configure multiple RADIUS server infrastructures) will be configured as a second NPS RADIUS server.

Additional lab setup

Install NPAS Role in 70411SRV1 and 70411SRV4
Log on to 70411SRV1 and run the commands below:

```
Install-WindowsFeature -Name npas-policy-server -ComputerName
70411SRV4 -IncludeAllSubFeature -IncludeManagementTools

Install-WindowsFeature -Name npas-policy-server -ComputerName
70411SRV1 -IncludeAllSubFeature –IncludeManagementTools
```

4.1.0 Configure multiple RADIUS server infrastructures

NPS configuration has three options: Standard, Advanced and Template Configuration.

1. Standard Configuration - Allows you to configure the following:
    a) **RADIUS Server for Dial-Up of VPN connections**: When you configure NPS as a RADIUS for Dial-Up of VPN connection, you create network policies that allow NPS to authenticate, and authorize connections from Dial-Up or VPN network access servers (Also called RADIUS clients). There are yet two options under this configuration:
        i)   **Dial-Up Connections**: NPS can authenticate and authorise connection requests made by dial-up clients connecting through the NPS server.
        ii) **Virtual Private Network (VPN) Connections**: When you deploy VPN Servers on your network, NPS can authenticate and authorize connection requests made by VPN clients.
    b) **RADIUS Server for 802.1X Wireless or Wired Connections:** When you configure NPS as a RADIUS Server for 802.1X Wireless or Wired Connections, you create network policies that allow NPS to authenticate, and authorize connections from Wireless access points and authenticating switches (Also called RADIUS clients). Configuring NPS as 802.1X Wireless connection offers two options:
        i)   **Secure Wireless Connections**: NPS can authenticate and authorize connection requests made by wireless clients connecting through access points deployed on the network.
        ii) **Secure Wired (Ethernet) Connections**: NPS may also be configured to authenticate and authorize connection requests made by Ethernet clients connecting 802.1X Ethernet switches.
    c) **Network Access Protection (NAP)**: NPS may be configured as a NAP Health Policy Server using the standard configuration option on the NPS console. This configuration provides the option to create health policies that allow NPS to validate the configuration of NAP-Capable client computers before they connect to the network. Clients that are not compliant with health policy may be placed in a restricted network and automatically updated to bring them into compliance. To setup NPS as a NAP Health Policy Server, the following connection options are available to choose from:
        i)   Dynamic Host Configuration Protocol (DHCP).
        ii) IPSec with Health Registration Authority.
        iii) IEEE 802.1X (Wired).
        iv) IEEE 802.1X (Wireless).
        v)   Virtual Private Network (VPN).

vi) Remote Desktop Gateway (RD Gateway).

With the connection options available for NAP Health Policy Server configuration, it becomes apparent that NAP Health Policy Server cannot work as a stand-alone server, but acts as health policy server for any of the connection types discussed above. That is NPS as:

1. RADIUS Server for Dial-Up of VPN connection
2. RADIUS Server for 802.1X Wireless or Wired Connections

So while NPS configured as **RADIUS Server, authenticates** and **authorizes** client connection requests from dial-up, VPN, 802.1X Wireless, 802.1X Wireless, 802.1X Ethernet switches clients, NAP Health Policy Server **validates** the configuration of NAP-Capable client computers before they connect to your network. When NPS is configured as a NAP Health Policy Server, it performs all the functionalities combined.

3. Advanced Configuration – This configuration option provide an alternative way to configure NPS. The following options are available with advanced configuration:

   a) **RADIUS server**: To configure NPS as a RADIUS server, complete the following tasks:
      i) Specify RADIUS clients.
      ii) Create Network policies and
      iii) Configure NPS to record accounting information. We will cover each of these in greater details later.

   b) **RADIUS proxy:** If NPS is configured as a RADIUS proxy, the server forwards connection requests to other RADIUS servers that are members of a remote RADIUS server group. To configure NPS as a RADIUS proxy, create connection request policies that determine how NPS forwards connection requests to other RADIUS servers. You can also configure NPS to forward accounting data to one or more computers in a remote RADIUS server group. To configure NPS as a RADIUS proxy, complete the following tasks:
      i) Specify RADIUS clients.
      ii) Create Network Request policies
      iii) Configure NPS to record accounting information
      iv) Add RADIUS Servers to Remote RADIUS server group

   c) **Network Access Protection (NAP) policy server**: When you configure NPS as a NAP policy server, NPS evaluates statements of health (SoH) sent by NAP-capable client computers requesting access to the network. NPS also acts as a RADIUS server when configured with NAP, performing authentication and authorization for connection requests. You can configure NAP policies and settings in NPS, including system health validators (SHVs), health policy, and remediation server groups. Remediation server groups provide a platform for client computers to update their configuration so as to become compliant with your organization's network policy. To configure NPS as a NAP, the following tasks should be completed:

i) Specify RADIUS clients.
ii) Create Network policies.
iii) Create Network Request policies.
iv) Configure NPS to record accounting information.

There are three additional tasks required to complete the configuration of NPS as a NAP:

v) **Health Policies**: Controls the configuration required for NAP-Capable computers to access the network.
vi) **System Health Validators**: Allows you to specify the health settings required on NAP-Capable computers to determine compliance.
vii) **Remediation Server Groups**: Allows you to specify Remediation Servers that provide services and updates to non-compliant NAP-Capable computers.

4. Template Configuration - NPS templates allow you to create an NPS component configuration for reuse later. The templates are not applied to the NPS server configuration until you select the template in the appropriate location in the NPS console. For example, you can create an **IP filters** template and then apply the same IP filters configuration to multiple network policies by simply selecting the template. NPS template may be created for:

a) Shared Secrets
b) RADIUS Clients
c) Remote RADIUS Servers
d) Health Policies
e) Remediation Server Groups
f) IP Filters:

Configure multiple RADIUS server infrastructures

In this section, we will specify 70411SRV3 (our VPN server configured in the previous chapter) as a RADIUS client on 70411SRV1 and 70411SRV4. We will also create Network policies. To complete these tasks, use **Advanced Configuration** option in the NPS console and follow the plan below:

1. Specify RADIUS clients.
2. Create Network policies and
3. Configure NPS to record accounting information. (To be completed in section 4.1.3)
4. Repeat Configurations steps 1 and 2 on 70411SRV4

Detailed task procedure outlined below:

1. To specify RADIUS clients:
    a) Log on to 70411SRV1 and open **Network Policy Server.**
    b) On the Network Policy Server console, on the left pane expand **RADIUS clients and servers** then right-click **RADIUS clients** and select **New.** The **New RADIUS Client** configuration page opens.
    c) Complete the following tasks on the **Settings** tab:
        i)   **Friendly name** field: Enter 70411SRV3.
        ii) **Address (IP or DNS)** field: Enter 70411SRV3 and click **Verify** and on the **Verify Address** dialogue, click **Resolve.** Confirm that it resolves to 192.168.0.34, and then click **Ok.**
        iii) Below Shared secret, click Manual then enter 704111srv3secret.
    d) Complete the following tasks on the **Advanced** tab:
        i)   On the **Vendor Name** drop down, select **Microsoft.**
        ii) Note the other options available.
    e) When you finish click **Ok** to save changes.
2. Create Network policies:
    a) On the Network Policy Server console, expand **Policies,** right-click **Network Policies** and click **New.**
    b) On the policy Name field, enter RAS Policy for 70411SRV3, then on the Type of Network Access Server drop down list, select Remote Access Server (VPN-Dial up) and click **Next.**
    c) On the Specify Conditions screen, click Add, then scroll down to RADIUS client Properties group, locate Client Friendly Name and click Add. On the Client Friendly Name field, enter 70411SRV3 then click Ok.
    d) On the **Specify Conditions** screen, click **Next.**
    e) On the Specify Access Condition screen, select Access Granted, and click Next.
    f) On the **Configure Authentication Methods** screen, click **Add** below **EAP Types,** then complete the following tasks:
        i)   On the Add EAP, select Microsoft: Secure Password (EAP-MSCHAPv2).
        ii) Click **Ok.**
    g) On the Configure Authentication Methods screen, click **Next.**
    h) On the **Configure Constraints** screen, note the available constraints - additional parameters of the Network Policy that are required to match the connection request then click **Next.**
    i) On the **Configure Settings** screen, note the available settings that can be configured and click **Next** then click **Finish.**
3. Repeat Configurations steps 1 and 2 on 70411SRV4.

4.1.1 Configure RADIUS clients

On the **RADIUS Clients and Servers** node of NPS console, RADIUS clients or Remote RADIUS Server Groups can be added. RADIUS clients specify the network access servers that provide accesses to your network while Remote RADIUS Server Groups specify where to forward connection requests when NPS is configured as a RADIUS proxy.

A Network Access Server may also act as a RADIUS client, sending connection requests and accounting messages to a RADIUS server for authentication, authorization, and accounting. Client computers, such as wireless portable computers and other computers running client operating systems, are not RADIUS clients. RADIUS clients are network access servers, such as wireless access points, 802.1X-capable switches, virtual private network (VPN) servers, and dial-up servers. These devices use the RADIUS protocol to communicate with RADIUS servers such as Network Policy Server (NPS) servers.

To deploy NPS as a RADIUS server, a RADIUS proxy, or a Network Access Protection (NAP) policy server, you must configure RADIUS clients in NPS console.

RADIUS Access-Request messages

RADIUS clients create RADIUS Access-Request messages and forward them to a RADIUS proxy or RADIUS server, or they forward Access-Request messages to a RADIUS server that they have received from another RADIUS client (Acting as RADIUS Proxy) but have not created themselves. RADIUS clients do not process Access-Request messages by performing authentication, authorization, and accounting. Only RADIUS servers perform these functions.

NPS, however, can be configured as both a RADIUS proxy and a RADIUS server simultaneously, so that it processes some Access-Request messages and forwards other messages.

RADIUS client properties

When you add a RADIUS client to the NPS configuration through the NPS snap-in or through the use of the netsh commands for NPS, you are configuring NPS to receive RADIUS Access-Request messages from either a network access server or a RADIUS proxy. When you configure a RADIUS client in NPS, you can designate the following properties:

1. **Client name:** A friendly name for the RADIUS client, which makes it easier to identify when using the NPS snap-in or netsh commands for NPS.
2. **IP address:** The Internet Protocol version 4 (IPv4) address or the Domain Name System (DNS) name of the RADIUS client.

3. **Client-Vendor:** The vendor of the RADIUS client. Otherwise, you can use the RADIUS standard value for Client-Vendor.
4. **Shared secret:** A text string that is used as a password between RADIUS clients, RADIUS servers, and RADIUS proxies. When the Message Authenticator attribute is used, the shared secret is also used as the key to encrypt RADIUS messages. This string must be configured on the RADIUS client and in the NPS snap-in.
5. **Message Authenticator attribute:** If the RADIUS Message Authenticator attribute is present it is verified. If it fails verification, the RADIUS message is discarded. If the client settings require the Message Authenticator attribute and it is not present, the RADIUS message is discarded. It is recommended to use Message Authenticator attribute.

Note

The Message Authenticator attribute is required and enabled by default when you use EAP Authentication.

6. **Client is NAP-capable:** A designation that the RADIUS client is compatible with Network Access Protection (NAP), and NPS sends NAP attributes to the RADIUS client in the Access-Accept message.

We have specified 70411SRV3 as a RADIUS client in the previous section. In this section, we will configure 70411SRV3 to send authentication requests to 70411SRV1 and 70411SRV4.

To Configure NPS RADIUS clients

1. Log on to 70411SRV1 and open **Remote Access**.
2. On the Remote Access console, click **Edit** under **Step 3 Remote Access Server**.
3. On the Remote Access Setup Wizard click **Next** 4 times until you get to VPN Configuration.
4. On the VPN Configuration screen, click Authentication tab, then select Use RADIUS Authentication.
5. Below Add **RADIUS Servers (queried in order from the highest to the lowest score),** double-click the empty space beside *, the **Add RADIOUS Server** dialogue box opens. Complete the following tasks:
   a) On the **Server name** filed enter 70411SRV1.
   b) Beside **Shared Secret** click **Change** then enter the shared secret generated in section 4.1.0 (704111srv3secret) twice and click **Ok**.
6. Repeat step 5 to add 70411SRV4 as a RADIUS Server with an initial score of 20.
7. When you finish, click **Finish.**
8. To save the changes to the RAS configuration, click **Finish** below the RAS setup diagram.

4.1.2 Manage RADIUS templates

In section 4.1.0, we listed **Templates** as a configuration option for Network Policy Server. The following types of templates were discussed:

1. Shared Secrets
2. RADIUS Clients
3. Remote RADIUS Servers
4. IP Filters
5. Health Policies
6. Remediation Server Groups

In section 4.2, we will treat NPS templates in details but in this section, we will concentrate on the three templates specific to RADIUS server and clients. Follow the procedure below to manage RADIUS templates:

1. To create a Shared Secret template:
   a) Log on to 70411SRV1 and open **Remote Access**.
   b) On the console tree, expand **Template Management** then right-click **Shared Secrets** and select **New**. The **New RADIUS Shared Secret Template** configuration page opens. Complete the following tasks:
      i) On Template name, enter RADIUSServers&Clients.
      ii) On Manual Shared Secret, enter RAD1USS&C.
      iii) When you finish click **Ok.**
2. To create a RADIUS Client template:
   a) On the console tree, expand **Template Management,** right-click **RADIUS Clients** and select **New**. The **New RADIUS Clients** configuration page opens.
   b) Complete the following tasks:
      i) On Friendly name, enter RADIUSClientstemplate.
      ii) **On Address (IP or DNS)**, enter 70411SRV3, and then click **Verify**, **Resolve** and **Ok.**
      iii) On **Shared Secret**, select **RADIUSServers&Clients** from the Shared Secret drop down.
      iv) Click **Advanced** tab and under **Vendor name**, select **Microsoft**.
      v) When done, click **Ok** to create the template.
3. To create a RADIUS Client template:
   a) On the console tree, expand **Template Management** then right-click **Remote RADIUS Servers** and select **New**. The Remote RADIUS Server Template wizard opens.
   b) On the Specify RADIUS Server Template Name and Address screen, complete the following tasks:
      i) On Template Name, enter RADIUSServerstemplate.
      ii) On **Server,** enter 70411SRV4; click **Verify, Resolve,** and then **Ok.**

      iii) Click **Next**.
- c) On the Specify Authentication/Accounting settings screen:
  - i) Note the default **Authentication port** as 1812.
  - ii) Select RADIUSServers&Clients from the Select an existing Shared Secret template drop down.
  - iii) Note the default **Accounting port** as 1813.
  - iv) Click **Next**.
- d) On the **Specify Load Balancing Settings,** accept the defaults (RADIUS server priority and weight will be discussed in detail in section 4.1.5) then click **Next** and **Finish.**

4.1.3 Configure RADIUS accounting

There are three types of accounting logging for Network Policy Server (NPS):

1. **Event logging:** Used primarily for auditing and troubleshooting connection attempts. You can configure NPS event logging from NPS server properties in the NPS console.
2. **Logging user authentication and accounting requests to a local file:** Used primarily for connection analysis and billing purposes. This logging method is also useful as a security investigation tool because it provides a method of tracking the activity of a malicious user after an attack. Local file logging is configured using the Accounting Configuration wizard.
3. **Logging user authentication and accounting requests to a Microsoft SQL Server XML-compliant database:** Enables multiple servers running NPS to have one data source. This logging method also provides the advantages of using a relational database.

The **Accounting Configuration wizard** in the NPS console provides the following four accounting configuration settings:

1. **Log to a SQL Server Database:** By using this setting, you can configure a data link to a SQL Server that allows NPS to connect to and send accounting data to the SQL server. In addition, the wizard can configure the database on the SQL Server to ensure that the database is compatible with NPS SQL server logging.
2. **Log to a text file on the local computer:** Configures NPS to log accounting data to a text file.
3. **Simultaneously log to SQL Server database and to a text file:** Configures the SQL Server data link and database. This method also configures text file logging so that NPS logs simultaneously to the text file and the SQL Server database.
4. **Log to a SQL Server database using text file logging for failover:** Configures the SQL Server data link and database. This method also configures text file logging so that NPS logs to the text file when SQL Server logging fails.

In addition to these settings, SQL Server and text logging provides the option to specify whether NPS continues to process connection requests if logging fails. This is configured in the **Logging failure action** section of the local file logging properties or SQL Server logging properties. This configuration may also be completed via the Accounting Configuration wizard.

Each logging configuration method provide an option to log information about Accounting requests, Authenticating requests, Periodic accounting status and Periodic authentication status.

To configure NPS RADIUS Accounting

To run the Accounting Configuration Wizard, complete the following steps:

1. Log on to 70411SRV1 and open the NPS console.
2. In the console tree, click **Accounting** and in the details pane, click **Configure Accounting**. The **Accounting Configuration Wizard** opens. Click **Next**.
3. On the Select Accounting Options screen, select Log to a text file on local computer, click **Next**.
4. On the **Configure Local File Logging** screen, note the Logging information you can configure, the default Log File Directory location (%Windir%\system32\LogFiles) and the Logging failure action, and then click **Next**.
5. On the **Summary** screen, click **Next**, and then **close**.

4.1.4 Configure certificates

When connection authentication requests are forward (from a RAS server) to an NPS server configured as a RADIUS server, certificate-based authentication may deployed on the RAS servers. When certificate-based authentication is enabled, servers running NPS must have a server certificate. During the authentication process, these servers send their server certificate to client computers as proof of identity. To configure certificates for NPS, the following tasks must be completed:

1. **Install the Active Directory Certificate Services Server role**: We have deployed a Certificate Authority (CA) on 70411SRV3.
2. **Configure a server certificate template**: The CA issues certificates based on a certificate template, so template for the NPS server certificate must be configured before the CA can issue a certificate. When certificate autoenrollment is configured, all servers running NPS on the network will automatically receive a server certificate when Group Policy on the server running NPS is refreshed. If you add more servers later, they will automatically receive a server certificate, too.

3. **Configure Certificate Auto-enrolment via Group Policy**: When Group Policy is refreshed; the servers running NPS receive two certificates:
   a) NPS Server certificate: This certificate is used by NPS to prove its identity to client computers that attempt to connect to your network.
   b) The issuing Certificate Authority certificate: Automatically installed on the servers running NPS in the Trusted Root Certification Authorities certificate store. NPS uses this certificate to determine whether to trust certificates it receives from other computers. For example, if you deploy Extensible Authentication Protocol-Transport Layer Security (EAP-TLS), client computers use a certificate to prove their identities to the server running NPS. When the server receives a certificate from a client computer, trust for the certificate is established because the server running NPS finds the issuing CA certificate in its own Trusted Root Certification Authorities certificate store.
4. **Deploy certificate-based authentication**: We will configure the RAS server (70411SRV3) for certificate-based authentication. This is not part of the NPS template deployment but I have included it for illustration. Rather than autoenrolling an NPS server certificate, you might want to enroll the certificate by using one of the following methods:
   a) Manually import an NPS server certificate from floppy disk or compact disc into the NPS certificate store.
   b) Use the Certificate Services Web enrollment tool to obtain the NPS server certificate.

To configure certificate

1. Configure a server certificate template and autoenrollment:
   a) Log on to 70411SRV3 and open a blank **MMC**.
   b) On the File menu, click **Add/Remove Snap-in**. The **Add or Remove Snap-ins** dialog box opens.
   c) In **Available snap-ins**, double-click **Certification Authority**, then select **Local computer (the computer this console is running on)** and click **Finish**. The Certification Authority dialog box closes, returning to the Add or Remove Snap-ins dialog box.
   d) In Available snap-ins, double-click Certificate Templates, and then click Ok.
   e) In the console tree, highlight **Certificate Templates**. All of the certificate templates are displayed in the details pane.
   f) In the details pane, click the **RAS and IAS Server** template.
   g) On the Action menu, click **More Actions** and click **Duplicate Template**.

    h) On the **Duplicate Template** dialog box, accept the defaults template version presented. Complete the following tasks:
- i) On the General tab, in Display Name and Template name fields, type NPSCertificate.
- ii) Click the Security tab. In Group or user names, click RAS and IAS Servers.
- iii) In **Permissions** for RAS and IAS servers, under **Allow,** select the **Enroll and Autoenroll permission** check boxes, and then click **Ok.**

    i) On the MMC console, double-click **Certification Authority**, double-click 70411Lab-70411SRV3-CA, and then click **Certificate Templates**.

    j) On the Action menu, click More Actions then point to **New**, and click **Certificate Template to Issue**. The Enable Certificate Templates dialog box opens.

    k) In Enable Certificate Templates, click NPSCertificate, and then click Ok.

2. Configure Certificate Auto-enrolment via Group Policy:
   a) Log on to 70411SRV (DC) and open **Group Policy Management.**
   b) Right-click Default Domain Policy select Edit.
   c) Navigate to Computer Configuration\Policies\Windows Settings\Security Settings and select **Public Key Policies**.
   d) In the details pane, double-click **Certificate Services Client - Auto-Enrollment**. The Certificate Services Client - Auto-Enrollment Properties dialog box opens.
   e) In the Certificate Services Client - Auto-Enrollment Properties dialog box, in Configuration Model, select **Enabled**.
   f) Select the **Renew expired certificates, update pending certificates**, and **remove revoked certificates** check boxes.
   g) Select the **Update certificates that use certificate templates** check box, and then click **Ok.**

3. Deploy certificate-based authentication:
   a) Log on to 70411SRV3 and open **Remote Access.**
   b) In **Step 2 Remote Access Server**, click **Edit**. Click **Next** thrice until you get to the **Authentication** screen.
   c) On the Authentication screen, click **Use computer certificate**s check box. Click **Browse** and select **70411Lab-70411SRV3-CA** then click **Ok.**
   d) Click **Next** and then **Finish.**

4.1.5 Configure a RADIUS server and RADIUS proxy (2012 R2 Objective)

This section we will discuss NPS as a RADIUS server and then as a RADIUS proxy. This section is further divided into two subsections.

Configure a RADIUS server

Network Policy Server (NPS) can be used as a Remote Authentication Dial-In User Service (RADIUS) server to perform authentication, authorization, and accounting for RADIUS clients. A RADIUS client can be an access server, such as a dial-up server or wireless access point, or a RADIUS proxy. When NPS is used as a RADIUS server, it provides the following:

1. A central authentication and authorization service for all access requests that are sent by RADIUS clients. NPS uses a Microsoft Active Directory Domain Services (AD DS) domain, or the local Security Accounts Manager (SAM) user accounts database to authenticate user credentials for connection attempts. To authorise users, NPS validates the dial-in property settings of the user account and checks network policies.
2. A central accounting recording service for all accounting requests that are sent by RADIUS clients. Accounting requests are stored in a local log file or a Microsoft SQL Server database. Accounting information may then be analysed as required.

Note

The access server also sends Accounting request messages when a connection is established, connection is closed, or an access server is started and stopped.

NPS may act as a RADIUS server in the conditions outlined below:

1. You are using a Windows AD DS domain, or the local SAM user accounts database as your user account database for access clients.
2. You are using Routing and Remote Access on multiple dial-up servers, VPN servers, or demand-dial routers and you want to centralize both the configuration of network policies and connection logging for accounting.
3. You are outsourcing your dial-up, VPN, or wireless access to a service provider. The access servers use RADIUS to authenticate and authorize connections that are made by members of your organization.
4. You want to centralize authentication, authorization, and accounting for a heterogeneous set of access servers.

As already stated several times in this chapter, to configure NPS as a RADIUS Server, three tasks needs to be completed using the Advanced Configuration method. We have configured RADIUS clients in the previous lab (Under

RADIUS clients). We will configure Network Policies and Accounting later in this chapter.

Configure a RADIUS Proxy

When used as a RADIUS proxy, NPS is a central switching or routing point through which RADIUS access and accounting messages flow. NPS records information in an accounting log about the messages that are forwarded. For NPS to function as a RADIUS Proxy, Remote RADIUS Server Groups has to be defined.

Remote RADIUS Server Groups also need to be defined if NPS is configured as a NAP (More in section 4.4). In this scenario a remote Health Registration Authority (HRA) server is configured with a remote RADIUS server group containing the list of NAP health policy servers used to validate the health of NAP client computers. If the NAP enforcement point is located on the same server as the NAP health policy server, then you do not need to configure remote RADIUS server groups.

To summarize the points discussed above, remote RADIUS server groups will be added to NPS:

1. When you configure NPS as a Proxy Server: Allows you to specify where to forward connection requests.
2. When you configure NPS as a NAP health policy server and the NAP health policy server is located on a server different from the NAP enforcement server. The health policy server must then be added to the remote RADIUS server groups on the NAP enforcement server, and a connection request policy must be configured to forward connection requests to the remote RADIUS server group.

To Configure Remote RADIUS Server Groups

1. Log on to 70411SRV1 and open **Network Policy Server**.
2. On the NPS console tree, expand RADIUS Clients and Server then highlight Remote RADIUS Server Groups.
3. Right-click **Remote RADIUS Server Groups**, and then click **New**.
4. On the **New Remote RADIUS Server Group** dialog box, under **Group name**, type **RADIUS Servers** and then click **Add**. The **Add RADIUS Server** configuration window opens.
5. On the Add RADIUS Server dialog box, under Select an existing Remote RADIUS Server template, select **RADIUSServertemplate** created earlier, click Ok.
6. On the New Remote RADIUS Server Group dialog box, click Ok.

RADIUS server priority and weight

To load balance RADIUS servers, there must be more than one RADIUS server per remote RADIUS server group. Load balancing behavior is determined by **Priority** and **Weight** configured for each RADIUS server. **Priority** and **Weight** configured are configured on the **Load Balancing** tab of the RADIUS server properties. Additional information about on Priority and Weight are provided below:

1. **Priority**: Specifies the order of importance assigned to RADIUS servers. Priority level must be assigned a value that is an integer, such as 1, 2, or 3. The lower the number, the higher priority the NPS proxy gives to the RADIUS server. For example, if the RADIUS server is assigned the highest priority of 1, the NPS proxy sends connection requests to the RADIUS server first; if servers with priority 1 are not available, NPS then sends connection requests to RADIUS servers with priority 2, and so on. You can assign the same priority to multiple RADIUS servers, and then use the **Weight** setting to load balance between them.

2. **Weight**: NPS uses Weight setting to determine how many connection requests to send to each group member when the group members have the same priority level. Weight setting must be assigned a value between 1 and 100, and the value represents a percentage value. For example, if the remote RADIUS server group has two members with same priority level of 1 and a weight rating of 50, the NPS proxy forwards 50 percent of the connection requests to each RADIUS server.

4.1.6 Configure NPS templates (2012 R2 Objective)

Network Policy Server (NPS) templates create reusable configuration elements, such as RADIUS clients or shared secrets. These may be reused on the local NPS server or exported for use on other NPS servers. NPS templates are designed to reduce the amount of time and cost it takes to configure NPS on one or more servers.

The following NPS template types are available for configuration in Templates Management: Shared Secrets, RADIUS Clients, Remote RADIUS Servers, IP Filters, Health Policies and Remediation Server Groups.

In section 4.1.2 we created templates that are specific for a RADIUS server. The tasks in this section will cover IP Filters, Health Policies and Remediation Server Groups templates.

To configure NPS templates

1. Create a template for IP Filters:
   a) Log on to 70411SRV1 and open NPS console.
   b) Expand **Templates Management**, then right-click **IP Filters**, and click **New**. The **New IP Filters Template** page opens.
   c) On the Template Name field, type IPv4 IP Filters Template.
   d) Review the different filters you can configure, and when done click **Ok.**

2. Create templates for Health Policies: Expand **Templates Management**, then follow the steps below to create a Health Policy for Compliant computers:
   a) Right-click Health Policies and click **New**. The Create New Health Policy page opens.
   b) On the **Policy** name field, type **Compliant Template**.
   c) Below Client SHV check drop-down, select Client passes all SHV check checks.
   d) Click the **Windows Security Health Validator** box then click **Ok** to create the health policy template.
3. Create a Health Policy template for non-Compliant computers:
   a) Right-click Health Policies and click New. The Create New Health Policy page opens.
   b) On the Policy name field, type Non-Compliant Template.
   c) Below Client SHV check drop-down, select Client fails one or more SHV check checks.
   d) Click the **Windows Security Health Validator** box then click **Ok** to create the health policy template.
4. Create templates for Remediation Server Groups:
   a) Expand Templates Management, then right-click Remediation Server Groups, and click New. The New Remediation Server Group page opens.
   b) On the **Group name** field, type **RSG Template**.
   c) Below Remediation Servers, click **Add** and complete the following tasks:
      i) On the **Friendly name** field enter 70411SRV1 (This is our WSUS server).
      ii) On the **IP Address or DNS** field enter 70411SRV1, then click **Resolve** and **Ok** twice.

4.2 Configure NPS policies

Introduction

We have covered Connection request policies in previous sections. Connection request policies allow you to designate whether connection requests are processed locally or forwarded to remote RADIUS servers. In this section, we will be covering Network and Health Policies.

After NPS authenticates users or computers connecting to the network, it performs authorization to determine whether to grant the user or computer permission to the network. Authorization is performed when NPS checks the dial-in properties of user accounts in Active Directory and when NPS evaluates the connection request against the network policies configured in the NPS console.

We already noted that NPS processes authorization requests from users by considering the settings on the user's **Dial-in** tab. These settings are discussed below:

1. If the value of **Network Access Permission** is **Deny access**, the user is always denied access to the network by NPS, regardless of any settings in network policy.
2. If the value of **Network Access Permission** is **Allow access**, the user is allowed network access unless there is a network policy that explicitly denies access to the user.
3. If the value of **Network Access Permission** is **Control access through NPS Network Policy**, NPS makes authorization decisions based solely on network policy settings.

Note

For ease of administration of network access, it is recommended that the Network Access Permission setting is always set to Control access through NPS Network Policy. By default, if your forest functional level is Windows Server 2008, when you create a new user account, the value of Network Access Permission is set to Control access through NPS Network Policy.

You can also specify connection settings in an NPS network policy that are applied after the connection is authenticated and authorized. For example, you can define IP filters for the connection that specify the network resources to which the user has permission to connect.

In this section, we will cover following exam objectives:

4.2.0 Configure connection request policies
4.2.1 Configure network policies for VPN clients
4.2.2 Manage NPS templates
4.2.3 Import and export NPS policies

Lab Plan
We will continue with the lap plan specified in the previous section.

Additional lab setup
None

4.2.0 Configure connection request policies

Connection requests policies allow you to designate whether connection requests are processed locally or forwarded to Remote RADIUS Servers. For Network Access Protection (NAP) with VPN or 802.1X, you must configure PEAP authentication in connection Requests Policy.

To configure a connection request policy

1. Log on to 70411SRV1 and open **Network Policy Server.**
2. On the Network Policy Server console tree, expand **Policies** then right-click **Connection Request Policies** and select New. The New Connection Request Policy Wizard opens.
3. In the Specify Connection Request Policy Name and Connection Type field, under Policy name, enter **Connection request for VPN Clients**.
4. Under Type of network access server, select Remote Access Server (VPN-Dial up), and then click **Next**.
5. On the **Specify Conditions** window, click **Add**.
6. On the **Select Condition** dialogue box, scroll down to **RADIUS client properties** group, select **Client Friendly Name** and then click **Add**. On the **Client Friendly Name** dialogue box, type 70411SRV3 and click **Ok.**
7. On the **Specify Conditions** Window click **Next**.
8. On the Specify Connection Requests Forwarding page, under settings, highlight **Authentication**, and on the details pane, click **Forward requests to the following remote RADIUS server group**. Ensure that **RADIUS Servers group** is selected.
9. Still under settings, highlight Accounting, click the check box Forward accounting requests to this remote RADIUS server group. Ensure that RADIUS Servers group is selected and click Next.
10. On the **Configure Settings** Page, review the different settings and note possible configurations then click **Next** and **Finish.**

To configure Protected EAP (PEAP) authentication

1. Log on to 70411SRV4 and open **Network Policy Server.**
2. On the Network Policy Server console tree expand Policies, right-click **Connection Request Policies** and select New. The **New Connection Request Policy** Wizard opens.
3. On the Specify Connection Request Policy Name and Connection Type field, under Policy name, enter Connection request for VPN Proxies.
4. Under Type of network access server, select Remote Access Server (VPN-Dial up), and then click **Next**.
5. On the **Specify Conditions** window, click **Add**.

6. On the **Select Condition** dialogue box, scroll down to **RADIUS client properties** group, select **Client Friendly Name** and click **Add.** On the **Client Friendly Name** dialogue box, enter 70411SRV1 and click **Ok.**
7. On the **Specify Conditions** Window click **Next**.
8. On the Specify Connection Requests Forwarding page, under settings, highlight Authentication, and on the details pane, click Authenticate requests on this server.
9. Still under **settings**, highlight **Accounting**, notice that **Forward accounting requests to this remote RADIUS server group** is disabled, this is because accounting requests will also be processed locally. Click **Next.**
10. On the Specify Authentication Methods screen, click Override network policy authentication settings check box and complete the following tasks:
    a) Below **EAP Types**, click **Add** and on the **Add EAP** dialogue, highlight **Microsoft: Protected EAP (PEAP)** and click **Ok**.
    b) Check Microsoft Encrypted Authentication version 2 (MS-CHAP-v2).
    c) Click **Next**.
11. On the **Configure Settings** Page, review the different settings and note all possible configurations, then click **Next** and **Finish**.

4.2.1 Configure network policies for VPN clients

Network policies designate what is authorized to connect to the network and the circumstances under which connection is allowed or denied. If multiple network policies are configured in NPS, the policies are an ordered list of rules. NPS evaluates the policies in listed order from first to last. If there is a network policy that matches the connection request, NPS uses the policy to determine whether to grant or deny access to the user or computer requesting the connection. It is, therefore, important to ensure that rules created in one policy do not unintentionally counteract the rules in a different policy.

To illustrate the point, assuming your organization has limited wireless resources so members of the **Domain Users** group are denied access when connecting through Wireless Access Points. In order to grant users access to the Wireless Access point, you create another security group, **Wireless Users** and grant the group access to your Wireless Access Point. If the network policy that denies wireless access to **Domain Users** is evaluated before the Wireless Users policy is evaluated, NPS denies access to members of the Wireless Users group when they attempt to connect by wireless; even though your intention is to grant them access. To ensure this does not happen, move the Wireless Users network policy higher in the list of policies in the NPS console so that it is evaluated before the Domain Users policy is evaluated.

In this circumstance, when a member of the Wireless Users group attempts to connect, NPS evaluates the Wireless Users policy first and then authorizes the connection. When NPS receives a wireless connection attempt from a member of the Domain Users group that is not a member of the Wireless Users group, the connection attempt does not match the Wireless Users policy, so that policy is not evaluated by NPS. Instead, NPS moves down to the Domain Users wireless policy, and then denies the connection to the member of the Domain Users group.

In the sections below, we will configure Network Policies for VPN clients to manage **Multilink and bandwidth allocation, IP filters, encryption** and **IP Settings**. These settings are located under **Routing and Remote Access: Multilink and Bandwidth Allocation Protocol (BAP)**.

BAP configure how multiple dial-up connections from one computer are managed and whether the number of connections should be reduced based on capacity.

IP Filters settings create IPv4 and IPv6 filters to control the IP traffic that the client computer can send or receive.

Encryption settings specify the encryption level required between the client computer and the server running Routing and Remote Access service. If non-Microsoft network access servers are used for VPN and dial-up connections, encryption settings selected must be supported by the servers.

IP Settings specify the client IP address assignment rules for the network policy.

To configure Network Policy settings for VPN clients

1. Log on to 70411SRV1 and open **Network Policy Server.**
2. On the **Network Policy Server** console tree expand **Policies,** and highlight **Network Policies**. On the details pane, double-click **RAS Policy for 70411SRV3**.
3. On the **RAS Policy for 70411SRV3** Properties, click **Settings** tab and configure the following under **Routing and Remote Access**:
   a) To configure Multilink and Bandwidth Allocation Protocol (BAP):
      i) Highlight Multilink and Bandwidth Allocation Protocol (BAP) and on the details pane,
      ii) Configure **Multilink** settings - Specify how you would like to handle multiple connections to the network. Available options are listed below:
         (1) Server settings determine Multilink usage.
         (2) Do not allow Multilink connections.
         (3) Specify Multilink settings (Maximum number of ports allowed).
      iii) Select Specify Multilink settings and beside Maximum number of ports allowed, enter 10.

      iv) Configure **Bandwidth Allocation Protocol** settings – If the lines of a Multilink connection fall below the following percentage of capacity for the specified period of time, reduce the connection by one line: Note available options:

        (1) Percentage of capacity.

        (2) Period of time.

        (3) Require BAP for dynamic Multilink requests.

  b) To Configure **IP filters**:

     i) Highlight **IP filters** - you can perform the following tasks:

        (1) Select an existing IP Filter template.

        (2) Configure Input Filters and Output Filters for IPv4 and IPv6 addresses.

     ii) To configure IPv4 packets this interface sends:

        (1) Click **Input Filters**, and on the **Inbound Filters** dialogue click **New**,

        (2) Note that you have only **Destination network** highlighted, click **Cancel** twice.

     iii) To configure IPv4 packets this interface receives:

        (1) Click **Output Filters**, and on the **Outbound Filters** dialogue click **New**,

        (2) Note that you have only **Source network** highlighted, click **Cancel** twice.

  c) To configure **Encryption**:

     i) Highlight **Encryption**: Encryption settings are supported by computers running Microsoft Routing and Remote Access Service. The following Encryption types can be configured:

        (1) Basic encryption (MPPE 40-bit).

        (2) Strong encryption (MPPE 56-bit).

        (3) Strongest encryption (MPPE 128-bit).

        (4) No encryption

  d) To configure **IP Settings:**

     i) Highlight **IP Settings**: Specify the client IP address assignment for this policy. The following are supported options:

        (1) Server must supply an IP address.

        (2) Client may request an IP address.

        (3) Server settings determine IP address assignment (This is the default).

        (4) Assign a static IPv4 address.

4. On the **RAS Policy for 70411SRV3** Properties, click **Ok** to save your changes.

4.2.2 Manage NPS templates

Templates Management provides a node in the NPS console where you can create, modify, delete, duplicate, and view the use of NPS templates. NPS templates are designed to reduce the amount of time and cost that it takes to configure NPS on one or more servers.

Note

NPS templates and Templates Management are available only in Windows Server 2012 and Windows Server 2012 R2. NPS templates and Templates Management are not available in Windows Server 2008.

The following NPS template types are available for configuration in Templates Management:

Shared Secrets: Makes it possible to specify reusable shared secrets (by selecting the template in the appropriate location in the NPS console) when you configure RADIUS clients and servers.

RADIUS Clients: Configures RADIUS client templates that are reusable.

Remote RADIUS Servers: Configures RADIUS Servers templates that are reusable.

IP Filters: Configures Internet Protocol version 4 (IPv4) and Internet Protocol version 6 (IPv6) filters templates that are reusable.

Health Policies: These templates provide option to create health policy settings that are reusable.

Remediation Server Groups: These templates provide option to create remediation server group settings that are reusable.

Netsh command for NPS may be used to configure NPS templates. When Netsh command is used to change the settings of a configuration element, a reference to a template that is applied to the current configuration element is removed.

Note that from the NPS Console, you can perform the following tasks when you right-click Template Management: Import Templates from a Computer, Import Templates from a File and Export Templates to a File.

4.2.3 Import and export NPS policies

It is possible to export the entire NPS configuration; including RADIUS clients and servers, network policy, connection request policy, registry settings, and logging configuration from one NPS server. These settings may then be imported to another NPS server. NPS configuration Export and import may be accomplished by using the netsh command, via Windows interface (NPS console) and Windows PowerShell.

Using the netsh command

Netsh nps export command requires the **exportPSK** parameter with the value **YES**. This parameter and value explicitly state that you understand that you are exporting the NPS server configuration, and that the exported XML file contains unencrypted shared secrets for RADIUS clients and members of remote RADIUS server groups.When the **netsh import** command is run, NPS is automatically refreshed with the updated configuration settings. You do not need to stop NPS on the destination computer to run the **netsh import** command, however if the NPS console or NPS MMC snap-in is open during the configuration import, changes to the server configuration are not visible until you refresh the view.

Note

If SQL Server logging is configured on the source NPS server, SQL Server logging settings are not exported to the XML file. After you import the file to another NPS server, you must manually configure SQL Server logging.

Using Windows interface (NPS console)

You can perform the same task described above from the NPS MMC console.

Using Windows Powershell

Beginning with Windows Server 2012, you can export and import the NPS configuration using Windows PowerShell. The command syntax are shown below:

```
Export-NpsConfiguration [-Path] <String> [ <CommonParameters>]
Import-NpsConfiguration [-Path] <String> [ <CommonParameters>]
```

To export and import NPS Configuration including Policies.

1. To export NPS configuration: Log on to 70411SRV1 and run the following PowerShell command:

```
Export-NpsConfiguration -Path C:\Npsconfig.xml
```

2. To import the configuration: Log on to 70411SRV4 and run the following PowerShell command:

```
Import-NpsConfiguration -Path "\\70411SRV1\C$\Npsconfig.xml"
```

4.3 Configure Network Access Protection (NAP)

Introduction

Network Access Protection (NAP) utilizes a number of components on the server and client to allow administrators much greater control over which computers are allowed to connect to the network. Specifically, NAP may be configured to prevent systems that may be at risk, such as systems without up-to-date security patches, systems not running antivirus software and antimalware software with current definitions, or systems without an active host firewall, from connecting to the network and potentially putting other systems at risk.

NAP can be used with client computers running Windows XP SP3 and above. These operating systems support the NAP Agent. NAP Agent is the component on the client that collects and manages health information. When the NAP Agent service is installed and running, the client can communicate its health status to the NAP servers. The health status information is based on the state of the client's configuration and can include such information as: The firewall status, Antivirus signature status, status of service packs and security updates. NAP is Microsoft's implementation of a "health" enforcement solution; it protects the network from health "issues" that remote clients may have. It does this by checking the identity of each remote client and determines whether the client is in compliance with the organization's health policies. The health information that each client sends to the NAP server is called a statement of health or SoH.

The server evaluates this information based on the policies and settings that have been configured. It uses this information, along with group membership, to determine whether and at what level of access the client will be allowed to connect to the corporate network. Clients that are out of compliance with the policies can be brought into compliance through NAP's mechanisms. NAP does this by performing a network health analysis, verifying the effectiveness of existing security policies, and helping administrators to identify risks by creating a health profile for the network. This improves the overall health of the network by enforcing compliance with your network health policies and restricting access to non-compliant computers.

In this section, we will cover following exam objectives:

4.3.0 Configure System Health Validators (SHVs)

4.3.1 Configure health policies

4.3.2 Configure NAP enforcement using DHCP and VPN

4.3.3 Configure isolation and remediation of non-compliant computers

4.3.4 Configure NAP client settings

Lab Plan

We will require the following servers to perform the tasks in this section: 70411SRV1, 70411SRV3 and 70411SRV4.

Additional lab setup

Install DHCP role on 70411SRV4 and configure scopes.

Log on to **70411SRV4** and run the following PowerShell command to install DHCP:

```
Install-WindowsFeature -Name DHCP -IncludeAllSubFeature –
IncludeManagementTools
```

When the installation completes, authorize the DHCP server.

Configure DHCP scope failover on 70411SRV3

1. Log on to 70411SRV3 and open DHCP from Server Manager.
2. On the DNCP console, expand **70411SRV3.70411Lab.com** then expand **IPv4.**
3. Under IPV4, right-click Scope [192.168.0.0] and click Configure Failover.
4. On the **Configure Failover** wizard click **Next**.
5. On the Specify the partner server to use for failover, click Add Server.
6. On the **Add Server** page, type 70411SRV4 and click **Ok.**
7. On the **Configure Failover** wizard click **Next**.
8. On the **Create a new failover relationship**, accept all defaults and enter P@ssw0rd as the **Shared secret** then click **Next** and **finish**.

4.3.0 Configure System Health Validators (SHVs)

System health validators (SHVs) define configuration requirements for computers that attempt to connect to a network. SHVs configuration specify the settings required for NAP-capable client computers. SHVs work in conjunction with one or more health policies.

To configure Windows Security Health Validator

1. Log on to 70411SRV1 and open **Network Policy Server**.
2. Expand Network Access Protection, and then expand System Health Validators.
3. At the middle pane, under **Name**, double-click **Windows Security Health Validator**.
4. Highlight **Windows Security Health Validator** and in the details pane, click **Settings**.
5. On the **Settings** Page, Double-click **Default Configuration**. The Windows Security Health Validator page settings open.
6. On the left pane, highlight **Windows 8/Windows 7/Windows Vista** and on the details pane, review options available for configuration:
   a) **Firewall Settings**: Checks that firewall is enabled for all network connections.
   b) **Antivirus Settings**: Provides two configuration options:
      i) An antivirus application is on.
      ii) Antivirus is up to date.
   c) **Spyware Protection Settings**: Two configurations available in this category:
      i) An antispyware application is on.
      ii) antispyware is up to date.
   d) **Security Update Settings**: You can configure to restrict access for clients that do not have all available security updates installed. You can specify the minimum severity level required for updates. Below are available severity options:
      i) Low and above.
      ii) Moderate and above.
      iii) Important and above.
      iv) Critical Only.
   e) You are able specify the minimum number of hours allowed since the client has checked for security updates (Maximum allowed is 72 hours, default set is 22 hours)
   f) Finally, you can configure how clients receive security updates. Updates can be received from:
      i) Windows Update.
      ii) Windows Server Update Services.

7. On the left pane, highlight **Windows XP** and on the details pane, review options you can configure: All options described above are also available for Windows XP, except **Spyware Protection Settings**.
8. Click **Ok** to close the Windows Security Health Validator dialog box.

Exam Tip

Note that the **Windows Security Health Validator** settings for Windows XP do not have option for **Spyware Protection Settings.** This is only available for **Windows 8/Windows 7/Windows Vista** settings. Also note the available options for client security update settings. You can configure clients to update security via Windows Update, Windows Server Update Services or both. By default, only Windows Update is checked.

4.3.1 Configure health policies

Health policies define which SHVs are evaluated, and how they are used to validate the configuration of computers that attempt to connect to a network. Based on the results of SHV checks, health policies classify client health status.

In the tasks below, you will create two health policies for compliant and non-compliant clients. You will then create two Network Policies to determine how NPS respond to compliant and non-compliant clients.

To Configure health and Network policies

1. To Configure health policies, complete the tasks below:
    a) From the NPS Console on 70411SRV1, expand **Polices**.
    b) Right-click **Health Policies**, and then click **New**.
    c) On the **Create New Health Policy** dialog box, check Select an existing template, and select the Compliant Template.
    d) On the Edit **Policy Name** field, enter **Compliant** and click **Ok**.
    e) Right-click **Health Policies**, and click **New**.
    f) On the Create New Health Policy dialog box, check Select an existing template, and select Non-Compliant Template.
    g) On the Edit **Policy Name** field enter **Non-compliant** and click **Ok**.
2. To configure a network policy for compliant client computers, complete the tasks below:
    a) From the NPS Console on 70411SRV1, expand **Polices,** right-click **Network Policies**, and click **New**.
    b) On the Specify Network Policy Name and Connection Type window, On the Policy name field, enter Compliant-Full-Access, and then click **Next**.
    c) On the Specify Conditions window, click Add.
    d) On the **Select condition** dialog box, double-click **Health Polices**.

e) On the **Health   Policies** dialog   box,   under **Health   policies,** select **Compliant**, and then click **Ok**.

f) On the **Specify   Conditions** window,   verify   that **Health   Policy** is specified,   under **Conditions** with   a   value   of **Compliant**,   then click **Next**.

g) On the **Specify   Access   Permission** window,   verify   that **Access granted** is selected, and then click **Next** three times.

h) On the Configure Settings window, click **NAP   Enforcement**, then select Allow Full Network access and select Enable auto-remediation of client computers.

i) On the Completing New Network Policy window, click **Next** then **Finish**.

3. Configuring a network policy for non-compliant client computers:

a) From the NPS Console on 70411SRV1, expand **Polices,** right-click **Network Policies**, and click **New**.

b) On the Specify Network Policy Name and Connection Type window, under **Policy   name**,   enter **Non-Compliant-limited-Access**,   and then click **Next**.

c) On the **Specify Conditions** window, click **Add**.

d) On the **Select condition** dialog box, double-click **Health Polices**.

e) On   the **Health   Policies** dialog   box,   under **Health   policies**, select **Non-**Compliant, then click **Ok**.

f) On the **Specify   Conditions** window,   verify   that **Health   Policy** is specified under **Conditions** with   a   value   of **Non-**Compliant,   then click **Next**.

g) On the **Specify   Access   Permission** window,   verify   that **Access granted** is selected, then click **Next** three times.

h) On the **Configure Settings** window, click **NAP   Enforcement** then select **Allow Limited access**. Configure the following:

   i) Under Remediation Server Group and Troubleshooting URL, click Configure.

   ii) Beside Remediation Server Group click New Group and on the New Remediation Server Group dialogue click Select an existing template. RSG Template template is selected.

   iii) Click Edit Group name and enter Remediation Servers then click Ok.

   iv) On the New Remediation Server Group dialogue click Ok.

i) On the New **Network Policy** page, click **Next** and **Finish**.

4.3.2 Configure NAP enforcement using DHCP and VPN

Network Access Protection (NAP) enforcement can be configured for 802.1X Wired, 802.1X Wireless, DHCP, TS Gateway and VPN. For the purposes of the exam, we shall concentrate on NAP enforcement using DHCP and VPN.

To configure NAP enforcement using DHCP

High-level plan below:

1. Configure NPS as a RADIUS proxy - Create Remote RADIUS Server Group.
2. Enable DHCP Scopes for NAP.
3. Create New Connection Request for DHCP.
4. Configure the DHCP-NPS proxy servers as RADIUS clients.
5. Create a Group for a Network Policy.
6. Enable the Network Access Protection Service on Clients.
7. Enable and Disable NAP Enforcement Clients.
8. Enable Security Center in Group Policy.
9. Configure Remediation Server Groups.
10. Configure the Windows Security Health Validator.
11. Configure Policies that enforce NAP for DHCP.
12. Ensure that NPS network policy constraints allow computer health checks.

Detailed configuration steps are outlined below:

1. Create Remote RADIUS Server Group on 70411SRV1: Task completed in previous section. We have a Remote RADIUS Server Group called **RADIUS Servers,** with 70411SRV4 (Current DHCP Server) as the only member.
2. Enable DHCP Scopes for NAP:
   a) Log on to 70411SRV4 and open DHCP management console.
   b) Expand 70411SRV4.70411Lab.com, then expand IPv4 node.
   c) Right-click Scope [192.168.0.0] and click Properties.
   d) On the Scope [192.168.0.0] Properties, click **Network Access Protection** tab.
   e) On the Network Access Protection tab, select **Enable for this scope** and click **Ok**.

Note

To enable Network Access Protection for all scopes: Right-click **IPv4,** select **Properties** then click **Network Access Protection** tab, and click **Enable on all scopes.**

3. Create New Connection Request for DHCP:
    a) Log on to 70411SRV1 and open NPS console.
    b) On the console tree, expand **Policies,** then right-click **Connection Requests Policies** and select **New.**
    c) On the New Connection Requests Policy, **Policy name** field enter **ConnectionRequestsDHCP**. On the **Type of network access server** drop-down, select **DHCP Server** and click **Next**.
    d) On the **Specify Conditions** screen, click **Add** and on the **Select condition** window, double-click **Client Friendly Name**.
    e) On the Client Friendly Name field, type 70411SRV3 and click Ok.
    f) On the **Specify Conditions** screen, click **Next**.
    g) On the **Specify Connection Request Forwarding** screen, configure the following:
        i) Under settings, select Authentication and on the details pane select Forward requests to the following remote RADIUS server group for authentication, then select RADIUS Servers Group from the drop down.
        ii) Under settings click **Accounting** and on the details pane, forward requests to **RADIUS Servers Group** as well. Click **Next** twice and then **Finish**.
4. Configure the DHCP-NPS proxy servers as RADIUS clients:
    a) Log on to 70411SRV4 and open NPS console.
    b) On the NPS Console, expand **RADIUS Clients and Servers,** right-click **RADIUS Clients** and select **New.**
    c) On the **New RADIUS Client,** click **Settings** tab, complete the following tasks:
        i) On **Friendly name** enter 70411SRV1.
        ii) On Address (IP or DNS) enter 70411SRV1, and click Verify, Resolve then Ok.
        iii) On **Shared Secret** enter that **Manual** is selected, then on the shared secret boxes, enter **P@ssW0rd** as the shared secret and click **Ok.**
    d) On the **New RADIUS Client,** click **Advanced** tab and complete the following tasks:
        i) On **Vendor name** drop-down, select **Microsoft**.
        ii) On Additional Options, check RADIUS client is NAP-Capable and click Ok.
5. Create a Group for a Network Policy (Necessary to perform authorization by group):
    a) Log on to 70411SRV and open Active Directory Users and Computers.
    b) Navigate to Users container, right-click it and point to **New**, select **Group**.

   c) On the New Object – Group screen, complete the following tasks:

      i) On the Group name field, enter **NAPCompliant Clients**.

      ii) Under Group Scope select **Global**.

      iii) Under Group type select **Security**.

   d) Click **Ok.**

   e) Repeat the steps above to create a **Non-NAPComplaint Clients** group.

6. Enable the Network Access Protection Service on Clients: This task will be completed in section 4.3.4.

7. Enable and Disable NAP Enforcement : This task will be completed in section 4.3.4.

8. Enable Security Center in Group Policy:

   a) Log on to 70411SRV and open **Group Policy Management.**

   b) On the GPMC console, navigate to 70411Lab.com domain, right-click **Default Domain Policy** and click **Edit.**

   c) Navigate to Computer Configuration\Administrative Templates\Windows Components, and then highlight Security Center, on the details pane, double-click Turn on Security Center (Domain PCs only), click Enabled, and then click Ok.

Note

When Security Center is turned on, it monitors essential security settings and notifies the user when the computer might be at risk. Security Center can only be turned off for computers that are joined to a Windows domain. When a computer is not joined to a Windows domain, the policy setting will have no effect. If you enable this policy setting, Security Center is turned on for all users. If you disable this policy setting, Security Center is turned off for domain members.

9. Configure Remediation Server Groups: We already created a Remediation Server Group, **Remediation Servers,** with 70411SRV1 (WSUS Server) as member.

10. Configure the Windows Security Health Validator: Already completed in a previous section.

11. Configure Policies that enforce NAP for DHCP:

   a) Log on to 70411SRV1 and open NPS console.

   b) On the console, click **NPS (Local)** and on the details pane, below the **Standard Configuration** scenario ensure that **Network Access Protection (NAP)** is selected, then click **Configure NAP**, to launch the **NAP Configuration wizard.**

   c) On the Network connection method screen, select Dynamic Host Configuration Protocol (DHCP). On the Policy Name, edit the default name and change it to NAP Policies for DHCP then click Next.

d) On the Specify NAP Enforcement Servers Running DHCP Server screen, below RADIUS clients, complete the following tasks:

    i) Click **70411SRV3** (If it appears on the list) and select **Edit.**

    ii) On the Friendly name, under Address (IP or DNS) field, enter 70411SRV4, , and click Verify, Resolve, then Ok.

    iii) Below Shared Secret, Select an existing Shared Secret template, then select RADIUSServers&Clients and click Ok.

e) On the Specify NAP Enforcement Servers Running DHCP Server screen, click Next.

f) On the **Specify DHCP Scopes** screen, click **Next**. (The policy applies to all NAP-enabled scopes at the selected DHCP server).

g) On the Configure Machine Groups, below Machine Groups, click Add and on the Select Group window, enter NAPComplaint Clients and click Ok.

h) On the Configure Machine Groups window, click Next.

i) On the Specify NAP Remediation Server Group and URL screen, below Remediation Server Group drop-down, select Remediation Servers then click Next.

j) Review the settings on the **Define NAP Health Policy** screen and confirm that the following information are available:

    i) System Health Validator in use: Windows Security Health Validator.

    ii) Auto-remediation of client computers: Enabled.

    iii) Network access restrictions for NAP-ineligible client computers: Deny full access to NAP-ineligible client computers. Allow access to a restricted network.

k) On the **Define NAP Health Policy** screen, click **Next.** Review the summary page and click **Finish.**

12. Ensure that NPS network policy constraints allow computer health checks:

a) Still Logged on to 70411SRV1 and NPS console open, complete the following tasks:

    i) Highlight **Network Policies,** on the details pane highlight **NAP Policies for DHCP Compliant** policy and click the **constraints** tab.

    ii) On the left pane, click **Authentication Methods** and on the details pane, ensure that **Perform machine health check only** check box is selected, click **Cancel.**

    iii) Repeat the task above for NAP Policies for DHCP Noncompliant and NAP Policies for DHCP Non NAP-Capable policies.

To configure NAP enforcement using VPN

Most of the tasks performed for NAP enforcement using DHCP are applicable to VPN. The final task will be to create NAP policies for VPN.

1. Log on to 70411SRV1 and open NPS console.
2. On the console, click **NPS (Local)** and on the details pane, below the **Standard Configuration** scenario, ensure that **Network Access Protection (NAP)** is selected, then click **Configure NAP,** to launch the **NAP Configuration wizard.**
3. On the **Network connection method** screen, select **Virtual Private Network (VPN)** and on the **Policy Name**, edit the default name and change it to **NAP Policies for VPN**, then click **Next**.
4. On the **Specify NAP Enforcement Servers Running VPN Server** screen, below **RADIUS clients**, 70411SRV3 will be listed as RADIUS client, click **Next**.
5. On the Configure User Groups and Machine Groups screen, click Next.
6. On the **Configure an Authentication Method** screen, perform the following tasks:
   a) Review the certificate issued to 70411SRV1 by your Certificate Authority (CA), 70411SRV3.
   b) Note the available EAP types to use with PEAP. The authentication type determines the kind of credentials that NPS can accept from client computers and users (either a username and password or a certificate). Available authentication types are discussed below:
      i) **Secure Password (PEAP-MS-CHAP v2):** This authentication type permits users to type password-based credentials during authentication.
      ii) **Smart Card or other certificates (EAP-TLS):** This authentication type requires certificates on smart cards or in the client computer certificate store. For this authentication type, you MUST deploy your own trusted root certificate. Secure Password (PEAP-MS-CHAP v2) is selected by default.
7. On the Configure an Authentication Method screen, click **Next**.
8. On the Specify NAP Remediation Server Group and URL screen, below Remediation Server Group drop-down, select Remediation Servers and click **Next**.
9. Review the settings in the **Define NAP Health Policy** screen and confirm that the information is as detailed below:
   a) System Health Validator in use: Windows Security Health Validator.
   b) Auto-remediation of client computers: Enabled.
   c) Network access restrictions for NAP-ineligible client computers: Deny full access to NAP-ineligible client computers. Allow access to a restricted network.

10. On the **Define NAP Health Policy** screen, click **Next.** Review the summary page and click **Finish.**

Note

Protected Extensible Authentication Protocol (PEAP) is the authentication method available for NAP enforcement using VPN. PEAP is the authentication method used with wireless access points and authentication switches. To configure PEAP, you must select a server certificate on the NPS server and you must configure an authentication type.

4.3.3 Configure isolation and remediation of non-compliant computers using DHCP and VPN

When we ran the **Network Access Protection (NAP) Wizard** to configure NAP enforcement using VPN and DHCP, the wizard created a number of Connection Requests, Network and Health policies including policies for Noncompliant computers. These Noncompliant policies determine how NPS manage isolation and remediation of non-compliant computers.

To Review isolation and remediation of non-compliant computers

1. Review Policies for VPN Noncompliant computers:
   a) Log on to 70411SRV1 and open NPS console
   b) Navigate to **Policies** and highlight **Health Policies** and on the details pane examine the following policies:
      i) Double-click **NAP Policies for VPN Noncompliant** and review the following:
      ii) Note the **Client SHV checks option** selected: **Client fails one or more SHV checks** - This health policy evaluates a client against the SHV used in this health policy, Windows Security Health Validator for failures. If the client meets the criteria (Fails one or more SHV checks), a Network Policy decides what action(s) to take. Details below.
   c) Still on the **Policies** node, highlight **Network Policies** and on the details pane examine the following policies:
      i) Double-click NAP Policies for VPN Noncompliant.
      ii) On the General tab, note that Grant access if connection request matches this policy is selected.
      iii) Click Conditions tab: Below Condition, double-click Health Policy and note that NAP Policies for VPN Noncompliant health policy is used.
      iv) Click **Settings** tab and highlight **NAP Enforcement** and on the details pane, note that **Allow limited network access** is selected,

that Remediation servers are configured and auto-remediation of client computers is also configured.

v) Review the NAP Enforcement policy set for **the NAP Policies for VPN Compliant** network policy. This is set to **All full network access**.

2. Review Policies for DHCP Noncompliant computers: Same approach is used for DHCP Noncompliant computers.

Note

Isolation and remediation of non-compliant computers are performed by a combination of Health policies (compares the client's health status against the Security Health Validator (SHV)) and Network Policy that applies NAP enforcement by granting limited access to the non-compliant computers while the Remediation servers provide update via auto-remediation.

4.3.4 Configure NAP client settings

A NAP-client has a number of settings that may be enabled or disabled. These settings include the DHCP Quarantine, the EAP Quarantine, the RD Gateway Quarantine and IPsec Relying Party. This can be configured on a single computer by running NAPCLCFG or via group policy for multiple computers.

To Configure NAP client settings Using Group Policy

1. Log on to 70411SRV and open **Group Policy Management**.
2. On the GPMC console, navigate to **70411Lab.com** domain, right-click **Default Domain Policy** and click **Edit**.
3. To configure **NAP Service** complete the following tasks:
   a) Navigate to Computer Configuration\Policies\Windows Settings\Security Settings\System Services and double-click **Network Access Protection Agent**.
   b) On the Network Access Protection Agent Properties page, check **Enable this policy setting,** then select **Automatic** and click **Ok**.
4. To configure NAP Enforcement Client:
   a) Navigate to Computer Configuration\Policies \Windows Settings\Security Settings\Network Access Protection\NAP Configuration\Enforcement Clients.
   b) Notice that these policies are similar to the ones we configured with NAPCLCFG console. Enable the following:
      i) DHCP Quarantine enforcement client.
      ii) EAP Quarantine enforcement client.

Configure HRA Automatic Discovery

If you deploy a Health Registration Authority (HRA) server in your environment, you might need to configure NAP clients to automatically discovery HRA servers on the network using DNS service (SRV) records. The following requirements must be met in order to configure trusted server groups on NAP client computers using HRA automatic discovery:

1. Client computers must be running at least Windows XP with Service Pack 3 (SP3).
2. The HRA server must be configured with a Secure Sockets Layer (SSL) certificate.
3. The EnableDiscovery registry key must be configured on NAP client computers.
4. DNS SRV records must be configured.
5. The trusted server group configuration in either local policy or Group Policy must be cleared.

To Configure HRA Automatic Discovery

1. Configure the EnableDiscovery registry key on client computers, complete the following tasks:
   a) Log 70411SRV and open **Group Policy Management**.
   b) Expand Forest: 70411Lab.com, and navigate to Domains, 70411Lab.com.
   c) Beneath 70411Lab.com domain, right-click **Default Domain Policy** and click **Edit**. Group Policy Management Editor Opens.
   d) Under Computer Configuration, Expand Preferences\Windows Settings.
   e) Right-click **Registry,** point to **New** and select **Registry Wizard.**
   f) On the **Registry Browser,** complete the following tasks:
      i) On the **Action** drop-down, select **Create.**
      ii) On the **Hive** drop-down, select **HKEY_LOCAL_MACHINE.**
      iii) Beside the **Key Path** field, click the select box (3 doted grey boxes),
      iv) then   enter \SOFTWARE\Policies\Microsoft\NetworkAccessProtection\ClientConfig\Enroll\HcsGroups.
      v) On the Value Name Field enter EnableDiscovery.
      vi) On the **Value Type** drop-down, select **REG_ DWORD** and on the **Value data** field, enter 1.
      vii) Beneath **Base** box, select **Decimal.**
      viii) Click **Ok** to apply your changes.
2. Configure DNS SRV records:
   a) Log 70411SRV and open DNS Management console.

    b) In the console tree, open Forward Lookup
        Zones\70411Lab.com_sites\Default-First-Site-Name_tcp.

    c) Right-click **_tcp** and click **Other New Records**.

    d) On the Resource Record Type window, under Select a resource record type, click Service Location (SRV), and then click Create Record.

    e) On the **New Resource Record** window, next to **Service**, type **_hra**. Next to **Protocol**, type **_tcp.**

    f) Under **Host offering this service**, type 70411SRV3.70411Lab.com, and click **Ok**.

3. Clear the trusted server group configuration:

    a) Log 70411SRV and open Group Policy Management.

    b) Expand Forest: 70411Lab.com, and navigate to Domains, 70411Lab.com.

    c) Beneath 70411Lab.com domain, right-click Default Domain Policy and click Edit. Group Policy Management Editor Opens.

    d) On the console tree, navigate to
        Computer Configuration\Policies/Windows Settings\Security Settings\Network Access Protection\NAP Client Configuration\Health Registration Settings\Trusted Server Groups.

    e) Verify that no groups are listed in the details pane under **Trusted Server Groups**.

The task above should be performed by editing the group policy containing computers that you wish to Configure HRA Automatic Discovery. Step 1 can be configured directly on NAP client computers. In the previous task, I used group policy to demonstrate a possible enterprise deployment. The server provided under **Host offering this service**, in step 2 should be the HRA server. The server above is for illustration since we did not deploy a HRA server.

Exam Tip

It is important to note steps required to Configure HRA Automatic Discovery:

1. Configure the EnableDiscovery registry key on client computers.
2. Configure DNS SRV records.
3. Clear the trusted server group configuration.

The HRA server must be configured with a Secure Sockets Layer (SSL) certificate and Client computers must be running at least Windows XP with Service Pack 3 (SP3).

Chapter 5

Configure and Manage Active Directory

5.1 Configure Service Authentication

Introduction

Most Enterprise applications require accounts with the right access to run successfully. A major security challenge is selecting the appropriate type of account for these applications. On a local computer, an administrator can configure the application to run as Local Service, Network Service, or Local System. These service accounts are simple to configure and use, but are typically shared among multiple applications and services and cannot be managed on a domain level. The security loop up of using this approach is obvious.

On the other hand, if the application is configured to use a domain account, privileges can be isolated for these applications. Unfortunately, this approach requires manual password management. Alternatively, a custom solution may be created to manage passwords for these service accounts. Many server applications use this strategy to enhance security, but this strategy requires additional administration and complexity. In these deployments, service administrators spend a considerable amount of time on maintenance tasks such as managing service passwords and service principal names (SPNs), which are required for Kerberos authentication. In addition, these maintenance tasks can disrupt service.

In Windows 7 and Windows Server 2008 R2, managed service account (MSA) was introduced as an integral part of the operating system. MSA resolves some of the challenges faced by administrators using the native service accounts to manage applications. Managed service accounts are managed domain accounts that provide the following features to simplify service administration:

1. Automatic password management (automatically updated every 30 days)
2. Simplified Service Principal Name (SPN) management, including delegation of management to other administrators. Additional automatic SPN management is available at the Windows Server 2008 R2 domain functional level.

Virtual accounts are managed local accounts that provide the following features to simplify service administration:

1. No password management is required.
2. The ability to access the network with a computer identity in a domain environment.

In Windows Server 2012 and Windows 8, group managed service account (gMSA), was introduced to resolve the limitations associated with managed service accounts. gMSA was designed to provide crucial applications such as Exchange or IIS with the isolation of their own accounts, while eliminating the need for an administrator to manually administer the SPN and credentials for these accounts.

In this section, we will cover following exam objectives:

5.1.0 Create and configure Service Accounts
5.1.1 Create and configure Managed Service Accounts
5.1.2 Create and configure Group Managed Service Accounts
5.1.3 Manage Service Principal Names (SPNs)
5.1.4 Configure Kerberos delegation
5.1.5 Configure virtual accounts (2012 R2 Objective)

Lab Plan

We will run most tasks on the domain controllers.

Additional lab setup

None

5.1.0 Create and configure Service Accounts

A service account is a user account that is created to isolate a service or application. To create and configure a service account, it is important to apply the principle of "least privilege". This means granting the service account the minimum required access. Creating one service account per application is recommended as against using a single service account for multiple services. Other considerations when creating a service account are discussed below:

Service Account Lockout: If a service account is used by multiple applications and the password is changed, an administrator will be required to update the password on all the applications. If the administrator forgets to update it on one of the applications, the application will attempt to use the old password and in the process, may lock out the account. This will disrupt all the services / applications using the service account. From Windows Server 2003 Service Pack 1 upwards, Active Directory will check the last two passwords used. If there is a match, the service account will not be locked. This helps prevent one service application bringing down all other applications using the same service account.

Service account password expiration: If a service account password was to expire, this will prevent the service account from running the application until the password is changed. So a service account password should be configured not to expire.

To create and configure a service account.

1. Log on to 70411SRV and open Active Directory Users and Computers.
2. To create a service account: Navigate to the **Users** container and right click it, then select **New**, and point to **User**. On the **New Object – User wizard**, complete the following tasks:
    a) On the **First name** filed, enter **DFS**.
    b) On the **Last Name** field, enter **Namespace**.
    c) On the **User Logon name** field, enter **DFSNService** (Appending "Service" will help identify the account as being used by a service as against a standard login account).
    d) When you finish, click **Next.**
    e) On the next screen, perform the following tasks:
        i)   Enter a password for the service account.
        ii) Uncheck User must change password at next log on.
        iii) Check User cannot change password and Password never expires.
        iv) When you finish, click **Next** and then **Finish.**
3. Create a Service Account group and add **DFSNService** as member: Still on **Active Directory Users and Computers,** right-click **Users** node,

select **New** and click **Group.** On the **New Object – Group** wizard, complete the following tasks:
a) On the Group name field, enter ServiceAccounts.
b) On Group scope, select **Global**.
c) On Group Type, select **Security.**
d) When you finish, click **Ok.**
e) Double-click **ServiceAccounts** and click **Member of** tab, click **Add** and type **Administrators,** then click **Ok.** This adds the **ServiceAccounts** group to the local administrator's group of 70411SRV.
f) Double-click **DFS Namespace** user and perform the following tasks:
    i)   Click Member of tab, add ServiceAccounts group.
    ii)   Select ServiceAccounts and click Set Primary Group.
    iii) Select **Domain Users** and click **Remove**.
    iv)   Click **Ok** to apply your changes and close DFS Namespace Properties.
4. Configure DFS Name service to use a service account: Log on to 70411SRV and open the **Services** MMC. Perform the following tasks:
    a) Double-click **DFS Namespace** service and click **Log on** tab.
    b) Select the option **This account,** then click **Browse**, and enter **DFSNService** then click **Ok.**
    c) At the password prompt, enter the domain password for the **DFSNService** service account and click **Ok.**
    d) Note the information: The account DFSNService@70411Lab.com has been granted Log On As A Service right and click **Ok**.
    e) Right-click **DFS Namespace** service and select **Restart.**

Note

In the task above, you removed DFSNService as member of the Users group and only member of the ServiceAccounts group. This ensures the service account does not have unnecessary privileges.

5.1.1 Create and configure Managed Service Accounts

Manually managing service accounts in an enterprise could get complicated and very time-consuming. Think of manually changing passwords for multiple service accounts to improve security. Managed service account feature introduced with Windows Server 2008 R2, simplifies service account management, removes the need to manage passwords for service accounts and provides a higher level of security.

MSA management in Active Directory uses the same principle as computer account management. Each domain computer has a computer account and a password. Computer account passwords are automatically updated without any manual intervention. This eliminates the need to manually manage MSAs. Note the following about Managed Service Accounts:

1. Passwords changed automatically every 30 days.
2. The password is randomly generated using 120 characters.
3. MSAs are bound only to one computer.
4. MSAs can be placed into groups. This provides a work-around to give them access to other resources on the network.
5. Automatic Service Principal Name (SPN) registration.
6. The following requirements MUST be met to use MSAs:
   a) Domain functional level MUST be set to at least Windows Server 2008 R2
   b) The client using the MSA must be running at least Windows Server 2008 R2 or Windows 7.
   c) Software requirements:
      i) .Net Framework 3.5.
      ii) Active Directory Module for Windows PowerShell.

To create and configure Managed Service Accounts

1. Confirm existence of Managed Service Account container:
   a) Log on to 70411SRV and open Active Directory Users and Computers.
   b) Expand 70411Lab.com domain and confirm that the Managed Service Account container exists.
2. Create a Managed Service Account:
   a) Log on to 70411SRV and open **Windows PowerShell** then perform the following tasks:
      i) To add a new KDS "root key.", run any of the commands below:

Add-KdsRootKey –EffectiveTime ((get-date).addhours(-10))

Add-KDSRootKey –EffectiveImmediately

Note

Key Distribution Service (KDS) is a service in Windows Server 2012. KDS is implemented in kdssvc.dll and is required to create and use Managed or Group Managed Service Accounts (MSAs). The PowerShell command above added a KDS to the domain.

---

      ii) Create a Managed service account for WSUS Service called **MSAWSUSSVS** by running the following commands:

New-ADServiceAccount -name "MSAWSUSSVS" -DNSHostName
"MSAWSUSSVS.70411Lab.com" -enable $true –
PrincipalsAllowedToRetrieveManagedPassword 70411SRV1$

    iii) Open Active Directory Users and Computers and refresh the **Managed Service Accounts** node. The new MSA created above, MSAWSUSSVS should be listed.

3. Associate the new MSA with a target computer in Active Directory: From Windows PowerShell, run the following commands:

Add-ADComputerServiceAccount -identity 70411SRV1 -ServiceAccount
MSAWSUSSVS

4. Install the Managed Service Account: This command MUST be run on the local computer where you intend to use the MSA:
    a) Log on to 70411SRV1 and perform the following tasks:
    b) Install Active Directory Module for Windows PowerShell:
        i) Launch **Add Roles and Features** from Server Manager.
        ii) On the Features screen, expand Remote Server Administration Tools\Role Administration Tools\AD DS and AD LDS Tools.
        iii) Check Active Directory Module for Windows PowerShell.
        iv) Click Next then Install.
    c) To install the MSA created in step 2 by running the following PowerShell commands:

Install-ADServiceAccount MSAWSUSSVS

5. Associate the new MSA with the **DFS Namespace** service:
    a) Still logged on to 70411SRV1, add MSAWSUSSVS to the Local Administrators group.
    b) Open the **Services** MMC, and complete the following tasks:
        i) Double-click **WSUS Service** service and click **Log on** tab.
        ii) Select the option **This account,** then click **Browse**, change **Location** to **Entire Directory** then type **MSAWSUSSVS** and click **Ok.** The account name will display with a $ sign, 70411LAB\MSAWSUSSVS$.
        iii) Leave both password fields **BLANK** and click **Ok.**
        iv) Note the information: The account 70411LAB\MSAWSUSSVS$ has been granted Log On As A Service right and click **Ok.**
        v) Right-click **WSUS Service** service and select **Restart.**

The following PowerShell cmdlets can be used to manage MSAs:

1. **Get-ADServiceAccount**: Gets one or more Active Directory managed service accounts or group managed service accounts.
2. **Remove-ADServiceAccount**: Removes an Active Directory managed service account or group managed service account object.

3. **Set-ADServiceAccount**: Modifies an Active Directory managed service account or group managed service account object.
4. **Uninstall-ADServiceAccount:** Uninstalls an Active Directory managed service account from a computer or removes a cached group managed service account from a computer.

Note

The PrincipalsAllowedToRetrieveManagedPassword switch is required when you run the New-ADServiceAccount command let. If you do not specify this switch, you will receive an error. Without the PrincipalsAllowedToRetrieveManagedPassword switch, error 2947 will also be logged on the Directory Services event log with details "An attempt to fetch the password of a group managed service account failed."

5.1.2 Create and configure Group Managed Service Accounts

As discussed in section 5.1.1, Managed Service Accounts (MSAs) has a lot to offer, including automatic password management and automatic SPN registration. Even with these great features, MSAs have some limitations as outlined below:

1. Not supported for applications like Exchange or SQL.
2. Cannot be shared across multiple hosts.
3. Cannot be used to run a scheduled task.

Group Managed Service Account (gMSA) introduced in Windows Server 2012, resolves these problems. The benefits of gMSAs are outlined below:

1. A single gMSA can be used on multiple hosts.
2. A gMSA can be used for scheduled tasks.
3. A gMSA can be used for IIS Application Pools, SQL 2012 and other applications.

It is important to check with each application vendor to confirm compatibility with gMSA. Windows Server 2012 schema has a new object class called gMSAs- msDSGroupManagedServiceAccount. This object class is derived from the computer class with five additional attributes outlined below:

1. Governs which computers (groups of computers) are allowed to retrieve gMSA password and make use of the gMSA.
2. A binary blob containing (among other things) the current password, previous password and password change interval.
3. Key identifier used by Key Distribution Service (KDS) to generate current password.
4. Key identifier from previous password.

Unlike the previous MSAs, the password for gMSAs are generated and maintained by the Key Distribution Service (KDS) on Windows Server 2012 DCs. This allows multiple hosts to use the same gMSA. Member servers that wish to use the gMSA, simply query the DC for the current password. Usage of the gMSA is restricted only to those computers specified in the security descriptor, **msDS-GroupMSAMembership**. Group managed service accounts requirements are outlined below:

1. At least one Windows Server 2012 Domain Controller.
2. A Windows Server 2012 or Windows 8 machine with the Active Directory PowerShell module, to create and manage the gMSA.
3. A Windows Server 2012 or Windows 8 domain member to use the gMSA.

To create a gMSA, we will follow the plan outline below:

1. Create the KDS Root Key - Already created in the previous section.
2. Create and Configure the gMSA.
3. Configure the gMSA on host (s).

To Create and configure Group Managed Service Accounts

1. Create the KDS Root Key - Created in the previous section.
2. Create and Configure a gMSA:
   a) To create a security group - For computer objects of the hosts that will be allowed to use the gMSA, complete the tasks below:
      i) Log on to 70411SRV and open Active Directory Users and Computers.
      ii) Navigate to Users container.
      iii) Right-click **Users** container and point to **New** then select **Group**. The New Object - Group wizard opens. Complete the following tasks:
         (1) On Group name field, enter gMSAComputers.
         (2) On Group scope, select Global.
         (3) On Group type, select Security.
         (4) Click Ok.

Note

Using a security group to manage gMSA hosts gives more administrative flexibility with downside: Computers (hosts) will need to be re-booted after adding or removing them from the group. To complete the task below, Active Directory module for Windows PowerShell MUST be installed on 70411SRV1 and 70411SRV3.

     iv) Double-click **gMSAComputers** group and add 70411SRV1 and 70411SRV3 as members.

     v) Reboot 70411SRV1 and 70411SRV3.

  b) Create a Managed service account for WSUS Service called **ManagedDFSNService** by running the following commands:

```
New-ADServiceAccount -name "gMSAWSUSSVS" -DNSHostName
"gMSAWSUSSVS.70411Lab.com" -enable $true -
PrincipalsAllowedToRetrieveManagedPassword gMSAComputers
```

  c) Associate the new gMSA with a target computer in Active Directory: From Windows PowerShell, run the following commands:

```
Add-ADComputerServiceAccount -identity 70411SRV1 -ServiceAccount
gMSAWSUSSVS

Add-ADComputerServiceAccount -identity 70411SRV3 -ServiceAccount
gMSAWSUSSVS
```

  d) Install the Managed Service Account on the hosts that runs the service: Log on to 70411SRV1 and 70411SRV3, and run the following commands:

```
Install-ADServiceAccount gMSAWSUSSVS
```

  e) Configure gMSAWSUSSVS to be used by services in 70411SRV1 and 70411SRV3:

     i) Log on to 70411SRV1 and 70411SRV3 each to perform the following tasks:

     ii) Open Internet Information Services (IIS) Manager.

     iii) Expand the server name and navigate to **Application Pools**, then right-click **WsusPool** and click **Advanced Settings**.

     iv) High-light **identity box** (Beneath Generate Process Model Event), and click on the **edit** sign to the right.

     v) On the **Application pool identity** window that opens, click **Custom Account**, then click **Set** and enter **70411Lab\gMSAWSUSSVS$** as User Name. Leave the password fields blank and click **Ok** thrice.

     vi) Under **Application Pool Tasks**, right-click **WsusPool** and click **Stop**, and then click **Start**.

5.1.3 Manage Service Principal Names (SPNs)

A service principal name (SPN) is the name by which a client uniquely identifies an instance of a service. If multiple instances of a service are installed on computers throughout a forest, each instance must have its own SPN. A given service instance may have multiple SPNs if there are multiple names that clients might use for authentication. For example, an SPN always includes the name of the host computer on which the service instance is running, so a service instance might register an SPN for each name or alias of its host.

Service principal names are associated with the security principal (users or groups) in whose security context the service executes. SPNs are used to support **Mutual authentication** between a client application and a service. An SPN is assembled from information that a client knows about a service. Or, it can obtain information from a trusted third party, such as Active Directory.

Before the Kerberos authentication service can use an SPN to authenticate a service, the SPN must be registered on the account object that the service instance uses to log on. A given SPN can be registered on only one account.

SPN Format

The SPN syntax has four elements: two required elements and two optional elements, that can be used, if necessary, to produce a unique name. The basic syntax of service principal name is as follows:

< service type >/< instance name >:< port number >/< service name >

The elements of the syntax have the following meanings:

1. **Service type**: Type of service, such as "www" for World Wide Web service or "ldap" for Lightweight Directory Access Protocol.
2. **Instance name**: Name of the instance of the service. Depending upon the service type, it is either the name or IP address of the host running the service.
3. **Port number**: TCP/IP port used by the service on the host. This is required only if the port used is different from the default for the service type.
4. **Service name**: The name can be the DNS name of a host, of a replicated service, or of a domain; or it can be the distinguished name of a service connection point object or of an RPC service object.

The components present in a service's SPNs depend on how the service is identified and replicated. There are two basic SPN scenarios: **Host-based** services and **Replicable** services.

Host-Based Service is a service that is identified by the name of the host on which the service runs. In such cases, the service principal name of the service will have the following format:

< service type >/< host name >:< port number >

Or, if the service is using the default port for the service type specified by service type , then the SPN can be abbreviated to the following:

< service type >/< host name >

Replicable services (service principal name for services named in a directory service - like AD DS), has the following syntax:

< service type >/< host name >:< port number >/< distinguished name >

The elements of the syntax have the following meanings:

1. **Service type:** Type of service for example, print.
2. **Distinguished name**: Distinguished name of an instance of the service in Active Directory. For example, "cn=testservice,dc=gov,dc=uk".
3. **Host name**: DNS name of the host running an instance of distinguished name.
4. **Domain name**: Name of the domain that contains the account running the service specified by distinguished name (formed from the "dc=" components of distinguished name).

For example, the service principal name for the print service for the Sample Council in building 10 at Reskit, whose distinguished name is "cn=bldg26,dc=ntdom,dc=reskit,dc=com", which is running on nonstandard port number 1234 on host "prt1.ntdom.reskit.com", is as follows:

For example, the SPN for a print service on the sampledomain.gov.uk domain, running on non-standard port number 557 on host printserver.sampledomain.gov.uk with a DN of "cn=location1,dc=sampledomain,dc=gov,dc=uk", will be configured as follows:

Print/printserver.London.sampledomain.gov.uk: 557/
cn=location1,dc=sampledomain,dc=gov,dc=uk

In the next task, you will create a Web Server Service account (WebServerService) for a web server 70411SRV1 and add a Service Principal Name for the web service to the service account. Keep a tab on this because you will create a Kerberos delegation for a Web Server Service (WebServerService) on 70411SRV1 in the next section.

To create a Service Principal Name for a Service account.

1. Log on to 70411SRV (DC) and open Active Directory Users and Computers.
2. To display the Attribute Editor of Active Directory objects, click **View** and select **Advanced Features**.
3. To create a Service Account: Right-click **Users** node, point to **New** and select **User**. Then complete the following tasks:
   a) On the **First name** field, enter **WebServer.**
   b) On the **Last name** filed, enter **Service.**

     c)   On the **User logon name** field, enter **WebServerService,** then click **Next** and complete the wizard.

4.   To create an SPN for the Web service account, complete the tasks below:

     a)   Right-click **WebServerService** and click **Properties**.

     b)   Click **Attribute Editor** tab then locate and highlight **ServicePrincipalName**.

     c)   Below the **Attributes** window, click **Edit** and on the **Multi-valued String Editor**, below **Value to add** field, type the following:

---

www/70411SRV1.70411Lab.com:8080/CN=70411SRV1,OU=WINSRV2012 R2,DC=70411Lab,DC=com.

---

     d)   When you finish, click **Add** and then **Ok.**

     e)   To save your changes and close the **Properties** of 70411SRV1 click **Ok.**

5.   To confirm that this SPN was added successfully, open an elevated command prompt and execute the command below:

Setspn -l WebServerService.

Note

After adding the SPN to the service account, the Delegation tab will become available on the WebServerService properties. The Delegation tab will not show on a User's account until you add a SPN to the account.

Setspn Command Line Tool

Setspn is a command-line tool that was introduced from Windows Server 2008 onwards. It is available if you have the Active Directory Domain Services (AD DS) server role installed. **Setspn** command line tool may also be used to manage SPNs.

Setspn Format: The format of an SPN is shown below:

serviceclass/host:port/servicename.

Setspn command switches and examples:

l (small letter 'L'): List the SPNs that an object has registered with Active Directory.

Example: To list the SPNs of a computer named 70411SRV, execute:

---

setspn -l 70411SRV

---

r: Resets incorrect SPNs for an AD computer object.

Example: To reset the SPNs of a computer named 70411SRV, execute:

---

setspn -r 70411SRV

-d: Removes an SPN.

Example: To remove the SPN for the Web service on a computer named 70411SRV.70411Lab.com, execute:

```
setspn -d 70411SRV.70411Lab.com 70411SRV
```

-s: Adds an SPN to an AD computer or user object.

Example: If there is an Active Directory domain controller with the host name server1.70411Lab.com that requires an SPN for the Lightweight Directory Access Protocol (LDAP), execute:

```
setspn -s ldap/ server1.70411Lab.com server1
```

Exam Tip

It is very important to understand the various setspn switches.

5.1.4 Configure Kerberos delegation

Kerberos is a secure ticket-based protocol for authenticating a service request. Kerberos is integral to the Active Directory security structure. Delegation is permitting another computer or service to allow a Kerberos ticket to be created for another service on the originating user's behalf. This can be done at the computer level by using full delegation or with constrained delegation. Constrained delegation means that the Kerberos delegation can only be executed against a limited set of services.

From Windows Server 2003 and higher, the **ms-DS-Allowed-To-Delegate-To** attribute is added to service accounts to help enforce constrained delegation. The ms-DS-Allowed-To-Delegate-To attribute lists the service principal names (SPNs) of other service accounts that a given service account is allowed to delegate to. When a Windows Server KDC processes a service ticket request via the constrained delegation extension, it will verify that the target service account is listed in the ms-DS-Allowed-To-Delegate-To attribute.

In the following task, you will create a Service Account (**WebServerService**) for the www service on 70411SRV1 web server. You will then authorize 70411SRV1 to request Kerberos authentication using the Service account by adding it to the **ms-DS-Allowed-To-Delegate-To** attribute of **WebServerService** account. Finally, you will configure constrained delegation on 70411SRV1 and add **WebServerService** as a delegated service.

To Configure Kerberos delegation

1. Log on to 70411SRV (DC) and open Active Directory Users and Computers.

2. To authorize 70411SRV1 to request Kerberos authentication:
   a) Navigate to **WINSRV2012R2** OU, on the details pane, right-click **70411SRV1** and click **Properties,** and then click the **Attribute Editor** tab.
   b) On the **Attribute Editor** tab, locate the **ms-DS-Allowed-To-Delegate-To** attribute and highlight it, then click **Edit.**
   c) On the **Multi-valued String Editor,** below **Value to add** field, type the   following: www/70411SRV1.70411Lab.com:8080/CN=70411SRV1,OU=WINSRV2012R2,DC=70411Lab,DC=com.
   d) When you finish, click **Add** and then **Ok.**
   e) To save your changes and close the **Properties** of **70411SRV1** click **Ok.**
3. To configure constrained delegation:
   a) Navigate to **WINSRV2012R2** OU, on the details pane, open the **properties** of 70411SRV1, then click the **Delegation** tab.
   b) On the Delegation tab, select the option **Trust this computer for delegation to specific services only** (This is called Constrained delegation), then select **Use Kerberos only**.
   c) Below Services to which this account can present delegated credentials, click Add.
   d) On the **Add Services** screen, click **Users or Computers.** On the search box, enter **WebServerService** and click **Check Names** then click and **Ok.**
   e) Back on the **Add Services** screen highlight **www,** below **Service Type** and click **Ok.**
   f) On the **properties** of 70411SRV1, click **Ok.**

Note

When you click the search box in step 3-(d) above, only security principals (Users or Computers) that have SPN configured will be displayed. When you enter a security principal that does not have a SPN, it will return an error.

Exam Tip

Important to note that the Delegation tab will not be available for an Active Directory account unless Service Principal Name is added as seen in the previous section.

5.1.5 Configure virtual accounts (2012 R2 Objective)

Virtual accounts require very minimal management. They cannot be created or deleted, nor do they require any password management. Both Managed Service Accounts (MSA) and virtual accounts were capabilities introduced in Windows Server 2008 R2 and Windows 7. Virtual accounts in Windows Server 2012 are "managed local accounts" that provide the following features to simplify service administration:

1. No password management is required.
2. The ability to access the network with a computer identity in a domain environment.

To configure an IIS application pool to use a virtual account

1. Log on to 70411SRV1 and open Internet Information Services (IIS) Manager.
2. Expand 70411SRV1, then high-light **Application Pools**. Right-click **WsusPool** and click **Advanced Settings**.
3. High-light **identity** (under Generate Process Model Event L), and click on the **edit** sign to the right.
4. On the **Application Pool Identity** Page, select **Built-In account**, then select **NetworkService** from the drop down list. Click **Ok** twice
5. Under **Application Pool Tasks**, right-click **WsusPool** click **Stop**, and then click **Start**. If it fails to start, wait for a while and start it again.

5.2 Configure Domain Controllers

Introduction

Active Directory operates a multi-master database model. Multi-master means that all domain controllers hold writable copies of the Active Directory Database. The multi-master database model has some exceptions. Some objects cannot use the multi-master replication model. These objects that do not support multi-master replication model are handled by one domain controller. These single-master role holders are called Flexible single master operations (FSMO) holders. These single-master roles role holders will normally process single-master operations and replicate to other domain controllers.

Sometimes, a domain controller holding a FSMO role might need to be taken off line for maintenance. Under such circumstances, the administrator might need to transfer the role to another domain controller to ensure that the FSMO role continuous to be available in the domain. Some other time, the FSMO DC may become permanently damaged. In such circumstances, the role will have to be seized.

Though all DCs maintain writable copies of the AD database, there are circumstances, say in a non-secure branch office where an administrator might want to deploy a Read-only domain controller (RODC).
In versions of Microsoft Windows Server prior to Windows Server 2012, the process of adding an additional virtual domain controller involved copying data either across the network or using a media. A Windows Server 2012 Virtual Domain Controller running on a Hyper-V Version 3.0 and VMware vSphere 5.1, supports cloning and safe restore capabilities.

In this section, we will cover following exam objectives:

5.2.0 Configure Universal Group Membership Caching (UGMC)
5.2.1 Transfer and seize operations master
5.2.2 Install and configure a read-only domain controller (RODC)
5.2.3 Configure Domain Controller cloning

Lab Plan

We will complete all tasks in this section using the following servers: 70411SRV, 70411RODC, 70411SRV4 and 70411SRV5.

Additional lab setup

None

5.2.0 Configure Universal Group Membership Caching (UGMC)

In a multi-domain forest, when a user logs on to a domain, a global catalog server must be contacted to determine the universal group memberships of the user. A universal group can contain users from other domains, and it can be applied to access control lists (ACLs) on objects in all domains in the forest. Therefore, universal group memberships must be ascertained at domain logon so that the user is granted the appropriate access in the domain and in other domains during the logon session. Only global catalog servers store the memberships of all universal groups in the forest. If a global catalog server is not available in the site when a user logs on to a domain, the domain controller must contact a global catalog server in another site.

In multi-domain forests that do not have a global catalog servers on remote sites, the need to contact a global catalog server over a potentially slow wide area network (WAN) connection can be problematic and a user may be unable to log on to the domain if a global catalog server is not available. In this situation, Universal Group Membership Caching (UGMC) may be enabled on domain controllers running Windows Server 2012 on the remote site. So, when the domain controller contacts a global catalog server for the user's initial domain logon, the domain controller retrieves universal group memberships for the user. On subsequent logon requests by the same user, the domain controller uses cached universal group memberships and does not have to contact a global catalog server.

To enable or disable universal group membership caching

1. Log on to 70411SRV and open Active Directory Sites And Services.
2. Expand **Sites**, then high-light **Default-First-Site-Name**. On the details pane, right-click **NTDS Site Settings**, and click **Properties**.
3. On the Site Settings tab, check Enable Universal Group Membership Caching.
4. Beside **Refresh Cache From** drop-down list, choose a site from which to cache universal group memberships.
5. The selected site must have a working global catalog server. To disable universal group membership caching, clear the **Enable Universal Group Membership Caching** check box on the Site Settings tab.
6. Click **Ok**.

If universal group membership is cached locally, any domain controller can resolve logon requests locally without having to go through a global catalog server. This allows for faster logons and makes managing server outages much easier because the domain does not rely on a single server or a group of servers for logons. This solution also reduces replication traffic. Instead of replicating the entire global catalog periodically over the network, only the universal group membership information in the cache is refreshed. By default, a refresh occurs every eight hours on each domain controller that's caching membership locally.

Universal group membership caching is site-specific. Remember, a site is a physical directory structure consisting of one or more subnets with a specific IP address range and network mask. The domain controllers running Windows Server and the global catalog they are contacting must be in the same site. If there are multiple sites in a domain, configure local caching in each site. Additionally, users in the site must be part of a Windows domain running in Windows Server 2003 or higher functional mode.

5.2.1 Transfer and seize operations master

There are five unique Flexible single master operations (FSMO) roles in an Active Directory forest:

1. **Schema** Master: AD schema is a definition of object classes and attributes. For example, a User is a class, while attributes of the user class are First Name, Last Name, Display Name, etc. The Schema Master Domain Controller is responsible for updating changes to the AD schema and replication to other domain controllers. The Schema master role is forest-wide and there is one for each forest.
2. **Domain naming Master**: The Domain naming master role is forest-wide and there is one for each forest. This role is required to add or remove domains or application partitions to or from a forest.
3. **RID Master**: The RID master is responsible for processing RID pool requests from all domain controllers in a particular domain. When a DC creates a security principal object such as a user or group, it attaches a unique Security ID (SID) to the object. This SID consists of a domain SID (the same for all SIDs created in a domain), and a relative ID (RID) that is unique for each security Principal SID created in a domain.
4. Each DC in a domain is allocated a pool of RIDs that it is allowed to assign to the security principals it creates. When a DC's allocated RID pool falls below a threshold, that DC issues a request for additional RIDs to the domain's RID master. The domain RID master responds to the request by retrieving RIDs from the domain's unallocated RID pool and assigns them to the pool of the requesting DC. At any one time, there can be only one domain controller acting as the RID master in the domain.
5. **PDC Emulator Master:** The PDC emulator master is necessary to synchronize time in an enterprise and it is authoritative for the domain in the enterprise. This role is domain-wide and there is one for each domain.

The domain controller that owns this role also performs the following functions:

a) Password changes performed by other DCs in the domain are replicated preferentially to the PDC emulator.

b) Authentication failures that occur at a given DC in a domain because of an incorrect password are forwarded to the PDC emulator before a bad password failure message is reported to the user.

c) Account lockout is processed on the PDC emulator.

d) Editing or creation of Group Policy Objects (GPO) is always done from the GPO copy found in the PDC Emulator's SYSVOL share, unless configured not to do so by the administrator.

6. **Infrastructure master:** When an object in one domain is referenced by another object in another domain, it represents the reference by the GUID, the SID (for references to security principals), and the DN of the object being referenced.

    The infrastructure FSMO role holder is the DC responsible for updating an object's SID and distinguished name in a cross-domain object reference. At any one time, there can be only one domain controller acting as the infrastructure master in each domain. When the run post-deployment task via Server Manager and promote a Windows Server 2012 to a DC, the Wizard assigns all 5 FSMO roles to the first domain controller in the forest root domain. The first domain controller in each new child or tree domain is assigned the three domain-wide roles. Domain controllers continue to own FSMO roles until they are reassigned by using one of the following methods:

    a) An administrator reassigns the role by using a GUI administrative tool.

    b) An administrator reassigns the role by using the **ntdsutil /roles** command.

    c) An administrator gracefully demotes a role-holding domain controller by using the Active Directory Installation Wizard. This wizard reassigns any locally-held roles to an existing domain controller in the forest.

It is recommended to transfer FSMO roles in the following scenarios:

1. The current role holder is operational and can be accessed on the network by the new FSMO owner.

2. You are gracefully demoting a domain controller that currently owns FSMO roles that you want to assign to a specific domain controller in your Active Directory forest.

3. The domain controller that currently owns FSMO roles is to be taken offline for scheduled maintenance and you need specific FSMO roles to be assigned to another DC. This may be required to perform operations

that connect to the FSMO owner. This would be especially true for the PDC Emulator role but less true for the RID master role, the Domain naming master role and the Schema master roles.

It is recommended to seize FSMO roles in the following scenarios:

1. The current role holder is experiencing an operational error that prevents an FSMO-dependent operation from completing successfully and the role cannot be transferred.
2. A domain controller that owns an FSMO role is force-demoted by using the dcpromo /forceremoval command.
3. The operating system on the computer that originally owned a specific role no longer exists or has been reinstalled.

Note

To transfer RID, Infrastructure and PDC Master roles, use ntdsutil or Active Directory Users and Computers. To transfer Domain Naming Master role, use ntdsutil or Active Directory Domains and Trusts. Schema Master role can be transferred using ntdsutil and Active Directory Schema snap-in. To access Active Directory Schema snap-in via MMC, first execute the command regsvr32 schmmgmt.dll then open Active Directory Schema from MMC.

As replication occurs, non-FSMO domain controllers in the domain or forest gain full knowledge of changes that are made by FSMO-holding domain controllers. If you must transfer a role, the best candidate domain controller is one that is in the appropriate domain that last inbound-replicated, or recently inbound-replicated a writable copy of the "FSMO partition" from the existing role holder. For example, the Schema master role-holder has a distinguished name path of CN=schema,CN=configuration,dc=<forest root domain>, and this means that roles reside in and are replicated as part of the CN=schema partition. If the domain controller that holds the Schema master role experiences a hardware or software failure, a good candidate role-holder would be a domain controller in the root domain and in the same Active Directory site as the current owner. Domain controllers in the same Active Directory site perform inbound replication every 5 minutes or 15 seconds.

A domain controller whose FSMO roles have been seized should not be permitted to communicate with existing domain controllers in the forest. In this scenario, it is recommended to either format the hard disk and reinstall the operating system on such domain controllers or forcibly demote such domain controllers on a private network and then remove their metadata on a surviving domain controller in the forest by using the **ntdsutil /metadata cleanup** command.

The risk of introducing a former FSMO role holder, whose role has been seized into the forest is that the original role holder may continue to operate as before until it inbound-replicates knowledge of the role seizure. Known risks of two domain controllers owning the same FSMO roles include creating security principals that have overlapping RID pools, and other problems.

To transfer the FSMO roles

1. Log on to 70411SRV and open command prompt.
2. On the command prompt, type **ntdsutil** and press the **ENTER** key.
3. On the **ntdsutil** prompt, type **roles**, and press the **ENTER** key.
4. On the **fsmo maintenance** prompt, type **connections** and press the **ENTER** key.
5. On the server connections prompt type **connect to server 70411SRV2**, and press the **ENTER** key.
6. On the **server connections** prompt, type **q**, and press the **ENTER** key.
7. On the **fsmo maintenance** prompt, type **Transfer RID master**, then press the **ENTER** key.

Note

For a list of roles that you can transfer, type ? at the fsmo maintenance prompt, and then press ENTER. To transfer a specific role, type Transfer <Role name>. For example, to transfer the RID master role, type transfer rid master. The one exception is for the PDC emulator role, whose syntax is transfer pdc, not transfer pdc master.

8. Respond Yes to the Role Transfer Confirmation Dialog.
9. On the **fsmo maintenance** prompt, type **q**, and press the **ENTER** key to return to the ntdsutil prompt. Type **q**, and then press **ENTER** to quit the Ntdsutil utility.
10. To confirm that 70411SRV2 is now the RID Operations Master holder:
    a) Open Active Directory Users and Computers.
    b) Right-click 70411Lab.com and select **Operations Masters**.
    c) At the **Operations Masters** window, the RID tab is selected; confirm that 70411SRV2 is listed as owner. Note also that by clicking the **Change** button, you can transfer the role back to 70411SRV.
    d) Click PDC and Infrastructure tabs in sequence and confirm that the PDC Emulator and Infrastructure Master roles are still held by 70411SRV.

Note

In the task below, please respond **No** to step 8.

To seize the FSMO roles

1. Log on to 70411SRV2 and open command prompt.
2. On the command prompt, type **ntdsutil** and press the **ENTER** key.
3. On the **ntdsutil** prompt, type **roles**, and press the **ENTER** key.
4. On the **fsmo maintenance** prompt, type **connections** and press the **ENTER** key.
5. On the server connections prompt, type connect to server 70411SRV, and press the ENTER key.
6. On the **server connections** prompt, type **q**, and press the **ENTER** key.
7. On the **fsmo maintenance** prompt, type **Seize RID master**, and press the **ENTER** key.
8. Respond No to the Role **Seizure Confirmation Dialog** window.

Note

It is not recommended to host the Infrastructure master role on a global catalog server. If the Infrastructure master runs on a global catalog server, the server stops updating object information because it does not contain any references to objects that it does not hold. This is because a global catalog server holds a partial replica of every object in the forest.

Exam Tip

There is no option to seize a FSMO role from a GUI tool. FSMO role seizer can only be performed using ntdsutil. FSMO role transfer can be accomplished with either a GUI tool or ntdsutil utility.

5.2.2 Install and configure a read-only domain controller (RODC)

A Read Only Domain Controller (RODC) is a domain controller that hosts a read only copy of the Active Directory Database. These servers are normally installed in remote office locations where the physical security of the server may not be guaranteed. Since the server only hosts a read only copy of the AD data store, the confidential data will not be compromised even if the servers were stolen. RODCs store the same objects as Read Write Domain Controllers (RWDC) except for the user passwords.

Active directory clients can access the RODC to access AD data but clients will not be able to make any changes to the RODC directly. If a change is required, the client will be referred to a Read-write Domain Controller (RWDC). As noted earlier in this chapter, a RWDC hosts a writable copy of AD database.

A RODC can be installed in two ways: By pre-staging a computer account in AD and without pre-staging a computer account in AD.

Installing a RODC by Pre-staging

This is a two-stage process:

1. Stage an unoccupied computer account in AD.
2. Attach an RODC to that computer account.

As with most tasks in Windows Server 2012 R2, this can be accomplished via Server Manager or Windows PowerShell. The following cmdlet creates a read-only domain controller (RODC) account that can be used to install an RODC in Active Directory:

Add-ADDSReadOnlyDomainControllerAccount

After pre-staging a computer account in AD, the RODC will be installed with the cmdlet below:

Install-ADDSDomainController

For the purposes of this guide, we will use Server Manager and GUI tools to stage and deploy our RODC. I may provide example PowerShell cmdlets to perform similar tasks as well. Before you proceed with the next task, start 70411RODC.

To install a RODC by Pre-staging

1. Stage an unoccupied computer account in AD:
    a) Log on to 70411SRV and open Active Directory Administrative Center.
    b) Double-click **70411Lab (Local),** and on the details pane, double-click **Domain Controllers**.
    c) On the Tasks list (To the right), double-click Pre-create a Read-only domain controller account. The Active Directory Domain Services Installation Wizard opens.
    d) On the Welcome screen, check the box Use Advanced Mode Installation (select this option to show password replication policy options), then click Next.
    e) On the Network Credentials screen, accept My current logged on credentials (membership in the Domain Admins group is required), click **Next**.
    f) On the **Specify the Computer Name**, enter **70411RODC** (The domain controller you configure and attach to this account later must have the same name, or the promotion operation will not detect the staged account), then click **Next**.
    g) On the **Select a site** screen click **Next**.
    h) On the Additional Domain Controller Options dialog, check DNS Server and Global Catalog boxes, and then click **Next**.

Note

Microsoft recommends that read-only domain controllers provide DNS and GC services, so both are installed by default; one intention of the RODC role is for branch office scenarios where the wide area network may not be available and without DNS and global catalog services, computers in the branch will not be able to use AD DS resources and functionalities.

i)   On the Specify the Password Replication Policy, accept the defaults and click **Next**.

The Specify the Password Replication Policy window enables you to modify the default list of accounts that are allowed to cache their passwords on the read-only domain controller. Accounts in the list configured with **Deny** or that are not in the list (implicit deny), do not cache their password. Accounts that are not allowed to cache passwords on the RODC and cannot connect and authenticate to a writable domain controller cannot access resources or functionality provided by Active Directory.

j)   On the Delegation of RODC Installation and Administration, read the notes on the wizard, and click **Next**.

The Delegation of RODC Installation and Administration dialog enables you to configure a user or group containing users who are allowed to attach the server to the RODC computer account.

k)   On the **Summary** screen, click **Next** (The **Active Directory Domain Services** Installation Wizard creates the staged read-only domain controller in Active Directory. You cannot cancel this operation after it starts)

l)   Click **Finish**.

The following Powershell command will perform the task completed above:

```
Add-addsreadonlydomaincontrolleraccount -DomainControllerAccountName
70411RODC -DomainName 70411Lab.com -SiteName Default-First-Site-
Name
```

2.   Attach the staged computer account:
a)   Log on to 70411RODC and open Server Manager.
b)   From Server Manager, click **Add Roles and Features** and click **Next**.
c)   On the Select Installation type page, ensure that Role-based or feature-based installation is selected, and then click **Next**.
d)   On the **Server Roles** page, select **Active Directory Domain Services** and click **Add Features** when prompted to select features, and then click **Next** thrice.
e)   On the final page, click **Install.**

f) After AD DS installation, from **Server Manager** click the yellow triangle with a black exclamation mark, then click **promote this server to a domain controller**.

g) On the Deployment Configuration screen, select add a domain controller to an existing domain, and on the Domain box type 70411Lab.com.

h) On the **Credentials for deployment operation** window, click **change**, then enter your domain admin username and password in the format **domainname\adminname**, then enter the password and click **Ok**.

i) On the Deployment Configuration page click **Next**.

j) On the **Domain Controller Options** page, select **Use Existing RODC account** and type the directory services restore mode password, then click **Next**.

k) On the Additional Options page, click **Next**.

Note

The Additional Options page provides configuration options to name a domain controller as the replication source, or you can use any domain controller as the replication source. You can also choose to install the domain controller using backed up media - Install from media (IFM) option.

The Install from media checkbox provides an option to a browse to a backup media. Click **Verify** to ensure the provided path is a valid media. Media used by the IFM option is created with Windows Server Backup or Ntdsutil.exe from an existing Windows Server 2012 computer only; you cannot use a Windows Server 2008 R2 or previous operating system to create media for a Windows Server 2012 domain controller.

l) On the **Paths** page, click **Next**.

m) Review options page and click **Next**.

n) When pre-requisite check completes, click **install**.

The following Powershell command will perform the task completed above:

```
Install-ADDSDomainController –DomainName 70411Lab.com –
UseExistingAccount –Credential (Get-Credential).
```

The command will prompt for a SafeModeAdministratorPasword.

Install RODC without Staging

RODC can be installed without pre-staging a computer account in Active Directory. This is performed via post-AD installation tasks. It may also be completed using Windows PowerShell. To install a RODC with this method, run the following command:

> Install-AddsDomainController –ReadOnlyReplica -Domain 70411Lab.com -
> SiteName TechtrinitRoot -Credentials (Get–Credentials)

5.2.3 Configure Domain Controller cloning

Prior to Windows Server 2012, Active Directory Domain Controllers virtualization required additional careful steps to avoid actions that may corrupt AD database. For example, care had to be taken to avoid applying an old snapshot that could possibly cause USN rollback to occur and risk AD corruption.

Beginning with Windows Server 2012, Microsoft incorporated a new VM-Generation-ID unique identifier as an additional attribute of a Domain Controller's AD computer object as well as the VM container that is running the virtualized DC instance. When a virtualized DC starts up, Windows Server 2012 and Windows Server 2012 R2 checks for a match between the VM-Generation-ID recorded on the VM instance and the VM-Generation-ID recorded on the DC's computer object in AD. If there is a mismatch, Windows Server determines that a possible virtualization snapshot or imaging event has occurred and it dumps the current RID pool and USN for fresh information to protect the state of Active Directory.

Requirements for cloning a DC

The following requirements must be met to successfully clone a Virtual Domain Controller:

1. A Virtualization platform that supports VM-Generation-ID (VMGID). VMGID is currently supported on Hyper-V Version 3.0 on Windows Server 2012. The following versions of VMWre vSphere are also supported:
    a) vSphere 5.0 Patch 4 (Build 821926, 9/27/2012)
    b) vSphere 5.1 (Build 799733, 9/10/2012)
2. Windows Server 2012 operating system running as a Guest Domain Controller.
3. PDC Emulator running on a Windows Server 2012 Domain Controller before the cloning process begins.
4. Forest Functional Level to be Windows Server 2003 or higher.
5. Minimum Schema version of 56 (Windows Server 2012 schema).
6. **Cloneable Domain Controllers** group and permissions set on Domain Naming Context of the Source Virtual Domain Controller.

The PDC Emulator must be running on a Windows Server 2012 Domain Controller and is required for the following reasons:

1. A special Cloneable Domain Controllers group is created in Active Directory and permissions are set for this group on the root of the domain naming context. By default, the group has no members in it. If

the PDC Emulator is transferred from an earlier domain controller to Windows Server 2012, the Cloneable Domain Controllers group is created if it does not exist already.

2. For the cloning Domain Controller to create the computer object for the Domain Controller that is being cloned, it uses the DRSUAPI RPC protocol to contact the PDC Emulator.

Improperly cloning domain controllers in a production environment can result in issues that are difficult to resolve. I strongly recommend that you test the steps below in an isolated lab environment to make sure that you are comfortable with the process and expected results before attempting to perform these steps in a production environment.

Exam Tip

It is very important to note that before a Domain Controller can be cloned, the PDC emulator FSMO role MUST be held by a Windows Server 2012 DC.

To clone a Domain Controller

1. Preparing the environment - Run some prerequisite checks:
    a) Check availability of VM-Generation-ID Driver:
        i)   Log on to 70411SRV4 and perform the following tasks:
        ii)   Open Computer Management and highlight Device Manager,
        iii) On the details pane, expand **Systems Devices**.
        iv)   Confirm the Microsoft Hyper-V Generation Counter exists.
        v)   To drill further:
              (1) Write-click the Microsoft Hyper-V Generation Counter driver, and click properties,
              (2) From Drivers tab, click Driver details, and verify that the driver is "vmgencounter.sys" (This is the driver that makes vDC cloning and snapshot restore possible in Windows Server 2012).
    b) Verify Schema version:
        i)   Log on to 70411SRV (or to any DC in the forest)
        ii)   Run **regedit**, and browse to HKLM\System\CurrentControlSet\Services\NTDS\Parameters, and verify that "Schema Version" REG_DWORD value is 69 (This is the Windows Server 2012 R2 version of the schema. Windows Server 2012 AD DS schema version is 56 (Minimum required for AD cloning).
    c) Verify Forest Functional Level:
        i)   Log on to 70411SRV (or to any DC in the forest) and open **Active Directory Users and Computers**.
        ii)   Right-click 70411Lab.com and click Properties.

        iii) On the **General** tab, verify the **Forest functional level**. (Minimum should be Windows Server 2003).
- d) Check the vDC source Operating System:
  - i) Log on to 70411SRV4 (the source vDC) and open command prompt.
  - ii) Execute **winver** command and verify that source vDC is a Windows Server 2012 R2 (Minimum requirement is Windows Server 2012).
- e) Verify that the server running PDC FSMO role is a Windows Server 2012 DC.
- f) Ensure that PDC and RID master are available during cloning process:
  - i) Transfer all FSMO roles to 70411SRV.
- g) Authorizing a domain controller as a source for the cloning:
  - i) Log on to 70411SRV and open Active Directory Users and Computers.
  - ii) Add 70411SRV4 (the source vDC) to the **Cloneable Domain Controllers** security group.
- h) Review the list of applications and Services: Every application or service running on a computer creates Security Identifiers to identify some of its internal components. It is a necessary action to check if there is any application running on the domain controller that will be impacted by the cloning process.
  - i) To get the list of applications and services installed on 70411SRV4, run the following PowerShell command:

```
Get-ADDCCloningExcludedApplicationList -GenerateXml
```

        ii) The generated configuration file will be written to C:\Windows\NTDS\CustomDCCloneAllowList.xml

Exam Tip

Note the name of the xml file created to check application compatibility - CustomDCCloneAllowList.xml. Also note the name of the xml file created in step 2(a) below when you configure the source DC - DCCloneConfig.xml.

        iii) To review the file, double-click it to open with Internet Explorer.
        iv) The following applications / services were listed, for me (Yours may differ):
          (1) DHCP
          (2) IAS
          (3) WLMS (windows licensing monitoring service)
2. Configuring the source domain controller:

a) Run the following PowerShell command on 70411SRV4 to generate the DCCloneConfig.xml file:

New-ADDCCloneConfigFile -Static -IPv4Address "192.168.0.40" -
IPv4DNSResolver "192.168.0.81" -IPv4SubnetMask "255.255.255.0" -
CloneComputerName "70411SRV6" -IPv4DefaultGateway "192.168.0.1" -
SiteName "Default-First-Site-Name"

The command generates a clone configuration file and stores it in this location C:\Windows\NTDS\DCCloneConfig.xml

3. Exporting, Importing and renaming the source domain controller as a new virtual machine:
   a) Stop the Source VM - Take it offline: Run the command from the Hyper-V host:

Stop-VM –Name 70411SRV4 –TurnOff

   b) To Export the Virtual Machine of Source Domain Controller, run the command below on the Hyper-V host:

Export-VM -Name 70411SRV4 -Path D:\ExportedSourceDC

   c) To Import and generate a new VM-Generation-ID:

Import-VM -Path "D:\ExportedSourceDC\70411SRV4\Virtual
Machines\71A66E85-5295-441E-9C4D-F3900F2870E3.xml" -Copy -
GenerateNewId -VhdDestinationPath "D:\Labfiles\VHD-
Used\70411SRV6"

4. Start the cloned Domain Controller
   a) Open Hyper-V manager and confirm that there are now two versions of 70411SRV4.
   b) Highlight each and determine the create time stamp.
   c) Rename the one with the most recent stamp time as 70411SRV6.
   d) Boot 70411SRV6. The DC cloning process will proceed to completion.
   e) Confirm configuration of 70411SRV6:
      i) Log on to 70411SRV6 with your domain account.
      ii) Note computer name, IP, DNS, and Gateway.
      iii) Confirm that the information in the previous step are the same with the details used in the New-ADDCCloneConfigFile command in step 2.

Note

The DC cloning process summary: When the cloned DC starts, it checks the VM-GenerationID. If a mismatch is detected, the next step is to check for the configuration file (DCCloneConfig.xml we created earlier). If the DCCloneConfig.xml exists, the cloning process starts. If the config file doesn't exist, it is assumed that this is a restored snapshot and the restore process starts.

5.3 Maintain Active Directory

Introduction

In section 5.2, we concentrated on maintenance tasks related to domain controllers. In contrast, there are tasks specific to maintaining Active Directory. Maintaining Active Directory Directory Services (AD DS) involves a variety of tasks like backup and restore, optimization, and metadata clean-up.

In this section, we will cover following exam objectives:

5.3.0 Back up Active Directory and SYSVOL
5.3.1 Perform Active Directory restore
5.3.2 Manage Active Directory offline
5.3.3 Configure and restore objects by using the Active Directory Recycle Bin (2012 R2 Objective)
5.3.4 Perform object- and container-level recovery
5.3.5 Configure Active Directory snapshots
5.3.6 Clean up metadata

Lab Plan

We will use 70411SRV, 70411SRV2 and 70411SRV4, 70411SRV6 (Domain Controllers) for most tasks in this section.

Additional lab setup

Install **Windows Backup** feature (Add Roles and Features in Server Manager), under features.

1. Log on to 70411SRV and open **Server Manager,**
2. From **Manage** menu, click **Add Roles and Features**. The Add Roles and Features Wizard opens. Click **Next** four times until you get to the **Features** screen.
3. On the Features screen, select **Windows Server Backup** and click **Next,** then **Install.**
4. Repeat the steps above on 70411SRV2 and 70411SRV4.
5. Create two shared folders **E:\WSBackup** and **E:\WSSBackup** in 70411SRV4, and grant **domain admins Full Control.**

Log on to 70411SRV2 and Create an AD user account called **ADAuthRestore** (Check **User cannot change password,** and **Password never expires**).

Complete the following tasks:

1. Log on to 70411SRV and open Active Directory Users and Computers.

2. Right-click **70411Lab.com,** point to **New** and select **Organizational Unit**.
3. On the **Name** field of the New Object-Organizational Unit wizard, enter **RecycleBinTestL1** and click **Ok.**
4. Right click **RecycleBinTest** OU, point to **New** and select **Organizational Unit**.
5. On the **Name** field of the New Object-Organizational Unit wizard, enter **RecycleBinTestL2** and click **Ok.**
6. Right-click **RecycleBinTestL1** OU, point to New and select User.
7. On the New Object - User wizard, enter the following.
   a) First Name field, enter **OUL1User1.**
   b) Log on name filed, enter **OUL1User1,**
   c) Click **Next,** enter a password, click **Next** and then **Finish.**
8. Repeat step 7 to create **OUL1User2,** under the **RecycleBinTestL1** OU.
9. Right-click **RecycleBinTestL2** OU, point to **New** and select **User.**
10. On the **New Object - User** wizard, enter the following.
    a) First Name field, enter **OUL2User1.**
    b) Log on name filed, enter **OUL2User1,**
    c) Click **Next,** enter a password, click **Next** and **Finish.**

From 70411SRV, Create an AD User, **TombstonetestUser** on the Users Container.

5.3.0 Back up Active Directory and SYSVOL

It is recommended to schedule Backup of Active Directory Domain Services (AD DS) for a set of domain controllers identified as critical. Though AD DS recovery is not performed routinely, it might sometimes be necessitated by a failure; recovery from such failure in some situations may only be achieved by restoring the directory to a previous state.

Note

Restoring from a backup is not always the best or only option to recover AD DS. Directory restore is recommended to be used as a last resort.

Windows Server Backup tool is used to back up AD DS in Windows Server 2012. Windows Server Backup tool was introduced in Windows Server 2008; replaced Ntbackup, the tool used in earlier versions of the Windows Server operating system. Ntbackup cannot backup servers running Windows Server 2012.

Windows Server Backup tool is a feature in Windows Server 2012 and Windows Server 2012 R2. To use this tool, the Windows Server Backup Feature must be installed. Windows Server Backup Features has two install components:

1. **Windows Server Backup (Wbadmin.msc):** A Graphical User Interface (GUI) snap-in that is available on the **Administrative Tools** menu. You can use the Windows Server Backup GUI to perform critical-volumes backups and full server backups.
2. **Command-line Tools:** Required to install the Wbadmin.exe command-line tool for Windows Server Backup. Command-line Tools are a set of Windows PowerShell tools.

To use one of the wizards for backing up critical volumes, you must know which volumes to select, or you can allow the wizard to select them when you specify that you want to enable system recovery. When you use the command-line tool for backing up critical volumes, the tool selects the correct volumes automatically. To back up system state, you must use the Wbadmin.exe command-line tool.

Contents of Windows Server backup type

The following list describes the backup types and the data that they contain:

1. **System state:** Includes all the files that are required to recover AD DS. System state includes at least the following data, plus additional data, depending on the server roles that are installed:
   a) Registry.
   b) COM+ Class Registration database.

    c) Boot files.
    d) Active Directory Certificate Services (AD CS) database.
    e) Active Directory database (Ntds.dit) file and log files.
    f) SYSVOL directory.
    g) Cluster service information.
    h) Microsoft Internet Information Services (IIS) metadirectory.
    i) System files under Windows Resource Protection.

2. **Critical volumes / Bare Metal recovery**: Includes all volumes that contain system state files:
    a) The volume that hosts the boot files, which consist of the Bootmgr file and the Boot Configuration Data (BCD) store.
    b) The volume that hosts the Windows operating system and the registry.
    c) The volume that hosts the SYSVOL tree.
    d) The volume that hosts the Active Directory database.
    e) The volume that hosts the Active Directory database log files.

3. **Full server:** Includes all volumes on the server, including USB drives. The backup does not include the volume where the backup is stored.

The DNS server stores settings in the registry. Therefore, system state or critical-volume backup is required for DNS recovery, regardless of whether the zone data is Active Directory-integrated or stored in the file system.

System state or critical-volumes backup may be used to restore a domain controller on which the backup was generated or to create a new additional domain controller in the same domain by installing from backup media. System state or critical-volumes backup cannot restore a different domain controller or to restore a domain controller onto different hardware. You can only use a full server backup to restore a domain controller onto different hardware.

Backup frequency

The frequency of backups depends on criteria that vary for individual Active Directory environments. In most Active Directory environments, users, computers, and administrators make daily changes to directory objects, such as group membership or Group Policy. For example, computer accounts, including domain controller accounts, change their passwords every 30 days by default. Therefore, every day a percentage of computer passwords changes for domain controllers and domain client computers. Rolling the computer password of a domain controller back to a former state affects authentication and replication.

A percentage of user passwords might also expire on a daily basis, and if they are lost as a result of domain controller failure, they must be reset manually. Generally, no external record of these changes exists except in AD DS.

Therefore, the more frequently domain controllers are backed up, the fewer problems that may arise if it becomes necessary to restore these information. The more Active Directory objects and domain controllers that exist in an AD environment, the more frequent backups should be. For example, in a large organization, to recover from the inadvertent deletion of a large organizational unit (OU) by restoring the domain from a backup that is days or weeks old, you might have to re-create hundreds of accounts that were created in that OU since the backup was made. To avoid re-creating accounts and potentially performing large numbers of manual password resets, ensure that recent system state backups are always available to recover recent Create, Modify, and Delete operations.

Backup frequency criteria

Backup frequency may be determined using the following criteria:

1. Small environments with a single domain controller in the forest or domains that exist in a single physical location (that is, domains that have a single point of failure): create backups at least daily.
2. Medium (10 to 49 domain controllers) and large environments (50 to 1,000 or more domain controllers): Create backups of each unique directory partition in the forest on two different computers at least daily with an emphasis on backing up application directory partitions, empty root domains, domains in a single geographic site, and sites that have large populations of users or that host mission-critical work.
3. Make backups with increasing frequency until you are confident that if you lose the objects that were created or modified since the last backup, the loss would not create a disruption of your operations.
4. Major changes to the environment should always be immediately followed by a new system state backup.

Note

Microsoft recommends at least two domain controllers for each domain in an Active Directory forest.

Backup latency interval

After performing an initial Active Directory backup on a domain controller, Event ID 2089 provides warnings about the backup status of each directory partition that a domain controller stores, including application directory partitions. Specifically, Event ID 2089 is logged in the Directory Service event log when partitions in the Active Directory forest are not backed up with sufficient frequency, and it continues daily until a backup of the partition occurs.

This event serves as a warning to administrators and monitoring applications to make sure that domain controllers are backed up well before the tombstone lifetime expires. By monitoring this event, domain administrators can ensure that backups occur with sufficient frequency. Sufficient frequency is determined by the backup latency interval.

The value for the backup latency interval is stored as a **REG_DWORD** value in the **Backup Latency Threshold (days)** registry entry in HKEY_LOCAL_MACHINE\SYSTEM\CurrentControlSet\Services\NTD S\Parameters. By default, the value of **Backup Latency Threshold (days)** is half the value of the tombstone lifetime of the forest. In a Windows Server 2012 forest, half the tombstone lifetime is 90 days. However, it is recommended to take backups at a much higher frequency than the default value of **Backup Latency Threshold (days).**

By setting a minimum backup frequency, changing the Backup Latency Threshold (days) registry entry setting to reflect that frequency, and monitoring Event ID 2089, a suitable backup frequency can be established.

To set a different **Backup Latency Threshold (days)** value, use Registry Editor (Regedit.exe) to create the entry as a **REG_DWORD** and provide the appropriate number of days.

To perform Active Directory Backup

1. Log on to 70411SRV4 and open **Server Manager**.
2. From Tools menu, click Windows Server Backup.
3. On the left pane, right-click **Local Backup** and select **Backup once**.
4. On the **Backup Once** Wizard, on the **Backup options** page, click **Different options**, and then click **Next**.
5. Click **Next** to select **Different options** page and click **Next** again.
6. On the **Select backup configuration** page, click **Custom**, and then click **Next**.
7. On the Select backup items page, click Add Items.
8. On the **Select items** menu, select **System State**, then expand **C:**, expand **Windows**, then check **SYSVOL** folder and click **Ok**. (**SYSVOL** is part of **System state** but we will require the SYSVOL backup to perform SYSVOL restore later).
9. On the Select backup items page, click **Next**.
10. On the Specify Destination Type screen, click Local Drives, and click Next.
11. On the **Confirmation** screen, click **Backup.**
12. When backup completes, click **Close.**

Note

Windows Server Backup appears on the Administrative Tools menu by default, even if the Windows Server Backup feature is not installed. If Windows Server Backup is not installed, when you open Windows Server Backup, a message appears, notifying you that the tool is not installed and providing the instructions for installing Windows Server Backup.

To Schedule Active Directory Backup

1. Log on to 70411SRV and open **Server Manager**.
2. From Tools menu, click Windows Server Backup.
3. On the left pane, right-click **Local Backup** and select **Backup Schedule**.
4. On the **Getting Started** screen, click **Next**.
5. On Select **Backup Configuration** screen, select **Custom** and click **Next**.
6. On the Select backup items page, click Add Items.
7. On the **Select items** menu, select **System State,** then Expand **C:**, expand **Windows** and check **SYSVOL** folder and click **Ok**.
8. On the **Select backup items** page, click **Next**.
9. On the **Specify Backup Time** screen, note that you can backup once a day or select multiple times of the day, select **Once a day** and click **Next.**
10. On the **Specify Destination Type** screen, note all the available options:
    a) **Back up to a hard disk that is dedicated for backups (recommended):** Choose this option for the safest way to store backups. The hard disk that you use will be formatted and then dedicated to only store backups.
    b) **Back up to a volume:** Choose this option if you cannot dedicate an entire disk for backups. Note that the performance of the volume may be reduced by up to 200 percent while it is used to store backups. Microsoft recommends not to store other server data on the same volume.
    c) **Backup to a shared network folder**: Choose this option if you do not want to store backups locally on the server. Note that you will only have one backup at a time because when you create a new backup it overwrites the previous backup.
11. Select **Backup to a shared network folder,** click **Next** and respond **Ok** to the Warning message.
12. On the **Specify Remote Folder** screen, **Location** field, enter \\70411SRV4\WSBackup.
13. Below **Access control,** review the ACL options:
    a) **Do not inherit**: This option makes the backup accessible only for the user whose credentials are provided in the next step. (This option is greyed out).
    b) **Inherit**: This option makes the backup accessible to everybody who has access to the specified remote shard folder.

14. Below Access control, Select Inherit and click Next.
15. On the **Windows Security** dialogue, provide an account that is a member of the **Domain Admins** group in the format **70411Lab\<account name>** and password, then click **Ok.**
16. On the **Confirmation** screen, click **Finish.**
17. When backup completes, click **Close.**

When configuring a scheduled backup, on the network share access control, the Do not inherit option is not available. This as well as **Inherit** option were available when we configured one off backup.

Before you perform the next task, ensure that the user account **ADAuthRestore** has replicated to 70411SRV6. To force replication, log on to 70411SRV2 and execute: **repadmin /syncall /AdP**.

It is important that you perform the next task as you will require the backup in section 5.3.1

To perform a system state backup using wbadmin.exe

1. Log on to 70411SRV2 and open command prompt.
2. To backup system state to the local drive E:, run the command below:

```
wbadmin start systemstatebackup -backupTarget:E: -quiet
```

Specifying the -quiet parameter, suppresses any prompts.

3. To delete an AD object, complete the following tasks:
   a) Open Active Directory Users and Computers and navigate to the Users container.
   b) On the details pane, right-click ADAuthRestore and delete it

5.3.1 Perform Active Directory restore

Recovery from Active Directory corruption or inconsistency may be accomplished by performing a restore operation to return AD DS to its state at the time of the backup. As noted earlier in this section, recovering AD DS from an error or failure condition using backup should be undertaken as a last resort. Assuming that a restore operation is appropriate to recover a domain controller, requirements for recovering AD DS relate to the age of the backup.

Before restoring a domain controller from a backup, it is important to consider the following:

1. Tombstone lifetime of the forest: Tombstone lifetime is the number of days that deletions are retained in the directory. The backup must not be older than the tombstone lifetime. In forests that are created on servers running Windows Server 2003 with Service Pack 1 and upwards, the default value of the tombstone lifetime is 180 days.

Important

Always check the tombstone lifetime value before you use a backup to restore AD DS. Even if you are sure of the default value for your environment, the tombstone lifetime value might have been changed administratively in AD DS.

2. Do not modify system clocks in an attempt to improperly extend the useful life of a system state backup. Skewed time can cause serious problems in cases where directory data is time sensitive.

To determine the tombstone lifetime for the 70411Lab forest using ADSIEdit

1. Log on to 70411SRV and open **ADSI Edit** from Server Manager.
2. In **ADSI Edit** Window, right-click **ADSI Edit**, and then click **Connect to**.
3. For Connection Point, click Select **a well known Naming Context**, and then select **Configuration** from the drop-down list and click **Ok**.
4. Double-click **Configuration**, the container **CN=Configuration,DC=70411Lab, DC=com** opens
5. Expand **CN=Configuration,DC=70411Lab, DC=com\CN=Services** and highlight **CN=Windows NT**.
6. On the details pane right-click **CN=Directory Service**, and then click **Properties**.
7. In the Attribute column, click **tombstoneLifetime**.
8. Note the value in the Value column. If the value is <not set>, the value is 180 days.

Important

In step 3 above, if you want to connect to a different domain controller, under Computer, click Select or type a domain or server: (Server | Domain [:port]). Provide the server name or the domain name and Lightweight Directory Access Protocol (LDAP) port (389), and then click Ok.

Exam Tip

It is important to note the connection point you require in ADSI Edit to view tombstonelifetime attribute - "a well known Naming Context".

Tombstone Lifetime attribute may also be determined using the dsquery command as illustrated below:

```
dsquery * "cn=directory service,cn=windows
nt,cn=services,cn=configuration,dc=70411Lab,dc=com" -scope base -attr
tombstonelifetime
```

The command will display the tombstonelifetim attribute value.

AD DS restore using backup may be accomplished in the following ways:

1. **Non-authoritative restore**: Use this process to restore AD DS to its state at the time of the backup, and then allow Active Directory replication to update the restored domain controller to the current state of AD DS.

2. **Authoritative restore**: Use this process to recover objects that have been deleted from AD DS. Authoritative restore does not allow replication to overwrite the restored deletions. Instead, the restored objects replicate authoritatively to the other domain controllers in the domain.

Note

Be aware that additions of data that are made between the time of the backup and the authoritative restore process are not removed during the restore process. Authoritative restore focuses only on the deleted objects. Additional data is merged during the restore process.

If AD DS recovery from backup is not possible, you must reinstall AD DS. Sometimes restoring from backup is possible but not feasible. For example, if a domain controller is needed quickly, it is sometimes faster to reinstall AD DS than to recover the domain controller. In cases of hardware failure or file corruption, you might have to reinstall the operating system and then either reinstall or restore AD DS.

To perform a **nonauthoritative** or **authoritative** restore you must boot the server into Directory Services Repair Mode (DSRM), one of the options available from the Advanced Boot Options menu which you access by pressing F8 at the beginning of the boot process. To access the Advanced Boot Options menu on a Hyper-V guest, reboot the guest and press F5 to access the Windows Boot Manager screen. Then in the Windows Boot Manager screen, press F8 to access advanced boot options.

To Perform Non-Authoritative AD DS Restore

1. Reboot 70411SRV4 and press **F5** (Function + F5, for some laptops) as the Hyper-V guest is starting up. This will load the Windows Boot Manager screen.
2. On the Windows Boot Manager screen, highlight Windows Server 2012 R2 and click F8 (Function+F8, for some laptops) to load the Advanced boot options.
3. On the Advanced boot options, select Directory Services Repair Mode (DSRM) and hit the Enter key.
4. At the log on screen, perform the following tasks:
   a) To Log in using the local administrator account, specify **.\Administrator** as the username.
   b) Open a command prompt.
   c) To see a list of available backups, execute the command:

WBADMIN GET VERSIONS -backupTarget:E:

   d) To begin recovery, execute the command: (Change the version to yours)

WBADMIN start systemstaterecovery -backuptarget:E: -Version:< version Identification>

Replace **Version ID** with **Version identifier** from the previous command.

   e) Respond **Y**, to the start the system state recovery operation.
   f) Windows PowerShell way: Run the commands below to accomplish the task with PowerShell: To load the available backup set in the variable $Backup, run the commands:

$Backup = Get-WBBackupSet

   g) To start systemstaterecovery with the backup set, run the command;

Start-WBSystemStateRecovery -BackupSet $Backup

   h) Respond **Y**, to start system state recovery to original location.
5. When the recovery completes, restart the DC
6. When you log into the DC, press **Enter** to complete the recovery operation
7. Confirm that the object deleted earlier, **ADAuthRestore** was not restored.

Important

You may also use Bcdedit.exe to restart a server in DSRM. The command is: bcdedit /set safeboot dsrepair.

To Perform an Authoritative AD DS Restore

Authoritative restores are conducted the same way as outlined in the previous task, except that **Ntdsutil** is used to mark objects as **authoritative**. You can mark objects one at a time, or you can mark entire subtrees.

1. To perform non-authoritative restore, complete the tasks below:
   a) Restart 70411SRV2 and complete the following tasks:
   b) Press **F5** (Function + F5, for some laptops) as the Hyper-V guest is starting up. This will load the **Windows Boot Manager screen.**
   c) On the Windows Boot Manager screen, highlight Windows Server 2012 R2 and click F8 (Function+F8, for some laptops) to load the Advanced boot options.
   d) On the Advanced boot options, select Directory Services Repair Mode (DSRM) and press the Enter key.
   e) Log on with local administrator account by specify **.\Administrator** as the username.
   f) Open command prompt and perform the following tasks:
      i) To load the available backup set in the variable $Backup, run the command:

```
$Backup = Get-WBBackupSet
```

      ii) To start systemstaterecovery with the backup set, run the command

```
Start-WBSystemStateRecovery -BackupSet $Backup
```

You can also run the command in one go as shown below:

```
Start-WBSystemStateRecovery -BackupSet ((Get-WBBackupSet))
```

      iii) Respond **Y**, to start system state recovery to original location.
      iv) When the non-authoritative restore completes, **DO NOT REBOOT** the DC and continue with step 2 below.
2. To mark a deleted object as authoritative, open a command prompt and complete the tasks below:
   a) Enter **ntdsutil** at the command prompt.
   b) At the ntdsutil prompt, enter **activate instance ntds**, and then enter **authoritative restore**.
   c) To mark ADRestoretest account deleted earlier as authoritative, at the ntdsutil prompt type: restore object " CN=ADRestoretest,CN=Users,DC=70411Lab,DC=com"
   d) At the Authoritative Restore Confirmation Dialog box, click Yes
   e) Exit ntdsutil.
3. Reboot the DC in normal mode and log on to the domain.
4. After the restart, confirm that the object deleted earlier, **ADRestoretest** was restored.

Note

The format for step 2 above is as follows: Enter *restore object "dn"* to restore a single object, where dn is the object's distinguished name. Enter *restore subtree "dn"* to restore a subtree, where dn is the subtree's distinguished name. The process specifies the location of an LDIF file if backlinked objects are being restored.

Reanimating Active Directory Tombstone Objects

So far, we have discussed how to recover deleted Active Directory objects using authoritative or non-authoritative restore. These methods require taking the domain controller offline and restarting in Directory Services Repair Mode. Tombstone reanimation provides the option to recover deleted objects without taking a DC offline. Also, a deleted object's identity information, such as its objectGUID and objectSid attributes may be recovered using this method.

Tombstone reanimation was introduced in Windows Server 2003 Active Directory to simplify certain data recovery scenarios. This feature takes advantage of the fact that Active Directory keeps deleted objects in the database for a period of time before physically removing them.

How to recover a deleted object using tombstone reanimation

LDP.exe is a Windows Explorer-like utility for working with Active Directory. Even though tombstones are invisible to normal directory operations, you can find tombstone objects in Active Directory using LDAP search operations and special LDAP extensions called controls. LDP.exe utility can perform LDAP search operations.

To recover a deleted object using tombstone reanimation

1. Log on to 70411SRV and open Active Directory Users and Computers.
2. Navigate to **Users** container and delete **TombstonetestUser** (Created earlier).
3. To open **LDP.exe**:
   a) Open cmd in elevated mode (Admin privileges).
   b) At the command prompt, execute:

```
LDP.exe
```

4. To connect to the DC:
   a) Click **Connection** and select **Connect**.

  b) At the **Connect** dialogue, confirm that 70411SRV is in the **Server** field and on the **Port field,** enter **389,** then click **Ok**

5. To display the Deleted Objects container:

  a) Click **Connection** and select **Bind.**

  b) On the **Bind** dialogue, ensure that **Bind as currently logged on user** is selected and click **Ok.**

  c) Click **Options** and select **Controls.**

  d) On the **Controls** dialog box, expand the **Load Predefined** pull-down menu, click **Return deleted objects**, and then click **Ok.**

6. To authenticate to a DC and confirm that deleted object container is loaded:

  a) Click **View,** and select **Tree,** and in **BaseDN,** type **DC=70411Lab,DC=com** and click **Ok.**

  b) Expand DC=70411Lab,DC=com and confirm that CN=Deleted Objects,DC=70411Lab,DC=com container is listed.

7. To restore a deleted object:

  a) Double-click CN=Deleted Objects,DC=70411Lab,DC=com container.

  b) Expand CN=Deleted Objects,DC=70411Lab,DC=com container.

  c) Locate the deleted object CN=TombstonetestUser, right-click it and select modify.

  d) In the Modify dialog box, complete the following tasks:

   i) On **Edit Entry** Attribute, type **isDeleted**. Leave the **Values** box empty.

   ii) Under **Operation**, click **Delete**, and then click **Enter.**

   iii) On Edit Entry Attribute, select isDeleted and type distinguishedName.

   iv) On **Values,** type **CN=TombstonetestUser,CN=Users,DC=70411Lab,DC=com** (the original distinguished name (also known as DN) of the Active Directory object).

   v) Under Operation, click Replace.

   vi) Make sure that the **Extended** check box is selected, click **Enter,** and then click **Run.**

8. To confirm deleted object restore:

  a) Open Active Directory Users and Computers and navigate to **Users** container.

  b) Confirm that **TombstonetestUser** now exists.

SYSVOL Restore and Recovery

In a Multi-domain controller environment, there might be occasions when one or more Domain Controllers are out of date with SYSVOL replication. Each Domain Controller has its own folder where GPOs and scripts are saved. This folder is located under **%WINDIR%\SYSVOL\domain**. There are 2 folders in this location:

Policies: Group Policies are saved in this location - %WINDIR%\SYSVOL\domain\Policies.

Scripts: Logon scripts or other files are saved in this location - %WINDIR%\SYSVOL\domain\Scripts shared as NETLOGON.

If SYSVOL replication to a particular DC stops, the DC will no longer be up to date. The Domain Controller with PDC Emulator operation master role will always have updated copy of the SYSVOL; so it is the best place to look for the updated copy. Any other DC that is out of sync will have to be updated using Non-Authoritative SYSVOL Restore. SYSVOL replication in Windows Server 2012 is performed using DFS Replication (DFSR) and the procedures apply to SYSVOL replication using DFSR.

Non-Authoritative SYSVOL Restore is applicable when a single or a couple of DCs are not updated. There are some other times when all of Domain Controllers do not run and share SYSVOL where Group Policies and logon scripts are located. In this situation, performing Authoritative SYSVOL Restore is recommended. Authoritative SYSVOL restore should be performed on the Domain Controller holding **PDC Emulator operation master role**. One of the functions of PDC emulator FSMO role holder is to manage and maintain GPOs. When you create or modify existing GPO, it is done directly on this Domain Controller.

To Perform Non-Authoritative SYSVOL Restore

1. Log on to 70411SRV6 and open Server Manager.
2. Confirm that **DFS Management Tools** is installed:
    a) Open Server Manager, click **Manage** and select **Add Roles and Features**.
    b) Click **Next** four times until you reach **Features** page.
    c) On the Features page, expand Remote Server Administration Tools\Role Administration Tools\File Services Tool\ and conform that DFS Management Tools is installed.
    d) Cancel Add Roles and Features Wizard.
3. Disable DFS Replication (DFSR):
    a) Still logged on to 70411SRV6, open **ADSI Edit**.
    b) Right-click **ADSI Edit** and select **Connect to.**
    c) On the Connect Settings window, select a **well known Naming Context** and choose Default Naming Context, then click **Ok**.

d) On the ADSI Edit MMC, double-click Default Naming Context [70411SRV6.70411Lab.com]. DC=70411Lab,DC=com opens.

e) Highlight DC=70411Lab,DC=com, and on the details pane, double-click OU=Domain Controllers. Double-click CN=70411SRV6, then CN=DFSR-LocalSettings, CN=Domain System Volume.

f) Right-click CN=SYSVOL Subscription and select Properties.

g) Double-click **msDFSR-Enabled,** select **False** and click **Ok.**

h) On the CN=SYSVOL Subscription Properties, click **Ok** to save changes.

4. Force Active Directory Replication: Open elevated command prompt and execute the command:

```
repadmin /syncall /AdP
```

5. Synchronize with the global information store:

```
dfsrdiag PollAD
```

6. Confirm SYSVOL replication state: Check **DFS Replication** event log for event ID 4114 which indicates that SYSVOL is no longer replicated.

7. Enable DFS Replication (DFSR): Repeat step 3 to enable DFS Replication.

8. Force Active Directory Replication:

```
repadmin /syncall /AdP
```

9. Confirm SYSVOL replication state: Check **DFS Replication** Event ID 4602 in the DFSR event log indicating SYSVOL has been initialized.

To Perform Authoritative SYSVOL Restore

1. Log on to 70411SRV6 and perform the following tasks:

a) Transfer PDC FSMO role to 70411SRV6.

b) Stop DFSR Service, execute the following command:

```
net stop DFSR
```

c) Disable DFS Replication (DFSR):
   i) Open **ADSI Edit** (Server Manager – Tools).
   ii) Right-click **ADSI Edit** and select **Connect to.**
   iii) On the Connect Settings window, select a well known Naming Context and choose Default Naming Context, click Ok.
   iv) On the ADSI Edit MMC, double-click Default Naming Context, [70411SRV6.70411Lab.com]. DC=70411Lab,DC=com opens
   v) Highlight DC=70411Lab,DC=com, in the details pane double-click OU=Domain Controllers. Double-click CN=70411SRV6, then CN=DFSR-LocalSettings, CN=Domain System Volume.
   vi) Right-click CN=SYSVOL Subscription and select Properties.
   vii) Double-click **msDFSR-Enabled**, select **False** and click **Ok.**

viii) On the CN=SYSVOL Subscription Properties, click Ok to save changes.

   d) Configure DFS Replication Option:
- i) Right-click CN=SYSVOL Subscription and select Properties.
- ii) Double-click msDFSR-options, enter the value 1 and click **Ok** to save changes.

2. Log on to all DCs and perform the following tasks:
   a) Stop DFSR Service, execute the following command:

```
net stop DFSR
```

   b) Disable DFS Replication (DFSR): Repeat the task completed in 1-3 above on all DCs.

3. Log on to 70411SRV6 and perform the following tasks:
   a) Force Active Directory Replication:

```
repadmin /syncall /AdP
```

   b) Start DFSR Service:

```
net start DFSR
```

   c) Confirm SYSVOL replication state: Check **DFS Replication** event log for event ID 4114 which indicates that SYSVOL is no longer replicated.

   d) Enable DFS Replication (DFSR): Reverse of steps 1-3 above **(msDFSR-Enabled = TRUE)**

   e) Force Active Directory Replication:

```
repadmin /syncall /AdP
```

   f) Synchronize with the global information store:

```
dfsrdiag PollAD
```

   g) Confirm SYSVOL replication state: You will see Event ID 4602 in the **DFS Replication** event log indicating SYSVOL has been initialized. It will also contain the information "This member is the designated primary member for this replicated folder".

4. Log on to all DCs and perform the following tasks:
   a) Start DFSR Service, execute the following command:

```
net start DFSR
```

   b) Enable DFS Replication (DFSR): Reverse of steps 1-3 above **(msDFSR-Enabled = TRUE)**.

   c) Synchronize with the global information store:

```
dfsrdiag PollAD.
```

Note

To perform authoritative SYSVOL restore, set msDFSR-Enabled=FALSE, and msDFSR-options=1 on the DC you want to mark as authoritative, set msDFSR-Enabled=FALSE, leave msDFSR-options=<not set> (default) on all other DCs.

5.3.2 Manage Active Directory offline

Most day to day tasks involving Active Directory will be performed with AD DS online. But some tasks relating to optimizing AD DS database, like defragmentation and relocation AD DS database, can only be performed when Active Directory Directory Service is offline.

As more and more items are added to the AD database, over time it may become defragmented and may require manual defragmentation to improve performance.

Although Active Directory performs regular online defragmentation, it is sometimes necessary to perform an offline defragmentation. In previous versions of AD DS, conducting offline tasks required rebooting the DC in Directory Services Repair Mode (DSRM) and then rebooting again into normal mode when finished. From Windows Server 2008, it is possible to stop the AD DS service and other services that depend on it, perform maintenance tasks such as offline defragmentation, and then restart the services. The ability to perform offline tasks by simply stopping AD DS provides some benefits. The server will still provide some services such as shared network folders and print services while others such as user authentication and replication will not be available.

To optimize AD database (Offline Defragmentation)

1. Log on to 70411SRV6 and perform the following tasks:
2. Stop Active Directory Domain Services:
    a) Open Server Manager, click **Tools** and select **Services.** The Services MMC snap-in opens.
    b) Right-click **Active Directory Domain Services** and select **Stop.** Note the dependent services that will also stop:
        i)   Kerberos Key Distribution Center.
        ii) Intersite Messaging.
        iii) DNS Server.
        iv) DFS Replication.
    c) Respond **Yes** to the **Stop Other Services** Dialogue box
3. Create a temporary directory for AD Database: Navigate to C:\Windows\NTDS and create a folder called **NTDSBackup.**
4. Perform Offline Defragmentation:
    a) Open an elevated command prompt.

b) At the command prompt, enter **ntdsutil**, and press enter.

c) On the ntdsutil prompt, enter **Activate Instance NTDS**. Then enter **files**.

d) On the **file maintenance** prompt, enter **info** to display information about the path to the AD DS database and log files. The following information is displayed:

i)   Database: C:\Windows\NTDS\ntds.dit - <DB size in Mb>.

ii) Backup dir: C:\Windows\NTDS\dsadata.bak.

iii) Working dir: C:\Windows\NTDS.

iv) Log dir: C:\Windows\NTDS - < DB size in Mb> total.

e) To defrag AD Database, on the **file maintenance** prompt enter:

compact to C:\Windows\NTDS\NTDSBackup

f) When the defragmentation completes:

i)   Rename **ntds.dit** in the directory C:\Windows\NTDS to **ntds_old.dit**.

ii) Copy **ntds.dit** from C:\Windows\NTDS\NTDSBackup\ to C:\Windows\NTDS.

g) On the **file maintenance** prompt enter **q**, then **q** at the **ntdsutil** prompt.

h) Reboot 70411SRV6:

shutdown /r.

i) After the reboot, confirm that Active Directory Domain Services and all dependent services listed above started successfully.

j) Check the following logs for errors / Information:

i)   DFS Replication.

ii) Directory Service.

iii) DNS Server.

To relocate AD DS Database and Logs

1. Log on to 70411SRV6 and perform the following tasks:

2. Stop Active Directory Domain Services:

a) Open Server Manager, click **Tools** and select **Services.** Services MMC snap-in opens

b) Right-click **Active Directory Domain Services** and select **Stop.** Note the dependent services that will also stop:

i)   Kerberos Key Distribution Center.

ii) Intersite Messaging.

iii) DNS Server.

iv) DFS Replication.

c) Respond **Yes** to the **Stop Other Services** Dialogue box.

3. Create a directory structure in drive E for AD Database E:\Windows\NTDS.

4. To relocate the AD Database and log file:
   a) Open an elevated command prompt.
   b) At the command prompt, enter **ntdsutil**, and press enter.
   c) On the ntdsutil prompt, enter **Activate Instance NTDS**. Then enter **files**.
   d) On the **file maintenance** prompt, enter **info** to display information about the path to the AD DS database and log files. The following information is displayed:
      i) Database: C:\Windows\NTDS\ntds.dit - <DB size in Mb>.
      ii) Backup dir: C:\Windows\NTDS\dsadata.bak.
      iii) Working dir: C:\Windows\NTDS.
      iv) Log dir: C:\Windows\NTDS - < DB size in Mb> total.
   e) On the **file maintenance** prompt, complete the following tasks:
      i) To move the database, execute:

> move db to E:\Windows\NTDS

      ii) To move the log files, execute:

> move logs to E:\Windows\NTDS

   f) On the **file maintenance** prompt enter **q**, then **q** at the **ntdsutil** prompt.
   g) Start Active Directory Domain Services and confirm that all dependent services listed above started successfully.
   h) Check the following logs for errors / Information:
      i) DFS Replication
      ii) Directory Service
      iii) DNS Server

Note

The feature that allows stopping of Active Directory Domain Services without affecting other services on the server is called **Restartable Active Directory Domain Services**.

5.3.3 Configure and restore objects by using the Active Directory Recycle Bin (2012 R2 Objective)

Prior to Windows Server 2008 R2, the only option available to recover accidentally deleted objects was authoritative restore from backup. The major drawback to this method was that it had to be performed in Directory Services Restore Mode (DSRM). When a DC is in DSRM, the domain controller being restored had to remain offline. Another shortcoming of authoritatively restoring Active Directory objects from AD DS backups was that any changes to the objects that occurred between the backup time and the restore time could not be recovered.

Active Directory Recycle Bin, introduced with Windows Server 2008 R2, helps minimize directory service downtime by enhancing your ability to preserve and restore accidentally deleted Active Directory objects without restoring Active Directory data from backups, restarting AD DS, or rebooting domain controllers. Although tombstone reanimation (discussed earlier) provides the option to recover deleted objects without taking a DC offline, the method is not as robust as AD Recycle Bin.

How Active Directory Recycle Bin works

When you enable Active Directory Recycle Bin, all link-valued and non-link-valued attributes of the deleted Active Directory objects are preserved and the objects are restored in their entirety to the same consistent logical state that they were in immediately before deletion. It is important to understand two concepts:

Deleted objects

After you enable **Active Directory Recycle Bin**, when an Active Directory object is deleted, the system preserves all the object's link-valued and non-link-valued attributes and the object becomes "logically deleted", a new state introduced in Windows Server 2008 R2. A deleted object is moved to the **Deleted Objects container**, with its distinguished name mangled. A deleted object remains in the Deleted Objects container in a logically deleted state throughout the duration of the deleted object lifetime. Within the deleted object lifetime, you can recover a deleted object.

Recycled objects

After the deleted object lifetime expires, the logically deleted object is turned into a recycled object and most of its attributes are stripped away. A "recycled object," a new state introduced in Windows Server 2008 R2, remains in the Deleted Objects container until its recycled object lifetime expires. After the recycled object lifetime expires, the garbage-collection process physically deletes the recycled Active Directory object from the database.

Deleted object lifetime and recycled object lifetime

The **deleted object lifetime** is determined by the value of the **msDS-deletedObjectLifetime** attribute. The recycled object lifetime is determined by the value of the legacy **tombstoneLifetime** attribute. By default, **msDS-deletedObjectLifetime** is set to null. When **msDS-deletedObjectLifetime** is set to null, the deleted object lifetime is set to the value of the recycled object lifetime. By default, the recycled object lifetime, which is stored in the tombstoneLifetime attribute, is also set to null. In Windows Server 2012 R2, when **tombstoneLifetime** is set to null, the recycled object lifetime defaults to 180 days.

Active Directory Recycle Bin can be enabled with the following tools: Active Directory Administrative Center, Enable-ADOptionalFeature PowerShell cmdlet (This is the recommended method.), Ldp.exe.

To enable Active Directory Recycle Bin using PowerShell

1. Log on to 70411SRV and open **Active Directory Module for Windows PowerShell** with elevated privileges. (Server Manager – Tools).
2. At the Active Directory Module for Windows PowerShell prompt, run the following command:

```
Enable-ADOptionalFeature –Identity 'CN=Recycle Bin
Feature,CN=Optional Features,CN=Directory Service,CN=Windows
NT,CN=Services,CN=Configuration,DC=70411Lab,DC=com' -Scope
ForestOrConfigurationSet -Target '70411Lab.com'
```

3. Respond **Y** to the warning.

To set the msDS-deletedObjectLifetime attribute

1. Log on to 70411SRV and open **ADSI Edit** from Server Manager.
2. On the **ADSI Edit** Window, right-click **ADSI Edit**, and then click **Connect to**.
3. For Connection Point, click Select **a well known Naming Context**, and then select **Configuration** from the drop-down list then click **Ok**.
4. Double-click **Configuration**, then highlight the container **CN=Configuration,DC=70411Lab, DC=com** to open it.
5. Expand   CN=Configuration,DC=70411Lab,DC=com\CN=Services\ and highlight CN=Windows NT.
6. On the details pane right-click CN=Directory Service, and then click Properties.
7. On the Attribute column, click msDS-deletedObjectLifetime.
8. This value is set at <not set> by default.

5.3.4 Perform object- and container-level recovery

When Active Directory objects are deleted, they are placed in the Deleted Objects container. By default, the CN=Deleted Objects container is not displayed. The **Ldp.exe** administration tool can be used to display the Deleted Objects container in AD DS. As illustrated earlier in this chapter, Ldp.exe may also be used to restore a single, deleted Active Directory object.

The **Get-ADObject** and **Restore-ADObject** Active Directory module for Windows PowerShell cmdlets can also restore deleted Active Directory object. The recommended approach is to use the Get-ADObject cmdlet to retrieve the deleted object and then pipe the output to the Restore-ADObject cmdlet. It is possible use the **Get-ADObject** and **Restore-ADObject** cmdlets to restore multiple objects, for example in nested Organizational Units.

To display the Deleted Objects container

1. Log on to 70411SRV and open a command prompt.
2. At the command prompt, type **ldp.exe**. The LDP console opens.
3. On the **Options** menu, click **Controls**.
4. On the Controls dialog box, expand the **Load Predefined** pull-down menu, and click **Return deleted objects**, then click **Ok**.
5. To verify that the Deleted Objects container is displayed:
   a) To connect and bind to the server that hosts the forest root domain of the AD DS environment, complete the following tasks:
      i)   From **Connections** menu, click **Connect.**
      ii) On the **Server** field, enter 70411SRV and click **Ok**.
      iii) From **Connections** menu, click **Bind**.
      iv) Under Bind Type, select Bind as currently logged on user, then click Ok.
   b) Click **View**, then click **Tree**, and in **BaseDN**, select **DC=70411Lab,DC=com** and click **Ok**.
   c) On the console tree, expand DC=70411Lab,DC=com, and locate the CN=Deleted Objects,DC=70411Lab,DC=com container.

To restore a single, deleted Active Directory object

1. Log on to 70411SRV and open **Active Directory Module for Windows PowerShell** with administrative privileges.
2. Delete an object: Open **Active Directory Users and Computers** and delete the "ADFS Service" account under the **Users** container.
3. To confirm that the object is in the deleted objects container, execute the command:

```
Get-ADObject -Filter {displayName -eq "ADFS Service"} -
IncludeDeletedObjects
```

4. To restore the deleted object, run the following command:

> Get-ADObject -Filter {displayName -eq "ADFS Service"} -
> IncludeDeletedObjects | Restore-ADObject

5. To confirm that the ADFS Service account was restored, open **Active Directory Users and Computers,** navigate to the **Users** container, refresh it and view contents on the details pane.

Note

You can also restore a deleted object from the **Deleted Objects** container in **Active Directory Administrative Center**. This is achieved by right-clicking the object and selecting **Restore**.

Restoring multiple, deleted Active Directory objects

When we prepared for the lab at the beginning of this section, we created an OU hierarchy with the following structure:

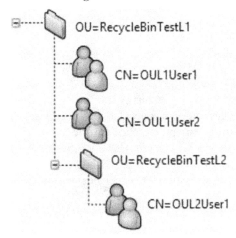

Figure 5.3.0 – Multiple AD OU Hierarchy

Restoring multiple deleted objects is not as straight forward as restoring a single object. For example, in Figure 5.3.0 above, when the **RecycleBinTest1** OU is deleted, all its objects (total of five objects, including itself) are moved to the **Deleted Objects** container, with their distinguished names mangled. The Deleted Objects container displays all logically deleted objects in a flat hierarchy as its direct children.

The recommended approach to restoring a nested OU to its original state is to use the **Get-ADObject** Active Directory module cmdlet to retrieve the deleted objects one hierarchy level at a time and then to pass those objects through the pipeline to the **Restore-ADObject** cmdlet. If the administrator is not familiar with the original hierarchy of the OU, the administrator must first use the **Get-ADOBject** cmdlet to perform several investigation steps.

Before you proceed, open Active Directory Users and Computers, and delete the OU hierarchy, **RecycleBinTestL1,** confirm deletion and subtree deletion. Confirm that the deleted OU is now in the **Deleted Objects** container in the **Active Directory Administrative Center.** If the object is not displayed, you might need to close and reopen **Active Directory Administrative Center.** Notice that the objects do not appear in their original hierarchical format in the **Deleted Objects** container. It is in a mangled structure.

To restore multiple, deleted Active Directory objects

1. Perform investigative steps:
    a) Log on to 70411SRV and open Active Directory Module for Windows PowerShell.
    b) Search for a the user account OUL1User1 with the Get-ADOBject cmdlet, using the msDS-lastKnownRDN attribute in the ldapFilter parameter and constructing the command so that the lastKnownParent attribute of OUL1User1 is returned, as follows:

```
Get-ADObject -SearchBase "CN=Deleted Objects,DC=70411Lab,DC=com"
-ldapFilter:"(msDs-lastKnownRDN=OUL1User1)" -IncludeDeletedObjects -
Properties lastKnownParent
```

This will display some useful information, like DistinguishedName and LastKnownParent. This information can also be obtained from the **Deleted Objects** container in the **Active Directory Administrative Center.**

    c) From the output of the Get-ADObject, you know that the user OUL1User1, belongs to the OU RecycleBinTestL1. You may want to make further investigation by searching for all the objects in the **Deleted Objects** container whose **lastKnownParent** value is **RecycleBinTestL1**, using the following command:

```
Get-ADObject –SearchBase "CN=Deleted
Objects,DC=70411Lab,DC=com" -Filter {lastKnownParent -eq
'OU=RecycleBinTestL1\\0ADEL:a37f5b4a-7275-4294-9d09-
94fd0cb2a7f4,CN=Deleted Objects,DC=70411Lab,DC=com'} -
IncludeDeletedObjects -Properties lastKnownParent | ft
```

Note

The information contained in the lastKnownParent filter above is obtained from the lastKnownParent output in the last command. Mine is " OU=RecycleBinTestL1\0ADEL:a37f5b4a-7275-4294-9d09-94fd0cb2a7f4,CN=Deleted   Objects,DC=70411Lab,DC=com".   It   is important to escape the slash (\) in the mangled distinguished name that is used in the Get-ADObject cmdlet with another slash.

2.   The last command will return a list in a tabular form as shown below:

```
Deleted Distinguished LastKnownPar Name              ObjectClass  ObjectGUID
        Name          ent
------- ------------- ------------ ----              -----------  ----------
True    OU=Recycle... OU=Recycl... RecycleBi...      organizat... d4e2e5d0-...
True    CN=OULiUse... OU=Recycl... OULiUser1...       user        591b1035-...
True    CN=OULiUse... OU=Recycl... OULiUser2...       user        37b0e5aa-...
```

Important

It is critical to begin restoring objects from the highest level of the hierarchy because deleted objects must be restored to a live parent. In the example above, the RecycleBinTestL1 OU must be restored first as all our investigations point to it as the lastKnownParent for all the objects we intend to restore. It is a simple logic as you will not attempt to restore an object to a non-existent object.

3.   To restore the deleted objects:
   a)   Restore the **RecycleBinTestL1** OU by running the following command at the Active Directory Module for Windows PowerShell prompt:

```
Get-ADObject -ldapFilter:"(msDS-LastKnownRDN=RecycleBinTestL1)" -IncludeDeletedObjects | Restore-ADObject
```

   b)   Confirm RecycleBinTestL1 was restored successfully by checking Active Directory Users and Computers.
   c)   Next step will be to restore all direct children (Users and OUs) of the RecycleBinTestL1 OU. In this example, we will restore, RecycleBinTestL2 OU and the two users, OUL1User1 and OUL1User2:

```
Get-ADObject -SearchBase "CN=Deleted Objects,DC=70411Lab,DC=com" -Filter {lastKnownParent -eq "OU=RecycleBinTestL1,DC=70411Lab,DC=com"} -IncludeDeletedObjects | Restore-ADObject
```

   d)   Confirm that the child objects of **RecycleBinTestL1** OU were restored successfully.

e) Final step will be to restore all direct children to the **RecycleBinTestL2** OU:

Get-ADObject -SearchBase "CN=Deleted Objects,DC=70411Lab,DC=com" -Filter {lastKnownParent -eq OU=RecycleBinTestL2,OU=RecycleBinTestL1,DC=70411Lab,DC=com"} - IncludeDeletedObjects | Restore-ADObject

f) Confirm that the entire OU hierarchy is now fully restored.

Exam Tip

It is important to understand how a deleted nested object MUST be restored: From top to bottom. In the actual exam, it might appear in the form of drag and drop. You might be given an OU structure like in our example with the objects on the pane. You may be required to drag and drop the components in the order you would restore them.

5.3.5 Configure Active Directory snapshots

Active Directory snapshot was introduced in Windows Server 2008. It is designed to allow administrators to take snapshots of the Active Directory database. A snapshot is an offline, read-only copy of the AD database. Creating a snapshot before making any major Active Directory modification offers a copy of the database to fall back should the need arise. When an AD snapshot is taken before a change, the administrator can compare settings within the live database against the settings contained in the copy. Data may also be exported from the snapshot into the live Active Directory database.

When an AD snapshot is mounted and connected to, the contents of the snapshot at point of creation may be accessed. For example, it will be possible to view what objects existed and other types of information. However, it is not possible to move or copy objects or information from the snapshot to the live database directly. To perform such tasks, you will need to manually export the relevant objects or attributes from the snapshot, and manually import them into the live AD database. This provides an alternative way to recover objects as against taking down the DC, rebooting into DSRM, and restoring the System State from a backup.

To create Active Directory snapshot

1. Log on to 70411SRV and open an elevated command prompt.
2. Create a snapshot:
   a) At the command prompt, execute **Ntdsutil**.
   b) At the Ntdsutil prompt, execute activate instance ntds.
   c) At the **Ntdsutil** prompt, type **snapshot**.
   d) To create a snapshot, at the **snapshot** prompt, type **create**.

e)   To list all snapshots, at the **snapshot** prompt, type **list all**.

The last command lists available snapshots. Typically, you will see two Active Directory snapshots listed. The first snapshot bears the current date and time. This is the snapshot you have just created. The **create** command generated a snapshot with information similar to "Snapshot set {1d2fd434-68cc-43b3-9bbd-dcbf97fb2aff} generated successfully." If you compare this information to the one generated by the **list all** command, you will notice a similarity.

Exam Tip

Note the order of ntdsutil snapshot commands: activate instance ntds, snapshot, create

3.   Mounting an Active Directory snapshot:
   a)   To mount the first snapshot, enter the command **mount 1** at the snapshot prompt.
   b)   The command will execute and display where the snapshot was mounted.
   c)   Mine was mounted at: C:\$SNAP_201403151542_VOLUMEC$\
   d)   If you open the above directory, you notice it contains all the information on drive C:\ of the current domain controller.
   e)   On the **snapshot** prompt, type **q**. At the **Ntdsutil** prompt, type **q**.
4.   Connecting to an Active Directory mounted snapshot:
   a)   To expose the snapshot, execute the command:

```
dsamain -dbpath
"C:\$SNAP_201403151542_VOLUMEC$\Windows\NTDS\ntds.dit"
ldapport 1002
```

The above command will allow you to access the database using port 1002. Do not close the command prompt.

   b)   To connect to the exposed AD database using Active Directory users and Computers:
      i)   Open Active Directory users and Computers.
      ii)   On the console tree, right-click Active Directory Users and Computers [70411SRV.70411Lab.com], and then click Change Domain Controller.
      iii) Click "<Type a Directory Server name[:port] here>", field and enter 70411SRV:1002, then click **Ok**.
5.   Disconnecting from the Active Directory snapshot: To disconnect the exposed snapshot, at the command prompt from step 4(a), Press Ctrl+C and the snapshot will be disconnected.
6.   Unmounting the snapshot:
   a)   Open elevated command prompt

b) At the command prompt, execute **Ntdsutil**.

c) At the **Ntdsutil** prompt, type **snapshot**.

d) To list mounted snapshots, at the snapshot prompt, enter **List mounted**.

e) Notice that the snapshot was mounted on point 2.

f) To umount the snapshot, at the **snapshot** prompt, enter **Unmount 2**.

g) To delete the snapshot, at the **snapshot** prompt, type **Delete 2**.

h) On the **snapshot** prompt, type **q**. On the **Ntdsutil** prompt, type **q**.

Note

After you successfully mount an AD snapshot, you will need to expose the snapshot with the DSAMAIN command. After using DSAMAIN to expose the AD snapshot, you can use any GUI tool that can connect to the specified port, tools such as Active Directory Users and Computers (DSA.msc), ADSIEDIT.msc, LDP.exe or others. You can also connect to it by using command line tools such as LDIFDE or CSVDE, tools that allow you to export information from that database.

5.3.6 Clean up metadata

Metadata cleanup is necessary if you force-remove Active Directory Domain Services (AD DS) from a domain controller. It removes data from AD DS that identifies a domain controller to the replication system, including File Replication Service (FRS) and Distributed File System (DFS) Replication connections. It also removes attempts to transfer or seize any operations master roles that the retired domain controller holds.

Metadata cleanup can be performed using Active Directory Users and Computers and/or Active Directory Sites and Services. You may also complete metadata cleanup task using Ntdsutil. Deleting a domain controller computer account from the Domain Controllers organizational unit (OU), performs metadata cleanup of the server automatically. Previously, you had to perform a separate metadata cleanup procedure. You can also use the Active Directory Sites and Services console (Dssite.msc) to delete a domain controller's computer account, which also completes metadata cleanup automatically. However, Active Directory Sites and Services remove the metadata automatically only when you first delete the NTDS Settings object below the computer account in Dssite.msc.

Note

For the above GUI tools to perform automatic metadata cleanup, you have to use the versions that come with at least Windows Server 2008 or Windows Server 2008 R2. As long as you are using the Windows Server 2008, Windows Server 2008 R2, or RSAT versions of Dsa.msc or Dssite.msc, you can clean up metadata automatically for domain controllers running earlier versions of Windows operating systems.

In the task below, we will perform metadata cleanup for two domain controllers: 70411SRV4 and 70411SRV6.

To perform metadata cleanup

1. Identify replication partners for 70411SRV6:
   a) Open Active Directory Sites and Services on any domain controller.
   b) Expand Default-First-Site-Name\Servers\70411SRV6.
   c) Right-click **NTDS Settings** beneath 70411SRV6 and select **Properties**, then click the **Connections** tab.
   d) Note the servers listed in the **Replicated From** and **Replicated To** sections.
2. To perform Metadata cleanup using GUI tools:
   a) Log on to 70411SRV and open Active Directory Users and Computers.
   b) On the left pane, highlight **Domain Controllers** container and on the details pane, right-click **70411SRV6** and click **Delete**.
   c) Click **Yes** to confirm delete.
   d) On the **Deleting Domain Controller** warning, click "Delete this Domain Controller anyway. It is permanently offline and can no longer be removed using the removal wizard and click Delete".
   e) Another warning appears informing you that "This Active Directory Domain Controller is a global catalog, do you want to continue this deletion", click **Yes**.
   f) Because this server also holds a FSMO role, another warning appears informing you that "The selected server currently holds one or more FSMO roles. In order to proceed with the deletion, the roles must be removed to a new server". Click **Ok** to move the PDC Emulator FSMO role to 70411SRV.
3. To confirm metadata cleanup:
   a) Open Active Directory Sites and Services.
   b) Expand **Default-First-Site-Name** and refresh the **Servers** node.
   c) Highlight 70411SRV6 and confirm that NTDS Settings no longer exists.
   d) Right-click 70411SRV6 and delete it.

Note

When you perform metadata cleanup using Active Directory Users and Computers, NTDS Settings was removed, completing metadata cleanup. To enforce metadata cleanup using Active Directory Sites and Services, it is essential to delete the NTDS Settings beneath the server first, before deleting the server itself. If you use AD Users and computers first, you will have to delete the computer account from AD Sites and services. If you use AD Sites and services, you will have to complete the task in step 2 above.

4. To perform Metadata cleanup for 70411SRV4 using Ntdsutil:
    a) Open a command prompt as an administrator.
    b) At the command prompt, type **ntdsutil** then press enter.
    c) At the ntdsutil: prompt, type **metadata cleanup**, and press enter.
    d) At the metadata cleanup prompt, type **connections**, and then press enter.
    e) At the server connections prompt, type **connect to server 70411SRV** and press enter.
    f) At the server connections prompt, type **q** and press enter.
    g) At the metadata cleanup prompt, type **select operation target** and press enter.
    h) At the Selected Operations Target prompt, type **list domains** and press Enter. (Lists all the domains in the forest with a number associated to each.)
    i) At the Select Operations Target prompt, type **select domain 0** and press enter. "0" should point to DC=70411Lab,DC=com.
    j) At the Select Operations Target prompt, type **list sites** and press Enter. (Lists all the sites in the forest with a number assigned to each.)
    k) At the Select Operations Target prompt, type **select site 0**, where number "0" is the site containing the failed domain controller, then press Enter.
    l) At the Select Operations Target prompt, type **list servers in site** and press Enter.
    m) At the Select Operations Target prompt, type **select server 2**, and press Enter. Where "2" is the number for 70411SRV4 from the output of the previous command.
    n) At the Select Operations Target prompt, type **quit** and presses enter.
    o) At the Metadata Cleanup prompt, type **remove selected server** and press enter.
    p) On the Server Remove Confirmation Dialogue select **Yes**.
    q) At the metadata cleanup prompt, type **q** and press enter.
    r) At the ntdsutil prompt, type q and press enter.
5. Confirm metadata cleanup for 70411SRV4:

a) Open Active Directory Sites and Services.
b) Expand Default-First-Site-Name\ and refresh the **Servers** node.
c) Highlight 70411SRV4 and confirm that NTDS Settings no longer exists.
d) Right-click 70411SRV4 and delete it.
e) Shutdown 70411SRV4 and 70411SRV6.

The Server Remove Confirmation Dialogue in step 4, warning message contains the following information: The server in question should already be off-line permanently and never return to service. If it comes back on-line, the server object will be revived. In addition to cleaning up the Active Directory object using Ntdsutil, or the GUI tools, it is essential to clean up the DNS records for the failed domain controller. Remove all DNS records from DNS, including all domain controller records, GC server records, and PDC emulator records. (The last two will exit only if the domain controller was configured with these roles.) If you do not clean up the DNS records, clients will continue to receive the DNS information and try to connect to the domain controller. This can result in slower connections to Active Directory as clients fail over to use alternate domain controllers.

6. Clean up DNS Entries:
    a) Log on to 70411SRV and open DNS Manager.
    b) Expand **Forward Lookup Zones** then right-click 70411Lab.com and click **Properties**.
    c) On the 70411Lab.com Properties, click **Name Servers** tab.
    d) Remove 70411SRV4 and 70411SRV6 from the list and click **Ok**.
    e) Expand 70411Lab.com zone, then _sites, Default-First_Site-Name, and finally highlight _tcp.
    f) With **_tcp** highlighted, on the details pane, ensure that there is no entry for any of the servers.

5.4 Configure Account Policies

Introduction

Account policies can be configured at domain or local computer level. Group Policy settings for Password, Account Lockout and Kerberos Policies are referred collectively as **Account Policies settings**. Account Policies settings are included in the built-in Default Domain Controllers Policy Group Policy object (GPO). In this section, we will consider Account Policies settings, delegation and Password Settings Objects (PSOs).

Each domain can have one Account Policies setting. The Default Domain Policy is the policy that is enforced by the domain controllers in the domain by default. The Account Policies setting must either be defined in the Default Domain Policy or in a new policy that is linked to the root of the domain and given precedence over the Default Domain Policy. These domain-wide Account Policies settings (Password Policy, Account Lockout Policy, and Kerberos Policy) are enforced by the domain controllers in the domain. Therefore, domain controllers always retrieve the values of these Account Policies settings from the Default Domain Policy GPO.

The only exception to this rule is when another Account Policies setting is defined for an organizational unit (OU). The Account Policies settings for the OU affect the local policy on any computers that are contained in the OU. For example, if an OU policy defines a maximum password age that differs from the domain-level Account Policies settings, the OU policy is applied and enforced only when users log on to the local computer. The default local computer policies apply only to computers that are in a workgroup or in a domain where neither an OU Account Policies setting nor a domain policy applies.

In this section, we will cover following exam objectives:

5.4.0 Configure domain user password policy

5.4.1 Configure local user password policy

5.4.2 Configure account lockout settings

5.4.3 Configure Kerberos policy settings (Server 2012 R2 Objective)

5.4.4 Configure and apply Password Settings Objects (PSOs)

5.4.5 Delegate password settings management

Lab Plan:

We will use 70411SRV (Domain Controller) and 70411SRV1 for most tasks in this section.

Additional lab setup

Create the following security groups under the Users node, using Active Directory users and Computers:

PSOLocalGroup (Domain local group), **PSOGlobalGroup** (Global group), **PSOUnivGroup** (Universal group).

Also create two global security groups called **PSODelegateGroup1** and **PSODelegateGroup2**. Create four user accounts called **PSODelegateUser1**, **PSODelegateUser2**, **PSOTestUser** and **PSOTestUser1**.

Add PSODelegateUser1 as a member of the PSODelegateGroup1 group, PSODelegateGroup2 as member of PSODelegateGroup2. From the member of tab of PSODelegateUser1 user, set PSODelegateGroup1 as primary group, remove Domain Users group. Repeat task for PSODelegateUser2.

From the **member of** tab of PSODelegateGroup1, add **Remote Desktop Users** group. Repeat for **PSODelegateGroup2.**

5.4.0 Configure domain user password policy

In Windows and many other operating systems, the most common method to authenticate a user's identity is to use a secret passphrase or password. A secure network environment requires all users to use strong passwords (ones that have at least 10 characters and include a combination of letters, numbers, and symbols). These passwords help prevent the compromise of user accounts and administrative accounts by unauthorized people who use either manual methods or automated tools to guess weak passwords. Strong passwords that are changed regularly reduce the likelihood of a successful password attack.

Fine-grained password policies, introduced from Windows Server 2008 provide organizations with a way to define different password and account lockout policies for different sets of users in a domain. Prior to Windows Server 2008, only one password policy and account lockout policy could be applied to all users in the domain.

Fine-grained password policies apply only to user objects (or inetOrgPerson objects if they are used instead of user objects) and global security groups. Fine-grained password policies include attributes for all the settings that can be defined in the Default Domain Policy (except Kerberos settings) as well as account lockout settings. When you specify a fine-grained password policy you must specify all of these settings. By default, only members of the Domain Admins group can set fine-grained password policies. However, you can also delegate the ability to set these policies to other users. To use this feature, the domain functional level must be Windows Server. Fine-grained password policies cannot be applied to an organizational unit (OU) directly.

Note

Fine-grained password policies apply only to user objects and global security groups. PSOs cannot be applied to an organizational unit (OU) directly.

Password Policies can be configured via group policy. The settings are located in: Computer Configuration\Policies\Windows Settings\Security Settings\Account Policies\Password Policy. The following 6 Policies are available on the Password Policy node:

1. **Enforce password history:** Determines the number of unique new passwords that have to be associated with a user account before an old password can be reused. The value must be between 0 and 24 passwords. This policy enables administrators to enhance security by ensuring that old passwords are not reused continually.

Default: 24 on domain controllers, 0 on stand-alone servers.

2. **Maximum password age**: Determines the period of time (in days) that a password can be used before the system requires the user to change it. You can set passwords to expire after a number of days between 1 and 999, or you can specify that passwords never expire by setting the number of days to 0. If the maximum password age is between 1 and 999 days, the Minimum password age must be less than the maximum password age. If the maximum password age is set to 0, the minimum password age can be any value between 0 and 998 days.

Default: 42.

Note

It is security best practices to have passwords expire every 30 to 90 days, depending on your environment. This way, an attacker has a limited amount of time in which to crack a user's password and have access to your network resources.

3. **Minimum password age**: Determines the period of time (in days) that a password must be used before the user can change it. You can set a value between 1 and 998 days, or you can allow changes immediately by setting the number of days to 0. The minimum password age must be less than the Maximum password age, unless the maximum password age is set to 0, indicating that passwords will never expire. Configure the minimum password age to be more than 0 if you want **Enforce password history** policy to be effective. Without a **minimum password age**, users can cycle through passwords repeatedly until they get to an old favourite. The default setting does not follow this recommendation, so that an administrator can specify a password for a user and then require the user to change the administrator-defined password when the user logs on. If the password history is set to 0, the user does not have to choose a new password. For this reason, Enforce password history is set to 1 by default.

4. **Minimum password length**: Determines the least number of characters that a password for a user account may contain. You can set a value of between 1 and 14 characters, or you can establish that no password is required by setting the number of characters to 0.

Default: 7 on domain controllers, 0 on stand-alone servers.

5. **Password must meet complexity requirements**: Determines whether passwords must meet complexity requirements. If this policy is enabled, passwords must meet the following minimum requirements:
    a) Not contain the user's account name or parts of the user's full name that exceed two consecutive characters.
    b) Be at least six characters in length.
    c) Contain characters from three of the following four categories:

i)   English uppercase characters (A through Z).
ii) English lowercase characters (a through z).
iii) Base 10 digits (0 through 9).
iv) Non-alphabetic characters (for example, !, $, #, %).

d) Complexity requirements are enforced when passwords are changed or created.

Default: Enabled on domain controllers, Disabled on stand-alone servers.

6. **Store passwords using reversible encryption**: Determines whether the operating system stores passwords using reversible encryption. This policy provides support for applications that use protocols that require knowledge of the user's password for authentication purposes. Storing passwords using reversible encryption is essentially the same as storing plaintext versions of the passwords. For this reason, this policy should never be enabled unless application requirements outweigh the need to protect password information. This policy is required when using Challenge-Handshake Authentication Protocol (CHAP) authentication through remote access or Internet Authentication Services (IAS). It is also required when using Digest Authentication in Internet Information Services (IIS).

Default: Disabled.

5.4.1 Configure local user password policy

Local password policy can be configured on a stand-alone member server or a server that is a member of a workgroup. To locate and configure the local password policy, open **Administrative Tools** and then **Local Security Policy.** Navigate to **Account Policy\Password Policy.** Note that unlike the **Password Policies** for a domain, which is **"Not Defined",** by default, the local **password policies** default settings are configured already.

5.4.2 Configure account lockout settings

More than a few unsuccessful password submissions during an attempt to log on to a computer might represent an attacker's attempts to determine an account password by trial and error. The Windows operating system can track logon attempts, and you can configure the operating system to disable the account for a preset period of time after a specified number of failed attempts. Account lockout policy settings control the threshold for this response and what action to take after the threshold is reached. The settings can be configured in the following location within the Group Policy Management Console: Computer Configuration\Windows Settings\Account Policies\Account Lockout Policy. Available policies are discussed below:

1. **Account lockout duration:** This security setting determines the number of minutes a locked-out account remains locked out before automatically becoming unlocked. It ranges from 0 minutes through 99,999 minutes. If the account lockout duration is set to 0, the account will be locked out until an administrator explicitly unlocks it. If an account lockout threshold is defined, the account lockout duration must be greater than or equal to the reset time.

Default: None, because this policy setting only has meaning when an Account lockout threshold is specified.

2. **Account lockout threshold:** Security setting determines the number of failed logon attempts that causes a user account to be locked out. A locked-out account cannot be used until it is reset by an administrator or until the lockout duration for the account has expired. You can set a value between 0 and 999 failed logon attempts. If you set the value to 0, the account will never be locked out. Failed password attempts against workstations or member servers that have been locked using either CTRL+ALT+DELETE or password-protected screen savers count as failed logon attempts.

Default: 0

3. **Reset account lockout counter after:** Security setting determines the number of minutes that must elapse after a failed logon attempt before the failed logon attempt counter is reset to 0 bad logon attempts. The available range is 1 minute to 99,999 minutes. If an account lockout threshold is defined, this reset time must be less than or equal to the Account lockout duration.

Default: None, because this policy setting only has meaning when an Account lockout threshold is specified.

5.4.3 Configure Kerberos policy settings (2012 R2 Objective)

In Windows Server 2003 with Service Pack 1 (SP1) and later, the Kerberos authentication protocol provides the default mechanism for domain authentication services. Kerberos also provides the authorization data that is necessary for a user to access a resource and perform a task on that resource. If the lifetime of Kerberos tickets is reduced, the risk of a legitimate user's credentials being stolen and successfully used by an attacker decreases. However, authorization overhead increases. The following 5 Policies are available under Kerberos Policy node:

1. **Enforce user logon restrictions:** This security setting determines whether the Kerberos V5 Key Distribution Center (KDC) validates every

request for a session ticket against the user rights policy of the user account. Validation of each request for a session ticket is optional, because the extra step takes time and it may slow network access to services.

Default: Enabled.

2. **Maximum lifetime for service ticket:** This security setting determines the maximum amount of time (in minutes) that a granted session ticket can be used to access a particular service. The setting must be greater than 10 minutes and less than or equal to the setting for Maximum lifetime for user ticket.

3. If a client presents an expired session ticket when it requests a connection to a server, the server returns an error message. The client must request a new session ticket from the Kerberos V5 Key Distribution Center (KDC). Once a connection is authenticated, however, it no longer matters whether the session ticket remains valid. Session tickets are used only to authenticate new connections with servers. Ongoing operations are not interrupted if the session ticket used to authenticate the connection expires during the connection.

Default: 600 minutes (10 hours).

4. **Maximum lifetime for user ticket:** This security setting determines the maximum amount of time (in hours) that a user's ticket-granting ticket (TGT) may be used.

Default: 10 hours.

5. **Maximum lifetime for user ticket renewal:** This security setting determines the period of time (in days) during which a user's ticket-granting ticket (TGT) may be renewed.

Default: 7 days.

6. **Maximum tolerance for computer clock synchronization:** This security setting determines the maximum time difference (in minutes) that Kerberos V5 tolerates between the time on the client clock and the time on the domain controller running Windows Server 2012 R2 that provides Kerberos authentication.

7. To prevent "replay attacks," Kerberos V5 uses time stamps as part of its protocol definition. For time stamps to work properly, the clocks of the client and the domain controller need to be in sync as much as possible. In other words, both computers must be set to the same time and date. Because the clocks of two computers are often out of sync, administrators can use this policy to establish the maximum acceptable difference to Kerberos V5 between a client clock and domain controller clock. If the difference between a client clock and the domain controller clock is less

than the maximum time difference that is specified in this policy, any time stamp that is used in a session between the two computers is considered to be authentic.

Default: 5 minutes.

Note

This setting is not persistent on pre-Vista platforms. If you configure this setting and then restart the computer, this setting reverts to the default value.

Exam Tip

It is very important to understand the policies outline above and how they apply including the default values and configurations.

5.4.4 Configure and apply Password Settings Objects (PSOs)

Password Setting Object (PSO) is another name for Fine Grain Password Policies. PSOs allow the use of different password policies based on security group membership. As mentioned earlier, in Active Directory domains before Windows Server 2008 one password and account lockout policy could be specified for all users in the domain. From Windows Server 2008, fine-grained password policies specify multiple password policies and apply different password restrictions and account lockout policies to different sets of users within a single domain.

To store fine-grained password policies, Windows Server 2008 onwards includes two new object classes in the Active Directory Domain Services (AD DS) schema:
Password Settings Container and Password Settings.
The Password Settings Container (PSC) object class is created by default under the System container in the domain. It stores the Password Settings objects (PSOs) for that domain. This container cannot be renamed, moved, or deleted. Password Settings objects (PSOs) can be applied to users or global security groups with the following tools: Active Directory module for Windows PowerShell, Active Directory and Computers, ldifde and Active Directory Administrative Center (ADAC).

To create and apply a Password Settings Object using ADAC

1. Log on to 70411SRV and open Active Directory Administrative Center.
2. Change ADAC view to **Tree View.**
3. Expand **70411Lab (local),** then expand **Systems** container.
4. To create a Password Settings Object:

5. Right-click Password Settings Container, point to New and select Password Settings.
6. On the **Create Password Settings** window, note the following:
   a) **Precedence**: Password settings with a lower precedence number will override ones with higher number.
   b) **Enforce minimum password length**: Similar to minimum password length discussed earlier. It is enabled by default with a value of 7.
   c) **Enforce password history**: Enabled by default with a value of 24.
   d) Password must meet complexity requirements: Also enabled by default.
   e) **Protect from accidental deletion**: When checked, an AD object will be protected from accidental deletion.
   f) Store password using reversible encryption: Disabled by default.
   g) **Enforce minimum password age**: Enabled by default with a value of 1.
   h) **Enforce maximum password age:** Enabled by default with a value of 42.
   i) **Enforce account lockout policy**: Disabled by default. Enabling this option enables additional items for configuration:
      i) **Number of failed log on attempts allowed**: Similar to Account lockout threshold discussed earlier.
      ii) **Reset failed logon attempts counter after (Mins)**: Similar to the same policy discussed in section 5.4.1. This provides two additional options: Account will be locked out:
         (1) For a duration of (mins) or.
         (2) Until an administrator manually unlocks the account.
7. On the **Name** field, enter **PSOTest1** and on the **Precedence** field, enter 5.
8. To apply the PSO to a group or user:
   a) Below **Directly Applies To,** click **Add.** Note that in the search box that opens, only **Users or Group** are available object types.
   b) To confirm that PSO can only be assigned to global groups, enter each of the groups created at the beginning of this section: PSOLocalGroup (Domain local group), PSOGlobalGroup (Global group), PSOUnivGroup (Universal group).
   c) Confirm that you are only able to find the global group PSOGlobalGroup.
   d) When you find the global group, click **Ok.**
   e) Click **Add,** and on the search box enter PSOTestUser and click **Ok.**
9. On the Create Password Settings: PSOTest1, click **Ok.**

Note

Note the options not enabled by default when you create a new PSO: Enforce account lockout policy and Store password using reversible encryption. Also note that PSOs can only be assigned to Global groups or user accounts.

Exam Tip

Very important to note that PSOs can only be assigned to Global groups or user accounts. You cannot assign PSOs to OUs, computers, Universal or Domain Local Groups.

To create a Password Settings Object using Windows PowerShell

Stilled logged on to70411SRV, open Active Directory Module for Windows Powershell and type the following commands:

```
New-ADFineGrainedPasswordPolicy -Name "PSOTest2" -Precedence 10 -
ComplexityEnabled $TRUE -LockOutDuration "0:00:30:00" -
LockOutObservationWindow "0:00:30:00" -LockOutThreshold 0 -
MaxPasswordAge "20:00:00:00" -MinPasswordAge "5:00:00:00" -
PasswordHistoryCount 24 -ReversibleEncryptionEnabled $FALSE
```

To Review the properties of PSOTest2

1. Close and reopen Active Directory Administrative Center.
2. Select **Tree View** and Navigate to **70411Lab (local)\Systems** container.
3. Highlight **Password Settings Container,** on the details pane, right-click **PSOTest2** and click **properties.**
4. Review the different properties of the PSO and confirm that it is not applied to any group or user.

Understanding PSO Precedence and Resultant PSO

A PSO can be linked to more than one group or user and an individual group or user can have more than one PSO linked to it. As we know, a user can belong to multiple groups. So when more than one PSO is applied to a user or group, which PSO and lockout policy will apply? One and only one PSO determines the password and lockout settings for a user - this PSO is called the resultant PSO.

Each PSO has an attribute that determines the PSOs precedence. The precedence value is any number greater than 0, where the number 1 indicates the highest precedence. If multiple PSOs apply to a user, the PSO with the highest precedence takes effect. The rules that determine precedence are as follows:

1. If multiple PSOs apply to groups to which the user belongs, the PSO with the highest precedence wins.
2. If one or more PSOs are linked directly to the user, PSOs linked to groups are ignored, regardless of their precedence. The user-linked PSO with highest precedence wins.
3. If one or more PSOs have the same precedence value, Active Directory must make a choice. It picks the PSO with the lowest globally unique identifier (GUID). GUIDs are like serial numbers for Active Directory objects. No two objects have the same GUID. GUIDs have no particular meaning; they are just identifiers. So picking the PSO with the lowest GUID is, in effect, an arbitrary decision. You should configure PSOs with unique, specific precedence values so that you avoid this situation.

Compare user account settings with PSO settings

This section is included strictly for the exam purposes. There might be question about what can be configured via the Accounts tab of a user account property and what can be configured using Password Settings Object. We will examine the options available on the Account tab of a user.

To proceed, open Active Directory Users and Computers and open the properties of PSOTestUser, created earlier. Click **Account** tab. The following can be configured:

1. **User must change password at next log on**: This forces the user to change password at next log on.
2. **User cannot change password**: User will never be able to change password from a client computer. When this box is checked, only an administrator can change the account's password using and Active Directory Administration tool like Active Directory Users and computers.
3. **Password never expires**: Simply does what it says.
4. Store password using reversible encryption: We already explained this earlier.
5. **Account is disabled:** Disables the user account. Not available on a PSO.
6. Smart card is required for interactive log on: This option is not available on a PSO.
7. Account is sensitive and cannot be delegated: Not available on a PSO.
8. **Do not require Kerberos preauthentication**: Only available via the user's properties, not available on a PSO.
9. I omitted some options that are obvious. Now let's examine the properties of **PSOTest1** PSO:
10. **Enforce minimum password length**: This option can only be configured using a PSO.
11. **Enforce password history**: This option can only be configured using a PSO.

12. **Password must meet complexity requirements**: This option can only be configured using a PSO.
13. **Store password using reversible encryption**: Can be configured on the users account and on a PSO.
14. **Enforce minimum password age**: This option can only be configured using a PSO.
15. **Enforce maximum password age:** If set to zero, password will not expire. This is similar to the **Password never expires** option on a user account
16. **Enforce account lockout policy:** This option can only be configured using a PSO.

Exam Tip

It is very important to note what you can configure under a user's accounts properties and what you can configure using PSO. For the purposes of the exam, you might be required to drag and drop these properties to the right column.

To apply PSOs to users or global security groups

1. Log on to 70411SRV and Open Active Directory Users and Computers.
2. On the **View** menu, ensure that **Advanced Features** is checked.
3. On the console tree, expand 70411Lab.com domain, then expand **Systems** Container and click **Password Settings Container**.
4. On the details pane, right-click **PSOTest1**, and then click **Properties**.
5. Click the Attribute Editor tab.
6. Select the **msDS-PsoAppliesTo** attribute, and then click **Edit**.
7. On the Multi-valued Distinguished Name Security Principal Editor note the following:
   a) The user and group we added when we created this PSO appear on the list.
   b) You can add a Windows account or a DN.

Note

To disable account lockout policies, assign the msDS-LockoutThreshold attribute the value of 0.

5.4.5 Delegate password settings management

By default, only members of the Domain Admins group can create PSOs. Members of this group have the **Create Child** and **Delete Child** permissions on the **Password Settings Container** object. In addition, by default only members of the Domain Admins group have Write Property permissions on the PSO. Therefore, only members of the Domain Admins group can apply a PSO to a group or user object.

The **Password Settings Container** contains all Password Settings Objects. If you grant a user or group access to the **Password Settings Container,** the user will have access to all PSOs except if you exclusively remove that access. To delegate access to a specific PSO, modify the security descriptor of the PSO accordingly.

Note

You do not have to have permissions on the user object or group object to be able to apply a PSO.

To delegate access to a PSO

1. Log on to 70411SRV and open Active Directory Administrative Center.
2. Ensure that Tree View is selected, and navigate to Systems\Password Settings Container.
3. To delegate **Create all child objects** and **Write** access to the PSODelegateGroup1 group:
   a) Highlight **Password Settings Container**, on the Task pane, below Password Settings Container and click **Properties**.
   b) On the Password Settings Container Properties, click **Extensions** tab and click **Add**.
   c) On the search box, type **PSODelegateGroup1** and click **Ok.**
   d) On the Permissions for **PSODelegateGroup1**, beneath **Allow** column, check the box beside **Create all child objects** and **Write**.
   e) Click **Ok** to save your changes.
4. To delegate apply a PSO to the PSODelegateGroup2 group:
   a) Right-click Password Settings Container and click Properties.
   b) On the Password Settings Container Properties, click **Extensions** tab and click **Add**.
   c) On the search box, type **PSODelegateGroup2** and click **Ok.**
   d) On the Password Settings Container Properties, **Extensions** tab, confirm that **PSODelegateGroup2** has **Read** access, click **Ok.**
   e) Right-click **PSOTest1** and select **Properties**.
   f) On the **PSOTest1** Properties, click **Extensions** tab and click **Add**.
   g) On the search box, type **PSODelegateGroup2** and click **Ok.**
   h) On the Permissions for **PSODelegateGroup2**, beneath Allow column, check **Write**.
   i) Click **Ok** to save your changes.

Note

To proceed with the next task, it is very important to log on to 70411SRV1 member server as PSODelegateUser1.

To Test PSO delegation

1. To confirm that PSODelegateUser1 can create PSOs:
   a) Log on to the domain from 70411SRV1 member server as **PSODelegateUser1** and open **ADSI Edit**.
   b) Right-click ADSI Edit and click **Connect to....**
   c) On the Connection Settings dialogue, ensure that **Select a well known Naming Context** is selected and click **Ok**.
   d) Double-click Default naming context [70411SRV.70411Lab.com]. When it loads, expand it.
   e) Click **DC=70411Lab, DC=com** and expand it.
   f) Click **CN=Systems** and expand it.
   g) Click **CN=Password Settings Container.** When it loads, right-click it, point to **New** and select **Object.**
   h) On the Create Object wizard, select **msDS-PasswordSettings** and click **Next.**
   i) On the **Attribute: cn value** field, type **PSOTest3** and click **Next.**
   j) On the Attribute: msDS-PasswordSettingsPrecedence value enter 15 and **click Next.**
   k) On the Attribute: msDS-PasswordReversibleEncryptionEnables value, enter FALSE and click **Next.**
   l) On the Attribute: msDS-PasswordHistoryLenght value, enter 24 and click **Next.**
   m) On the Attribute: msDS-PasswordComplexityEnable value, enter TRUE and click **Next.**
   n) On the Attribute: msDS-MinimumPasswordLength value, enter 7 and click **Next.**
   o) On the Attribute: msDS-MinimumPasswordAge value, enter 1:00:00:00 and click **Next.**
   p) On the Attribute: msDS-MaximumPasswordAge value, enter 42:00:00:00 and click **Next.**
   q) On the Attribute: msDS-LockoutThresholdvalue enter, 10 and click **Next.**
   r) On the Attribute: msDS-LockoutObservationWindow, enter 0:00:30:00 and click **Next.**
   s) On the Attribute: msDS-LockoutDuration, enter 0:00:30:00 and click **Next.**
   t) Click **Finish** to create the POS.
2. To confirm that PSODelegateUser1 cannot delete child objects in the **Password Settings Container:** Right-click **PSOTest1** and select **delete.** You will receive an error message.
3. To confirm that PSODelegateGroup2 can assign a PSO but cannot create:

a) Log on to the domain from 70411SRV1 member server as **PSODelegateUser2** and open **ADSI Edit.**
b) Navigate to **CN=Systems** Container.
c) Attempt to create a new PSO called PSOTest4, with msDS-PasswordSettingsPrecedence value of 20. You will receive "**Access is denied**" message.
d) Click Cancel.
e) Right-click CN=PSOTest1 PSO and click **Properties.**
f) On the **Attribute Editor** tab, locate and highlight **msDS-PSOAppliesTo** attribute, then click **Edit.**
g) On the Multi-valued Distinguised Name With Security Principal Edit dialogue, click Add Windows Account.
h) On the search box, enter **PSOTestUser1** and click **Ok.**
i) On the Multi-valued Distinguised Name With Security Principal Edit dialogue, click Ok.
j) On the CN=PSOTest1 Properties, click **Ok.**

4. To confirm that PSODelegateGroup2 cannot apply any of the other PSOs to a user or group:
a) Right-click CN=PSOTest2 PSO and click **Properties.**
b) Notice that the **Attribute Editor** tab is blank because this user does not have access to this object.

Note

If a user does not have a **Read** permission to the **Password Settings Container**, it will not be available to the user. So, even though you grant the user **Write** access to a PSO within the container, the user will not be able to apply the PSO to a user or group. The way to delegate **Apply** access to a PSO to a user is to grant **Read** access to the **Password Settings Container** and **Write** access to the specific PSO.

Chapter 6

Configure and Manage Group Policy

6.1 Configure Group Policy Processing

Introduction

Client's settings in an Active Directory infrastructure may be configured via Group Policies. There are three components of Group Policy Objects:

1. **Group Policy Container (GPC)**: Exists within Active Directory.
2. **Group Policy Template (GPT)**: Where the actual content of the GPOs resides.
3. **Client-Side Extensions (CSEs)**: A third component, known as Client-Side Extensions (CSEs) is be found on client devices and are necessary for the clients to properly process the Group Policies assigned to them.

Group Policy Container (GPC) holds a list of all GPOs in Active Directory. To view GPC, open **Active Director Users and Computers** and enable **Advanced Features.** Expand the domain for example, 70411Lab.com then navigate to **Systems\Policies** container. The **Policies** container for my domain, as at the time of writing is as shown below:

Figure 6.1.0 - Group Policy Container (Can also be viewed using ADSI Edit)
Right-click any of the GPOs shown above, select Properties and view the **Attribute Editor** tab. There are some key attributes that we need to note. Some important attributes are listed below:

displayName: This attribute is the human-friendly name of the GPO.
gPCFileSysPath: This attribute points clients to the location of the GPO content. Collectively, this is known as the Group Policy Template, which is housed in the SYSVOL share.

gPCMachineExtensionNames: Here is the list of Client-Side Extensions (CSEs) that will be needed by the client in order to process all of the machine-side settings configured for this GPO.

gPCUserExtensionNames: This attribute contains the list of CSEs that will be needed to process the user-side settings. As there are no user-side settings configured in this GPO, the attribute is not populated (therefore, it is not displayed).

Another important attribute that will be relevant to our discussion in this section is **gPLink**. Every container (Sites, Domains and OUs) where GPOs can be assigned will have this attribute. GPC is in Active Directory merely represents the attributes relevant to the GPO content. The content of the GPO resides in a Group Policy Template (GPT). On a local domain controller, its actual location is **%windir%\SYSVOL\domain\Policies**.

The content of the GPT from my test lab, as at the time of writing is shown in Figure 6.1.1

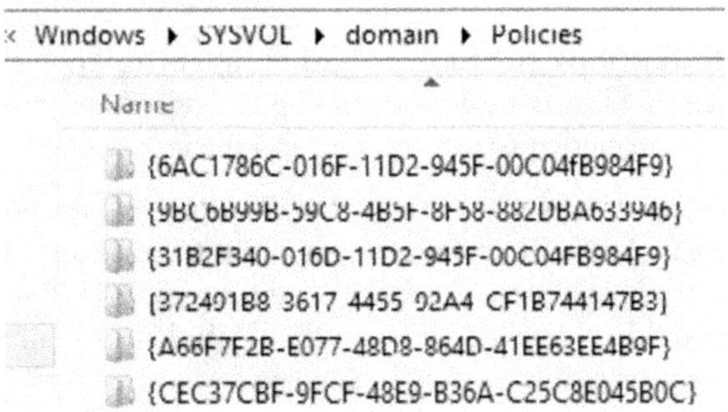

x Windows ▸ SYSVOL ▸ domain ▸ Policies

Name

{6AC1786C-016F-11D2-945F-00C04fB984F9}
{9BC6B99B-59C8-4B5F-8F58-882DBA633946}
{31B2F340-016D-11D2-945F-00C04fB984F9}
{372401B8 3617 4455 92A4 CF1B744147B3}
{A66F7F2B-E077-48D8-864D-41EE63EE4B9F}
{CEC37CBF-9FCF-48E9-B36A-C25C8E045B0C}

Figure 6.1.1 - Group Policy Template

Notice that the contents of the GPC and the GPT are exactly the same.

In this section, we will cover following exam objectives:

6.1.0 Configure processing order and precedence
6.1.1 Configure blocking of inheritance
6.1.2 Configure enforced policies
6.1.3 Configure security filtering and WMI filtering
6.1.4 Configure loopback processing
6.1.5 Configure client-side extension (CSE) behavior
6.1.6 Configure and manage slow-link processing
6.1.7 Configure and manage Group Policy caching (2012 R2 Objective)
6.1.8 Force Group Policy update (2012 R2 Objective)

Lab Plan:

We will use 70411SRV (Domain Controller) for most tasks in this section.

Additional lab setup

None

6.1.0 Configure processing order and precedence

Clients can have local Group Policy Objects (GPOs). These policies are configured locally on a client machine and are always processed. There are also GPOs linked to a client from Active Directory domain. While the client knows that it needs to process its local GPO, it is not as clear which GPOs in the directory structure apply to it.

Within the directory, GPOs can be linked to the following levels: Sites, Domains or Organizational Unit. GPO processing is initiated from the client side rather than being pushed from your Domain Controllers. In our introduction, we mentioned that every container where GPO can be linked has an attribute called **gPLink**. A client identifies which GPOs are assigned to it from within Active Directory by looking at the **gPLink** attribute of the various containers where it belongs. This attribute, when populated, points to the name and location of the GPO that the client must consider. GPOs will be processed based on the location of a client in the Active Directory infrastructure. Precedence follows the order outlined below:

1. Local
2. Site
3. Domain
4. Organizational Unit

Local GPOs are processed first, followed by GPOs linked to the site, domain and then OU, in that order. What this means is that if you configure a GPO on your PC but an administrator configures a GPO on the domain, your local GPO will be overwritten. So, to determine which GPO applies to a client, place it in the relevant container with the above processing precedence in mind. There might be circumstances where a container has more than one GPOs assigned to it. You can determine processing order by manually configuring it.

To configure processing order

1. Log on to 70411SRV and open Group Policy Management.
2. Beneath Domains, high-light 70411Lab.com.
3. If you have followed the labs in this guide, you should have three GPOs:
   a) Default Domain Policy.
   b) DirectAccess Client Settings.
   c) DirectAccess Server Settings.
4. To view and change the processing order, click the **Linked Group Policy Objects** tab. The first column will show the **Link Order.**
5. Highlight any of the GPOs and use the arrow buttons on the left to move them up or down.

6. Click the **Group Policy Inheritance** tab to view the precedence of the GPOs.

6.1.1 Configure Blocking of Inheritance

You can block inheritance for a domain or organizational unit. Blocking inheritance prevents Group Policy objects (GPOs) that are linked to higher sites, domains, or organizational units from being automatically inherited by the child-level.

To block group policy inheritance

1. Log on to 70411SRV and open Group Policy Management Console.
2. On the Group Policy Management Console tree, Expand **Forest: 70411Lab.com**, expand **Domains.**
3. To block inheritance at the domain, right-click **70411Lab.com** and click **Block Inheritance**.
4. To block inheritance for an OU, right-click the OU, WINSRV2012R2 and click **Block Inheritance**.
5. To confirm that you cannot block inheritance at site level:
   a) Right-click **Sites** and click **Show Sites**.
   b) On the **Show Sites** dialogue, check the box beside **Default-First-Site-Name** and click **Ok.**
   c) Right-click **Default-First-Site-Name** site and confirm that **Block Inheritance** option is not available.

Note

You can only block inheritance at the Domain and OU level, not site or on the individual GPO. An object that is configured to Block Inheritance will have a blue circle with white exclamation mark.

6.1.2 Configure Enforced Policies

Group policy blocking and enforcement provide the ability for an administrator to control how group policies are applied. They reduce the number of group policies an administrator will need to deploy. Block Inheritance may be used to stop any GPO up in the hierarchy from applying to a child object. But there are instances when the domain administrator wants to ensure that administrators responsible for any child OUs is not able to block a particular GPO.

Enforced policies take precedence over Block Inheritance, so all Enforced GPOs will override any GPO configured to Block Inheritance.

To configure enforced policies

1. Log on to 70411SRV and open Group Policy Management Console.
2. On the Group Policy Management Console tree, Expand **Forest: 70411Lab.com**, then expand **Domains**, and finally expand **70411Lab.com** domain. The following GPOs will be listed:
   a) Default Domain Policy.
   b) DirectAccess Client Settings.
   c) DirectAccess Server Settings.
3. To ensure that the **Default Domain Policy** GPO is applied to all objects in the domain, regardless of any **Block Inheritance** enabled, right-click **Default Domain Policy** and click **Enforced**.
4. To link a GPO to a site:
   a) Expand Sites container, right-click Default-First-Site-Name and select Link an Existing GPO.
   b) On the Select GPO dialogue, select DirectAccess Server Settings and click **Ok**.
5. To enforce GPO at Site-Level: Expand **Site\Default-First-Site-Name** and select **Enforced.**

Note

A GPO that is **Enforced** will have a gold locked key beside it. Unlike **Block Inheritance**, which is enabled on the object (Domain or OU), **Enforced** is enabled on the individual GPO.

Exam Tip

It is very important to understand how Enforced GPOs interact with GPOs configured to Block Inheritance. Also note the looks: An object that is configured to Block Inheritance will have a blue circle with white exclamation mark, while a GPO that is Enforced will have a gold locked key beside it. This question might be in form of drag and drop.

6.1.3 Configure security filtering and WMI filtering

Configure WMI filtering

Windows Management Instrumentation (WMI) filters settings dynamically determine the scope of Group Policy objects (GPOs), based on attributes of the target computer. When a GPO linked to a WMI filter is applied on a target computer, the filter is evaluated on the target computer. If the WMI filter evaluates to false, the GPO is not applied (unless the client computer is running Windows 2000, in which case the filter is ignored and the GPO is always applied). If the WMI filter evaluates to true, the GPO is applied.

To create a WMI filter

1. Log on to 70411SRV and open Group Policy Management Console.
2. On the Group Policy Management Console tree, Expand **Forest: 70411Lab.com**, then expand **Domains**, finally expand **70411Lab.com** domain.
3. Right-click **WMI Filters** and click **New. The New WMI Filter** dialogue opens
4. In the **New WMI Filter** dialog box, complete the following tasks:
   a) On the **Name** field, type **Win7and2008R2.**
   b) On the **Description** field, enter "WMI Filter for computers running Windows 7, Windows Vista, Windows Server 2008, and Windows Server 2008 R2".
   c) Under Queries, click **Add**.
   d) On the **WMI Query** dialog box, leave the default namespace (root\CIMv2) and on the **Query** field, enter the following and click **Ok**.

---
select * from Win32_OperatingSystem where Version like "6.%"
---

5. If you receive a warning, click **Ok.**
6. After adding all queries, click **Save**.

To link a WMI filter to a Group Policy object

1. In the Group Policy Management Console (GPMC) console tree, double-click **Group Policy Objects.**
2. Click Default Domain Policy GPO.
3. In the results pane, on the **Scope** tab, under **WMI Filtering**, select **Win7and2008R2** from the drop-down list.
4. When prompted to confirm the selection, click **Yes.**

Configure security filtering

In order for a GPO to apply to an object, the object must have **Read** and **Apply Group Policy** rights on the GPO. By default, all GPOs have **Read** and **Apply Group Policy** for the **Authenticated Users** group. To specify which users or computers will or will not have a Group Policy Object applied to them, you can deny them either the **Apply Group Policy** or **Read** permission on that Group Policy Object.

These permissions allow administrators to limit the scope of a GPO to a specific set of computers within a site, domain, or OU.

To Configure Filtering for a Computer

1. Log on to 70411SRV and open Group Policy Management Console.

2. On the Group Policy Management Console tree, Expand **Forest: 70411Lab.com**, then expand **Domains**, and finally, expand **70411Lab.com** domain.
3. Expand Group Policy Objects container and high-light Default Domain Policy.
4. On the Details Pane, click **Scope** tab.
5. To filter by group:
   a) Beneath **Security Filtering,** highlight **Authenticated Users** and click **Remove**, then click **Ok** to confirm the removal.
   b) Click **Add,** and on the search box, enter **PSOUnivGroup** group then click **Ok.**
6. To confirm the actual permission granted to the **PSOUnivGroup** group:
   a) Click **Delegation** tab and click **Advanced** (Far right). The Default Domain Policy Settings properties open.
   b) Beneath Group or users names, highlight PSOUnivGroup.
   c) Beneath Permissions for PSOUnivGroup, confirm that Read and Apply group policy Permissions are granted.
   d) Click **Cancel**.

6.1.4 Configure loopback processing

Loopback processing is an advanced group policy option that is intended to keep the configuration of a computer the same regardless of the user logged on to the computer. This policy setting directs the system to apply the set of Group Policy objects for the computer to any user who logs on to a computer affected by the setting. It is intended for special-use computers, such as those in public places, laboratories, and classrooms, where user setting must be modified based on the computer in use.

By default, the user's Group Policy Objects determine which user settings apply. If Loopback processing policy setting is enabled, when a user logs on to a computer, the computer's Group Policy Objects will determine the set of Group Policy Objects that will apply. When Loopback processing option is configured, both the computer and user portions of the GPO should be enabled.

The **Configure User Group Policy loopback processing mode** policy is located under Computer Configuration\Policies\Administrative settings\System\Group Policy. This policy supports the following modes:
Replace Mode: Indicates that the user settings defined in the computer's Group Policy Objects replace the user settings normally applied to the user.
Merge Mode: Indicates that the user settings defined in the computer's Group Policy Objects and the user settings normally applied to the user are combined. If the settings conflict, the user settings in the computer's Group

Policy Objects take precedence over the user's normal settings. If you disable this setting or do not configure it, the user's Group Policy Objects determines which user settings apply.

To Configure loopback processing

1. Log on to 70411SRV and open Group Policy Management Console.
2. On the Group Policy Management Console tree, Expand **Forest: 70411Lab.com**, then expand **Domains**, and expand **70411Lab.com** domain.
3. Right-click **Default Domain Policy** and click **Edit**. The Group Policy Management Editor opens.
4. Navigate to Computer Configuration\Policies\Administrative settings\System\Group Policy. On the details pane double-click **Configure User Group Policy loopback processing mode**. Complete the following tasks:
   a) Select Enabled.
   b) Beneath **Options, Replace** is selected by default.
   c) Click **Ok** to save your changes.

6.1.5 Configure client-side extension (CSE) behaviour

When Group Policy processes on a Windows-based computer, client-side extensions (CSE) interpret the stored policy settings and make the appropriate changes to the environment. Policy settings are grouped into categories, such as Administrative Templates, Security Settings, Folder Redirection, Disk Quota, Software Installation, and the Group Policy preference extensions. The settings in each category require a specific CSE to process them, and each CSE has its own rules for processing settings.

Each client-side extension is identified by a subkey (on the client) under the following path:
HKEY_LOCAL_MACHINE\Software\Microsoft\Windows NT\CurrentVersion\Winlogon\GPExtensions

Foreground and background processing

Group Policy foreground processing applies when the computer starts or shuts down and when the user signs in or signs out. During foreground processing, policy settings can be applied asynchronously or synchronously.

Group Policy background processing applies during periodic refreshes after the computer has started or a user has signed in. All requested Group Policy refreshes that are performed by using **GPUpdate.exe** also run as background processing. During background processing, policy settings are only applied asynchronously.

Asynchronous and synchronous processing

Asynchronous processing refers to processes that do not depend on the outcome of other processes. Therefore, they can occur on different threads simultaneously. Synchronous processing refers to processes that depend on each other's outcome. Therefore, synchronous processes must wait for the previous process to finish before the next process can start. Asynchronous processing affects Group Policy in the following ways:

At startup: The client computer does not wait for the network to be fully initialized before sign-in is available to the user. Group Policy for the client computer processes when the network becomes available in parallel to startup and sign-in activities.

At sign-in: A user does not have to wait for Group Policy to finish processing before signing in.
For CSEs such as Folder Redirection, Software Installation, and Drive Maps preference extension, the outcome of Group Policy processing might adversely affect the user's experience. For example a program being uninstalled while the user is working with it. To keep this from happening, the CSE is designed to require synchronous processing to apply the new settings.

During asynchronous processing, the CSE signals the system to indicate that a synchronous application of Group Policy is required. A synchronous application of Group Policy occurs at the next startup (if it is signaled during the computer Group Policy refresh) or at the user's next sign-in (if it is signaled during the user Group Policy refresh).
Although the requirement to run a client-side extension in synchronous mode is not configurable, other default behavior for each CSE can be configured through policy settings. To configure the properties that are associated with a CSE, apply the Administrative Templates computer configuration policy settings that are created for this purpose. Some examples are **Disk Quotas, Folder Redirection,** and **Power Management.** These policies are located in **Computer Configuration\Policies\Administrative settings\System\.**
Policy settings that affect CSE properties can be configured in **Computer Configuration\Policies\Administrative settings\System\Group Policy**. In this node, 32 Policies can be configured for CSE behavior. When you open a policy that can be configured for CSE behavior and enable it, there will be three options, sometimes four that affects CSE behavior. The options are discussed below:

1. **Allows processing across a slow network connection**: Updates preference items even when the update is transmitted across a slow

network connection, such as a telephone line. Updates across slow connections can cause significant delays.

2. **Do not apply during periodic background processing**: Prevents the system from updating affected preference items in the background while the computer is in use. When background updates are disabled, preference item changes do not take effect until the next user logon or system restart.

3. **Process even if the Group Policy Objects have not changed**: Updates and reapplies the preference items even if the preference items have not changed. Many policy implementations specify that they are updated only when changed. However, you might want to update unchanged preference items, such as reapplying a desired preference setting in case a user has changed it.

4. **Allows background processing priority**: Defines state of Background processing priority. Available options are listed below:
   a) Normal
   b) Below Normal
   c) Lowest
   d) Idle

By default, background processing priority is "Idle."

To illustrate client-side-extension behavior configuration, we will consider two policies settings:

1. **Configure disk quota policy processing:** This policy setting affects all policies that use the disk quota component of Group Policy, such as those in Computer Configuration\Policies\Administrative Templates\System\Disk Quotas. This policy has the following configuration options that affects Client-Side-Extension behaviour:
   a) Allows processing across a slow network connection.
   b) Do not apply during periodic background processing.
   c) Process even if the Group Policy Objects have not changed.

2. **Configure Folder Options preference extension policy processing:** This policy setting allows you to configure when preference items in the **Folder Options** preference extension are updated. Folder Options policy is located in Computer Configuration\Policies\Preferences\ node.

3. This policy has the three options listed above plus an additional option - **Allow background processing priority**.

Exam Tip

It is important to understand the **Asynchronous** and **synchronous processing** in relation to application of group policies to a computer.

Fast Logon Optimization and CSE processing

When **Fast Logon Optimization** is enabled, Group Policy foreground processing runs asynchronously. When a CSE requires synchronous processing:

1. Policy settings do not apply during the asynchronous processing cycle.
2. The CSE that requires synchronous policy application can still be called during asynchronous policy application. Instead of applying policy settings, the CSE signals for synchronous processing to be applied at the next startup or sign-in.

If you do not want fast startup to apply to computers in your enterprise, you can apply a GPO that disables the **Computer Configuration/Policies/Administrative Templates/System/Shutdown/Require use of fast startup** policy setting. Be aware that disabling this policy setting results in full shutdowns and longer startup times for client computers. The enabled state of the **Require use of fast startup** policy setting does not take precedence over any Group Policy setting that disables hibernation.

To configure CSE behaviour for disk quota policy processing

1. Log on to 70411SRV and open Group Policy Management Console.
2. On the Group Policy Management Console tree, Expand **Forest: 70411Lab.com**, then expand **Domains**, expand **70411Lab.com** domain.
3. Right-click **Default Domain Policy** and click **Edit**. The Group Policy Management Editor opens.
4. To configure disk quota:
   a) Navigate to Computer Configuration\Policies\Administrative Templates\System\Disk Quotas. - At least one policy MUST be enabled here for the disk quota policy processing to affect CSE behaviour.
   b) Enable the Policies **Enable disk quotas**, Enforce disk quota limit and **Specify default quota limit and warning level** with the default levels.
   c) When done, click **Ok.**
5. To configure CSE behaviour for disk quota policy processing:
   a) Navigate to Computer Configuration\Policies\Administrative settings\System\Group Policy.

b) On the details pane, double-click **Configure disk quota policy processing** and select **Enabled**.
c) Below Options, check the box beside Do not apply during periodic background processing.
d) Click **Ok** to save your changes.

6.1.6 Configure and manage slow-link processing

Most group policy settings will apply despite the network conditions; others will not be applied if available network bandwidth is below a pre-set threshold. The default bandwidth threshold in a Windows Server 2012 R2 is 500Kbps. When a client is applying its Group Policies and it detects that the available bandwidth between it and the Domain Controller is less than 500 Kbps, it will only download and apply those settings within the GPO that are considered mandatory. In Windows Server 2012 R2, the following settings are not considered mandatory and are not downloaded on a slow links:

1. Disk Quota
2. Scripts
3. Folder Redirection
4. Software Installation
5. Wireless Network (IEEE 802.11) Policies
6. Wired Network (IEEE 802.3) Policies
7. Internet Explorer Maintenance Extension
8. EFS Recovery
9. IP Security

Slow Link Detection

Prior to Windows Server 2008, client computers used the Internet Control Message Protocol (ICMP) protocol to determine a slow link between the Group Policy client and the domain controller. The problem with this is that ICMP traffic is usually blocked in most networks, which prevents this Group Policies feature working. To overcome this difficulty, Microsoft introduced a new tool to detect slow links, starting with Windows Vista. This new mechanism is known as Network Location Awareness (NLA).

Slow link detection is configured using the policy setting **Configure Group Policy slow link detection.** This setting appears in the **Computer Configuration** and **User Configuration** folders. The setting in Computer Configuration defines a slow link for policies in the Computer Configuration folder. The setting in User Configuration defines a slow link for settings in the User Configuration folder. Another policy setting, **Disable detection of slow network connections** and related policies in Computer Configuration\Policies\Administrative Templates\System\User Profile also affects slow link detection behavior. If this policy setting enabled, the system does not detect slow connections or recognize any connections as being slow.

As a result, the system does not respond to slow connections to user profiles, and it ignores the policy settings that tell the system how to respond to a slow connection.

To configure and manage slow-link processing

1. Log on to 70411SRV and open Group Policy Management Console.
2. On the Group Policy Management Console tree, Expand **Forest: 70411Lab.com**, then expand **Domains**, and expand **70411Lab.com** domain.
3. Right-click **Default Domain Policy** and click **Edit**. The Group Policy Management Editor opens.
4. To configure Group Policy slow link detection, navigate to Computer Configuration\Policies\Administrative settings\System\Group Policy and on the details pane, double-click the policy **Configure Group Policy slow link detection** and complete the following tasks:
   a) Select **Enabled**.
   b) Beneath **Options**, note the default value (500Kbps)
   c) Click **Ok** to save your changes.
5. To disable detection of slow network connections, navigate to Computer Configuration\Policies\Administrative settings\System\User Profiles and on the details pane, double-click the policy **Disable detection of slow network connections.** Then complete the following tasks:
   a) Select **Disable**.
   b) Click **Ok** to save your changes.

In step 4 above, you can disable slow link detection by entering 0 in the **connection speed** box. You also have an option to configure **Always treat WWAN connections as a slow link** policy. If you disable this setting or do not configure it, the system uses the default value of 500 kilobits per second.

Exam Tip

Important to note the valid ways to disable slow link detection: Enable the Policy **Configure Group Policy slow link detection** and enter 0Kbps as the connection speed or Enable the Policy **Disable detection of slow network connections**. If you leave Configure **Group Policy slow link detection** in Not Configured or **Disabled** state, slow link detection will be on and use the default value of 500Kbps.

6.1.7 Configure and manage Group Policy caching (2012 R2 Objective)

Windows Server 2012 R2 introduces a new feature for Group Policy called Policy Caching. When this setting is enabled, the client will download the policies from a domain controller and store them locally. The policy setting that controls group policy catching is called **Configure Group Policy**

Caching and is located in Computer Configuration\Policies\Administrative settings\System\Group Policy.

If this policy setting is left at **Enable** or **Not Configured** state, Group Policy caches policy information after every background processing session. This cache saves applicable GPOs and the settings contained within them in the location c:\windows\system32\GroupPolicy\Datastore. When Group Policy runs in synchronous foreground mode, it refers to this cache, which enables it to run faster. When the cache is read, Group Policy attempts to contact a logon domain controller to determine the link speed. When Group Policy runs in background mode or asynchronous foreground mode, it continues to download the latest version of the policy information, and it uses a bandwidth estimate to determine slow link thresholds.

This policy provides an option to configure **Slow link value** and **Timeout value**. The slow link value determines how long Group Policy will wait for a response from the domain controller before reporting the link speed as slow. The default is 500 milliseconds. The timeout value determines how long Group Policy will wait for a response from the domain controller before determining that there is no network connectivity. This stops the current Group Policy processing. Group Policy will run in the background the next time a connection to a domain controller is established. Setting this value too high might result in longer waits for the user at boot or logon. The default is 5000 milliseconds.

If this policy setting is disabled, the Group Policy client will not cache applicable GPOs or settings that are contained within the GPOs. When Group Policy runs synchronously, it downloads the latest version of the policy from the network and uses bandwidth estimates to determine slow link thresholds. The policy setting **Enable Group Policy Caching for Servers** configures Group Policy caching behavior on Windows Server machines.

Note

The **Configure Group Policy Caching** setting behaves in the same way whether it is **Enabled** or **Not Configured**. To stop clients from caching group policies, you must **Disable** this policy. The default **Slow link** value is 500 milliseconds. **Timeout** has a default value of 5000 milliseconds. Group Policy caching is only supported in Windows Server 2012 R2, Windows 8.1 or Windows RT 8.1.

6.1.8 Force Group Policy update (2012 R2 Objective)

Prior to Windows Server 2012 and Windows 8, the only tool available to force a group policy update was the **GPUpdate** command. This command supersedes the now obsolete **/refreshpolicy** option for the **secedit** command.

From Windows Server 2012 and Windows 8, you can remotely refresh Group Policy settings for all computers in an organizational unit (OU) from one central location by using the Group Policy Management Console (GPMC). Or you can use the **Invoke-GPUpdate** Windows PowerShell cmdlet to refresh Group Policy for a set of computers, including computers that are not within the OU structure.

Remote Group Policy refresh updates all Group Policy settings, including security settings that are set on a group of remote computers, by using the functionality that is added to the context menu for an OU in the Group Policy Management Console (GPMC).

When you select an OU to remotely refresh the Group Policy settings on all the computers in that OU, the following operations are completed:

1. An Active Directory query returns a list of all computers that belong to that OU.
2. For each computer that belongs to the selected OU, a WMI call retrieves the list of signed in users.
3. A remote scheduled task is created to run **GPUpdate.exe /force** for each signed in user and once for the computer Group Policy refresh.

In point 3 above, the task is scheduled to run with a random delay of up to 10 minutes to decrease the load on the network traffic. This random delay cannot be configured when you use the GPMC, but you can configure the random delay for the scheduled task or set the scheduled task to run immediately when you use the **Invoke-GPUpdate** cmdlet.

Note

GPMC can remotely force Group policy updates on computers in an OU but the
Invoke-GPUpdate Windows PowerShell cmdlet can refresh Group Policy for a set of computers, including computers that are not within the OU structure.

Requirements for remote Group Policy refresh

To schedule a Group Policy refresh for domain-joined computers by using the GPMC or the Invoke-GPUpdate cmdlet, you must have firewall rules that enable inbound network traffic on the ports listed below:

TCP RPC dynamic ports, Schedule (Task Scheduler service): Required for remote Scheduled Tasks Management (RPC).

TCP port 135, RPCSS (Remote Procedure Call service): Required for remote Scheduled Tasks Management (RPC-EPMAP).

TCP all ports, Winmgmt (Windows Management Instrumentation service): Required for Windows Management Instrumentation (WMI-in).

Windows Server 2012 Group Policy added a Starter GPO called, **Group Policy Remote Update Firewall Ports**. This Starter GPO includes policy settings to configure the firewall rules that are specified above. It is a best practice to create a new GPO from this Starter GPO. Link the GPO to your domain at a higher precedence than the Default Domain GPO, and then use it to configure all the computers in the domain to enable a remote Group Policy refresh.

To Force Group Policy update

1. To configure firewall rules on each client that will be managed with remote Group Policy refresh:
    a) Log on to 70411SRV and open Group Policy Management Console.
    b) Expand Forest: 70411Lab.com\Domains.
    c) Click on **Starter GPOs** and on the details pane, click **Create Starter GPOs Folder**.
    d) Right-click the 70411Lab.com domain, and click Create a GPO in this domain, and link it here…
    e) On the New GPO dialog box, the name field enter Configure firewall rules for remote gpupdate.
    f) On the **Source Starter GPO** drop-down list, select the **Group Policy Remote Update Firewall Ports** Starter GPO, and click **Ok**.
    g) Click 70411Lab.com domain and on the details pane, click **Linked Group Policy Objects** and move the **Configure firewall rules for remote gpupdate** to a Link Order of 1.

Note

Step 1 above can be accomplished using the Use the New-GPO cmdlet with the -StarterGpoName parameter, and then pipe the output to the New-GPLink cmdlet. New-GPO –Name "Configure firewall rules for remote gpupdate" –StarterGpoName "Group Policy Remote Update Firewall Ports" | New-GPLink –target "dc=70411Lab,dc=com" –LinkEnabled yes

2. To schedule a Group Policy refresh to run on all computers in an OU by using GPMC:
   a) Right-click Domain Controllers OU and click Group Policy Update...
   b) Click **Yes** in the Force Group Policy update dialog box. This is the equivalent to running GPUpdate.exe /force from the command line.

Note

The **Remote Group Policy update results** window displays only the status of scheduling a Group Policy refresh for each computer located in the selected OU and any OUs contained within the selected OU. This display does not show the success or failure of the actual Group Policy refresh for each computer.

6.2 Configure Group Policy Settings

Introduction

Group policy allows administrators perform some specific tasks like folder redirection, scripts configuration, and software installation. You are also able to import security templates and custom administrative templates into group policy. This gives you the flexibility to deploy these templates to multiple computers and users in your enterprise.

In this section, we will cover following exam objectives:

6.2.0 Configure Group policy settings

6.2.1 Import security templates

6.2.2 Import custom administrative template file

6.2.3 Configure property filters for administrative templates

---

Lab Plan:

We will use 70411SRV (Domain Controller) for most tasks in this section.

Additional lab setup

1. Create the following folders on 70411SRV: E:\MSIPackages, E:\UserProfiles.
2. Share the folders with the default rights.
3. Download an MSI package for Firefox from http://www.frontmotion.com/Firefox/download_firefox.htm to E:\MSIPackages. I downloaded Firefox-27.0.1-ach.msi
4. Create a folder **ADMTemplates** in drive E:\
5. Download **Office 2010 Administrative Template files** from http://www.microsoft.com/en-gb/download/details.aspx?id=18968 to E:\ADMTemplates
6. Download all three files in the above link
7. Double-click the executable for your platform, and extract the files to E:\ADMTemplates
8. Download Administrative Templates for Internet Explorer 11 from http://www.microsoft.com/en-gb/download/details.aspx?id=40905 to E:\ADMTemplates
9. Download ADMX Migrator to E:\ADMXMigrator (http://fullarmor-admx-migrator.software.informer.com/1.3/)
10. Install ADMX Migrator on 70411Win7 (Your Windows 7 VM).

6.2.0 Configure Group policy settings

There are many Group policy settings in Windows Server 2012 R2. These settings give administrators control over what is allowed, or not allowed in an enterprise. For the purposes of exam 70411, we will cover Software installation Settings, Folder redirection Settings, Scripts Settings and Administrative template settings. Scripts and Software installation Settings can be configured on both the Computer and User Configuration nodes.

To configure Group Policy settings

1. Log on to 70411SRV and open Group Policy Management Console.
2. Open Default Domain Policy for editing.
3. To configure Software installation Settings:
   a) Navigate to Computer Configuration\Policies, and highlight **Software Settings**.
   b) On the details pane, right-click **Software installation** and click **Properties**. Complete the following tasks:
      i) On the **General** tab, enter \\70411SRV\MSIPackages as the Default package location.
      ii) Under **New packages,** note options available:
         (1) Display the Software dialogue box (Default).
         (2) Assign.
         (3) Advanced.
   c) Beneath the Installation user interface options, note available options:
      i) Basic.
      ii) Advanced (Default).

Note

Publish option is not available when configuring **Software installation** options under **Computer Configuration** node. All options including **Publish**, are available when you configure **Software installation** options under User Configuration node.

   d) Click **Advanced** tab: The advanced tab is used to configure options to automatically remove the applications when it is no longer managed, published OLE information in the active directory, and make 32-bit applications available on 64-bit platforms. The following options can be configured:
      i) Uninstall the applications when they fall out of the scope of management.
      ii) Include OLE information when deploying applications.
      iii) Make 32-bit x86 Windows Installer applications available to Win64 machines (Selected by default).

iv) Make 32-bit x86 down-level (ZAP) applications available to Win64 machines.

e) Click **File Extensions** tab: Provide the option to order precedence with which Windows will invoke applications when a user opens a document.

f) Click **Categories** tab: Provide the option to define application categories. This is the category where this application will be listed in Add/Remove programs. Add the following categories.
   i) MS Office
   ii) Legacy

g) On the Software installation properties click **Ok**.

h) Navigate to User Configuration\Policies, and highlight Software Settings.

i) On the details pane, right-click **Software installation** and click **Properties**. Note the following:
   i) **General** tab: Note that unlike when we configured **Software installation** options under **Computer Configuration** node, **Publish** is now available.
   ii) All other tabs provide the same options, click **Categories** tab and confirm that the two categories we created in the **Computer Configuration** node appears here as well.
   iii) On the **General** tab enter \\70411SRV\MSIPackages as the Default package location.

Note

OLE information: Specifies whether to deploy information about COM components with the package so that software on the client can install them from Active Directory as needed, in a manner similar to activation by file extension.

j) Click **Ok**.

k) To create a new package on the **User Configuration** node:
   i) Navigate to User Configuration\Policies, and expand Software Settings.
   ii) Right-click **Software installation** and point to **New** and select **Package**. The Default package location configured earlier opens. If it does not open, beside File names, enter \\70411SRV\MSIPackages and click **Open** to open the network location, then Select **Firefox-27.0.1-ach.msi** and click **Open**.
   iii) The Deploy Software dialogue box opens.
   iv) Note the available options, then select **Publish** and click **Ok**.

Note

To publish an application, it must be an MSI package and must be located in a network share.

---

l) To create a new package on the Computer Configuration node:
   i)   Navigate to **Computer Configuration\Policies**, and expand Software Settings.
   ii) Right-click **Software installation**, point to **New** and select **Package**. The Default package location configured earlier opens. If it does not open, beside File names, enter \\70411SRV\MSIPackages, then click **Open** to open the network location, Select **Firefox-27.0.1-ach.msi** and click **Open**.
   iii) The Deploy Software dialogue box opens.
   iv) Note the available options, select **Publish,** and click **Ok.**
4. To configure Folder redirection Settings:
   a) Navigate to User Configuration\Policies\Windows Settings and expand **Folder Redirection.** You can configure the following: AppData (Roaming), Desktop, Start Menu, Documents, Pictures, Music, Videos, Favourites, Contacts, Downloads, Links, Searches, and Saves Games.
   b) Review the properties of the package.
   c) Navigate to Computer Configuration\Policies, and highlight Software Settings.
   d) Right-click Mozilla Firefox (ach) and select Properties, then examine the following:
      i)   Click **Deployment** tab. Notice that only **Assigned** option is available. You can also configure to uninstall the application when it falls out of the scope of management.
      ii) Click **Upgrade** tab: You can add upgrades packages for this application.
      iii) Click **Categories** tab: You will see available categories, from the two we created earlier.
   e) Navigate to Navigate to User Configuration\Policies, and highlight Software Settings.
   f) Right-click Mozilla Firefox (ach) and select Properties, then examine the following:
      i)   Click **Deployment** tab: Notice that you can publish and assign the application, amend the installation interface, auto-install by file extension activation.
      ii) All other tabs are very similar to the package in **Computer Configuration** node.
5. Configure Folder Redirection Settings:

a) Navigate to User Configuration\Policies\Windows Settings\Folder Redirection.

b) In the details pane, right-click **Documents** click **Properties** and complete the following tasks:

    i) Click Target tab: On the Settings drop-down, select Basic - Redirect everyone's folder to the same location.

    ii) Beneath Target folder location, under the root path, select Create a folder for each user.

    iii) On the **Root Path field**, enter \\70411SRV\UserProfiles. Note the example displayed: For user Claire, this folder will be redirected to \\70411SRV\UserProfiles\Claire\Documents.

    iv) Click **Settings** tab: Note the options checked by default:

        (1) Grant the user exclusive rights to Documents.

        (2) Move the contents of the documents to the new location.

        (3) For **Policy Removal**: Leave the folder in the new location when policy is removed.

    v) On the **Settings** tab, the following are not enabled by default:

        (1) Also apply redirection policy to Windows 2000, Windows 2000 Server, Windows XP and Windows Server 2003 Operating systems.

c) When done, click **Ok** and respond **Yes** to the warding message.

Note

When configuring Folder Redirection, there is a second **option Advanced - Specify location for various user groups**. If this option is selected, the folder will be redirected to different location based on the security group membership of users. The **Advanced** option also disables all options in the **Settings** tab.

6. Configure Scripts Settings:

a) Navigate to Computer Configuration\Policies\Administrative Templates\System and highlight **Scripts** container. On the details pane, review the following Group Policy Settings:

    i) **Allow logon scripts when NetBIOS or WINS is disabled:** Allows user logon scripts to run when the logon cross-forest, DNS suffixes are not configured, and NetBIOS or WINS is disabled. This policy setting affects all user accounts interactively logging on to the computer.

    ii) **Specify maximum wait time for Group Policy scripts:** Determines how long the system waits for scripts applied by Group Policy to run. This setting limits the total time allowed for all logon, logoff, startup, and shutdown scripts applied by Group Policy to finish running. If the scripts have not finished running when the specified time expires, the system stops script processing and records an error event. To direct the system to wait until the scripts have finished, no matter how long they take, enable this policy and enter 0 on the options box.

iii) **Run Windows PowerShell scripts first at computer startup, shutdown:** This policy setting determines whether Windows PowerShell scripts are run before non-Windows PowerShell scripts during computer startup and shutdown. By default, Windows PowerShell scripts run after non-Windows PowerShell scripts. It determines the order in which computer startup and shutdown scripts are run within all applicable GPOs.

iv) **Run logon scripts synchronously:** Directs the system to wait for logon scripts to finish running before it starts the File Explorer interface program and creates the desktop.

v) **Display instructions in shutdown scripts as they run:** Displays the instructions in shutdown scripts as they run. Shutdown scripts are batch files of instructions that run when the user restarts the system or shuts it down. By default, the system does not display the instructions in the shutdown script.

vi) **Run logon scripts asynchronously:** This policy setting lets the system run startup scripts simultaneously. By default, the system waits for each startup script to complete before it runs the next startup script.

vii) **Display instructions in startup scripts as they run:** This policy setting displays the instructions in startup scripts as they run. Similar to the shutdown scripts display policy.

viii) **Run Windows PowerShell scripts first at user logon, logoff:** This policy setting determines whether Windows PowerShell scripts are run before non-Windows PowerShell scripts during user logon and logoff. By default, Windows PowerShell scripts run after non-Windows PowerShell scripts.

b) Navigate to User Configuration\Policies\Administrative Templates\System and highlight **Scripts** container. On the details pane, review the following Group Policy Settings:

i) **Run legacy logon scripts hidden:** This policy setting hides the instructions in logon scripts written for Windows NT 4.0 and earlier.

ii) **Display instructions in logoff scripts as they run:** This policy setting displays the instructions in logoff scripts as they run.

iii) Run Windows PowerShell scripts first at user logon, logoff: Same as same policy in Configuration settings.

6.2.1 Import security templates

The recommended practice for deploying security templates is to import them into a GPO and deploy the security template using GPO.

To import a Security template

1. To create and configure a Security template:
    a) Log on to 70411SRV and open a blank MMC.
    b) Click File and select Add or Remove Snap-ins.
    c) On the **Add or Remove Snap-ins** dialogue, select **Security Templates**, click **Add**, and then click **Ok**.
    d) Right-click **Security Templates** and select **New Template Search path**. Select C:\Windows\security\templates and click **Ok**.
    e) Expand   Security   Templates,   then   right-click C:\Windows\security\templates and select **New Template**. Enter **70411DCSectemplate** as the template name then click **Ok**.
    f) Beneath   C:\Windows\security\templates,   expand **70411DCSectemplate** and complete the following tasks:
        i) Expand **Account Policies** and highlight **Password Policy.** On the details pane, configure **Minimum password age** and **Maximum password age** with default values.
        ii) Highlight Account Lockout policy and on the details pane, configure Account lockout duration, Account lockout threshold, and Reset account lockout counter after policies with default values.
2. Confirm current security policy configuration:
    a) Log on to 70411SRV and open Group Policy Management Console.
    b) Expand Forest: 70411Lab.com\Domains\70411Lab.com.
    c) Expand Domain Controllers OU, and then right-click Default Domain Controllers Policy and click Edit, Group Policy Management Editor opens.
    d) Under   Computer   Configuration,   expand   Policies\Windows Settings\Security Settings.
    e) Expand Account Policies and highlight Password Policy.
    f) On the details pane, ensure that all the policies are left at **Not Defined.**
    g) Highlight **Account Lockout policy** and on the details pane, ensure that all the policies are left at **Not Defined.**
3. Import security template:
    a) Right-click Security Settings and click Import Policy.
    b) On the Import Policy From window, navigate to C:\Windows\security\templates and open **70411DCSectemplate** template.
    c) Right-click **Security Settings** and click **Reload**.

6.2.2 Import custom administrative template file

Administrative Templates are registry-based policy settings that appear in the Local Group Policy Editor under the Administrative Templates node. Administrative Templates are available on the Computer and User Configuration nodes. This hierarchy is created when the Local Group Policy Editor reads XML-based Administrative Template files (.admx).

Classic Administrative Template files (also known as ADM files) are not authored using XML. Earlier versions of the Local Group Policy Editor displayed these settings under the Administrative Templates node. The current version of Administrative Template files are authored using XML (known as ADMX files). The Local Group Policy Editor displays these settings under the Administrative Templates node.

However, the Local Group Policy Editor still recognizes ADM files and displays these settings under the Classic Administrative Templates node, which is a child node to Administrative Templates. These Classic Administrative Templates can be imported.

To Import custom administrative template file

1. Log on to 70411SRV and open Group Policy Management Console.
2. Expand Forest: 70411Lab.com\Domains\70411Lab.com.
3. Expand Domain Controllers OU, and then right-click **Default Domain Policy** and click **Edit,** Group Policy Management Editor opens.
4. Expand Computer Configuration\Policies.
5. To import a custom administrative template file:
   a) Right-click Administrative Templates: and select Add/Remove Templates.
   b) On the Add/Remove Templates dialogue, click **Add** and browse to E:\ADMTemplates\ADM\en-us.
   c) Select **word14.adm** and click **Open**.
   d) On the **Add/Remove Templates** dialogue, word14 template appears on the list
   e) Repeat the steps to add excel14.adm and inetres.adm (Internet Explorer 11) template.
   f) When you finish, click **Close**.
   g) Close and reopen the Group Policy Management Editor.
6. To View the imported template:
   a) Expand   User   Configuration\Policies\Administrative Templates:\Classic Administrative Templates (ADM).
   b) Beneath **Classic Administrative Templates (ADM),** that is two nodes: Microsoft Excel 2010 and Microsoft Word 2010 are now available for configuration.

Exam Tip

Note the difference between the current version of Administrative Template files - They are authored using XML (known as ADMX files) and are displayed on the Administrative Templates node. ADM files are not authored using XML, they are still recognized in the local group policy but displayed on the Classic Administrative Templates node, which is a child node to Administrative Templates.

Group Policy Central Store

In earlier Windows operating systems, all the default Administrative Template files were added to the ADM folder of a Group Policy object (GPO) on a domain controller. The GPOs are stored in the SYSVOL folder. The SYSVOL folder is automatically replicated to other domain controllers in the same domain. A policy file uses approximately 2 megabytes (MB) of hard disk space. This increases replication traffic because each domain controller stores a distinct version of a policy.

From Windows Vista and above, Administrative Template files are stored in a Central Store. This means that the ADM folder is not created in a GPO as in earlier versions of Windows. Therefore, domain controllers do not store or replicate redundant copies of .adm files. To take advantage of the benefits of .admx files, you must create a Central Store in the SYSVOL folder on a domain controller. The Central Store is a file location that is checked by the Group Policy tools. The Group Policy tools use any .admx files that are in the Central Store. The files in the Central Store are later replicated to all domain controllers in the domain.

To create a Central Store for .admx and .adm files, create a folder named **PolicyDefinitions** in the following location: \\FQDN\SYSVOL\FQDN\policies. After creating the PolicyDefinitions folder, copy all files from the PolicyDefinitions folder on a Windows 7 client computer to the PolicyDefinitions folder on the domain controller. The PolicyDefinitions folder on a Windows 7 computer resides in %windir%\ folder. The PolicyDefinitions folder on the Windows Vista-based computer stores all .admx files and .adml files for all languages enabled on the client computer. The .adml files on the Windows Vista-based computer are stored in a language-specific folder. For example, English (United States) .adml files are stored in a folder that is named "en-US."

To create a Central Store for 70411Lab.com

1. Log on to 70411SRV and open the Default Domain Policy using Group policy editor.
2. Confirm that Administrative Templates container is blank.

3. Open \\70411Lab.com\SYSVOL\70411Lab.com\Policies.
4. Create a folder called **PolicyDefinitions.**
5. Log on to 70411Win7 and copy the contents of
    C:\Windows\PolicyDefinitions to
6. \\70411Lab.com\SYSVOL\70411Lab.com\Policies\PolicyDefinitions.
7. Open the Default Domain Policy using Group policy editor and confirm
    that Administrative Templates is populated.

Note

Group Policy Central Store was introduced from Windows Vista.

Exam Tip

It is important to understand the procedure for creating a Group Policy
Central Store:
Step 1 - Create a PolicyDefinitions folder in
\\FQDN\SYSVOL\FQDN\policies.
Step 2 - Copy the contents of PolicyDefinitions folder on a Windows 7 client
computer to the PolicyDefinitions folder on the domain controller. Questions
in this category will often be framed like – "You have an .ADMX file that
contains group policy you wish to apply but it does not appear in Group
Policy…"

ADMX Migrator

ADMX Migrator is a snap-in for the Microsoft Management Console (MMC)
that simplifies the process of converting an existing Group Policy ADM
Template to the new ADMX format and provides a graphical user interface
for creating and editing Administrative templates.

To convert an .ADM file to .ADMX

1. Log on to 70411WIN7 and open ADMX Editor.
2. Right-click **ADMX Editor** on the left pane and click **Generate ADMX
    from ADM.**
3. Point to \\70411SRV\e$\ADMTemplates\ADM\en-us and open
    access14.adm.
4. When the conversion completes, click **Close.**
5. Note the location of the new ADMX file and respond **Yes** to load the file
    as an **ADMX TemplateB.** A new template called **access14** is loaded.
6. Copy the ADMX file into the central store and confirm that it appears in
    the **Administrative Template** container in group policy.

Exam Tip

For the purposes of exam 70411, it is important to note that the first step to
converting ADM to ADMX is to **Generate ADMX from ADM**.

6.2.3 Configure property filters for administrative templates

Filtering can be configured for Administrative Templates. Filtering determines what is and is not displayed. The Local Group Policy Editor allows you to change the criteria for displaying Administrative Template policy settings. By default, the editor displays all policy settings, including unmanaged policy settings. However, you can use property filters to change how the Local Group Policy Editor displays Administrative Template policy settings. Property filters for administrative templates can be filtered in three ways: With Property Filters, with Keyword Filters and with Requirement Filters.

Filter with Property Filters

There are three inclusive property filters that you can use to filter Administrative Templates. These property filters include:

1. **Managed**: There are two kinds of Administrative Template policy settings: **Managed** and **Unmanaged**. The Group Policy Client service governs Managed policy settings and removes a policy setting when it is no longer within scope of the user or computer.
2. The Group Policy Client service does not govern unmanaged policy settings. These policy settings are persistent. The Group Policy Client service does not remove unmanaged policy settings, even if the policy setting is not within scope of the user or computer. Typically, you use these types of policy settings to configure options for operating system components that are not policy enabled. You can also use unmanaged policy settings for application settings.
3. The Managed property filter has three states: **Any**, **Yes**, and **No**. Setting this property filter to **Any** causes the Local Group Policy Editor to display all Administrative Template policy settings. Setting this property filter to **Yes** causes the editor to show only **managed** Administrative Template policy settings, hiding all unmanaged Administrative Template policy settings. Setting this property filter to **No** causes the editor to show only unmanaged Administrative Template policy settings, hiding all managed Administrative Template policy settings.
4. **Configured**: You can configure Administrative Template policy settings to one of three states: **Not Configured**, **Enabled**, and **Disabled**. **Not Configured** is the default state for all policy settings. Policy settings set to **Not Configured** do not affect users or computers. Enabling an Administrative Template policy setting activates the policy setting. When Enabled, the action described in the title of the policy setting applies to the user or computer. When Disabled, the opposite action described in the title of the policy setting applies to the user or computer. Usually, **Not Configured** and **Disabled** policy settings produce the same results.

However, **Not Configured** policy settings do not apply to the user, but **Disabled** policy settings apply to a user.

5. The Configured property filter has three states: **Any**, **Yes**, and **No**. Setting this property filter to **Any** causes the Local Group Policy Editor to display all Administrative Template policy settings and is the default setting for this filter. Setting this property filter to **Yes** causes the editor to show only configured Administrative Template policy settings, hiding not configured policy settings. Setting this property filter to **No** causes the editor to show only not configured Administrative Template policy settings, hiding configured policy settings.

Note

Usually the **Not Configured** and **Disabled** policy settings produce the same results. However, **Not Configured** policy settings do not apply to the user, but **Disabled** policy settings apply to a user.

6. **Commented**: Each Administrative Template policy setting has a comment property. The Commented property allows you to enter text associated with a specific policy setting.
7. The Commented property filter has three states: **Any**, **Yes**, and **No**. Setting this property filter to **Any** causes the Local Group Policy Editor to display all Administrative Template policy settings and is the default setting for this filter. Setting this proper filter to **Yes** causes the editor to show only commented Administrative Template policy settings, hiding policy settings without comments. Setting this property filter to No causes the editor to show only Administrative Template policy settings without comments, hiding commented policy settings.

To Configure property filters for administrative templates

1. Log on to 70411SRV and open Group Policy Management Console.
2. Expand Forest: 70411Lab.com\Domains\70411Lab.com.
3. Expand Domain Controllers OU, and then right-click **Default Domain Policy** and click **Edit**, Group Policy Management Editor opens.
4. Expand Computer Configuration\Policies.
5. To configure filters for administrative template: Right-click **Administrative Templates:** and select **Filter Options.** Configure the following options:
   a) property filters: There are three inclusive:
      i) Managed
      ii) Configured
      iii) Commented

b) Check **Enable Keyword filters**. On the Filter for keywords field, enter **Office, Internet Explorer.**

c) Check **Enable Requirements filters** and beneath, check Internet Explorer 11, Windows Server 2003 Operating Systems, Windows Server 2008 Operating systems, Windows Server 2012 Operating Systems and Windows Server 2012 R2 Operating Systems.

d) When done, click **Ok.**

6.3 Manage Group Policy Objects (GPOs)

Introduction

In the previous section, we covered different aspects of Group Policy Settings configuration but there are other tasks that involve group policy management, like backup and restore, and delegation of Group Policy management.
In this section, we will cover following exam objectives:

6.3.0 Back up, import, copy, and restore GPOs

6.3.1 Create and configure Migration Table

6.3.2 Reset default GPOs

6.3.3 Delegate Group Policy management

Lab Plan

We will use 70411SRV (Domain Controller) for most tasks in this section.

Additional lab setup

Create two folders E:\GPOBackup and E:\GPOMigrationtable on 70411SRVCreate a new security group: LinkGPO in the Users Container Create a new security group: **CreateGPOs** in the Users Container

6.3.0 Back up, import, copy, and restore GPOs

In this section, we will cover some basic GPO management tasks.

To back up a Group Policy object

1. Log on to 70411SRV, open Group Policy Management Console.
2. Expand Forest: 70411Lab.com\Domains\70411Lab.com.
3. To back up all GPOs in the domain:
   a) Right-click Group Policy objects and click Back Up All.
   b) On the **Backup Group Policy object** dialog box, in the **Location** field, enter E:\GPOBackup.
   c) On the **Description** box, type **All GPO Backup for 70411Lab domain**, and then click **Back Up** (This description will apply to all GPOs being backed up).
   d) When the operation completes, click **Ok**.

To restore a deleted or previous version of an existing Group Policy object

1. Right-click **Group Policy Objects** node and then click **Manage Backups**.

2. On the **Manage Backups** dialog box, in the **Backup location** box, type **E:\GPOBackup**. You can also use **Browse** to locate the backup folder (The wizard is likely to load the location used for the last backup).
3. On the Backed up GPOs box, select Default Domain Controller Policy, and then click Restore.
4. When prompted to confirm the restore operation, click **Ok**.
5. When the operation completes, click **Ok** and then click **Close**.

Copy a Group Policy Object

Group Policy object (GPO) may be copied using the **drag-and-drop** or **right-click** method. Both methods are covered below.

To copy a Group Policy object (drag-and-drop method)

1. Log on to 70411SRV and open Group Policy Management Console.
2. Expand Forest: 70411Lab.com\Domains\70411Lab.com.
3. To create a copy of the GPO on the same domain:
   a) Expand the **Group Policy Objects** container.
   b) Drag and drop the **Default Domain Policy** to **Group Policy Objects** (See figure below for illustration). Accept the default permissions under **Specify the permissions for the new GPO** , and click **Ok**.
4. To create a copy of the GPO in a different domain:
   a) Expand the **Group Policy Objects** container.
   b) Double-click the destination domain, and then drag and drop the GPO you want to copy to **Group Policy objects**. Answer all the questions in the cross-domain copying wizard that appears, and then click **Finish**.

Figure 6.3.0 - Copy a GPO by drag-and-drop method

To copy a Group Policy object (right-click method)

1. Repeat steps 1-2 above, and expand the **Group Policy Objects** Container.
2. Right-click the **Default Domain Policy** GPO and then click **Copy**.
3. To create a copy of the GPO on the same domain, right-click **Group Policy Objects**, and select **Paste**. Accept the default permissions under **Specify the permissions for the new GPO**, and then click **Ok**.
4. To create a copy of the GPO in a different domain, double-click the destination domain, right-click Group Policy objects, and then click Paste. Answer all the questions in the cross-domain copying wizard, and then click **Finish**.

6.3.1 Create and configure Migration Table

A migration table is used to copy or import a Group Policy object (GPO) from one domain or forest to another. The key challenge when migrating Group Policy objects (GPOs) from one domain or forest to another is that some information in the GPO is actually specific to the domain or forest where the GPO is defined. When transferring the GPO to a new domain or forest, it may not always be desirable, or even possible, to use the same settings. A migration table references users, groups, computers, and UNC paths in the source GPO to new values in the destination GPO.

Migration table is created using the Migration Table Editor. The Migration Table Editor is accessed by right clicking **Group Policy Objects** Container in Group Policy Management Console. Migration table editor scans GPOs or backup GPOs, extracts all references to security principals and UNC paths, and automatically enter these items in the migration table as source name entries.

To automatically populate a migration table from a GPO

1. Open the migration table editor.
2. From the Tools menu, click Populate from GPO.
3. On the Look in this domain drop-down list, select the domain that contains the GPO.
4. On the Group Policy objects list, click the Default Domain Policy GPO. To populate the migration table, select Include security principals from the DACL on the GPO during scan if appropriate, then click Ok.

To automatically populate a migration table from a backup GPO

1. Open the migration table editor.

2. From the Tools menu, click Populate from Backup.
3. In the **Backup location** drop-down box, type the path of the **GPOBackup** folder that contains the backup GPO, or click **Browse** to locate the folder.
4. In the Backed up GPOs list, select Default Domain Policy GPO, select Show only the latest version of each GPO and Include security principals from the DACL on the GPO, and then click Ok.

To create a migration table

1. Log on to 70411SRV and open Group Policy Management Console.
2. Expand Forest: 70411Lab.com\Domains\70411Lab.com.
3. To create a migration table:
   a) Right-click Group Policy Objects Container and click Open Migration Table Editor.
   b) To Automatically populate source:
      i) From the **Tools** menu, click **Populate from Backup** (You can also populate from GPO).
      ii) On the **Backup Location**, ensure that E:\GPOBackup is selected, then highlight **Default Domain Policy** and click **Ok**.
4. Click **File**, and then click **Save**.
5. Save the migration table to E:\GPOMigrationtable\70411Lab.

6.3.2 Reset default GPOs

It is recommended not to modify the default domain policy or default domain controller policy unless necessary. Instead of modifying these default GPOs, create a new GPO at the domain level and set it to override the default settings in the default policies. If these default GPOs are modified, the default values can be restored using DCGPOFIX.exe command line tool. The DCGPOFIX.exe command restores the Default Domain Policy and Default Domain Controller Policy GPO's to default.

To Reset Default Domain Policy and Default Domain Controller Policy

1. Open and elevated command prompt and type DCGPOFIX.exe.
2. At the confirmation prompt, type **Y,** confirm the reset by entering **Y** again

Note

To reset the Domain GPO, type dcgpofix /target:Domain.
To reset the Default Domain Controller GPO, type dcgpofix /target:DC
To reset both the Domain and Default Domain Controller GPOs, type dcgpofix /target:both

6.3.3 Delegate Group Policy management

In Active Directory, administrators are automatically granted permissions for performing different Group Policy management tasks. Other individuals can be granted such permissions through delegation. The following Group Policy tasks can delegated:

1. Creating GPOs (Only available on the Group Policy Objects Container).
2. Managing individual GPOs (for example, granting Edit or Read access to a GPO).
3. Performing the following tasks on sites, domains, and OUs:
   a) Managing Group Policy links for a given site, domain, or OU.
   b) Performing Group Policy Modelling analyses for objects in that container (not applicable for sites).
   c) Reading Group Policy Results data for objects in that container (not applicable for sites).
4. Creating WMI filters.
5. Managing and editing individual WMI filters.

Note

Group Policy Permissions can be delegated as outlined below:

On Domains and OUs: Link GPOs, Perform Group Policy Modelling Analysis, and Read Group Policy Result Data.

On Sites: Link GPOs (Perform Group Policy Modelling Analysis, and Read Group Policy Result Data are not available on Sites container.)

On Group Policy Objects and Starter GPOs container: Create GPOs and Create Starter GPOs respectively.

On individual GPOs: Read, Edit Settings, Delete, and Modify.

On WMI Filters Container: Full Control, Creator Owner (Full Control required to add new WMI filters).

On individual WMI Filters: Full Control, Edit

To delegate Group Policy administrative tasks on a container

1. Log on to 70411SRV and open Group Policy Management Console.
2. Expand Forest: 70411Lab.com\Domains\70411Lab.com.
3. To delegate permission to the 70411Lab.com domain:
   a) Highlight **70411Lab.com,** and on the details pane, click **Delegation** tab.
   b) On the **Permission** drop-down, note the available permissions for delegation:
      i) Link GPOs.
      ii) Perform Group Policy Modelling Analysis.

        iii) Read Group Policy Result Data.

    c) Select **Link GPOs**, beneath **Groups and Users,** and note the options available for each Group or User:

        i) Permission can Apply To: This Container and All child containers or This Container Only.

        ii) Setting: Allow Or Deny.

    d) With 70411Lab.com domain still highlight:

        i) To modify permissions for existing users, click **Advanced.**

        ii) To grant permission to a new user or group, click **Add.**

        iii) On the search field, enter LinkGPO and click **Ok.** On the **Add Group or User** dialogue box, accept the default permission and click **Ok.**

4. To delegate **Create GPOs** permission:

        i) Highlight **Group Policy Objects** container, and on the details pane, click **Delegation** tab.

        ii) Beneath Groups and Users, click Add.

        iii) On the search field, enter Create GPOs and click **Ok.**

5. To delegate permission to the site:

    a) Expand **Sites** Container and highlight **Default-First-Site-Name**, on the details pane, click **Delegation** tab.

    b) On the **Permission** drop-down, note the available permissions for delegation: Link GPOs.

Exam Tip

Note that for Site permission delegation, the only available option is **Link GPOs**.

6.4 Configure Group Policy Preferences

Introduction

Group Policy preferences; include more than 20 new Group Policy extensions that expand the range of configurable settings within a Group Policy object (GPO). These new extensions are included in the Group Policy Management Editor window of the Group Policy Management Console (GPMC), under the Preferences item (located right under Computer or User Configuration). Examples of the new Group Policy preference extensions include folder options, mapped drives, printers, scheduled tasks, services, and Start menu settings.

Group Policy preferences provide better targeting, through item-level targeting and action modes. Additionally, rich user interfaces and standards-based XML configurations provide more power and flexibility over managed computers when you administer GPOs.

In addition to providing significantly more coverage, better targeting, and easier management, Group Policy preferences enable administrators to deploy settings to client computers without restricting the users from changing the settings. This capability provides the flexibility to decide which settings to enforce and which settings to not enforce. Settings that do not require enforcement can be deployed using Group Policy preferences.

In this section, we will cover following exam objectives:

6.4.0 Configure Group Policy preferences (GPP) settings

6.4.1 Configure item-level targeting

Lab Plan:

We will use 70411SRV (Domain Controller) for most tasks in this section.

Additional lab setup

Create a folder E:\GPPSCreate. Also create a new Security Group called **FolderMapGPPS** on the Users Container of Active Directory Users and Computers MMC.

6.4.0 Configure Group Policy preferences (GPP) settings

GPP Settings can be configured for a number of items but for the purposes of the exam, we will concentrate on the following items: Printers, network drive mappings, custom registry settings, Control Panel settings (Printers, power options, Internet Explorer settings), file and folder deployment, and shortcut deployment. GPP settings are available on both the Computers and Users container.

To Configure Group Policy preferences (GPP) settings

1. Log on to 70411SRV and open Group Policy Management Console.
2. Expand Forest: 70411Lab.com\Domains\70411Lab.com.
3. Right-click **Default Domain Policy** and select **Edit**.
4. Expand Computer Configuration\Preferences\Windows Settings.
5. To configure settings for: Custom registry settings, file and folder deployment, and shortcut deployment:
   a) Right-click **Registry** point to **New,** note the available options:
      i)   Registry Item
      ii) Collection Item and
      iii) Registry Wizard
   b) Select **Registry Wizard**. On the Registry Browser wizard, select **Local Computer** and click **Next**.
   c) Check the box beside **HKEY_LOCAL_MACHINE** and click **Finish**.
   d) Right-click **Folder** point to **New**, then select **Folder**.
   e) On the **Action** drop-down, note the available actions:
      i)   Update (Default)
      ii) Create
      iii) Replace
      iv) Delete
   f) On the **Action** drop-down, select **Create**
   g) On the **Path** field, enter E:\GPPS and click **Ok.**
   h) Repeat the same process to deploy files and shortcuts.
6. To Configure Control Panel settings:
   a) Expand User Configuration\Preferences\Windows Settings\Control Panel settings.
   b) Right-click Printers (Also available on the Computer Configuration node), point to New, note the available options:
      i)   Shared Printer
      ii) TCP/IP Printer
      iii) Local Printer

Note

Computer Configuration node for printers does not have option to create a shared printer. Drive Mapping is only available under User Configurations.

    c)   Select **Local Printer** and complete the following tasks:
        i)   On the **Name** field, enter **GPPSPrinter.**
        ii) On the **Port field,** select LPT1:
        iii) On the **Path** field, enter \\70411SRV
    d)   When you finish, click **Ok.**
    e)   Right-click Power Options, point to **New,** and note the available options:
        i)   Power Options (Windows XP)
        ii) Power Scheme (Windows XP)
        iii) Power Plan (At least Windows 7)
    f)   Select Power Plan (At least Windows 7) and click **Ok.**
7. To configure Drive Mappings:
    a)   Expand User Configuration\Preferences\Windows Settings\.
    b)   Right-click **Drive Maps**, point to **New**, then select **Mapped Drive**.
    c)   On the **Action** drop-down, select **Update**.
    d)   On the **Location** field enter \\70411srv\sysvol.
    e)   On the **Drive Letter** box, select **Use First Available**, **Starting at**: Then select **N** from the drop-down.
    f)   When you finish, click **Ok.**

6.4.1 Configure item-level targeting

Item-level targeting changes the scope of individual preference items to apply only to selected users or computers. Within a single Group Policy object (GPO), multiple preference items may be included, each customized for selected users or computers and each targeted to apply settings only to the relevant users or computers.

In the task below, you will configure the mapped drive in the previous section to apply only to the **FolderMapGPPS** security group.

To Configure item-level targeting

1. Expand User Configuration\Preferences\Windows Settings\ and highlight **Drive Maps**.
2. On the details pane, double-click N:\ (The drive mapped in the previous section) and click the **Common** tab.
3. Check the box beside **item-level targeting** and click **Targeting.**
4. On the **Targeting Editor** window, click **New Item** and select **Security Group** from the list.
5. Beside the **Group** field, click the grey box and on the Group search box, enter **FolderMapGPPS** then click **Ok.**

6. On the Targeting Editor window, check the Primary Group box, and either select User in Group or Computer in group.
7. Click **Ok** twice.

Note

A Security Group targeting item allows a preference item to be applied to Computers or Users only if the processing computer or user is a member of the group specified in the targeting item and optionally only of the specified group is the primary group for the processing computer or user

Exam Tip

For the purpose of the exam, it is very important to understand the use of the cmdlets and commands listed below:

GpFixUp: Fix domain name dependencies in Group Policy Objects and Group Policy links after a domain rename operation.
Import-GPO: Imports the Group Policy settings from a backed-up GPO into a specified GPO.
Backup-GPO: Backs up one GPO or all the GPOs in a domain.
Restore-GPO: Restores one GPO or all GPOs in a domain from one or more GPO backup files.
Get-GPOReport: Generates a report in either XML or HTML format that describes properties and policy settings for a specified GPO or for all GPOs in a domain.
GPResult: Displays the Resultant Set of Policy (RSoP) information for a remote user and computer.
Set-GPInheritance: Blocks or unblocks inheritance for a specified domain or organizational unit.
GPUpdate: Refreshes local and Active Directory-based Group Policy settings, including security settings.
Dcgpofix: Recreates the default Group Policy Objects (GPOs) for a domain.
Set-GPPermission: Grants a level of permissions to a security principal for one GPO or all the GPOs in a domain.
ADD-ADGroupMember: Add one or more members to an Active Directory group.
Gpedit.msc: Opens Group Policy Editor.
Set-GPLink: Sets the properties of the specified GPO link.

Note From The Author

Well done! You have gone through all the objectives for exam 70-411. I am confident that you have also picked up hands-on skills to administer Windows Server 2012 R2. You are on your way to accomplishing your goal of passing exam 70-411 in one shot. I would like to make four requests:

1. Think of ways in which you can apply the skills gained on your job.
2. Please visit Amazon's website to provide a review.
3. Tell your Facebook, LinkedIn friends and colleagues about this book.
4. Sign up to my blog – www.iTechguides.com/blog for post on Active Directory, PowerShell scripting and Windows Server Administration.

Good Luck with your exam and career!

References

Microsoft Technet (No Date) *Managing WSUS from the Command Line* [Online], Microsoft Technet. Available: http://technet.microsoft.com/en-us/library/cc720466(v=ws.10).aspx [Accessed 11 June 2014].

Microsoft Technet (Updated: October 17, 2013) *Windows Server Update Services Cmdlets in Windows PowerShell* [Online], Microsoft Technet. Available: http://technet.microsoft.com/en-us/library/hh826166.aspx [Accessed 11 June 2014].

Microsoft Technet (Updated: October 20, 2013) *DISM Operating System Package Servicing Command-Line Options* [Online], Microsoft Technet. Available: http://technet.microsoft.com/en-us/library/hh825265.aspx [Accessed 11 June 2014].

Microsoft Technet (Updated: October 20, 2013) *Enable or Disable Windows Features Using DISM* [Online], Microsoft Technet. Available: http://technet.microsoft.com/en-us/library/hh824822.aspx [Accessed 11 June 2014].

Microsoft Technet (Updated: October 20, 2013) *Service a Mounted Windows Image* [Online], Microsoft Technet. Available: http://technet.microsoft.com/en-us/library/hh825224.aspx [Accessed 11 June 2014].

Microsoft Technet (Updated: April 18, 2014) *Add and Remove Drivers Offline Using DISM* [Online], Microsoft Technet. Available: http://technet.microsoft.com/en-us/library/hh825070.aspx [Accessed 11 June 2014].

Microsoft Technet (No Date) *Data Collector Set Properties* [Online], Microsoft Technet. Available: http://technet.microsoft.com/en-us/library/cc749267.aspx [Accessed 11 June 2014].

Microsoft Technet (Updated: May 18, 2009) *Resource Availability Troubleshooting Getting Started Guide* [Online], Microsoft Technet. Available: http://technet.microsoft.com/en-us/library/dd883276(v=ws.10).aspx [Accessed 11 June 2014].

Justin (December 31, 2012) *Resource Monitor on Windows Server 2008R2 and 2012* [Online], Rackspace. Available: https://community.rackspace.com/products/f/25/t/420 [Accessed 11 June 2014].

Tony Voellm (April 22, 2009) *Monitoring Hyper-V Performance* [Online], Microsoft MSDN. Available: http://blogs.msdn.com/b/tvoellm/archive/2009/04/23/monitoring-hyper-v-performance.aspx [Accessed 11 June 2014].

Microsoft MSDN (No Date) *Measuring Performance on Hyper-V* [Online], Microsoft MSDN. Available: http://msdn.microsoft.com/en-us/library/cc768535%28v=bts.10%29.aspx [Accessed 11 June 2014].

Tony Voellm (December 18, 2009) *Hyper-V Performance FAQ R2* [Online], Microsoft   MSDN.   Available: http://blogs.msdn.com/b/tvoellm/archive/2009/12/18/hyper-v-performance-faq-r2.aspx [Accessed 11 June 2014].

Wikipedia (No Date) *Hyper-V* [Online], Wikipedia. Available: http://en.wikipedia.org/wiki/Hyper-V [Accessed 11 June 2014].

Microsoft Technet (No Date) *Event Subscriptions* [Online], Microsoft Technet. Available: http://technet.microsoft.com/en-us/library/cc749183.aspx [Accessed 11 June 2014].

Microsoft Technet (No Date) *Configure Computers to Forward and Collect Events* [Online], Microsoft Technet. Available: http://technet.microsoft.com/en-us/library/cc748890.aspx [Accessed 11 June 2014].

Microsoft Technet (No Date) *Create a New Subscription* [Online], Microsoft Technet.   Available: http://technet.microsoft.com/en-us/library/cc722010.aspx [Accessed 11 June 2014].

Microsoft MSDN (No Date) *Event Tracing Sessions* [Online], Microsoft MSDN. Available: http://msdn.microsoft.com/en-us/library/windows/desktop/aa363881(v=vs.85).aspx [Accessed 11 June 2014].

www.1ask2.com (No Date) *Event Trace Sessions and Startup Event Trace Sessions* [Online],   www.1ask2.com.   Available: http://www.1ask2.com/Windows7/Data%20Collector%20Sets.htm [Accessed 11 June 2014].

www.enduria.eu (No Date) *Key Performance Counters and their thresholds for Windows   Server*   [Online],   www.enduria.eu.   Available: http://www.enduria.eu/key-performance-counters-and-their-thresholds-for-windows-server-recommended-by-microsoft/ [Accessed 12 June 2014].

Microsoft Technet (Updated: February 25, 2010) *Staging folders and Conflict and Deleted   folders*   [Online],   Microsoft   Technet.   Available: http://technet.microsoft.com/en-us/library/cc782648(v=ws.10).aspx [Accessed 12 June 2014].Microsoft Technet (Updated: October 17, 2013) *DFS Namespace (DFSN) Cmdlets in Windows PowerShell* [Online], Microsoft Technet. Available: http://technet.microsoft.com/en-us/library/jj884270.aspx [Accessed 12 June 2014].

Microsoft Technet (Updated: November 20, 2013) *Export a Clone of the DFS Replication   Database*   [Online],   Microsoft   Technet.   Available: http://technet.microsoft.com/en-us/library/dn482443.aspx [Accessed 12 June 2014].

NedPyle (July 31, 2013) *DFS Replication in Windows Server 2012 R2: Revenge of the Sync*   [Online],   Microsoft   Technet.   Available: http://blogs.technet.com/b/filecab/archive/2013/07/31/dfs-replication-in-windows-server-2012-r2-revenge-of-the-sync.aspx [Accessed 12 June 2014].

Microsoft Technet (Updated: December 12, 2013) *DFS Replication: Copying Files to Preseed or Stage Initial Synchronization* [Online], Microsoft Technet. Available: http://technet.microsoft.com/en-us/library/dn495052.aspx [Accessed 12 June 2014].

www.arstechnica.com (January 29, 2009) *DFS-R: How do you know when an initial replication is done?* [Online], www.arstechnica.com. Available: http://arstechnica.com/civis/viewtopic.php?t=71768 [Accessed 12 June 2014].

Microsoft Technet (Published: June 3, 2009) *Enable Access-Based Enumeration on a Namespace* [Online], Microsoft Technet. Available: http://technet.microsoft.com/en-us/library/dd919212(v=ws.10).aspx [Accessed 12 June 2014].

Kyle Beckman (March 15, 2013) *File Server Resource Manager (FSRM) 1-7* [Online], 4sysops.com. Available: http://4sysops.com/archives/file-server-resource-manager-fsrm-part-1-install-frsm/ [Accessed 12 June 2014].

Microsoft Technet (Updated: June 24, 2013) *File Server Resource Manager Overview* [Online], Microsoft Technet. Available: http://technet.microsoft.com/library/dffba8a6-f9a8-4692-b043-63effb043ea3 [Accessed 12 June 2014].

John Joyner (January 15, 2013) *DIY SAN: Windows Server 2012 Storage Spaces and iSCSI target* [Online], www.techrepublic.com. Available: http://www.techrepublic.com/blog/data-center/diy-san-windows-server-2012-storage-spaces-and-iscsi-target/ [Accessed 12 June 2014].

Microsoft Technet (Updated: May 1, 2008) *Encrypting File System* [Online], Microsoft Technet. Available: http://technet.microsoft.com/en-us/library/cc749610%28v=WS.10%29.aspx [Accessed 12 June 2014].

Microsoft Technet (Updated: August 21, 2013) *BitLocker Overview* [Online], Microsoft Technet. Available: http://technet.microsoft.com/en-us/library/hh831713.aspx [Accessed 12 June 2014].

Microsoft Technet (Updated: July 3, 2013) *Security Auditing Overview* [Online], Microsoft Technet. Available: http://technet.microsoft.com/en-us/library/dn319078.aspx [Accessed 12 June 2014].

Microsoft Technet (No Date) *Encrypting File System* [Online], Microsoft Technet. Available: http://technet.microsoft.com/en-us/library/cc960620.aspx [Accessed 12 June 2014].

SBS Bloggers (March 9, 2010) *Help Secure your Business Information using Encrypting File System* [Online], Microsoft Technet. Available: http://blogs.technet.com/b/sbs/archive/2010/03/09/help-secure-your-business-information-using-encrypting-file-system.aspx [Accessed 12 June 2014].

Microsoft (No Date) *What's the difference between BitLocker Drive Encryption and Encrypting File System?* [Online], windows.microsoft.com. Available: http://windows.microsoft.com/en-gb/windows7/whats-the-difference-

between-bitlocker-drive-encryption-and-encrypting-file-system [Accessed 12 June 2014].
Microsoft Technet (Updated: November 11, 2009) *Using Smart Cards with BitLocker* [Online], Microsoft Technet. Available: http://technet.microsoft.com/en-us/library/dd875530(WS.10).aspx [Accessed 12 June 2014].
Serdar Yegulalp (June 21, 2011) *How to Encrypt your Windows 7 Hard Disk with BitLocker* [Online], www.networkcomputing.com. Available: http://www.networkcomputing.com/storage/how-to-encrypt-your-windows-7-hard-disk-with-bitlocker/d/d-id/1098451 [Accessed 12 June 2014].
Brian Westover (April 8, 2013) *How to Uninstall Windows 8, Install Windows 7 on Your PC* [Online], www.pcmag.com. Available: http://www.pcmag.com/article2/0,2817,2417361,00.asp [Accessed 12 June 2014].
Timothy Warner (May 3, 2013) *Security Auditing Enhancements in Windows Server 2012* [Online], 4sysops.com. Available: http://4sysops.com/archives/security-auditing-enhancements-in-windows-server-2012/ [Accessed 12 June 2014].
Microsoft Technet (Updated: November 11, 2009) *BitLocker: Use BitLocker Drive Encryption Tools to manage BitLocker* [Online], Microsoft Technet. Available: http://technet.microsoft.com/en-us/library/dd875530(WS.10).aspx [Accessed 12 June 2014].mszCool [mario] (February 3, 2010) *BitLocker: Bitlocker in a Windows 7 Guest running on a Hyper-V R2 environment (or any environment without a TPM)* [Online], Microsoft MSDN. Available: http://blogs.msdn.com/b/mszcool/archive/2010/02/03/bitlocker-in-a-windows-7-guest-running-on-a-hyper-v-r2-environment-or-any-environment-without-a-tpm.aspx [Accessed 12 June 2014].
Stanford IT Services (Modified: April 19, 2013) *Enable BitLocker* [Online], Stanford IT Services. Available: https://itservices.stanford.edu/service/encryption/wholedisk/bitlocker [Accessed 12 June 2014].
Microsoft (No Date) *What Group Policy settings are used with BitLocker?* [Online], windows.microsoft.com. Available: http://windows.microsoft.com/en-GB/windows7/what-group-policy-settings-are-used-with-bitlocker [Accessed 12 June 2014].
Microsoft Technet (Updated: October, 2012) *BitLocker Group Policy settings* [Online], Microsoft Technet. Available: http://technet.microsoft.com/fr-fr/library/jj679890.aspx [Accessed 12 June 2014].
Alan Burchill (January 9, 2010) *Best Practice: How to configure Group Policy to use Data Recovery Agents with "Bitlocker to Go" drives – Part 2* [Online], www.grouppolicy.biz. Available: http://www.grouppolicy.biz/tag/data-recovery-agent/ [Accessed 12 June 2014].

Microsoft (No Date) *Create a recovery certificate for encrypted files* [Online], windows.microsoft.com. Available: http://windows.microsoft.com/en-gb/windows/create-encrypted-files-recovery-certificate#1TC=windows-7 [Accessed 12 June 2014].

Microsoft MSDN (May 5, 2014) *Apply Updates to an Image Using DISM (Standard 7 SP1)* [Online], Microsoft MSDN. Available: http://msdn.microsoft.com/en-us/library/ff794819(v=winembedded.60).aspx [Accessed 12 June 2014].

Brian Hill (December 8, 2009) *How to build and maintain a tiered WSUS infrastructure* [Online], www.arstechnica.com. Available: http://arstechnica.com/business/2009/12/how-to-implement-and-maintain-a-tiered-wsus-infrastructure/ [Accessed 12 June 2014].

John Mueller (No Date) *Using AuditPol to audit Windows users and set policies* [Online], Wiley Publishing. Available: http://searchitchannel.techtarget.com/feature/Using-AuditPol-to-audit-Windows-users-and-set-policies [Accessed 12 June 2014].

safaribooksonline.com (No Date) *Use of Auditpol.exe to Configure Auditing* [Online], safaribooksonline.com. Available: http://my.safaribooksonline.com/book/certification/mcts/9780768686005/auditing-of-active-directory-services/ch07lev2sec7 [Accessed 12 June 2014].

Microsoft Technet (No Date) *DNS Overview* [Online], Microsoft Technet. Available: http://technet.microsoft.com/en-us/library/cc730775%28v=WS.10%29.aspx [Accessed 12 June 2014].

Microsoft Technet (No Date) *Set Aging and Scavenging Properties for the DNS Server* [Online], Microsoft Technet. Available: http://technet.microsoft.com/en-us/library/cc753217.aspx [Accessed 12 June 2014].

Microsoft Technet (No Date) *Adding Zones* [Online], Microsoft Technet. Available: http://technet.microsoft.com/en-us/library/cc754386(v=ws.10).aspx [Accessed 12 June 2014].

Microsoft Technet (No Date) *Understanding Forwarders* [Online], Microsoft Technet. Available: http://technet.microsoft.com/en-us/library/cc730756(v=ws.10).aspx [Accessed 12 June 2014].

Microsoft Technet (No Date) *Create a Zone Delegation* [Online], Microsoft Technet. Available: http://technet.microsoft.com/en-us/library/cc753500.aspx [Accessed 12 June 2014].

Microsoft Support (No Date) *Explanation of a DNS Zone Transfer* [Online], Microsoft Support. Available: http://support.microsoft.com/kb/164017 [Accessed 12 June 2014].

Microsoft Support (No Date) *Description of the DNS SRV Resource Record Type* [Online], Microsoft Support. Available: http://support.microsoft.com/kb/232025 [Accessed 12 June 2014].

Wikipedia.org (No Date) *SRV record* [Online], Wikipedia.org. Available: http://en.wikipedia.org/wiki/SRV_record [Accessed 12 June 2014].

Microsoft Technet (Updated: January 21, 2005) *Configuring round robin* [Online], Microsoft Technet. Available: http://technet.microsoft.com/en-us/library/cc787484(v=ws.10).aspx [Accessed 12 June 2014].

www.dummies.com (No Date) *Implementing Remote Access and Virtual Private Networks* [Online], www.dummies.com. Available: http://www.dummies.com/how-to/content/implementing-remote-access-and-virtual-private-net.html [Accessed 12 June 2014].

Microsoft Technet (Updated: August 26, 2013) *Installing and Configuring Web Application Proxy for Publishing Internal Applications* [Online], Microsoft Technet. Available: http://technet.microsoft.com/en-us/library/dn383650.aspx#BKMK_KI [Accessed 12 June 2014].

NedPyle (June 19, 2008) *Custom Certificate Request in Windows Vista* [Online], Microsoft Technet. Available: http://blogs.technet.com/b/askds/archive/2008/06/19/custom-certificate-request-in-windows-vista.aspx [Accessed 12 June 2014].

Microsoft Technet (No Date) *Enable RRAS as a LAN and WAN Router* [Online], Microsoft Technet. Available: http://technet.microsoft.com/en-us/library/dd458974.aspx [Accessed 12 June 2014].

Microsoft Technet (Updated: February 12, 2014) *Design Your DNS Infrastructure for DirectAccess* [Online], Microsoft Technet. Available: http://technet.microsoft.com/en-us/library/ee382323(v=ws.10).aspx [Accessed 12 June 2014].

Microsoft Corporation (August, 2012) *Test Lab Guide: Demonstrate DirectAccess Simplified Setup in an IPv4-only Test Environment in Windows Server 2012* [Online], Microsoft Corporation. Available: http://www.microsoft.com/en-us/download/details.aspx?id=29029 [Accessed 12 June 2014].

Microsoft Technet (Updated: February 12, 2014) *Overview of Routing and Remote Access* [Online], Microsoft Technet. Available: http://technet.microsoft.com/en-us/library/cc732635(v=ws.10).aspx [Accessed 12 June 2014].

Microsoft Technet (No Date) *Routing and Remote Access* [Online], Microsoft Technet. Available: http://technet.microsoft.com/en-us/library/cc731671(v=ws.10).aspx [Accessed 12 June 2014].

Microsoft Technet (Updated: October 1, 2009) *Design Packet Filtering for DirectAccess* [Online], Microsoft Technet. Available: http://technet.microsoft.com/en-us/library/ee382294(v=ws.10).aspx [Accessed 12 June 2014].

Mark Morowczynski [MSFT] (August 19, 2013) *How To Setup Your Own Direct Access Lab With Windows Server 2012* [Online], Microsoft Technet. Available: http://blogs.technet.com/b/askpfeplat/archive/2013/08/19/how-to-setup-your-own-direct-access-lab-with-windows-server-2012.aspx   [Accessed 12 June 2014].

Syscomlab (September 21, 2012) *DirectAccess for Windows Server 2012 Installation & Configuration* [Online], Syscomlab. Available: http://syscomlab.blog.com/2012/09/directaccess-for-windows-server-2012-guide/ [Accessed 12 June 2014].

Syscomlab (September 24, 2012) *How to get Windows 7 to work with DirectAccess Server 2012* [Online], Syscomlab. Available: http://syscomlab.blog.com/2012/09/how-to-get-windows-7-to-work-with-directaccess-server-2012/ [Accessed 12 June 2014].

Brajesh Panda (March 10, 2013) *Windows 2012 Direct Access – Windows 8 Client Testing* [Online], techontip. Available: http://techontip.wordpress.com/2013/03/10/windows-2012-direct-access-windows-8-client-testing/ [Accessed 12 June 2014].

Microsoft Technet (March 29, 2012) *Deploy a CA and NPS Server Certificate* [Online], Microsoft Technet. Available: http://technet.microsoft.com/en-US/library/cc730811.aspx [Accessed 12 June 2014].

Microsoft Technet (Updated: February 29, 2012) *Administering NPS* [Online], Microsoft Technet. Available: http://technet.microsoft.com/en-us/library/cc754554(v=ws.10).aspx [Accessed 12 June 2014].

Microsoft Technet (Updated: February 29, 2012) *Network Policy Server* [Online], Microsoft Technet. Available: http://technet.microsoft.com/en-us/library/cc732912.aspx [Accessed 12 June 2014].

Microsoft Technet (Updated: November 7, 2013) *Network Policy and Access Services Overview* [Online], Microsoft Technet. Available: http://technet.microsoft.com/library/hh831683.aspx [Accessed 12 June 2014].

Microsoft Technet (Updated: February 29, 2012) *Install a NAP Health Policy Server* [Online], Microsoft Technet. Available: http://technet.microsoft.com/en-us/library/dd296890(v=ws.10).aspx [Accessed 12 June 2014].

Microsoft Corporation (No Date) *Network Policy Server (NPS) Operations Guide* [Online], Microsoft Corporation. Available: http://www.microsoft.com/en-us/download/details.aspx?id=16417 [Accessed 12 June 2014].

Microsoft Technet (No Date) *Configuring NAP on the Network Policy Server (NPS)* [Online], Microsoft Technet. Available: http://technet.microsoft.com/en-us/library/dd182017.aspx [Accessed 12 June 2014].

Deb Shinder (February 27, 2013) *Understanding and Configuring Network Policy and Access Services in Server 2012 (Part 1)* [Online], www.windowsecurity.com. Available: http://www.windowsecurity.com/articles-tutorials/Windows_Server_2012_Security/understanding-configuring-network-policy-access-services-server-2012-part1.html   [Accessed 12 June 2014].

Deb Shinder (March 13, 2013) *Understanding and Configuring Network Policy and Access Services in Server 2012 (Part 2)* [Online], www.windowsecurity.com. Available: http://www.windowsecurity.com/articles-tutorials/Windows_Server_2012_Security/understanding-configuring-network-policy-access-services-server-2012-part2.html   [Accessed 12 June 2014].

Deb Shinder (March 27, 2013) *Understanding and Configuring Network Policy and Access Services in Server 2012 (Part 3)* [Online], www.windowsecurity.com. Available: http://www.windowsecurity.com/articles-tutorials/Windows_Server_2012_Security/understanding-configuring-network-policy-access-services-server-2012-part3.html   [Accessed 12 June 2014].

Microsoft Technet (Updated: March 29, 2012) *Health Registration Authority* [Online], Microsoft Technet. Available: http://technet.microsoft.com/en-us/library/cc732365.aspx [Accessed 13 June 2014].

Microsoft Technet (Updated: March 29, 2012) *Network Access Protection in NPS* [Online], Microsoft Technet. Available: http://technet.microsoft.com/en-us/library/cc754378.aspx [Accessed 13 June 2014].

Microsoft Technet (Updated: October 21, 2008) *Load Balancing with NPS Proxy* [Online], Microsoft Technet. Available: http://technet.microsoft.com/en-us/library/dd197433(v=ws.10).aspx [Accessed 13 June 2014].

Microsoft Technet (No Date) *Checklist: Configure NAP Enforcement for DHCP* [Online], Microsoft Technet. Available: http://technet.microsoft.com/en-us/library/cc772356(v=ws.10).aspx [Accessed 13 June 2014].

Microsoft Technet (No Date) *Checklist: Configure NAP Enforcement for VPN* [Online], Microsoft Technet. Available: http://technet.microsoft.com/en-us/library/cc770422(v=ws.10).aspx [Accessed 13 June 2014].

Microsoft Technet (No Date) *Network Policy Settings Properties* [Online], Microsoft Technet. Available: http://technet.microsoft.com/en-us/library/cc772474(v=ws.10).aspx [Accessed 13 June 2014].

Microsoft Technet (Updated: June 27, 2012) *Service Accounts Step-by-Step Guide* [Online], Microsoft Technet. Available: http://technet.microsoft.com/en-us/library/dd548356(v=ws.10).aspx [Accessed 13 June 2014].

Doug Symalla (December 16, 2012) *Windows Server 2012: Group Managed Service Accounts* [Online], Microsoft Technet. Available: http://blogs.technet.com/b/askpfeplat/archive/2012/12/17/windows-server-2012-group-managed-service-accounts.aspx [Accessed 13 June 2014].

Microsoft Technet (Updated: August 22, 205) *Create a Service Account* [Online], Microsoft Technet. Available: http://technet.microsoft.com/en-us/library/cc739458(v=ws.10).aspx [Accessed 13 June 2014].

itfreetraining (August 21, 2012) *MCITP 70-640: Service Accounts* [Online], www.youtube.com.   Available: https://www.youtube.com/watch?v=wHa_eh96UHg   [Accessed 13 June 2014].

Per Nygaard (May 03, 2011) *Authentication and Authorization* [Online], Microsoft   MSDN.   Available: http://blogs.msdn.com/b/autz_auth_stuff/archive/2011/05/03/kerberos-delegation.aspx [Accessed 13 June 2014].

Sonoma Partners (April 12, 2007) *Kerberos and Delegation Tips* [Online], Sonoma Partners.   Available: http://blog.sonomapartners.com/2007/04/kerberos_and_de.html [Accessed 13 June 2014].

Rhys Goodwin (No Date) *Active Directory and Kermsberos SPNs Made Easy!* [Online],   rhysgoodwin.com.   Available: http://blog.rhysgoodwin.com/windows-admin/active-directory-and-kerberos-spns-made-easy/ [Accessed 13 June 2014].

Microsoft MSDN (No Date) *Service Principal Names* [Online], Microsoft MSDN.   Available: http://msdn.microsoft.com/en-us/library/ms677949(v=vs.85).aspx [Accessed 12 June 2014].

Microsoft Technet (No Date) *Service Principal Names* [Online], Microsoft Technet.   Available: http://technet.microsoft.com/en-us/library/cc961723.aspx [Accessed 13 June 2014].

Microsoft Technet (Updated: August 31, 2012) *Setspn* [Online], Microsoft Technet.   Available: http://technet.microsoft.com/en-us/library/cc731241.aspx [Accessed 16 June 2014].

Microsoft Technet (Updated: October 15, 2008) *Enabling Universal Group Membership Caching in a Site* [Online], Microsoft Technet. Available: http://technet.microsoft.com/en-us/library/cc816797(v=ws.10).aspx [Accessed 16 June 2014].

Microsoft Technet (Updated: October 17, 2012) *Group Managed Service Accounts Overview*   [Online],   Microsoft   Technet.   Available: http://technet.microsoft.com/en-us/library/hh831782.aspx   [Accessed 16 June 2014].

Naresh Man Maharjan (October 30, 2012) *Migrating Active Directory Domain Controller from Windows Server 2008 R2 to Windows Server 2012* [Online], MS Server Pro.   Available: http://www.msserverpro.com/migrating-active-directory-domain-controller-from-windows-server-2008-r2-to-windows-server-2012/ [Accessed 16 June 2014].

Keith Mayer [MSFT] (August 6, 2012) *Virtualization-safe Technology and Domain Controller Cloning* [Online], Microsoft Technet. Available: http://blogs.technet.com/b/keithmayer/archive/2012/08/06/safely-cloning-an-active-directory-domain-controller-with-windows-server-2012-step-by-step-ws2012-hyperv-itpro-vmware.aspx#.UnpMPtLwn3s [Accessed 16 June 2014].

Tom Moser [MSFT] (October 1, 2012) *Virtual Domain Controller Cloning in Windows Server 2012* [Online], Microsoft Technet. Available: http://blogs.technet.com/b/askpfeplat/archive/2012/10/01/virtual-domain-controller-cloning-in-windows-server-2012.aspx [Accessed 16 June 2014].

Microsoft Support (No Date) *How to force an authoritative and non-authoritative synchronization for DFSR-replicated SYSVOL (like "D4/D2" for FRS)* [Online], Microsoft Support. Available: http://support.microsoft.com/kb/2218556 [Accessed 16 June 2014].

kpytko.pl (No Date) *Authoritative SYSVOL restore (DFS-R)* [Online], kpytko.pl. Available: http://kpytko.pl/2013/12/13/authoritative-sysvol-restore-dfs-r/ [Accessed 16 June 2014].

kpytko.pl (No Date) *Non-authoritative SYSVOL restore (DFS-R)* [Online], kpytko.pl. Available: http://kpytko.pl/2013/12/13/authoritative-sysvol-restore-dfs-r/ [Accessed 16 June 2014].

Microsoft Technet (Updated: October 15, 2008) *Introduction to Administering DFS-Replicated SYSVOL* [Online], Microsoft Technet. Available: http://technet.microsoft.com/en-us/library/cc794837(v=ws.10).aspx [Accessed 16 June 2014].

Tech-faq (No Date) *How to Maintain Active Directory* [Online], Tech-faq. Available: http://www.tech-faq.com/how-to-maintain-active-directory.html [Accessed 16 June 2014].Brien Posey (January 8, 2009) *Defragmenting an Active Directory Database* [Online], www.petri.co.il. Available: http://www.petri.co.il/defragmenting-active-directory-database.htm# [Accessed 16 June 2014].

Microsoft Technet (August 31, 2007) *Reanimating Active Directory Tombstone Objects* [Online], Microsoft Technet. Available: http://blogs.technet.com/b/tnmag/archive/2007/08/31/reanimating-active-directory-tombstone-objects.aspx [Accessed 16 June 2014].

Kevin R. Sharp (August 2001) *Defragmenting the Active Directory object database* [Online], searchwindowsserver.techtarget.com. Available: http://searchwindowsserver.techtarget.com/tip/Defragmenting-the-Active-Directory-object-database [Accessed 16 June 2014].

Microsoft Technet (Updated: January 6, 2009) *Scenario Overview for Restoring Deleted Active Directory Objects* [Online], Microsoft Technet. Available: http://technet.microsoft.com/en-us/library/dd379542(v=ws.10).aspx [Accessed 16 June 2014].

John Marlin (July 18, 2013) *Introducing the Active Directory Recycle Bin in Windows Server 2012* [Online], windowsitpro.com. Available: http://windowsitpro.com/active-directory/windows-server-2012-active-directory-recycle-bin [Accessed 16 June 2014].

NedPyle [MSFT] (August 27, 2009) *The AD Recycle Bin: Understanding, Implementing, Best Practices, and Troubleshooting* [Online], Microsoft Technet. Available: http://blogs.technet.com/b/askds/archive/2009/08/27/the-ad-recycle-bin-understanding-implementing-best-practices-and-troubleshooting.aspx [Accessed 16 June 2014].

Brien Posey (October 2009) *Working with Active Directory snapshots in Windows Server 2008* [Online], searchwindowsserver.techtarget.com. Available: http://searchwindowsserver.techtarget.com/tip/Working-with-Active-Directory-snapshots-in-Windows-Server-2008 [Accessed 16 June 2014].

Microsoft Technet (February 4, 2009) *Active Directory Snapshot, new feature in Windows 2008* [Online], Microsoft Technet. Available: http://blogs.technet.com/b/niraj_kumar/archive/2009/02/05/active-directory-snapshot-new-feature-in-windows-2008.aspx [Accessed 16 June 2014].

Microsoft Technet (Updated: November 1, 2012) *Clean Up Server Metadata* [Online], Microsoft Technet. Available: http://technet.microsoft.com/en-us/library/cc816907(v=ws.10).aspx [Accessed 16 June 2014].

Naresh Man Maharjan (October 10, 2011) *Metadata Cleanup Using NTDSUTIL in Windows Server 2008 R2* [Online], www.msserverpro.com. Available: http://www.msserverpro.com/metadata-cleanup-using-ntdsutil-in-windows-server-2008-r2/ [Accessed 16 June 2014].

www.kurtdillard.com (No date) *Chapter 5: Maintaining the Active Directory Environment* [Online], www.kurtdillard.com. Available: http://www.kurtdillard.com/StudyGuides/70-640/5.html [Accessed 16 June 2014].

Microsoft Technet (Updated: October 15, 2008) *Administering Domain Controllers* [Online], Microsoft Technet. Available: http://technet.microsoft.com/en-us/library/cc794748(v=ws.10).aspx [Accessed 16 June 2014].

Microsoft Technet (Updated: April 8, 2013) *Running Domain Controllers in Hyper-V* [Online], Microsoft Technet. Available: http://technet.microsoft.com/en-us/library/virtual_active_directory_domain_controller_virtualization_hyperv(v=ws.10).aspx [Accessed 16 June 2014].

Jason Yoder (No Date) *Create a New Password Setting Object in Windows Server 2012* [Online], mctexpert.blogspot.co.uk. Available: http://mctexpert.blogspot.co.uk/2012/07/create-new-password-setting-object-in.html [Accessed 16 June 2014].

Microsoft Technet (Updated: August 20, 2012) *AD DS Fine-Grained Password and Account Lockout Policy Step-by-Step Guide* [Online], Microsoft Technet. Available: http://technet.microsoft.com/en-us/library/cc770842(v=ws.10).aspx [Accessed 16 June 2014].

Microsoft Technet (Updated: June 23, 2011) *Account Policies* [Online], Microsoft Technet. Available: http://technet.microsoft.com/en-us/library/dd349793(v=ws.10).aspx [Accessed 16 June 2014].

Web-foro.com (No Date) *PSO Precedence and Resultant PSO* [Online], Web-foro.com. Available: http://web-foro.com/wl/CompanionContent/course/crse6425b_00_09_01_08.htm [Accessed 16 June 2014].

Mate Ivanszky (May 9, 2012) *Step-by-Step Fine-Grained Password Policy in Windows 2008* [Online], www.showmehowtodoit.com. Available: http://www.showmehowtodoit.com/2012/step-by-step-fine-grained-password-policy-in-windows-2008/ [Accessed 16 June 2014].

Kyle Beckman (May 22, 2012) *Folder Redirection – Part 4: Group Policy configuration* [Online], 4sysops.com. Available: http://4sysops.com/archives/folder-redirection-part-4-group-policy-configuration/ [Accessed 16 June 2014].

Jeremy Moskowitz (No Date) *Inside ADM and ADMX Templates for Group Policy* [Online], Microsoft Technet. Available: http://technet.microsoft.com/en-gb/magazine/2008.01.layout.aspx [Accessed 16 June 2014].

Microsoft Technet (Updated: April 3, 2013) *Group Policy processing and precedence* [Online], Microsoft Technet. Available: http://technet.microsoft.com/en-us/library/cc785665(v=ws.10).aspx [Accessed 16 June 2014].

Microsoft Technet (Updated: April 7, 2003) *Group Policy Processing* [Online], Microsoft Technet. Available: http://technet.microsoft.com/en-us/library/cc758898(v=ws.10).aspx [Accessed 16 June 2014].

Srachui (February 13, 2012) *Group Policy Basics - Part 1: Understanding the Structure of a Group Policy Object* [Online], Microsoft Technet. Available: http://blogs.technet.com/b/musings_of_a_technical_tam/archive/2012/02/13/understanding-the-structure-of-a-group-policy-object.aspx [Accessed 16 June 2014].

Srachui (February 15, 2012) *Group Policy Basics - Part 2: Understanding Which GPOs to Apply* [Online], Microsoft Technet. Available: http://blogs.technet.com/b/musings_of_a_technical_tam/archive/2012/02/15/understanding-the-structure-of-a-group-policy-object-part-2.aspx [Accessed 16 June 2014].

Srachui (February 22, 2012) *Group Policy Basics - Part 3: How Clients Process GPOs* [Online], Microsoft Technet. Available: http://blogs.technet.com/b/musings_of_a_technical_tam/archive/2012/02/22/understanding-the-structure-of-a-group-policy-object-part-3.aspx [Accessed 16 June 2014].

Microsoft Technet (Updated: June 24, 2013) *Understand the Effect of Fast Logon Optimization and Fast Startup on Group Policy* [Online], Microsoft Technet.

Available: http://technet.microsoft.com/en-us/library/jj573586.aspx [Accessed 16 June 2014].

Srachui (February 27, 2012) *GPOs and Slow Link Detection* [Online], Microsoft Technet.   Available: http://blogs.technet.com/b/musings_of_a_technical_tam/archive/2012/02/ 27/gpos-and-slow-link-detection.aspx [Accessed 16 June 2014].

NedPyle [MSFT] (October 23, 2009) *Group Policy Slow Link Detection using Windows Vista and later* [Online], Microsoft Technet. Available: http://blogs.technet.com/b/askds/archive/2009/10/23/group-policy-slow-link-detection-using-windows-vista-and-later.aspx [Accessed 16 June 2014].

Darren Mar-Elia (No Date) *Understanding Group Policy Caching in Windows 8.1* [Online], sdmsoftware.com. Available: http://sdmsoftware.com/group-policy-blog/group-policy/understanding-group-policy-caching-in-windows-8-1/ [Accessed 16 June 2014].

Rod Trent (November, 10 2013) *Group Policy Caching in Windows Server 2012 R2* [Online], windowsitpro.com. Available: http://windowsitpro.com/windows-server-2012-r2/group-policy-caching-windows-server-2012-r2 [Accessed 16 June 2014].

Microsoft Technet (Updated: June 24, 2013) *Force a Remote Group Policy Refresh (GPUpdate)* [Online], Microsoft Technet. Available: http://technet.microsoft.com/en-us/library/jj134201.aspx [Accessed 16 June 2014].

searchwindowsserver (November, 2005) *Deploying security templates* [Online], searchwindowsserver.techtarget.com.   Available: http://searchwindowsserver.techtarget.com/feature/Deploying-security-templates [Accessed 16 June 2014].Microsoft Technet (No Date) *Administrative Template Policy Settings* [Online], Microsoft Technet. Available: http://technet.microsoft.com/en-us/library/cc771104.aspx [Accessed 16 June 2014].

Trevor Sullivan (October 15, 2012) *PowerShell: Creating Active Directory Managed Service Accounts* [Online], trevorsullivan.net. Available: http://trevorsullivan.net/2012/10/15/powershell-creating-active-directory-managed-service-accounts/ [Accessed 16 June 2014].

NedPyle [MSFT] (September 10, 2009) *Managed Service Accounts: Understanding, Implementing, Best Practices, and Troubleshooting* [Online], Microsoft Technet. Available: http://blogs.technet.com/b/askds/archive/2009/09/10/managed-service-accounts-understanding-implementing-best-practices-and-troubleshooting.aspx [Accessed 16 June 2014].

Winsysadmin.com (January 21, 2012) *Installing a Read-Only Domain Controller (Pre-create RODC Account)* [Online], Winsysadmin.com. Available: http://www.winsysadmin.com/ad/ad47004.aspx [Accessed 16 June 2014].

Nirmal Sharma (April 1, 2013) *Cloning Virtual Domain Controllers in Windows Server 2012* [Online], http://www.serverwatch.com/. Available:

http://www.serverwatch.com/server-tutorials/cloning-virtual-domain-controllers-in-windows-server-2012.html [Accessed 16 June 2014].
Paulo Viralhadas [MSFT] (March 7, 2013) □ow to clone a virtual Domain Controller [Online], Microsoft Technet. Available: http://blogs.technet.com/b/reference_point/archive/2013/03/07/how-to-clone-a-virtual-domain-controller.aspx [Accessed 16 June 2014].
Jane Yan [MSFT] (October 8, 2012) iSCSI Target Storage (VDS□VSS) Provider [Online], Microsoft Technet. Available: http://blogs.technet.com/b/filecab/archive/2012/10/08/iscsi-target-storage-vds-vss-provider.aspx [Accessed 16 June 2014].
Allen St.Clair (December 13, 2012) Volume Shadow Copy Service error on Windows Server 2012 [Online], wp.secretnest.info. Available: http://wp.secretnest.info/?p=807#comment-8354 [Accessed 16 June 2014].
Brandon Lawson(June 11, 2013) Creating Fine Grained Password Policies [Online], brandonlawson.com. Available: http://www.brandonlawson.com/active-directory/creating-fine-grained-password-policies/#lightbox/0/ [Accessed 16 June 2014].
Microsoft Technet (Updated: January 6, 2009) Managing and Deploying Driver Packages [Online], Microsoft Technet. Available: http://technet.microsoft.com/en-us/library/dd348456(v=ws.10).aspx [Accessed 16 June 2014].
Lawrence Garvin (November 13, 2013) USI□ G P.ATC□ MA□ AG□R A□ D WSUS I□ A MI□□D OS □□ VIRO□ M□□ T [Online], thwack.solarwinds.com. Available: http://thwack.solarwinds.com/community/solarwinds-community/geek-speak_tht/blog/2013/11/13/using-patch-manager-on-server-2012-with-wsus-v3 [Accessed 16 June 2014].
Alan Burchill (December 6, 2011) □ow to reset the Default Domain Group Policy Ob□cts (DCGPOFI□) [Online], www.grouppolicy.biz. Available: http://www.grouppolicy.biz/2011/12/how-to-reset-the-default-domain-group-policy-objects-dcgpofix/ [Accessed 16 June 2014].
www.itgeared.com (October 28, 2011) Restoring the Default Domain GPOs [Online], www.itgeared.com. Available: http://www.itgeared.com/articles/1077-how-to-restore-default-domain-and/ [Accessed 16 June 2014].
Microsoft Technet (Updated: March 28, 2003) Delegating Administration of Group Policy [Online], Microsoft Technet. Available: http://technet.microsoft.com/en-us/library/cc781991(v=ws.10).aspx [Accessed 16 June 2014].
Microsoft Technet (Updated: April 17, 2012) Preference Item-Level Targeting [Online], Microsoft Technet. Available: http://technet.microsoft.com/en-us/library/cc733022.aspx [Accessed 16 June 2014].

Microsoft MSDN (Updated: February 29, 2012) *Configure □ RA Automatic Discovery* [Online], Microsoft MSDN. Available: http://msdn.microsoft.com/en-us/library/dd296901(v=ws.10).aspx [Accessed 16 June 2014].

Microsoft Support (No Date) *□ow to create the Central Store for Group Policy Administrative Template files in Windows Vista* [Online], Microsoft Support. Available: http://support.microsoft.com/kb/929841 [Accessed 16 June 2014].

Microsoft Technet (No Date) *□nterprise P□I Concepts* [Online], Microsoft Technet. Available: http://technet.microsoft.com/en-us/library/cc753754.aspx [Accessed 22 July 2014].

www.ingramcontent.com/pod-product-compliance
Lightning Source LLC
Chambersburg PA
CBHW070931050326
40689CB00014B/3156